Houghton
Mifflin
Harcourt

Texas
GoMath!
Grade 8

Edward B. Burger

Juli K. Dixon

Timothy D. Kanold

Matthew R. Larson

Steven J. Leinwand

Martha E. Sandoval-Martinez

Authors

Edward B. Burger, Ph.D., is the Francis Christopher Oakley Third Century Professor of Mathematics at Williams College, an educational and business consultant, and a former vice provost at Baylor University. He has authored or coauthored more than sixty-five articles, books, and video series; delivered over five hundred addresses and workshops throughout the world; and made more than fifty radio and television appearances. He is a Fellow of the American Mathematical Society as well as having earned many national honors, including the Robert Foster Cherry Award for Great Teaching in 2010. In 2012, Microsoft Education named him a "Global Hero in Education."

Juli K. Dixon, Ph.D., is a Professor of Mathematics Education at the University of Central Florida. She has taught mathematics in urban schools at the elementary, middle, secondary, and post-secondary levels. She is an active researcher and speaker with numerous publications and conference presentations. Key areas of focus are deepening teachers' content knowledge and communicating and justifying mathematical ideas. She is a past chair of the NCTM Student Explorations in Mathematics Editorial Panel and member of the Board of Directors for the Association of Mathematics Teacher Educators.

Timothy D. Kanold, Ph.D., is an award-winning international educator, author, and consultant. He is a former superintendent and director of mathematics and science at Adlai E. Stevenson High School District 125 in Lincolnshire, Illinois. He is a past president of the National Council of Supervisors of Mathematics (NCSM) and the Council for the Presidential Awardees of Mathematics (CPAM). He has served on several writing and leadership commissions for NCTM during the past decade. He presents motivational professional development seminars with a focus on developing professional learning communities (PLC's) to improve the teaching, assessing, and learning of students. He has recently authored nationally recognized articles, books, and textbooks for mathematics education and school leadership, including *What Every Principal Needs to Know about the Teaching and Learning of Mathematics.*

Matthew R. Larson, Ph.D., is the K-12 mathematics curriculum specialist for the Lincoln Public Schools and served on the Board of Directors for the National Council of Teachers of Mathematics from 2010-2013. He is a past chair of NCTM's Research Committee and was a member of NCTM's Task Force on Linking Research and Practice. He is the author of several books on implementing the Common Core Standards for Mathematics. He has taught mathematics at the secondary and college levels and held an appointment as an honorary visiting associate professor at Teachers College, Columbia University.

Steven J. Leinwand is a Principal Research Analyst at the American Institutes for Research (AIR) in Washington, D.C., and has over 30 years in leadership positions in mathematics education. He is past president of the National Council of Supervisors of Mathematics and served on the NCTM Board of Directors. He is the author of numerous articles, books, and textbooks and has made countless presentations with topics including student achievement, reasoning, effective assessment, and successful implementation of standards.

Martha E. Sandoval-Martinez is a mathematics instructor at El Camino College in Torrance, California. She was previously a Math Specialist at the University of California at Davis and former instructor at Santa Ana College, Marymount College, and California State University, Long Beach. In her current and former positions, she has worked extensively to improve fundamental pre-algebra and algebra skills in students who have historically struggled with mathematics.

© Houghton Mifflin Harcourt Publishing Company • Image Credits: (Timothy D. Kanold) Photo courtesy of Tim Kanold; (Juli K. Dixon) Photo courtesy of Juli Dixon; (Martha E. Sandoval) Carlos Delgado/AP Images for HMH.

Consulting Reviewers

Anne Papakonstantinou, Ed.D.
Director - Rice University School
Mathematics Project
Rice University
Houston, Texas

Richard Parr
Executive Director - Rice University
School
Mathematics Project
Rice University
Houston, Texas

Susan Troutman
Associate Director for Secondary
Programs - Rice University School
Mathematics Project
Rice University
Houston, Texas

Carolyn White
Associate Director for Elementary
and Intermediate Programs - Rice
University School Mathematics
Project
Rice University
Houston, Texas

Valerie Johse
Texas Council for Economics
Education (TCEE) consultant
Houston, Texas

Texas Reviewers

Margaret R. Barron
Mathematics Specialist
Brownsville Independent School
District
Brownsville, Texas

Susan Jones
Lake Travis Middle School
Austin, Texas

Lauren Lindley
Middle School Math Specialist
Aldine ISD
Aldine, Texas

Lance Mangham
Carroll ISD
Carroll, Texas

Mary Elizabeth Rigsby
Hamilton Middle School
Houston ISD
Houston, Texas

David Surdovel
21st Century Academic Coordinator
of Mathematics
Manor ISD
Manor, Texas

Andrew D. Werner
Science Facilitator
Socorro ISD
El Paso, Texas

© Houghton Mifflin Harcourt Publishing Company

UNIT 1

Expressions and the Number System

MODULE 1 Real Numbers

 **TEKS**

MODULE 2 Scientific Notation

 **TEKS**

UNIT 2 Proportional and Nonproportional Relationships and Functions

MODULE 3 Proportional Relationships

MODULE 4 Nonproportional Relationships

MODULE 5 · Writing Linear Equations

TEKS

MODULE 6 · Functions

TEKS

MODULE **7** Angle Relationships in Parallel Lines and Triangles

MODULE **8** The Pythagorean Theorem

 **Volume**

MODULE 10 Surface Area

© Houghton Mifflin Harcourt Publishing Company • Image Credits: (b) ©Lauree Feldman/Getty Images

UNIT 4 Equations and Inequalities

MODULE 11 Equations and Inequalities with the Variable on Both Sides

© Houghton Mifflin Harcourt Publishing Company • Image Credits: ©Image Source/Alamy Images

UNIT 5 Transformational Geometry

MODULE 12 Transformations and Congruence

TEKS

MODULE 13 Dilations, Similarity, and Proportionality

TEKS

© Houghton Mifflin Harcourt Publishing Company • Image Credits: (t) ©Gregory K. Scott/Getty Images

UNIT 6 Statistics and Samples

MODULE 14 Scatter Plots

MODULE 15 Sampling

UNIT 7 Personal Financial Literacy

MODULE 16 Managing Your Money and Planning for Your Future

Texas Essential Knowledge and Skills for Mathematics

Correlation for HMH Texas Go Math Grade 8

Standard	Descriptor	Citations
8.1	**Mathematical process standards. The student uses mathematical processes to acquire and demonstrate mathematical understanding. The student is expected to:**	*The process standards are integrated throughout the book. See, for example, the citations below.*
8.1.A	apply mathematics to problems arising in everyday life, society, and the workplace;	SE: 34, 95, 136–137, 209–210, 229, 298–299
8.1.B	use a problem-solving model that incorporates analyzing given information, formulating a plan or strategy, determining a solution, justifying the solution, and evaluating the problem-solving process and the reasonableness of the solution;	SE: 78–79, 270–271, 376–378
8.1.C	select tools, including real objects, manipulatives, paper and pencil, and technology as appropriate, and techniques, including mental math, estimation, and number sense as appropriate, to solve problems;	SE: 199, 221–222, 416, 421–422, 441–443
8.1.D	communicate mathematical ideas, reasoning, and their implications using multiple representations, including symbols, diagrams, graphs, and language as appropriate;	SE: 61, 90, 144–145, 164, 275, 309, 363–365
8.1.E	create and use representations to organize, record, and communicate mathematical ideas;	SE: 102–103, 118–119, 130, 156–157, 246, 304–305
8.1.F	analyze mathematical relationships to connect and communicate mathematical ideas; and	SE: 65, 72, 169–170, 234, 251, 339–341
8.1.G	display, explain, and justify mathematical ideas and arguments using precise mathematical language in written or oral communication.	SE: 110, 193–194, 257, 317, 333–335

Standard	Descriptor	Taught	Reinforced
8.2 Number and operations. The student applies mathematical process standards to represent and use real numbers in a variety of forms. The student is expected to:			
8.2.A	extend previous knowledge of sets and subsets using a visual representation to describe relationships between sets of real numbers;	SE: 15–18	SE: 19–20, 27, 47, 48, 240, 322
8.2.B	approximate the value of an irrational number, including π and square roots of numbers less than 225, and locate that rational number approximation on a number line;	SE: 9–12	SE: 13–14, 21–26, 27, 47, 48, 428
8.2.C	convert between standard decimal notation and scientific notation; and	SE: 33–36, 39–42	SE: 37–38, 43–44, 45, 49, 216, 408
8.2.D	order a set of real numbers arising from mathematical and real-world contexts.	SE: 22–24	SE: 25–26, 27, 48, 358
8.3 Proportionality. The student applies mathematical process standards to use proportional relationships to describe dilations. The student is expected to:			
8.3.A	generalize that the ratio of corresponding sides of similar shapes are proportional, including a shape and its dilation;	SE: 209–210, 212, 363–364, 366	SE: 213–214, 216, 284, 367, 381, 382
8.3.B	compare and contrast the attributes of a shape and its dilation(s) on a coordinate plane; and	SE: 364–366, 369–370	SE: 367–368, 385
8.3.C	use an algebraic representation to explain the effect of a given positive rational scale factor applied to two-dimensional figures on a coordinate plane with the origin as the center of dilation.	SE: 369–372	SE: 373–374, 381, 382, 386, 472
8.4 Proportionality. The student applies mathematical process standards to explain proportional and non-proportional relationships involving slope. The student is expected to:			
8.4.A	use similar right triangles to develop an understanding that slope, m, given as the rate comparing the change in y-values to the change in x-values, $\frac{(y_2 - y_1)}{(x_2 - x_1)}$, is the same for any two points (x_1, y_1) and (x_2, y_2) on the same line;	SE: 210–211	SE: 213–214
8.4.B	graph proportional relationships, interpreting the unit rate as the slope of the line that models the relationship; and	SE: 71–74	SE: 75–76, 178
8.4.C	use data from a table or graph to determine the rate of change or slope and y-intercept in mathematical and real-world problems.	SE: 65–68, 71–74, 95–96, 98, 170	SE: 69–70, 75–76, 83, 99–100, 123, 177, 178, 179

Standard	Descriptor	Taught	Reinforced
8.5 Proportionality. The student applies mathematical process standards to use proportional and non-proportional relationships to develop foundational concepts of functions. The student is expected to:			
8.5.A	represent linear proportional situations with tables, graphs, and equations in the form of $y = kx$;	SE: 59–62	SE: 63–64, 173–174, 177, 178, 408
8.5.B	represent linear non-proportional situations with tables, graphs, and equations in the form of $y = mx + b$, where $b \neq 0$;	SE: 89–92, 97, 101–104	SE: 93–94, 105–106, 123, 173–174, 178, 179, 180, 382, 466
8.5.C	contrast bivariate sets of data that suggest a linear relationship with bivariate sets of data that do not suggest a linear relationship from a graphical representation;	SE: 144–145, 146, 397, 398	SE: 147–148, 181, 182, 399–400
8.5.D	use a trend line that approximates the linear relationship between bivariate sets of data to make predictions;	SE: 142–143, 146, 401–404	SE: 147–148, 181, 405–406, 407, 408, 430
8.5.E	solve problems involving direct variation;	SE: 77–80	SE: 81–82, 83, 216
8.5.F	distinguish between proportional and non-proportional situations using tables, graphs, and equations in the form $y = kx$ or $y = mx + b$, where $b \neq 0$;	SE: 90, 92, 107–112	SE: 93–94, 113–114, 123, 173, 179
8.5.G	identify functions using sets of ordered pairs, tables, mappings, and graphs;	SE: 155–160, 163	SE: 161–162, 175, 182, 183, 240, 471
8.5.H	identify examples of proportional and non-proportional functions that arise from mathematical and real-world problems; and	SE: 164–166	SE: 167–168, 173, 175
8.5.I	write an equation in the form $y = mx + b$ to model a linear relationship between two quantities using verbal, numerical, tabular, and graphical representations.	SE: 129–132, 135–138, 141, 146, 169–170, 171–172, 402–403, 404	SE: 133–134, 139–140, 147–148, 149, 180, 181, 405, 407, 408, 429, 430

Standard	Descriptor	Taught	Reinforced
8.6 Expressions, equations, and relationships. The student applies mathematical process standards to develop mathematical relationships and make connections to geometric formulas. The student is expected to:			
8.6.A	describe the volume formula $V = Bh$ of a cylinder in terms of its base area and its height;	SE: 245, 248	SE: 250
8.6.B	model the relationship between the volume of a cylinder and a cone having both congruent bases and heights and connect that relationship to the formulas; and	SE: 251, 254	SE: 255–256
8.6.C	use models and diagrams to explain the Pythagorean theorem.	SE: 221–222	SE: 224
8.7 Expressions, equations, and relationships. The student applies mathematical process standards to use geometry to solve problems. The student is expected to:			
8.7.A	solve problems involving the volume of cylinders, cones, and spheres;	SE: 246–248, 252–254, 257–260	SE: 249–250, 255–256, 261–262, 263, 264, 282, 286, 428, 466
8.7.B	use previous knowledge of surface area to make connections to the formulas for lateral and total surface area and determine solutions for problems involving rectangular prisms, triangular prisms, and cylinders;	SE: 269–272, 275–278	SE: 273–274, 279–280, 281, 282, 287, 358, 471
8.7.C	use the Pythagorean Theorem and its converse to solve problems; and	SE: 222–224, 227–230	SE: 225–226, 231–232, 239, 240, 264, 284–285, 322
8.7.D	determine the distance between two points on a coordinate plane using the Pythagorean Theorem.	SE: 233–236	SE: 237–238, 239, 240, 285

Standard	Descriptor	Taught	Reinforced
8.8 Expressions, equations, and relationships. The student applies mathematical process standards to use one-variable equations or inequalities in problem situations. The student is expected to:			
8.8.A	write one-variable equations or inequalities with variables on both sides that represent problems using rational number coefficients and constants;	SE: 298–299, 300, 304–305, 306, 309–311, 312, 315–316, 318	SE: 301–302, 307, 313–314, 319, 321, 322, 323, 472
8.8.B	write a corresponding real-world problem when given a one-variable equation or inequality with variables on both sides of the equal sign using rational number coefficients and constants;	SE: 299–300, 305, 306, 311, 312, 317, 318	SE: 313, 324
8.8.C	model and solve one-variable equations with variables on both sides of the equal sign that represent mathematical and real-world problems using rational number coefficients and constants; and	SE: 297–299, 300, 303–305, 306	SE: 301–302, 307–308, 321, 322, 323, 358, 382
8.8.D	use informal arguments to establish facts about the angle sum and exterior angle of triangles, the angles created when parallel lines are cut by a transversal, and the angle-angle criterion for similarity of triangles.	SE: 193–196, 199–204, 207–210, 212	SE: 197–198, 205–206, 213–214, 215, 216, 240, 283–284
8.9 Expressions, equations, and relationships. The student applies mathematical process standards to use multiple representations to develop foundational concepts of simultaneous linear equations. The student is expected to:			
8.9	identify and verify the values of x and y that simultaneously satisfy two linear equations in the form $y = mx + b$ from the intersections of the graphed equations.	SE: 115–120	SE: 121–122, 123, 179, 180
8.10 Two-dimensional shapes. The student applies mathematical process standards to develop transformational geometry concepts. The student is expected to:			
8.10.A	generalize the properties of orientation and congruence of rotations, reflections, translations, and dilations of two-dimensional shapes on a coordinate plane;	SE: 333–336, 339–342, 345–348, 363–364, 366	SE: 337–338, 343–344, 349–350, 357, 358, 367, 383–384
8.10.B	differentiate between transformations that preserve congruence and those that do not;	SE: 363–366	SE: 367
8.10.C	explain the effect of translations, reflections over the x- or y-axis, and rotations limited to 90°, 180°, 270°, and 360° as applied to two-dimensional shapes on a coordinate plane using an algebraic representation; and	SE: 351–354	SE: 355–356, 357, 428
8.10.D	model the effect on linear and area measurements of dilated two-dimensional shapes.	SE: 369–370, 375–378	SE: 373–374, 379–380, 381, 382

Standard	Descriptor	Taught	Reinforced
8.11 Measurement and data. The student applies mathematical process standards to use statistical procedures to describe data. The student is expected to:			
8.11.A	construct a scatterplot and describe the observed data to address questions of association such as linear, non-linear, and no association between bivariate data;	SE: 395–398, 401–403	SE: 399–400, 405, 407, 408, 429, 430
8.11.B	determine the mean absolute deviation and use this quantity as a measure of the average distance data are from the mean using a data set of no more than 10 data points; and	SE: 413–417	SE: 418–420, 427, 428, 431
8.11.C	simulate generating random samples of the same size from a population with known characteristics to develop the notion of a random sample being representative of the population from which it was selected.	SE: 421–424	SE: 425–426, 427, 428, 431
8.12 Personal financial literacy. The student applies mathematical process standards to develop an economic way of thinking and problem solving useful in one's life as a knowledgeable consumer and investor. The student is expected to:			
8.12.A	solve real-world problems comparing how interest rate and loan length affect the cost of credit;	SE: 441–444	SE: 445–446, 465, 468
8.12.B	calculate the total cost of repaying a loan, including credit cards and easy access loans, under various rates of interest and over different periods using an online calculator;	SE: 441–444	SE: 445–446, 465, 466, 468, 471, 472
8.12.C	explain how small amounts of money invested regularly, including money saved for college and retirement, grow over time;	SE: 447–449	SE: 451–452
8.12.D	calculate and compare simple interest and compound interest earnings;	SE: 447–450	SE: 451–452, 465, 466, 467, 468, 471, 472
8.12.E	identify and explain the advantages and disadvantages of different payment methods;	SE: 453–454, 456	SE: 442, 443, 446, 457–458, 466, 471
8.12.F	analyze situations to determine if they represent financially responsible decisions and identify the benefits of financial responsibility and the costs of financial irresponsibility; and	SE: 455–456	SE: 457–458, 465, 467, 468
8.12.G	estimate the cost of a two-year and four-year college education, including family contribution, and devise a periodic savings plan for accumulating the money needed to contribute to the total cost of attendance for at least the first year of college.	SE: 459–462	SE: 463–464, 465, 466, 468, 472

Texas English Language Proficiency Standards (ELPS)

HMH Texas Go Math supports English language learners at all proficiency levels. The HMH Texas Go Math Student Edition provides integrated resources to assist all levels of learners, as shown in the correlation tables provided below.

In addition, students at various levels may benefit from additional program support:

Beginning - Students at a Beginning level are supported by *Spanish Student Edition, Spanish Assessment Resources*, Success for Every Learner and Leveled Practice A worksheets in *Differentiated Instruction, Math On the Spot* videos with Spanish closed captioning, and the *Multilingual Glossary*.

Intermediate - Students at the Intermediate level may use any of the resources above, and may also use Reading Strategies in *Differentiated Instruction*.

Advanced and Advanced High - Students at these levels will be successful as the *Student Edition* promotes vocabulary development through visual and context clues. The Multilingual Glossary may also be helpful.

ELPS	Student Edition Citations
c.1.A use prior knowledge and experiences to understand meanings in English	This standard is met in: Reading Startup in each module—Examples: 5, 31, 57, 87 Unpacking the TEKS in each module—Examples: 6, 32, 58, 88
c.1.D speak using learning strategies such as requesting assistance, employing non-verbal cues, and using synonyms and circumlocution (conveying ideas by defining or describing when exact English words are not known)	This standard is met in Math Talk in most lessons—Examples: 8, 65, 101, 129, 369, 441
c.2.C learn new language structures, expressions, **and basic and academic vocabulary heard during classroom instruction and interactions**	This standard is met in: Math Talk in most lessons—Examples: 8, 22, 101, 137, 369, 441 Reflect questions in most lessons—Examples: 33, 40, 130, 145, 370, 442
c.2.D monitor understanding of spoken language during classroom instruction and interactions and **seek clarification [of spoken language] as needed**	This standard is met in: Math Talk in most lessons—Examples: 130, 229, 315, 335, 369, 414 Reflect questions in most lessons—Examples: 72, 90, 228, 333, 370, 422
c.2.E use visual, contextual, and **linguistic support to enhance and confirm understanding of increasingly complex and elaborated spoken language**	This standard is met in Visualize Vocabulary in each module—Examples: 5, 31, 57, 87
c.2.I demonstrate listening comprehension of increasingly complex spoken English by following directions, retelling or summarizing spoken messages, **responding to questions and requests,** collaborating with peers, **and taking notes commensurate with content and grade-level needs**	This standard is met in: Math Talk in most lessons—Examples: 34, 65, 72, 135, 315, 369 My Notes in many lessons— Examples: 17, 91, 131, 201, 246, 310
c.3.B expand and internalize initial English vocabulary by learning and using high-frequency English words necessary for identifying and describing people, places, and objects, by retelling simple stories and basic information represented or supported by pictures, and by learning and using **routine language needed for classroom communication**	This standard is met in: Vocabulary Puzzle in each unit—Examples: 2, 54, 188, 292 Active Reading in each module—Examples: 5, 31, 57, 87 Unpacking the TEKS in each module—Examples: 6, 32, 58, 88 Reflect questions in most lessons—Examples: 35, 73, 102, 222, 245 Math Talk in most lessons—Examples: 16, 60, 101, 136, 164, 195 Explore Activities in many lessons—Examples: 59, 66, 95, 144, 155, 221

ELPS	Student Edition Citations
c.3.C speak using a variety of grammatical structures, sentence lengths, sentence types, and **connecting words with increasing accuracy and ease as more English is acquired**	This standard is met in Math Talk in most lessons—Examples: 96, 107, 137, 157, 270, 335
c.3.D speak using grade-level content area vocabulary in context to internalize new English words and build academic language proficiency	This standard is met in: Vocabulary Puzzle in each unit—Examples: 2, 54, 188, 292 Active Reading in each module—Examples: 5, 31, 57, 87 Math Talk in most lessons—Examples: 16, 41, 164, 234, 335, 396
c.3.E share information in cooperative learning interactions	This standard is met in: Math Talk in most lessons—Examples: 41, 164, 234, 396, 414 Explore Activities in many lessons—Examples: 95, 221, 269, 395, 401
c.3.F ask [for] and give information ranging from using a very limited bank of high-frequency, high-need, concrete vocabulary, including key words and expressions needed for basic communication in academic and social contexts, to using abstract and content-based vocabulary during extended speaking assignments	This standard is met in: Math Talk in most lessons—Examples: 96, 164, 234, 270, 335 Explore Activities in many lessons—Examples: 39, 59, 71, 90, 269, 401
c.3.H narrate, describe, and **explain with increasing specificity and detail as more English is acquired**	This standard is met in: Reflect questions in most lessons—Examples: 41, 90, 143, 228, 235, 364 Math Talk in most lessons—Examples: 65, 77, 141, 365, 369 Independent Practice exercises in each lesson—Examples: 63, 82, 99, 134, 232, 238
C.4.C develop basic sight vocabulary, derive meaning of environmental print, and comprehend English vocabulary and language structures used routinely in written classroom materials	This standard is met in: Vocabulary Puzzle in each unit—Examples: 2, 54, 188, 292 Active Reading in each module—Examples: 5, 31, 57, 87 Unpacking the TEKS in each module—Examples: 6, 32, 58, 88 Highlighted vocabulary at point of use in instruction—Examples: 15, 60, 95, 156, 193, 221
c.4.D use prereading supports such as graphic organizers, illustrations, and pretaught topic-related vocabulary and other prereading activities to enhance comprehension of written text	This standard is met in Active Reading in each module—Examples: 5, 31, 57, 87
c.4.F use visual and contextual support and support from peers and teachers to read grade-appropriate content area text, enhance and confirm understanding, and develop vocabulary, grasp of language structures, and background knowledge needed to comprehend increasingly challenging language	This standard is met through photographs, illustrations, and diagrams throughout instruction—Examples: 15, 35, 67, 77, 221, 245
c.4.G demonstrate comprehension of increasingly complex English by participating in shared reading, **retelling or summarizing material, responding to questions, and taking notes commensurate with content area and grade level needs**	This standard is met in: Math Talk in most lessons—Examples: 72, 96, 137, 157, 164, 203 Reflect questions in most lessons—Examples: 21, 40, 73, 156, 194, 199 Essential Question Check In exercises in each lesson—Examples: 18, 24, 68, 90, 98, 138 H.O.T.S. exercises in each lesson—Examples: 20, 38, 64, 94, 106, 148

Texas English Language Proficiency Standards **TX9**

Succeeding with HMH Texas Go Math

Actively participate in your learning with your write-in Student Edition. Explore concepts, take notes, answer questions, and complete your homework right in your textbook!

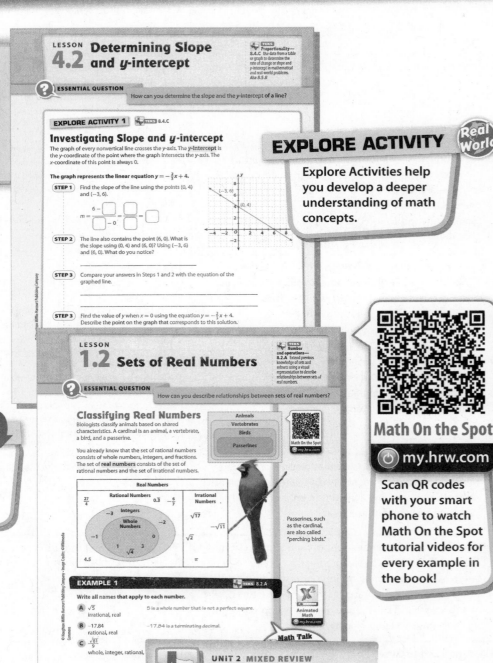

LESSON 4.2 Determining Slope and *y*-intercept

EXPLORE ACTIVITY — Real World

Explore Activities help you develop a deeper understanding of math concepts.

YOUR TURN

Your Turn exercises check your understanding of new concepts.

Math On the Spot
my.hrw.com

Scan QR codes with your smart phone to watch Math On the Spot tutorial videos for every example in the book!

UNIT 2 MIXED REVIEW
Texas Test Prep

Check your mastery of concepts through review and practice for the Texas test.

my.hrw.com

The Interactive Student Edition provides additional videos, activities, tools, and learning aids to support you as you study!

Practice skills and complete your homework online with the Personal Math Trainer. Your Personal Math Trainer provides a variety of learning aids that develop and improve your understanding of math concepts including videos, guided examples, and step-by-step solutions.

Personal Math Trainer
Online Assessment and Intervention

my.hrw.com

Math On the Spot

my.hrw.com

Math On the Spot video tutorials provide step-by-step instruction of the math concepts covered in each example.

Animated Math activities let you interactively explore and practice key math concepts and skills.

Animated Math

my.hrw.com

Mathematical Process Standards

8.1 **Mathematical process standards.** The student uses mathematical processes to acquire and demonstrate mathematical understanding.

8.1.A Everyday Life

The student is expected to apply mathematics to problems arising in everyday life, society, and the workplace.

Real-World Video

Cyclists adjust their rate of speed when approaching ramps and pipes so they can safely execute trick moves. Check out how unit rates can be used to solve problems involving speed, distance, and time.

my.hrw.com

CAREERS IN MATH

my.hrw.com

Go digital with your write-in student edition, accessible on any device.

8.1.B Use a Problem-Solving Model

The student is expected to use a problem-solving model that incorporates analyzing given information, formulating a plan or strategy, determining a solution, justifying the solution, and evaluating the problem-solving process and the reasonableness of the solution.

 Analyze Information

What are you asked to find?

What are the facts?

Is there any information given that you will not use?

 Formulate a Plan

What strategy or strategies can you use?

Have you solved any similar problems before?

 Solve

Follow your plan.

Show the steps in your solution.

 Justify and Evaluate

Did you answer the question?

Is your answer reasonable?

Are there other strategies that you could use?

8.1.C Select Tools

The student is expected to select tools, including real objects, manipulatives, paper and pencil, and technology as appropriate, and techniques, including mental math, estimation, and number sense as appropriate, to solve problems.

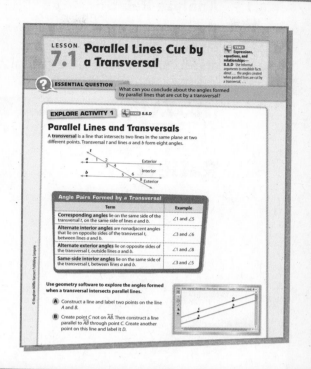

8.1.D Multiple Representations

The student is expected to communicate mathematical ideas, reasoning, and their implications, using multiple representations, including symbols, diagrams, graphs, and language as appropriate.

8.1.E Use Representations

The student is expected to create and use representations to organize, record, and communicate mathematical ideas.

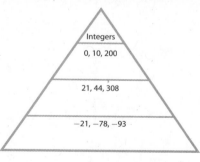

Integers

0, 10, 200

21, 44, 308

−21, −78, −93

© Houghton Mifflin Harcourt Publishing Company

8.1.F Analyze Relationships

The student is expected to analyze mathematical relationships to connect and communicate mathematical ideas.

FOCUS ON HIGHER ORDER THINKING

Reflect

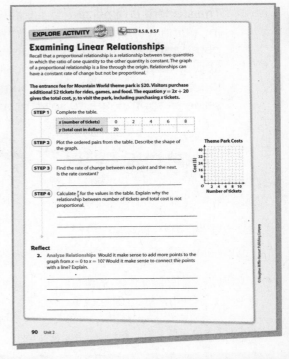

EXPLORE ACTIVITY TEKS 8.5.B, 8.5.F

Examining Linear Relationships

Recall that a proportional relationship is a relationship between two quantities in which the ratio of one quantity to the other quantity is constant. The graph of a proportional relationship is a line through the origin. Relationships can have a constant rate of change but not be proportional.

The entrance fee for Mountain World theme park is $20. Visitors purchase additional $2 tickets for rides, games, and food. The equation $y = 2x + 20$ gives the total cost, y, to visit the park, including purchasing x tickets.

STEP 1 Complete the table.

x (number of tickets)	0	2	4	6	8
y (total cost in dollars)	20				

STEP 2 Plot the ordered pairs from the table. Describe the shape of the graph.

STEP 3 Find the rate of change between each point and the next. Is the rate constant?

STEP 4 Calculate $\frac{y}{x}$ for the values in the table. Explain why the relationship between number of tickets and total cost is not proportional.

Reflect

2. **Analyze Relationships** Would it make sense to add more points to the graph from $x = 0$ to $x = 10$? Would it make sense to connect the points with a line? Explain.

90 Unit 2

8.1.G Justify Arguments

The student is expected to display, explain, and justify mathematical ideas and arguments using precise mathematical language in written or oral communication.

ESSENTIAL QUESTION

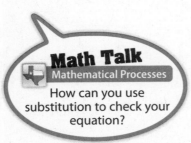

Math Talk
Mathematical Processes

How can you use substitution to check your equation?

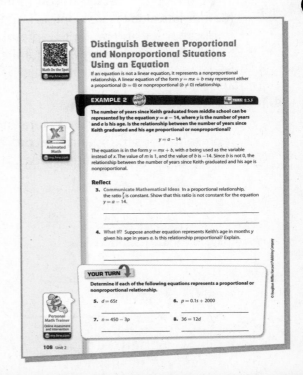

Distinguish Between Proportional and Nonproportional Situations Using an Equation

If an equation is not a linear equation, it represents a nonproportional relationship. A linear equation of the form $y = mx + b$ may represent either a proportional ($b = 0$) or nonproportional ($b \neq 0$) relationship.

EXAMPLE 2 TEKS 8.5.F

The number of years since Keith graduated from middle school can be represented by the equation $y = a - 14$, where y is the number of years and a is his age. Is the relationship between the number of years since Keith graduated and his age proportional or nonproportional?

$$y = a - 14$$

The equation is in the form $y = mx + b$, with a being used as the variable instead of x. The value of m is 1, and the value of b is −14. Since b is not 0, the relationship between the number of years since Keith graduated and his age is nonproportional.

Reflect

3. **Communicate Mathematical Ideas** In a proportional relationship, the ratio $\frac{y}{x}$ is constant. Show that this ratio is not constant for the equation $y = a - 14$.

4. **What If?** Suppose another equation represents Keith's age in months y given his age in years a. Is this relationship proportional? Explain.

YOUR TURN

Determine if each of the following equations represents a proportional or nonproportional relationship.

5. $d = 65t$

6. $p = 0.1s + 2000$

7. $n = 450 - 3p$

8. $36 = 12d$

108 Unit 2

Selected Response

1. Four sisters contributed equally to buy a present for their father. They received a 10% discount on the original price of the gift. After the discount was taken, each sister paid $13.50. What was the original price of the gift?

   Ⓐ $60.00   Ⓒ $54.00

   Ⓑ $59.40   Ⓓ $48.60

2. A store decreases the price of an item from $120 to $90. What is the percent decrease?

   Ⓐ 75%

   Ⓑ 30%

   Ⓒ $33\frac{1}{3}$%

   Ⓓ 25%

3. A coin-operated machine sells plastic rings. It contains 14 pink rings, 10 green rings, 9 purple rings, and 13 black rings. Valeria puts a coin into the machine. Find the theoretical probability that Valeria gets a pink ring rounded to the nearest thousandth.

   Ⓐ 0.562   Ⓒ 0.304

   Ⓑ 0.438   Ⓓ 0.280

4. A board is 9 feet $9\frac{1}{2}$ inches long. Jeff cuts as many pieces with a length of $11\frac{1}{4}$ inches as possible from the board. Assuming no waste, how long is the remaining piece of board?

   Ⓐ 10 in.   Ⓒ $4\frac{4}{9}$ in.

   Ⓑ 5 in.   Ⓓ $3\frac{1}{4}$ in.

5. An experiment consists of rolling two fair number cubes. What is the probability that the sum of the two numbers will be 8? Express your answer as a fraction in simplest form.

   Ⓐ $\frac{1}{12}$ Ⓒ $\frac{5}{36}$

   Ⓑ $\frac{1}{11}$ Ⓓ $\frac{1}{6}$

6. A deli offers a lunch special that comes with soup, a sandwich, and a drink. The soup choices are chicken noodle or creamy potato; the sandwich choices are ham, turkey, tuna, or veggie; and the drink choices are juice, coffee, or tea. How many different lunch spe-cials are in the sample space?

   Ⓐ 72   Ⓒ 24

   Ⓑ 27   Ⓓ 9

7. Roberto plays on the school baseball team. In the last 9 games, Roberto was at bat 32 times and got 11 hits. What is the experimental probability that Roberto will get a hit during his next time at bat? Express your answer as a fraction in simplest form.

   Ⓐ $\frac{32}{11}$ Ⓒ $\frac{21}{32}$

   Ⓑ $\frac{11}{32}$ Ⓓ $\frac{11}{21}$

8. What are the actual dimensions of the check-out area?

Floor Plan of Library

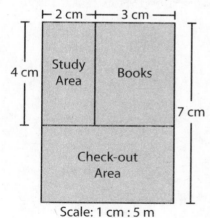

Scale: 1 cm : 5 m

   Ⓐ 25m × 15m   Ⓒ 15m × 35m

   Ⓑ 15m × 20m   Ⓓ 2m × 4m

9. Hue wants to buy two necklaces, one for her sister and one for herself. The necklace for her sister costs $43.25, and the necklace for herself costs $26.25. The sales tax on the purchases is 3%. Find the total cost of Hue's purchases, including sales tax.

(A) $71.59

(C) $67.42

(B) $69.50

(D) $2.09

10. Tell whether the data show a proportional relationship. If so, identify the constant of proportionality.

Number of Baskets	Cost
5	$15
7	$21
9	$27
13	$39
15	$45

(A) proportional; $k = \frac{1}{3}$

(B) proportional; $k = 3$

(C) not proportional

(D) proportional; $k = 10$

11. The graph shows the distance Jamie walks over time. Does she walk at a constant or variable speed? How fast is Jamie walking?

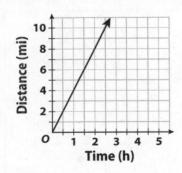

(A) variable speed; 8 mi/h

(B) constant speed; 4 mi/h

(C) constant speed; 2 mi/h

(D) constant speed; 8 mi/h

12. A map of Australia has a scale of 1 cm : 110 km. If the distance between Darwin and Alice Springs is 1444 kilometers, how far apart are they on the map, to the nearest tenth of a centimeter?

(A) 14.4 cm

(C) 11.1 cm

(B) 13.1 cm

(D) 1.3 cm

13. The ratio of adults to children attending a new exhibit at the museum on one day was 8:5. Based on this ratio, if 390 people attended that day, how many were children?

(A) 624

(C) 240

(B) 244

(D) 150

Gridded Response

14. The graph shows the proportional relationship between the total cost and the number of pounds of brown rice purchased.

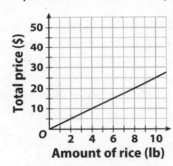

What would the total price in dollars be for 12.5 pounds of rice?

				•		
⓪	⓪	⓪	⓪		⓪	⓪
①	①	①	①		①	①
②	②	②	②		②	②
③	③	③	③		③	③
④	④	④	④		④	④
⑤	⑤	⑤	⑤		⑤	⑤
⑥	⑥	⑥	⑥		⑥	⑥
⑦	⑦	⑦	⑦		⑦	⑦
⑧	⑧	⑧	⑧		⑧	⑧
⑨	⑨	⑨	⑨		⑨	⑨

Selected Response

1. Stan made 14 of 20 free throws in basketball practice. Predict the number of free throws he would make if he attempted 100 free throws.

Ⓐ 40   Ⓒ 70

Ⓑ 50   Ⓓ 73

2. A manufacturer inspects 400 personal video players and finds that 399 of them have no defects. The manufacturer sent a shipment of 2000 video players to a distributor. Predict the number of players in the shipment that are likely to have no defects.

Ⓐ 5   Ⓒ 1950

Ⓑ 399   Ⓓ 1995

3. It costs $10 to go to Pete's Pottery Place to paint custom bowls at a cost of $3.50 per bowl. Janelle plans to paint bowls 5 days this month and to paint b bowls on each day so she can sell them at a craft fair. Which equation represents Janelle's total cost c for the month?

Ⓐ $c = 5(10b + 3.5)$ Ⓒ $c = 5(3.5b + 10)$

Ⓑ $c = 3.5(5b + 10)$ Ⓓ $c = 3.5(10b + 5)$

4. At the beginning of the year, Jason had $120 in his savings account. Each month he added $15 to his account. Write an equation for the amount of money A in Jason's savings account each month. Then use the equation to find the amount of money in his account at the end of the year.

Month	1	2	3	m
Amount	$135	$150	$165	$?

Ⓐ $A = 135 + 15m$; $315

Ⓑ $A = 135 + m$; $147

Ⓒ $A = 120 + 12m$; $300

Ⓓ $A = 15m + 120$; $300

5. Which equation is represented by the graph?

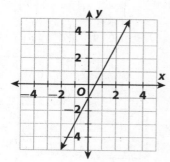

Ⓐ $y = 2x - 1$ Ⓒ $y = -2x + 1$

Ⓑ $y = -\frac{1}{2}x - 1$ Ⓓ $y = -x + 2$

6. The temperature of a pot of water is 62 °F. The temperature increases by 20 °F per minute when being heated.
Write an equation to represent the linear relationship.

Ⓐ $y = 62x + 20$ Ⓒ $y = 62 + 20$

Ⓑ $y = 20x + 62$ Ⓓ $y = (62 + 20)x$

7. Find the area of the circle to the nearest tenth. Use 3.14 for π.

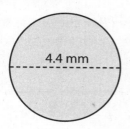

4.4 mm

Ⓐ 13.8 mm²   Ⓒ 47.7 mm²

Ⓑ 15.2 mm²   Ⓓ 60.8 mm²

8. For a history fair, a school is building a circular wooden stage that will stand 2 feet off the ground. Find the perimeter of the stage if the radius of the stage is 6 meters. Use 3.14 for π.

Ⓐ 18.84 m²   Ⓒ 113.04 m²

Ⓑ 37.68 m²   Ⓓ 452.16 m²

9. Samir built a cabinet in the shape of a rectangular prism. The cabinet was 36 inches wide, 3.5 feet tall, and 12 inches deep? What is the volume of the cabinet in cubic feet?

(A) 10.5 ft³

(C) 18 ft³

(B) 15 ft³

(D) 1512 ft³

10. Find the volume of the rectangular prism.

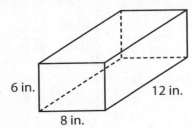

6 in.   12 in.   8 in.

(A) 60 in²

(C) 432 in²

(B) 192 in²

(D) 576 in²

11. Alicia and three friends are making a video to post online. The three friends all made video segments of equal length, and Alicia's video segment is less than 5 minutes long. Let s represent the length of each of the friend's segments. Write an inequality to represent the length ℓ of the full video.

(A) $\ell > 3s + 5$

(C) $\ell \geq 3s + 5$

(B) $\ell \leq 3s + 5$

(D) $\ell < 3s + 5$

12. The number line shows the solutions to an inequality. Which inequality does not match the graph?

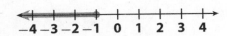

−4 −3 −2 −1 0 1 2 3 4

(A) $-x \geq 1$

(B) $2x - 3 \leq 5$

(C) $-2x + 1 \leq 3$

(D) $-x + 2 \geq 3$

13. Solve $4(a + 4) - 2 = 34$.

(A) $a = 8$

(C) $a = -5$

(B) $a = 5$

(D) $a = -8$

14. Carmen is an electrician. She charges an initial fee of $32, plus $33 per hour. If Carmen earned $197 on a job, how long did the job take?

(A) 132 hours

(C) 5 hours

(B) 5.1 hours

(D) 4 hours

15. Write and solve an equation to find the measure of the missing angle in the triangle.

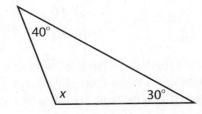

40° x 30°

(A) $40 - x = 30; x = 10°$

(B) $30 + 40 + x = 90; x = 20°$

(C) $x = 30 + 40; x = 70°$

(D) $30 + 40 + x = 180; x = 110°$

Gridded Response

16. Seth purchased a pair of jeans for $29.99 and two shirts for $8.50 each. The sales tax in his town in 6.5%. What was the total cost in dollars of Seth's purchase including sales tax? Round your answer to the nearest penny.

⓪	⓪	⓪	⓪	•	⓪	⓪
①	①	①	①		①	①
②	②	②	②		②	②
③	③	③	③		③	③
④	④	④	④		④	④
⑤	⑤	⑤	⑤		⑤	⑤
⑥	⑥	⑥	⑥		⑥	⑥
⑦	⑦	⑦	⑦		⑦	⑦
⑧	⑧	⑧	⑧		⑧	⑧
⑨	⑨	⑨	⑨		⑨	⑨

GRADE 8 PART 1

Benchmark Test

Personal
Math Trainer
Online
Assessment and
Intervention
my.hrw.com

Selected Response

1. Francine has a square mosaic that is made from small glass squares. If there are 196 small squares in the mosaic, how many are along an edge?

   Ⓐ 98 squares   Ⓒ 16 squares

   Ⓑ 49 squares   Ⓓ 14 squares

2. One of the following sets of ordered pairs represents a proportional relationship. Which equation represents that relationship?

   1: (0, 3), (3, 6), (6, 9), (9, 12)

   2: (0, 0), (2, 8), (4, 16), (5, 20)

   Ⓐ $y = x + 3$

   Ⓑ $y = x + 4$

   Ⓒ $y = 3x$

   Ⓓ $y = 4x$

3. Evaluate the expression $2\sqrt{-19 + 44}$.

   Ⓐ 10   Ⓒ 25

   Ⓑ 18.8   Ⓓ 50

4. Which of these functions is *not* a linear function?

   Ⓐ $y = x^2 - x$ Ⓒ $y = 1 - x$

   Ⓑ $y = \frac{x}{3}$ Ⓓ $y = \frac{2}{3}x - 2x$

5. You buy hats for $5 and sell them for $20 each. There are no other expenses. What does the graph of profits as a function of the number of hats sold look like?

   Ⓐ a line that goes up from left to right

   Ⓑ a line that goes down from left to right

   Ⓒ a curve that goes down from left to right

   Ⓓ a curve that goes up from left to right

6. Solve the equation.
$$-2z + 3 = -7z - 12$$

   Ⓐ $z = -15$ Ⓒ $z = -1.8$

   Ⓑ $z = -3$ Ⓓ $z = 1$

7. A passenger plane travels at about 7.97×10^2 feet per second. The plane takes 1.11×10^4 seconds to reach its destination. About how far must the plane travel to reach its destination?

   Ⓐ 8.85×10^8 feet   Ⓒ 8.85×10^6 feet

   Ⓑ 9.08×10^6 feet   Ⓓ 9.08×10^8 feet

8. Which is the best estimate of the slope of the graph shown?

Heating Oil Cost per Gallon

Cost ($) vs. Gallons

   Ⓐ 1   Ⓒ 4.5

   Ⓑ 4   Ⓓ 60

9. For which linear function is the rate of change the greatest?

   Ⓐ $y = -5x$

   Ⓑ {(−1, −2), (1, 2), (3, 6), (5, 10), (7, 14)}

   Ⓒ A fitness club charges a $200 membership fee plus monthly fees of $25.

   Ⓓ $y = 3x - 16$

10. Approximate $\sqrt{158}$ to the nearest hundredth.

   Ⓐ 12.57   Ⓒ 16.57

   Ⓑ 16.62   Ⓓ 8.52

11. For the given solid with base area B and volume V, which statement is *not* true?

   Ⓐ For a rectangular prism with length l, width w, and height h, $V = Bh$ where $B = lw$.

   Ⓑ For a rectangular pyramid with length l, width w, and height h, $V = \frac{1}{2} Bh$ where $B = lw$.

   Ⓒ For a cylinder with radius r and height h, $V = Bh$ where $B = \pi r^2$.

   Ⓓ For a cone with radius r and height h, $V = \frac{1}{3} Bh$ where $B = \pi r^2$.

12. Write a rule for the linear function represented by the table.

x	y
−3	12
−2	10
3	0
5	−4

   Ⓐ $y = -2x - 6$ Ⓒ $y = 0.5x + 6$

   Ⓑ $y = -2x + 6$ Ⓓ $y = 0.5x - 9$

13. A remote-controlled airplane descends at a rate of 2 feet per second. After 3 seconds it is 67 feet above the ground. Which equation in slope-intercept form models this situation?

   Ⓐ $y = -2x + 73$ Ⓒ $y = 2x + 61$

   Ⓑ $y = -2x + 67$ Ⓓ $y = -3x + 73$

14. What is the equation of the graph shown in slope-intercept form?

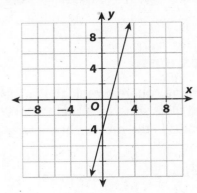

   Ⓐ $y = -4x - 4$ Ⓒ $y = 4x + 1$

   Ⓑ $y = 4x - 4$ Ⓓ $y = x - 4$

Gridded Response

15. The figure shows two parallel lines cut by a transversal.

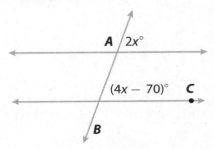

What is the measure in degrees of angle ABC?

				.		
⓪	⓪	⓪	⓪		⓪	⓪
①	①	①	①	①	①	①
②	②	②	②	②	②	②
③	③	③	③	③	③	③
④	④	④	④	④	④	④
⑤	⑤	⑤	⑤	⑤	⑤	⑤
⑥	⑥	⑥	⑥	⑥	⑥	⑥
⑦	⑦	⑦	⑦	⑦	⑦	⑦
⑧	⑧	⑧	⑧	⑧	⑧	⑧
⑨	⑨	⑨	⑨	⑨	⑨	⑨

Benchmark Test

Selected Response

1. Mahala is making a piece of jewelry that is in the shape of a right triangle. The two shorter sides of the piece of jewelry are 9 mm and 12 mm. Find the perimeter of the piece of jewelry.

(A) 15 mm

(C) 42 mm

(B) 36 mm

(D) 54 mm

2. The figure shown is dilated by a scale factor of 2.5 with the origin as the center of dilation. What are the coordinates of the image of the vertex at (2, −4) after the dilation?

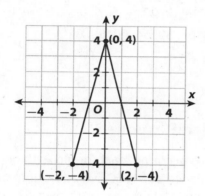

(A) (0.5, −1.5)

(C) (5, −10)

(B) (2, −1.5)

(D) (0.8, −1.6)

3. A bicyclist heads east at 19 km/h. After she has traveled 24.2 kilometers, another cyclist sets out from the same starting point in the same direction going 30 km/h. How long will it take the second cyclist to catch up to the first cyclist?

(A) 3.7 hours

(B) 3.2 hours

(C) 2.2 hours

(D) 1.7 hours

4. An artist is creating a large conical sculpture for a park. The cone has a height of 16 meters and a diameter of 25 meters. Find the volume of the sculpture to the nearest cubic meter. Use 3.14 for π.

(A) 164 m³

(C) 2,617 m³

(B) 654 m³

(D) 10,470 m³

5. A cylindrical barrel has a radius of 7.6 ft and a height of 10.8 ft. Tripling which dimension(s) will triple the volume of the barrel?

(A) height only

(B) radius only

(C) both height and radius

(D) neither height nor radius

6. Which linear equation is the closest approximation to the trend line that best represents the data?

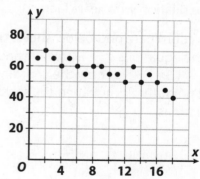

(A) $y = -2x + 65$

(C) $y = -1.5x + 70$

(B) $y = 0.5x + 70$

(D) $y = -0.5x + 65$

7. Which of the following transformations never changes the orientation of a figure?

(A) a reflection over the x-axis

(B) a reflection over the y-axis

(C) a rotation about the origin

(D) a translation that moves a figure both horizontally and vertically

8. Find the distance, to the nearest tenth, from $T(4, -2)$ to $U(-2, 3)$.

Ⓐ 3.3 units　　Ⓒ 7.8 units

Ⓑ 6.1 units　　Ⓓ 11 units

9. Find the volume of the cylinder. Use 3.14 for π. Round your answer to the nearest tenth.

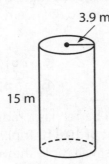

3.9 m

15 m

Ⓐ 183.7 m³　　Ⓒ 2755.4 m³

Ⓑ 716.4 m³　　Ⓓ 2865.6 m³

10. Which of the following is *not* a congruence transformation?

Ⓐ a reflection over the *x*-axis

Ⓑ a dilation with scale factor 0.5

Ⓒ a translation 1 unit left

Ⓓ a dilation with scale factor 1

11. The coordinate grid below shows the graphs of the equations $y = -0.5x + 1$ and $y = -1.5x - 1$. Identify the coordinates of any point that simultaneously satisfies both equations.

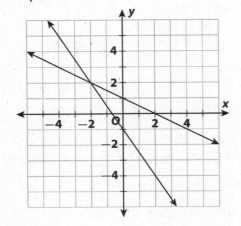

Ⓐ (0, 1)　　Ⓒ (−2, 2)

Ⓑ (2, −2)　　Ⓓ no such point

12. Which statement best describes the association between hours of sleep and reaction time shown in the scatter plot?

Sleep vs. Reaction Time

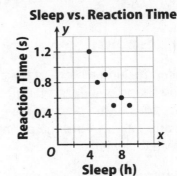

Ⓐ no association

Ⓑ negative and basically linear

Ⓒ positive and basically linear

Ⓓ positive and nonlinear

13. What is the mean absolute deviation of the data?

58, 61, 59, 64, 60, 59, 62, 61

Ⓐ 60.5　　Ⓒ 4

Ⓑ 6　　Ⓓ 1.5

Gridded Response

14. Two accounts each begin with an initial balance of $1000. No additional deposits are made. One account pays 4% annual simple interest, and the other account pays 4% interest compounded annually. What is the difference in the account balances in dollars and cents at the end of 10 years?

				.		
⓪	⓪	⓪	⓪		⓪	⓪
①	①	①	①		①	①
②	②	②	②		②	②
③	③	③	③		③	③
④	④	④	④		④	④
⑤	⑤	⑤	⑤		⑤	⑤
⑥	⑥	⑥	⑥		⑥	⑥
⑦	⑦	⑦	⑦		⑦	⑦
⑧	⑧	⑧	⑧		⑧	⑧
⑨	⑨	⑨	⑨		⑨	⑨

Expressions and the Number System

MODULE 1
Real Numbers
TEKS 8.2.A, 8.2.B, 8.2.D

MODULE 2
Scientific Notation
TEKS 8.2.C

CAREERS IN MATH

Astronomer An astronomer is a scientist who studies and tries to interpret the universe beyond Earth. Astronomers use math to calculate distances to celestial objects and to create mathematical models to help them understand the dynamics of systems from stars and planets to black holes. If you are interested in a career as an astronomer, you should study the following mathematical subjects:

• Algebra
• Geometry
• Trigonometry
• Calculus

Research other careers that require creating mathematical models to understand physical phenomena.

Unit 1 Performance Task

At the end of the unit, check out how **astronomers** use math.

UNIT 1
Vocabulary Preview

Use the puzzle to preview key vocabulary from this unit. Unscramble the circled letters to answer the riddle at the bottom of the page.

1. **TCREEFP SEAQUR**

2. **NOLRATAI RUNMEB**

3. **PERTIANEG MALCEDI**

4. **LAER SEBMNUR**

5. **NIISICFTCE OITANTON**

1. Has integers as its square roots. (Lesson 1-1)
2. Any number that can be written as a ratio of two integers. (Lesson 1-1)
3. A decimal in which one or more digits repeat infinitely. (Lesson 1-1)
4. The set of rational and irrational numbers. (Lesson 1-2)
5. A method of writing very large or very small numbers by using powers of 10. (Lesson 2-1)

Q: What keeps a square from moving?

A: _ _ _ _ _ _ _ _ _ _ _ _ _ _ _!

Real Numbers

ESSENTIAL QUESTION

How can you use real numbers to solve real-world problems?

Real-World Video

Living creatures can be classified into groups. The sea otter belongs to the kingdom Animalia and class Mammalia. Numbers can also be classified into groups such as rational numbers and integers.

my.hrw.com

© Houghton Mifflin Harcourt Publishing Company • Image Credits: ©Daniel Hershman/Getty Images

GO DIGITAL
my.hrw.com

my.hrw.com	**Math On the Spot**	**Animated Math**	**Personal Math Trainer**
Go digital with your write-in student edition, accessible on any device.	Scan with your smart phone to jump directly to the online edition, video tutor, and more.	Interactively explore key concepts to see how math works.	Get immediate feedback and help as you work through practice sets.

Are YOU Ready?

Complete these exercises to review skills you will need for this chapter.

Personal Math Trainer

Online Assessment and Intervention

my.hrw.com

Find the Square of a Number

EXAMPLE   Find the square of $\frac{2}{3}$.

$\frac{2}{3} \times \frac{2}{3} = \frac{2 \times 2}{3 \times 3}$ Multiply the number by itself.

$\phantom{\frac{2}{3} \times \frac{2}{3}} = \frac{4}{9}$ Simplify.

Find the square of each number.

1. 7 _____

2. 21 _____

3. −3 _____

4. $\frac{4}{5}$ _____

5. 2.7 _____

6. $-\frac{1}{4}$ _____

7. −5.7 _____

8. $1\frac{2}{5}$ _____

Exponents

EXAMPLE $5^3 = 5 \times 5 \times 5$ Use the base, 5, as a factor 3 times.

$ = 25 \times 5$ Multiply from left to right.

$ = 125$

Simplify each exponential expression.

9. 9^2 _____

10. 2^4 _____

11. $\left(\frac{1}{3}\right)^2$ _____

12. $(-7)^2$ _____

13. 4^3 _____

14. $(-1)^5$ _____

15. 4.5^2 _____

16. 10^5 _____

Write a Mixed Number as an Improper Fraction

EXAMPLE $2\frac{2}{5} = 2 + \frac{2}{5}$ Write the mixed number as a sum of a whole number and a fraction.

$\phantom{2\frac{2}{5}} = \frac{10}{5} + \frac{2}{5}$ Write the whole number as an equivalent fraction with the same denominator as the fraction in the mixed number.

$\phantom{2\frac{2}{5}} = \frac{12}{5}$ Add the numerators.

Write each mixed number as an improper fraction.

17. $3\frac{1}{3}$ _____

18. $1\frac{5}{8}$ _____

19. $2\frac{3}{7}$ _____

20. $5\frac{5}{6}$ _____

Reading Start-Up

© Houghton Mifflin Harcourt Publishing Company

Visualize Vocabulary

Use the ✔ words to complete the graphic. You can put more than one word in each section of the triangle.

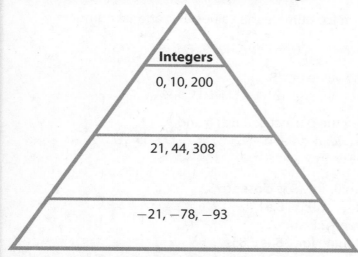

Integers

0, 10, 200

21, 44, 308

−21, −78, −93

Understand Vocabulary

Complete the sentences using the preview words.

1. One of the two equal factors of a number is a _____.

2. A _____ has integers as its square roots.

3. The _____ is the nonnegative square root of a number.

Vocabulary

Review Words

   integers *(enteros)*

✔ negative numbers *(números negativos)*

✔ positive numbers *(números positivos)*

✔ whole number *(número entero)*

Preview Words

   irrational numbers *(número irracional)*

   perfect square *(cuadrado perfecto)*

   principal square root *(raíz cuadrada principal)*

   rational number *(número racional)*

   real numbers *(número real)*

   repeating decimal *(decimal periódico)*

   square root *(raíz cuadrada)*

   terminating decimal *(decimal finito)*

Active Reading

Layered Book Before beginning the lessons in this module, create a layered book to help you learn the concepts in this module. Label the flaps "Rational Numbers," "Irrational Numbers," "Square Roots," and "Real Numbers." As you study each lesson, write important ideas such as vocabulary, models, and sample problems under the appropriate flap.

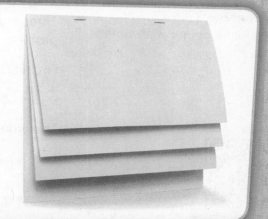

Unpacking the TEKS

Understanding the standards and the vocabulary terms in the standards will help you know exactly what you are expected to learn in this module.

 **TEKS 8.2.B**

Approximate the value of an irrational number, including π and square roots of numbers less than 225, and locate that rational number approximation on a number line.

Key Vocabulary

rational number *(número racional)*
Any number that can be expressed as a ratio of two integers.

irrational number *(número irracional)*
Any number that cannot be expressed as a ratio of two integers.

What It Means to You

You will learn to estimate the values of irrational numbers.

UNPACKING EXAMPLE 8.2.B

Estimate the value of $\sqrt{8}$.

8 is not a perfect square. Find the two perfect squares closest to 8.

8 is between the perfect squares 4 and 9.
So $\sqrt{8}$ is between $\sqrt{4}$ and $\sqrt{9}$.
    $\sqrt{8}$ is between 2 and 3.

8 is closer to 9, so $\sqrt{8}$ is closer to 3.
$2.8^2 = 7.84$ $2.9^2 = 8.41$
$\sqrt{8}$ is between 2.8 and 2.9
A good estimate for $\sqrt{8}$ is 2.85.

 **TEKS 8.2.D**

Order a set of real numbers arising from mathematical and real-world contexts.

Key Vocabulary

real number *(número real)*
A rational or irrational number.

What It Means to You

You can write decimal approximations of irrational numbers to help you order them.

UNPACKING EXAMPLE 8.2.D

Three students gave slightly different answers to the same problem: Avery $\sqrt{13}$, Lisa 3.7, and Jason $\frac{18}{5}$.

Find each value or approximation.

$\sqrt{13} \approx 3.6$, $3.7 = 3.7$, and $\frac{17}{5} = 3.4$

The order from greatest to least is

Lisa: 3.7, Avery: $\sqrt{13}$, Jason: $\frac{17}{5}$.

Visit **my.hrw.com** to see all the **TEKS** unpacked.

⏻ my.hrw.com

TEKS
Number and operations—8.2.B
Approximate the value of an irrational number, including π and square roots of numbers less than 225, and locate that rational number approximation on a number line.

? ESSENTIAL QUESTION

How do you express a rational number as a decimal and approximate the value of an irrational number?

Expressing Rational Numbers as Decimals

A **rational number** is any number that can be written as a ratio in the form $\frac{a}{b}$, where a and b are integers and b is not 0. Examples of rational numbers are 6 and 0.5.

6 can be written as $\frac{6}{1}$ 0.5 can be written as $\frac{1}{2}$

Every rational number can be written as a terminating decimal or a repeating decimal. A **terminating decimal**, such as 0.5, has a finite number of digits. A **repeating decimal** has a block of one or more digits that repeat indefinitely.

Math On the Spot
my.hrw.com

EXAMPLE 1

TEKS Prep for 8.2.B

Write each fraction as a decimal.

A $\frac{1}{4}$

$$\begin{array}{r} 0.25 \\ 4\overline{)1.00} \\ \underline{-8} \\ 20 \\ \underline{-20} \\ 0 \end{array}$$

$\frac{1}{4} = 0.25$

Remember that the fraction bar means "divided by." Divide the numerator by the denominator.

Divide until the remainder is zero, adding zeros after the decimal point in the dividend as needed.

$\frac{1}{3} = 0.3333333333333...$

B $\frac{1}{3}$

$$\begin{array}{r} 0.333 \\ 3\overline{)1.000} \\ \underline{-9} \\ 10 \\ \underline{-9} \\ 10 \\ \underline{-9} \\ 1 \end{array}$$

$\frac{1}{3} = 0.\overline{3}$

Divide until the remainder is zero or until the digits in the quotient begin to repeat.

Add zeros after the decimal point in the dividend as needed.

When a decimal has one or more digits that repeat indefinitely, write the decimal with a bar over the repeating digit(s).

Personal Math Trainer
Online Assessment and Intervention
⏻ my.hrw.com

Math On the Spot
⏻ my.hrw.com

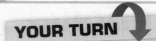

YOUR TURN

Write each fraction as a decimal.

1. $\frac{5}{11}$ _____ 2. $\frac{1}{8}$ _____ 3. $2\frac{1}{3}$ _____

Finding Square Roots of Perfect Squares

A number that is multiplied by itself to form a product is a **square root** of that product. Taking the square root of a number is the inverse of squaring the number.

$$6^2 = 36 \qquad \text{6 is one of the square roots of 36}$$

Every positive number has two square roots, one positive and one negative. The radical symbol $\sqrt{\ }$ indicates the nonnegative or **principal square root** of a number. A minus sign is used to show the negative square root of a number.

$$\sqrt{36} = 6 \qquad -\sqrt{36} = -6$$

The number 36 is an example of a perfect square. A **perfect square** has integers as its square roots.

EXAMPLE 2   **TEKS** Prep for 8.2.B

Find the two square roots of each number.

A 169

$\sqrt{169} = 13$ 13 is a square root, since $13 \cdot 13 = 169$.

$-\sqrt{169} = -13$ -13 is a square root, since $(-13)(-13) = 169$.

B $\frac{1}{25}$

Since 1 and 25 are both perfect squares, you can find the square root of the numerator and the denominator.

$\sqrt{\frac{1}{25}} = \frac{1}{5}$ 1 is a square root of 1, since $1 \cdot 1 = 1$, and 5 is a square root of 25, since $5 \cdot 5 = 25$.

$-\sqrt{\frac{1}{25}} = -\frac{1}{5}$ $-\frac{1}{5}$ is a square root, since $\left(-\frac{1}{5}\right) \cdot \left(-\frac{1}{5}\right) = \frac{1}{25}$.

 Math Talk
Mathematical Processes

Can you square an integer and get a negative number? Explain.

Reflect

4. **Analyze Relationships** How are the two square roots of a positive number related? Which is the principal square root?

_____

5. Is the principal square root of 2 a whole number? What types of numbers have whole number square roots?

_____

© Houghton Mifflin Harcourt Publishing Company

YOUR TURN

Find the two square roots of each number.

6. 64 _____   **7.** 100 _____   **8.** $\frac{1}{9}$ _____

9. A square garden has an area of 144 square feet. How long is each side?

_____

EXPLORE ACTIVITY 1   🦶 **TEKS** 8.2.B

Estimating Irrational Numbers

Irrational numbers are numbers that are not rational. In other words, they cannot be written in the form $\frac{a}{b}$, where a and b are integers and b is not 0.

Estimate the value of $\sqrt{2}$.

A Since 2 is not a perfect square, $\sqrt{2}$ is irrational.

B To estimate $\sqrt{2}$, first find two consecutive perfect squares that 2 is between. Complete the inequality by writing these perfect squares in the boxes.

C Now take the square root of each number.

D Simplify the square roots of perfect squares.

$\sqrt{2}$ is between _____ and _____.

E Estimate that $\sqrt{2} \approx 1.5$.

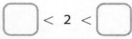

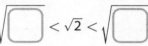

F To find a better estimate, first choose some numbers between 1 and 2 and square them. For example, choose 1.3, 1.4, and 1.5.

$1.3^2 =$ _____ $1.4^2 =$ _____ $1.5^2 =$ _____

Is $\sqrt{2}$ between 1.3 and 1.4? How do you know?

_____

Is $\sqrt{2}$ between 1.4 and 1.5? How do you know?

_____

$\sqrt{2}$ is between _____ and _____, so $\sqrt{2} \approx$ _____.

G Locate and label this value on the number line.

Reflect

10. How could you find an even better estimate of $\sqrt{2}$?

_____

11. Find a better estimate of $\sqrt{2}$. Draw a number line and locate and label your estimate.

$\sqrt{2}$ is between _____ and _____, so $\sqrt{2} \approx$ _____.

12. Estimate the value of $\sqrt{7}$ to the nearest hundredth. Draw a number line and locate and label your estimate.

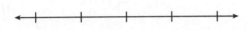

$\sqrt{7}$ is between _____ and _____, so $\sqrt{7} \approx$ _____.

EXPLORE ACTIVITY 2   TEKS 8.2.B

Approximating π

The number π, the ratio of the circumference of a circle to its diameter, is an irrational number. It cannot be written as the ratio of two integers.

In this activity, you will explore the relationship between the diameter and circumference of a circle.

A Use a tape measure to measure the circumference and the diameter of four circular objects using metric measurements. To measure the circumference, wrap the tape measure tightly around the object and determine the mark where the tape starts to overlap the beginning of the tape. When measuring the diameter, be sure to measure the distance across the object at its widest point.

B Record the circumference and diameter of each object in the table.

Object	Circumference	Diameter	circumference diameter

C Divide the circumference by the diameter for each object. Round each answer to the nearest hundredth and record it in the table.

D Describe what you notice about the ratio of circumference to diameter.

_____

_____

_____

Reflect

13. What does the fact that π is irrational indicate about its decimal equivalent?

_____

_____

14. Plot π on the number line.

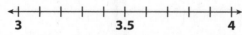

15. Explain Why... A CD and a DVD have the same diameter. Explain why they have the same circumference.

_____

_____

_____

_____

1. **Vocabulary** Square roots of numbers that are not perfect squares are

   _____

Write each fraction as a decimal. (Example 1)

2. $\frac{7}{8}$ _____

3. $\frac{17}{20}$ _____

4. $\frac{18}{25}$ _____

5. $2\frac{3}{8}$ _____

6. $5\frac{2}{3}$ _____

7. $2\frac{4}{5}$ _____

Find the two square roots of each number. (Example 2)

8. 49 _____

9. 144 _____

10. 400 _____

11. $\frac{1}{16}$ _____

12. $\frac{4}{9}$ _____

13. $\frac{9}{4}$ _____

Approximate each irrational number to the nearest 0.05 without using a calculator. (Explore Activity 1)

14. $\sqrt{34}$ _____

15. $\sqrt{82}$ _____

16. $\sqrt{45}$ _____

17. $\sqrt{104}$ _____

18. $-\sqrt{71}$ _____

19. $-\sqrt{19}$ _____

20. **Measurement** Complete the table for the measurements to estimate the value of π. Round to the nearest tenth. (Explore Activity 2)

Circumference (in.)	Diameter (in.)	circumference diameter
70	22	
110	35	
130	41	
200	62	

Describe what you notice about the ratio of circumference to diameter.

_____

? ESSENTIAL QUESTION CHECK-IN

21. Describe how to approximate the value of an irrational number.

   _____

   _____

   _____

1.1 Independent Practice

 TEKS 8.2.B

Personal Math Trainer

Online Assessment and Intervention

my.hrw.com

22. A $\frac{7}{16}$ -inch-long bolt is used in a machine. What is the length of the bolt written as a decimal?

_____

23. **Astronomy** The weight of an object on the moon is $\frac{1}{6}$ of its weight on Earth. Write $\frac{1}{6}$ as a decimal.

_____

24. The distance to the nearest gas station is $2\frac{3}{4}$ miles. What is this distance written as a decimal?

_____

25. A pitcher on a baseball team has pitched $98\frac{2}{3}$ innings. What is the number of innings written as a decimal?

_____

26. A Coast Guard ship patrols an area of 125 square miles. The area the ship patrols is a square. About how long is each side of the square? Round your answer to the nearest mile.

_____

27. Each square on Olivia's chessboard is 11 square centimeters. A chessboard has 8 squares on each side. To the nearest tenth, what is the width of Olivia's chessboard?

_____

28. The thickness of a surfboard relates to the weight of the surfer. A surfboard is $21\frac{3}{16}$ inches wide and $2\frac{3}{8}$ inches thick. Write each dimension as a decimal.

_____

_____

29. A gallon of stain can cover a square deck with an area of 300 square feet. About how long is each side of the deck? Round your answer to the nearest foot.

A = 300 ft²

_____

30. The area of a square field is 200 square feet. What is the approximate length of each side of the field? Round your answer to the nearest foot.

_____

31. **Measurement** A ruler is marked at every $\frac{1}{16}$ inches. Do the labeled measurements convert to terminating or repeating decimals?

_____

32. **Multistep** A couple wants to install a square mirror that has an area of 500 square inches. To the nearest tenth of an inch, what length of wood trim is needed to go around the mirror?

_____

33. **Multistep** A square photo-display board is made up of 60 rows of 60 photos each. The area of each square photo is 4 in. How long is each side of the display board?

Approximate each irrational number to the nearest hundredth without using a calculator. Then plot each number on a number line.

34. $\sqrt{24}$ _____

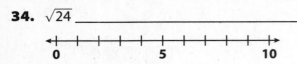

35. $\sqrt{41}$ _____

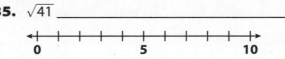

36. Represent Real-World Problems If every positive number has two square roots and you can find the length of the side of a square window by finding a square root of the area, why is there only one answer for the length of a side?

_____

_____

37. Make a Prediction To find $\sqrt{5}$, Beau found $2^2 = 4$ and $3^2 = 9$. He said that since 5 is between 4 and 9, $\sqrt{5}$ is between 2 and 3. Beau thinks a good estimate for $\sqrt{5}$ is $\frac{2+3}{2} = 2.5$. Is his estimate high or low? How do you know?

_____

_____

 **FOCUS ON HIGHER ORDER THINKING**

Work Area

38. Multistep On a baseball field, the infield area created by the baselines is a square. In a youth baseball league, this area is 3600 square feet. A pony league of younger children use a smaller baseball field with a distance between each base that is 20 feet less than the youth league. What is the distance between each base for the pony league?

_____

39. Problem Solving The difference between the square roots of a number is 30. What is the number? Show that your answer is correct.

_____

_____

40. Analyze Relationships If the ratio of the circumference of a circle to its diameter is π, what is the relationship of the circumference to the radius of the circle? Explain.

_____

_____

_____

_____

TEKS
Number and operations—
8.2.A Extend previous knowledge of sets and subsets using a visual representation to describe relationships between sets of real numbers.

? ESSENTIAL QUESTION

How can you describe relationships between sets of real numbers?

Classifying Real Numbers

Biologists classify animals based on shared characteristics. A cardinal is an animal, a vertebrate, a bird, and a passerine.

You already know that the set of rational numbers consists of whole numbers, integers, and fractions. The set of **real numbers** consists of the set of rational numbers and the set of irrational numbers.

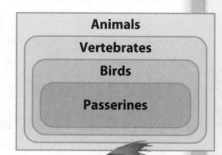

Animals
Vertebrates
Birds
Passerines

Math On the Spot
⟳ my.hrw.com

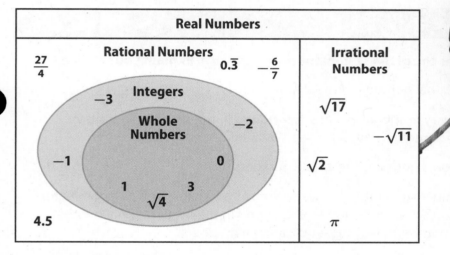

Real Numbers

Rational Numbers $\frac{27}{4}$ $0.\overline{3}$ $-\frac{6}{7}$

Integers -3

Whole Numbers

-1 0

1 3

$\sqrt{4}$

-2

4.5

Irrational Numbers

$\sqrt{17}$

$-\sqrt{11}$

$\sqrt{2}$

π

Passerines, such as the cardinal, are also called "perching birds."

EXAMPLE 1
TEKS 8.2.A

Write all names that apply to each number.

A $\sqrt{5}$ 5 is a whole number that is not a perfect square.
irrational, real

B -17.84 -17.84 is a terminating decimal.
rational, real

C $\frac{\sqrt{81}}{9}$ $\frac{\sqrt{81}}{9} = \frac{9}{9} = 1$
whole, integer, rational, real

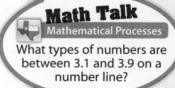
Animated Math
⟳ my.hrw.com

Math Talk
Mathematical Processes
What types of numbers are between 3.1 and 3.9 on a number line?

YOUR TURN

Write all names that apply to each number.

1. A baseball pitcher has pitched $12\frac{2}{3}$ innings.

_____

2. The length of the side of a square that has an

area of 10 square yards. _____

Math On the Spot

⏻ my.hrw.com

Understanding Sets and Subsets of Real Numbers

By understanding which sets are subsets of types of numbers, you can verify whether statements about the relationships between sets are true or false.

EXAMPLE 2
 TEKS 8.2.A

Tell whether the given statement is true or false. Explain your choice.

A All irrational numbers are real numbers.

True. Every irrational number is included in the set of real numbers. Irrational numbers are a subset of real numbers.

B No rational numbers are whole numbers.

False. A whole number can be written as a fraction with a denominator of 1, so every whole number is included in the set of rational numbers. Whole numbers are a subset of rational numbers.

Math Talk

Mathematical Processes

Give an example of a rational number that is a whole number. Show that the number is both whole and rational.

YOUR TURN

Tell whether the given statement is true or false. Explain your choice.

3. All rational numbers are integers.

_____

_____

_____

4. Some irrational numbers are integers.

_____

_____

Identifying Sets for Real-World Situations

Real numbers can be used to represent real-world quantities. Highways have posted speed limit signs that are represented by natural numbers such as 55 mph. Integers appear on thermometers. Rational numbers are used in many daily activities, including cooking. For example, ingredients in a recipe are often given in fractional amounts such as $\frac{2}{3}$ cup flour.

EXAMPLE 3 TEKS 8.2.A

Identify the set of numbers that best describes each situation. Explain your choice.

A the number of people wearing glasses in a room

The set of whole numbers best describes the situation. The number of people wearing glasses may be 0 or a counting number.

B the circumference of a flying disk has a diameter of 8, 9, 10, 11, or 14 inches

The set of irrational numbers best describes the situation. Each circumference would be a product of π and the diameter, and any multiple of π is irrational.

My Notes

Identify the set of numbers that best describes the situation. Explain your choice.

5. the amount of water in a glass as it evaporates

_____

_____

_____

6. the number of seconds remaining when a song is playing, displayed as a negative number

_____

_____

_____

Write all names that apply to each number. (Example 1)

1. $\frac{7}{8}$

   _____

2. $\sqrt{36}$

   _____

3. $\sqrt{24}$

   _____

4. 0.75

   _____

5. 0

   _____

6. $-\sqrt{100}$

   _____

7. $5.\overline{45}$

   _____

8. $-\frac{18}{6}$

   _____

Tell whether the given statement is true or false. Explain your choice.
(Example 2)

9. All whole numbers are rational numbers.

   _____

   _____

10. No irrational numbers are whole numbers.

   _____

Identify the set of numbers that best describes each situation. Explain your choice. (Example 3)

11. the change in the value of an account when given to the nearest dollar

   _____

   _____

12. the markings on a standard ruler

   _____

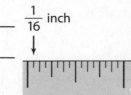

$\frac{1}{16}$ inch

IN.   1

© Houghton Mifflin Harcourt Publishing Company

? ESSENTIAL QUESTION CHECK-IN

13. What are some ways to describe the relationships between sets of numbers?

   _____

   _____

1.2 Independent Practice

 TEKS 8.2.A

Personal
Math Trainer

Online
Assessment and
Intervention

⏻ my.hrw.com

Write all names that apply to each number. Then place the numbers in the correct location on the Venn diagram.

14. $\sqrt{9}$ _____

15. 257 _____

16. $\sqrt{50}$ _____

17. $8\frac{1}{2}$ _____

18. 16.6 _____

19. $\sqrt{16}$ _____

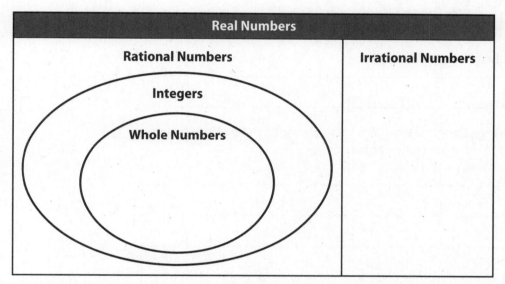

Identify the set of numbers that best describes each situation. Explain your choice.

20. the height of an airplane as it descends to an airport runway

_____

21. the score with respect to par of several golfers: 2, −3, 5, 0, −1

_____

_____

22. Critique Reasoning Ronald states that the number $\frac{1}{11}$ is not rational because, when converted into a decimal, it does not terminate. Nathaniel says it is rational because it is a fraction. Which boy is correct? Explain.

_____

_____

23. Critique Reasoning The circumference of a circular region is shown. What type of number best describes the diameter of the circle? Explain

your answer. _____

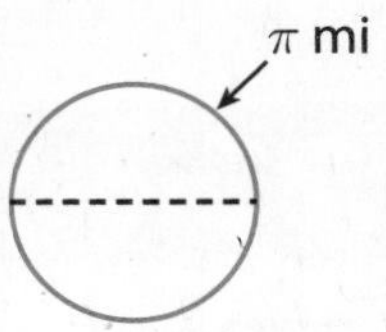

π mi

24. Critical Thinking A number is not an integer. What type of number can it be?

_____

25. A grocery store has a shelf with half-gallon containers of milk. What type of number best represents the total number of gallons?

_____

H.O.T. FOCUS ON HIGHER ORDER THINKING

26. Explain the Error Katie said, "Negative numbers are integers." What was her error?

_____

_____

27. Justify Reasoning Can you ever use a calculator to determine if a number is rational or irrational? Explain.

_____

_____

_____

_____

_____

_____

_____

28. Draw Conclusions The decimal $0.\overline{3}$ represents $\frac{1}{3}$. What type of number best describes $0.\overline{9}$, which is $3 \cdot 0.\overline{3}$? Explain.

_____

29. Communicate Mathematical Ideas Irrational numbers can never be precisely represented in decimal form. Why is this?

_____

_____

_____

Work Area

Ordering Real Numbers

TEKS
Number and operations—
8.2.D Order a set of real numbers arising from mathematical and real-world contexts.
Also 8.2.B

? ESSENTIAL QUESTION

How do you order a set of real numbers?

Comparing Irrational Numbers

Between any two real numbers is another real number. To compare and order real numbers, you can approximate irrational numbers as decimals.

Math On the Spot
my.hrw.com

EXAMPLE 1
TEKS 8.2.B

Compare $\sqrt{3} + 5$ ⬤ $3 + \sqrt{5}$. **Write** $<$, $>$, **or** $=$.

STEP 1 First approximate $\sqrt{3}$.

$\sqrt{3}$ is between 1 and 2, so $\sqrt{3} \approx 1.5$.

Next approximate $\sqrt{5}$.

$\sqrt{5}$ is between 2 and 3, so $\sqrt{5} \approx 2.5$.

> Use perfect squares to estimate square roots.
> $1^2 = 1$ $2^2 = 4$ $3^2 = 9$

STEP 2 Then use your approximations to simplify the expressions.

$\sqrt{3} + 5$ is between 6 and 7

$3 + \sqrt{5}$ is between 5 and 6

So, $\sqrt{3} + 5 > 3 + \sqrt{5}$

My Notes

Reflect

1. If $7 + \sqrt{5}$ is equal to $\sqrt{5}$ plus a number, what do you know about the number? Why?

   _____

2. What are the closest two integers that $\sqrt{300}$ is between?

   _____

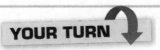

Compare. Write $<$, $>$, **or** $=$.

3. $\sqrt{2} + 4$ ◯ $2 + \sqrt{4}$

4. $\sqrt{12} + 6$ ◯ $12 + \sqrt{6}$

Personal Math Trainer

Online Assessment and Intervention

my.hrw.com

My Notes

Ordering Real Numbers

You can compare and order real numbers and list them from least to greatest.

EXAMPLE 2

 TEKS 8.2.D

Order $\sqrt{22}$, $\pi + 1$, and $4\frac{1}{2}$ from least to greatest.

STEP 1 First approximate $\sqrt{22}$.

$\sqrt{22}$ is between 4 and 5. Since you don't know where it falls between 4 and 5, you need to find a better estimate for $\sqrt{22}$ so you can compare it to $4\frac{1}{2}$.

To find a better estimate of $\sqrt{22}$, check the squares of numbers close to 4.5.

$4.4^2 = 19.36$ $4.5^2 = 20.25$ $4.6^2 = 21.16$ $4.7^2 = 22.09$

$\sqrt{22}$ is between 4.6 and 4.7, so $\sqrt{22} \approx 4.65$.

An approximate value of π is 3.14. So an approximate value of $\pi + 1$ is 4.14.

STEP 2 Plot $\sqrt{22}$, $\pi + 1$, and $4\frac{1}{2}$ on a number line.

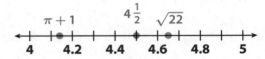

Read the numbers from left to right to place them in order from least to greatest.

From least to greatest, the numbers are $\pi + 1$, $4\frac{1}{2}$, and $\sqrt{22}$.

YOUR TURN

Order the numbers from least to greatest. Then graph them on the number line.

5. $\sqrt{5}$, 2.5, $\sqrt{3}$ _____

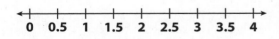

6. π^2, 10, $\sqrt{75}$ _____

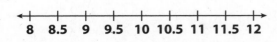

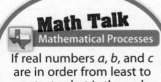

Math Talk
Mathematical Processes

If real numbers a, b, and c are in order from least to greatest, what is the order of their opposites from least to greatest? Explain.

Personal Math Trainer
Online Assessment and Intervention
my.hrw.com

© Houghton Mifflin Harcourt Publishing Company

Ordering Real Numbers in a Real-World Context

Calculations and estimations in the real world may differ. It can be important to know not only which are the most accurate but which give the greatest or least values, depending upon the context.

Math On the Spot
⏼ my.hrw.com

EXAMPLE 3  **TEKS** 8.2.D

Four people have found the distance in kilometers across a canyon using different methods. Their results are given in the table. Order the distances from greatest to least.

Distance Across Quarry Canyon (km)			
Juana	**Lee Ann**	**Ryne**	**Jackson**
$\sqrt{28}$	$\frac{23}{4}$	$5.\overline{5}$	$5\frac{1}{2}$

STEP 1 Approximate $\sqrt{28}$.

$\sqrt{28}$ is between 5.2 and 5.3, so $\sqrt{28} \approx 5.25$.

$\frac{23}{4} = 5.75$

$5.\overline{5}$ is 5.555..., so $5.\overline{5}$ to the nearest hundredth is 5.56.

$5\frac{1}{2} = 5.5$

STEP 2 Plot $\sqrt{28}$, $\frac{23}{4}$, $5.\overline{5}$, and $5\frac{1}{2}$ on a number line.

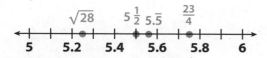

From greatest to least, the distances are:

$\frac{23}{4}$ km, $5.\overline{5}$ km, $5\frac{1}{2}$ km, $\sqrt{28}$ km.

YOUR TURN

7. Four people have found the distance in miles across a crater using different methods. Their results are given below.

Jonathan: $\frac{10}{3}$, Elaine: $3.\overline{45}$, José: $3\frac{1}{2}$, Lashonda: $\sqrt{10}$

Order the distances from greatest to least.

Personal Math Trainer
Online Assessment and Intervention
⏼ my.hrw.com

© Houghton Mifflin Harcourt Publishing Company

Guided Practice

Compare. Write <, >, or =. (Example 1)

1. $\sqrt{3} + 2 \bigcirc \sqrt{3} + 3$

2. $\sqrt{11} + 15 \bigcirc \sqrt{8} + 15$

3. $\sqrt{6} + 5 \bigcirc 6 + \sqrt{5}$

4. $\sqrt{9} + 3 \bigcirc 9 + \sqrt{3}$

5. $\sqrt{17} - 3 \bigcirc -2 + \sqrt{5}$

6. $10 - \sqrt{8} \bigcirc 12 - \sqrt{2}$

7. $\sqrt{7} + 2 \bigcirc \sqrt{10} - 1$

8. $\sqrt{17} + 3 \bigcirc 3 + \sqrt{11}$

9. Order $\sqrt{3}$, 2π, and 1.5 from least to greatest. Then graph them on the number line. (Example 2)

$\sqrt{3}$ is between _____ and _____, so $\sqrt{3} \approx$ _____.

$\pi \approx 3.14$, so $2\pi \approx$ _____.

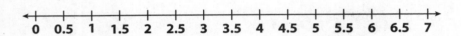

From least to greatest, the numbers are _____, _____,

_____.

10. Four people have found the perimeter of a forest using different methods. Their results are given in the table. Order their calculations from greatest to least. (Example 3)

_____

_____

Forest Perimeter (km)			
Leon	**Mika**	**Jason**	**Ashley**
$\sqrt{17} - 2$	$1 + \dfrac{\pi}{2}$	$\dfrac{12}{5}$	2.5

? ESSENTIAL QUESTION CHECK-IN

11. Explain how to order a set of real numbers.

_____

_____

_____

_____

_____

1.3 Independent Practice

 **TEKS** 8.2.B, 8.2.D

Personal
Math Trainer

Online
Assessment and
Intervention

my.hrw.com

Order the numbers from least to greatest.

12. $\sqrt{7}, 2, \dfrac{\sqrt{8}}{2}$

_____

13. $\sqrt{10}, \pi, 3.5$

_____

14. $\sqrt{220}, -10, \sqrt{100}, 11.5$

_____

15. $\sqrt{8}, -3.75, 3, \dfrac{9}{4}$

_____

16. Your sister is considering two different shapes for her garden. One is a square with side lengths of 3.5 meters, and the other is a circle with a diameter of 4 meters.

   a. Find the area of the square. _____

   b. Find the area of the circle. _____

   c. Compare your answers from parts **a** and **b**. Which garden would give your sister the most space to plant?

_____

_____

17. Winnie measured the length of her father's ranch four times and got four different distances. Her measurements are shown in the table.

Distance Across Father's Ranch (km)			
1	**2**	**3**	**4**
$\sqrt{60}$	$\dfrac{58}{8}$	$7.\overline{3}$	$7\dfrac{3}{5}$

   a. To estimate the actual length, Winnie first approximated each distance to the nearest hundredth. Then she averaged the four numbers. Using a calculator, find Winnie's estimate.

_____

_____

   b. Winnie's father estimated the distance across his ranch to be $\sqrt{56}$ km. How does this distance compare to Winnie's estimate?

_____

Give an example of each type of number.

18. a real number between $\sqrt{13}$ and $\sqrt{14}$ _____

19. an irrational number between 5 and 7 _____

20. A teacher asks his students to write the numbers shown in order from least to greatest. Paul thinks the numbers are already in order. Sandra thinks the order should be reversed. Who is right?

_____

_____

$$\sqrt{115}, \frac{115}{11}, \text{ and } 10.5624$$

21. Math History There is a famous irrational number called Euler's number, often symbolized with an *e*. Like π, it never seems to end. The first few digits of *e* are 2.7182818284.

a. Between which two square roots of integers could you find this number?

_____

b. Between which two square roots of integers can you find π?

_____

 **FOCUS ON HIGHER ORDER THINKING**

Work Area

22. Analyze Relationships There are several approximations used for π, including 3.14 and $\frac{22}{7}$. π is approximately 3.14159265358979…

a. Label π and the two approximations on the number line.

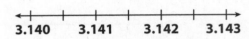

3.140   3.141   3.142   3.143

b. Which of the two approximations is a better estimate for π? Explain.

_____

c. Find a whole number *x* in $\frac{x}{113}$ so that the ratio is a better estimate for

π than the two given approximations. _____

23. Communicate Mathematical Ideas If a set of six numbers that include both rational and irrational numbers is graphed on a number line, what is the fewest number of distinct points that need to be graphed? Explain.

_____

_____

_____

24. Critique Reasoning Jill says that $12.\overline{6}$ is less than 12.63. Explain her error.

_____

Ready to Go On?

Personal Math Trainer
Online Assessment and Intervention
⏼ my.hrw.com

1.1 Rational and Irrational Numbers

Write each fraction as a decimal.

1. $\frac{7}{20}$ _____

2. $\frac{14}{11}$ _____

3. $1\frac{7}{8}$ _____

Find the two square roots of each number.

4. 81 _____

5. 1600 _____

6. $\frac{1}{100}$ _____

7. A square patio has an area of 200 square feet. How long is each side of the patio to the nearest 0.05? _____

1.2 Sets of Real Numbers

Write all names that apply to each number.

8. $\frac{121}{\sqrt{121}}$ _____

9. $\frac{\pi}{2}$ _____

10. Tell whether the statement "All integers are rational numbers" is true or false. Explain your choice.

_____

_____

1.3 Ordering Real Numbers

Compare. Write $<$, $>$, or $=$.

11. $\sqrt{8} + 3$ ◯ $8 + \sqrt{3}$

12. $\sqrt{5} + 11$ ◯ $5 + \sqrt{11}$

Order the numbers from least to greatest.

13. $\sqrt{39}, 2\pi, 6.\overline{2}$ _____

14. $\sqrt{\frac{1}{25}}, \frac{1}{4}, 0.\overline{2}$ _____

? **ESSENTIAL QUESTION**

15. How are real numbers used to describe real-world situations?

_____

_____

Personal
Math Trainer

my.hrw.com
Online
Assessment and
Intervention

Selected Response

1. The square root of a number is 9. What is the other square root?

- (A) −9
- (C) 3
- (B) −3
- (D) 81

2. A square acre of land is 4840 square yards. Between which two integers is the length of one side?

- (A) between 24 and 25 yards
- (B) between 69 and 70 yards
- (C) between 242 and 243 yards
- (D) between 695 and 696 yards

3. Which of the following is an integer but not a whole number?

- (A) −9.6
- (C) 0
- (B) −4
- (D) 3.7

4. Which statement is false?

- (A) No integers are irrational numbers.
- (B) All whole numbers are integers.
- (C) No real numbers are irrational numbers.
- (D) All integers greater than 0 are whole numbers.

5. Which set of numbers best describes the displayed weights on a digital scale that shows each weight to the nearest half pound?

- (A) whole numbers
- (B) rational numbers
- (C) real numbers
- (D) integers

6. Which of the following is not true?

- (A) $\sqrt{16} + 4 > \sqrt{4} + 5$
- (B) $3\pi > 9$
- (C) $\sqrt{27} + 3 > \frac{17}{2}$
- (D) $5 - \sqrt{24} < 1$

7. Which number is between $\sqrt{21}$ and $\frac{3\pi}{2}$?

- (A) $\frac{14}{3}$
- (C) 5
- (B) $2\sqrt{6}$
- (D) $\pi + 1$

8. What number is shown on the graph?

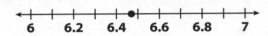

- (A) $\pi + 3$
- (C) $\sqrt{20} + 2$
- (B) $\frac{129}{20}$
- (D) $6.\overline{14}$

9. Which list of numbers is in order from least to greatest?

- (A) $3.3, \frac{10}{3}, \pi, \frac{11}{4}$
- (C) $\pi, \frac{10}{3}, \frac{11}{4}, 3.3$
- (B) $\frac{10}{3}, 3.3, \frac{11}{4}, \pi$
- (D) $\frac{11}{4}, \pi, 3.3, \frac{10}{3}$

Gridded Response

10. What is the decimal equivalent of the fraction $\frac{28}{25}$?

Scientific Notation

 ESSENTIAL QUESTION

How can you use scientific notation to solve real-world problems?

my.hrw.com

Real-World Video

The distance from Earth to other planets, moons, and stars is a very great number of kilometers. To make it easier to write very large and very small numbers, we use scientific notation.

GO DIGITAL

my.hrw.com

my.hrw.com

Go digital with your write-in student edition, accessible on any device.

Math On the Spot

Scan with your smart phone to jump directly to the online edition, video tutor, and more.

Animated Math

Interactively explore key concepts to see how math works.

Personal Math Trainer

Get immediate feedback and help as you work through practice sets.

Are YOU Ready?

Complete these exercises to review skills you will need for this chapter.

Personal Math Trainer

Online Assessment and Intervention

my.hrw.com

Exponents

EXAMPLE $10^4 = 10 \times 10 \times 10 \times 10$ Write the exponential expression as a product.
      $= 10,000$ Simplify.

Write each exponential expression as a decimal.

1. 10^2 _____   **2.** 10^3 _____   **3.** 10^5 _____   **4.** 10^7 _____

Multiply and Divide by Powers of 10

EXAMPLE $0.0478 \times 10^5 = 0.0478 \times 100,000$ Identify the number of zeros in the power of 10.
      $= 4,780$ When multiplying, move the decimal point to the *right* the same number of places as the number of zeros.

      $37.9 \div 10^4 = 37.9 \div 10,000$ Identify the number of zeros in the power of 10.
      $= 0.00379$ When dividing, move the decimal point to the *left* the same number of places as the number of zeros.

Find each product or quotient.

5. 45.3×10^3 **6.** $7.08 \div 10^2$ **7.** 0.00235×10^6 **8.** $3,600 \div 10^4$

_____   _____   _____   _____

9. 0.5×10^2 **10.** $67.7 \div 10^5$ **11.** 0.0057×10^4 **12.** $195 \div 10^6$

_____   _____   _____   _____

Reading Start-Up

Visualize Vocabulary

Use the ✔ words to complete the Venn diagram. You can put more than one word in each section of the diagram.

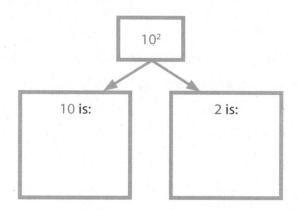

10^2

10 is:

2 is:

Understand Vocabulary

Complete the sentences using the preview words.

1. A number produced by raising a base to an exponent

   is a _____.

2. _____ is a method of writing very large or very small numbers by using powers of 10.

3. A _____ is any number that can be expressed as a ratio of two integers.

© Houghton Mifflin Harcourt Publishing Company

Vocabulary

Review Words
✔ base (base)
✔ exponent (exponente)
  integers (entero)
✔ positive number (número positivo)
  standard notation (notación estándar)

Preview Words
  power (potencia)
  rational number (número racional)
  real numbers (número real)
  scientific notation (notación científica)
  whole number (número entero)

Active Reading

Two-Panel Flip Chart Create a two-panel flip chart to help you understand the concepts in this module. Label one flap "Positive Powers of 10" and the other flap "Negative Powers of 10." As you study each lesson, write important ideas under the appropriate flap. Include sample problems that will help you remember the concepts later when you look back at your notes.

Unpacking the TEKS

Understanding the TEKS and the vocabulary terms in the TEKS will help you know exactly what you are expected to learn in this module.

TEKS 8.2.C

Convert between standard decimal notation and scientific notation.

Key Vocabulary

scientific notation *(notación científica)*
A method of writing very large or very small numbers by using powers of 10.

What It Means to You

You will convert very large numbers to scientific notation.

UNPACKING EXAMPLE 8.2.C

There are about 55,000,000,000 cells in an average-sized adult. Write this number in scientific notation.

Move the decimal point to the left until you have a number that is greater than or equal to 1 and less than 10.

5.5 0 0 0 0 0 0 0 0 0   *Move the decimal point 10 places to the left.*

5.5   *Remove the extra zeros.*

You would have to multiply 5.5 by 10^{10} to get 55,000,000,000.

$$55{,}000{,}000{,}000 = 5.5 \times 10^{10}$$

TEKS 8.2.C

Convert between standard decimal notation and scientific notation.

What It Means to You

You will convert very small numbers to scientific notation.

UNPACKING EXAMPLE 8.2.C

Convert the number 0.00000000135 to scientific notation.

Move the decimal point to the right until you have a number that is greater than or equal to 1 and less than 10.

0.0 0 0 0 0 0 0 0 1 3 5   *Move the decimal point 9 places to the right.*

1.35   *Remove the extra zeros.*

You would have to multiply 1.35 by 10^{-9} to get 0.00000000135.

$$0.00000000135 = 1.35 \times 10^{-9}$$

Visit **my.hrw.com** to see all the **TEKS** unpacked.

my.hrw.com

© Houghton Mifflin Harcourt Publishing Company

Scientific Notation with Positive Powers of 10

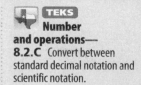

TEKS
Number and operations— 8.2.C Convert between standard decimal notation and scientific notation.

 ESSENTIAL QUESTION

How can you use scientific notation to express very large quantities?

EXPLORE ACTIVITY  TEKS 8.2.C

Using Scientific Notation

Scientific notation is a method of expressing very large and very small numbers as a product of a number greater than or equal to 1 and less than 10, and a power of 10.

The weights of various sea creatures are shown in the table. Write the weight of the blue whale in scientific notation.

Sea Creature	Blue whale	Gray whale	Whale shark
Weight (lb)	250,000	68,000	41,200

A Move the decimal point in 250,000 to the left as many places as necessary to find a number that is greater than or equal to 1 and less than 10.

What number did you find? _____

B Divide 250,000 by your answer to **A**. Write your answer as a power of 10.

_____

C Combine your answers to **A** and **B** to represent 250,000.

$$250,000 = \boxed{} \times 10^{\boxed{}}$$

Repeat steps **A** through **C** to write the weight of the whale shark in scientific notation.

$$41,200 = \boxed{} \times 10^{\boxed{}}$$

Reflect

1. How many places to the left did you move the decimal point to write

41,200 in scientific notation? _____

2. What is the exponent on 10 when you write 41,200 in scientific notation?

_____

Writing a Number in Scientific Notation

To translate between standard notation and scientific notation, you can count the number of places the decimal point moves.

Writing Numbers in Scientific Notation

When the number is greater than or equal to 10, use a positive exponent.	$84{,}000 = 8.4 \times 10^4$	The decimal point moves 4 places.

EXAMPLE 1

 TEKS 8.2.C

The distance from Earth to the Sun is about 93,000,000 miles. Write this distance in scientific notation.

STEP 1 Move the decimal point in 93,000,000 to the left until you have a number that is greater than or equal to 1 and less than 10.

9.3 0 0 0 0 0 0.   Move the decimal point 7 places to the left.

9.3   Remove extra zeros.

STEP 2 Divide the original number by the result from Step 1.

10,000,000   Divide 93,000,000 by 9.3.

10^7 Write your answer as a power of 10.

STEP 3 Write the product of the results from Steps 1 and 2.

$93{,}000{,}000 = 9.3 \times 10^7$ miles   Write a product to represent 93,000,000 in scientific notation.

Math Talk
Mathematical Processes

Is 12×10^7 written in scientific notation? Explain.

YOUR TURN

Write each number in scientific notation.

3. 6,400

4. 570,000,000,000

_____   _____

5. A light-year is the distance that light travels in a year and is equivalent to 9,461,000,000,000 km. Write this distance in scientific notation.

_____

© Houghton Mifflin Harcourt Publishing Company

Writing a Number in Standard Notation

To translate between scientific notation and standard notation, move the decimal point the number of places indicated by the exponent in the power of 10. When the exponent is positive, move the decimal point to the right and add placeholder zeros as needed.

Math On the Spot
my.hrw.com

EXAMPLE 2

TEKS 8.2.C

My Notes

Write 3.5×10^6 in standard notation.

STEP 1 Use the exponent of the power of 10 to see how many places to move the decimal point.

6 places

STEP 2 Place the decimal point. Since you are going to write a number greater than 3.5, move the decimal point to the *right*. Add placeholder zeros if necessary.

3 500 000.

The number 3.5×10^6 written in standard notation is 3,500,000.

Reflect

6. Explain why the exponent in 3.5×10^6 is 6, while there are only 5 zeros in 3,500,000.

_____

_____

_____

7. What is the exponent on 10 when you write 5.3 in scientific notation?

_____

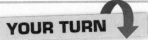

Write each number in standard notation.

8. 7.034×10^9

_____

9. 2.36×10^5

_____

10. The mass of one roosting colony of Monarch butterflies in Mexico was estimated at 5×10^6 grams. Write this mass in standard notation.

_____

Personal Math Trainer

Online Assessment and Intervention

my.hrw.com

Write each number in scientific notation. (Explore Activity and Example 1)

1. 58,927
Hint: Move the decimal left 4 places.

_____

2. 1,304,000,000
Hint: Move the decimal left 9 places.

_____

3. 6,730,000

_____

4. 13,300

_____

5. An ordinary quarter contains about 97,700,000,000,000,000,000,000 atoms.

_____

6. The distance from Earth to the Moon is about 384,000 kilometers.

_____

Write each number in standard notation. (Example 2)

7. 4×10^5
Hint: Move the decimal right 5 places.

_____

8. 1.8499×10^9
Hint: Move the decimal right 9 places.

_____

9. 6.41×10^3

_____

10. 8.456×10^7

_____

11. 8×10^5

_____

12. 9×10^{10}

_____

13. Diana calculated that she spent about 5.4×10^4 seconds doing her math homework during October. Write this time in standard notation. (Example 2)

_____

14. The town recycled 7.6×10^6 cans this year. Write the number of cans in standard notation. (Example 2)

_____

? ESSENTIAL QUESTION CHECK-IN

15. Describe how to write 3,482,000,000 in scientific notation.

_____

_____

_____

_____

2.1 Independent Practice

 8.2.C

Personal Math Trainer

Online Assessment and Intervention

my.hrw.com

Paleontology Use the table for problems 16–21. Write the estimated weight of each dinosaur in scientific notation.

Estimated Weight of Dinosaurs	
Name	**Pounds**
Argentinosaurus	220,000
Brachiosaurus	100,000
Apatosaurus	66,000
Diplodocus	50,000
Camarasaurus	40,000
Cetiosauriscus	19,850

16. Apatosaurus _____

17. Argentinosaurus _____

18. Brachiosaurus _____

19. Camarasaurus _____

20. Cetiosauriscus _____

21. Diplodocus _____

22. A single little brown bat can eat up to 1000 mosquitoes in a single hour. Express in scientific notation how many mosquitoes a little brown bat might eat in 10.5 hours.

_____

23. **Multistep** Samuel can type nearly 40 words per minute. Use this information to find the number of hours it would take him to type 2.6×10^5 words.

_____

_____

24. **Entomology** A tropical species of mite named *Archegozetes longisetosus* is the record holder for the strongest insect in the world. It can lift up to 1.182×10^3 times its own weight.

a. If you were as strong as this insect, explain how you could find how many pounds you could lift.

_____

_____

_____

b. Complete the calculation to find how much you could lift, in pounds, if you were as strong as an *Archegozetes longisetosus* mite. Express your answer in both scientific notation and standard notation.

_____

_____

25. During a discussion in science class, Sharon learns that at birth an elephant weighs around 230 pounds. In four herds of elephants tracked by conservationists, about 20 calves were born during the summer. In scientific notation, express approximately how much the calves weighed all together.

_____

26. **Classifying Numbers** Which of the following numbers are written in scientific notation?

0.641×10^3 9.999×10^4

2×10^1 4.38×5^{10}

_____

© Houghton Mifflin Harcourt Publishing Company

27. Explain the Error Polly's parents' car weighs about 3500 pounds. Samantha, Esther, and Polly each wrote the weight of the car in scientific notation. Polly wrote 35.0×10^2, Samantha wrote 0.35×10^4, and Esther wrote 3.5×10^4.

a. Which of these girls, if any, is correct?

_____

b. Explain the mistakes of those who got the question wrong.

_____

_____

_____

28. Justify Reasoning If you were a biologist counting very large numbers of cells as part of your research, give several reasons why you might prefer to record your cell counts in scientific notation instead of standard notation.

_____

_____

_____

 **FOCUS ON HIGHER ORDER THINKING**

29. Draw Conclusions Which measurement would be least likely to be written in scientific notation: number of stars in a galaxy, number of grains of sand on a beach, speed of a car, or population of a country? Explain your reasoning.

_____

_____

30. Analyze Relationships Compare the two numbers to find which is greater. Explain how you can compare them without writing them in standard notation first.

$$4.5 \times 10^6 \qquad 2.1 \times 10^8$$

_____

_____

31. Communicate Mathematical Ideas To determine whether a number is written in scientific notation, what test can you apply to the first factor, and what test can you apply to the second factor?

_____

_____

Scientific Notation with Negative Powers of 10

TEKS
Number and operations—8.2.C
Convert between standard decimal notation and scientific notation.

? ESSENTIAL QUESTION

How can you use scientific notation to express very small quantities?

EXPLORE ACTIVITY  **TEKS** 8.2.C

Negative Powers of 10

You can use what you know about writing very large numbers in scientific notation to write very small numbers in scientific notation.

A typical human hair has a diameter of 0.000025 meter. Write this number in scientific notation.

A Notice how the decimal point moves in the list below. Complete the list.

$2.345 \times 10^0 = 2.345$ It moves one place to the right with each increasing power of 10.

$2.345 \times 10^1 = 23.45$

$2.345 \times 10^2 = 234.5$

$2.345 \times 10^{\boxed{}} = 2345.$

$2.345 \times 10^0 = 2.345$ It moves one place to the left with each decreasing power of 10.

$2.345 \times 10^{-1} = 0.2345$

$2.345 \times 10^{-2} = 0.02345$

$2.345 \times 10^{\boxed{}} = 0.002345$

B Move the decimal point in 0.000025 to the right as many places as necessary to find a number that is greater than or equal to 1 and

less than 10. What number did you find? _____

C Divide 0.000025 by your answer to **B**. _____

Write your answer as a power of 10. _____

D Combine your answers to **B** and **C** to represent 0.000025 in

scientific notation. _____

Reflect

1. When you move the decimal point, how can you know whether you are increasing or decreasing the number?

_____

2. Explain how the two steps of moving the decimal and multiplying by a power of 10 leave the value of the original number unchanged.

_____

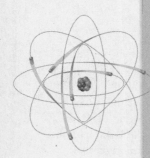
Writing a Number in Scientific Notation

To write a number less than 1 in scientific notation, move the decimal point right and use a negative exponent.

Writing Numbers in Scientific Notation

| When the number is less than 1, use a negative exponent. | $0.0\,7\,8\,3 = 7.83 \times 10^{-2}$ | The decimal point moves 2 places. |

EXAMPLE 1  TEKS 8.2.C

The average size of an atom is about 0.00000003 centimeter across. Write the average size of an atom in scientific notation.

Move the decimal point as many places as necessary to find a number that is greater than or equal to 1 and less than 10.

STEP 1 Place the decimal point. 3.0

STEP 2 Count the number of places you moved the decimal point. 8

STEP 3 Multiply 3.0 times a power of 10. 3.0×10^{-8}

Since 0.00000003 is less than 1, you moved the decimal point to the right and the exponent on 10 is negative.

The average size of an atom in scientific notation is 3.0×10^{-8}.

Reflect

3. **Critical Thinking** When you write a number that is less than 1 in scientific notation, how does the power of 10 differ from when you write a number greater than 1 in scientific notation?

_____

YOUR TURN

Write each number in scientific notation.

4. 0.0000829

_____

5. 0.000000302

_____

6. A typical red blood cell in human blood has a diameter of approximately 0.000007 meter. Write this diameter

in scientific notation. _____

Writing a Number in Standard Notation

To translate between scientific notation and standard notation with very small numbers, you can move the decimal point the number of places indicated by the exponent on the power of 10. When the exponent is negative, move the decimal point to the left.

Math On the Spot
⏱ my.hrw.com

EXAMPLE 2  TEKS 8.2.C

Platelets are one component of human blood. A typical platelet has a diameter of approximately 2.33×10^{-6} meter. Write 2.33×10^{-6} in standard notation.

STEP 1 Use the exponent of the power of 10 to see how many places to move the decimal point. **6 places**

STEP 2 Place the decimal point. Since you are going to write a number less than 2.33, move the decimal point to the *left*. Add placeholder zeros if necessary. 0.0 0 0 0 0 2 3 3

The number 2.33×10^{-6} in standard notation is 0.00000233.

Math Talk
Mathematical Processes

Describe the two factors that multiply together to form a number written in scientific notation.

Reflect

7. **Justify Reasoning** Explain whether 0.9×10^{-5} is written in scientific notation. If not, write the number correctly in scientific notation.

_____

_____

_____

8. Which number is larger, 2×10^{-3} or 3×10^{-2}? Explain.

_____

YOUR TURN

Write each number in standard notation.

9. 1.045×10^{-6} 10. 9.9×10^{-5}

_____ _____

11. Jeremy measured the length of an ant as 1×10^{-2} meter. Write this length in standard notation.

_____

Personal Math Trainer
Online Assessment and Intervention
⏱ my.hrw.com

© Houghton Mifflin Harcourt Publishing Company

Write each number in scientific notation. (Explore Activity and Example 1)

1. 0.000487
Hint: Move the decimal right 4 places.

_____

2. 0.000028
Hint: Move the decimal right 5 places.

_____

3. 0.000059

_____

4. 0.0417

_____

5. Picoplankton can be as small as 0.00002 centimeter.

_____

6. The average mass of a grain of sand on a beach is about 0.000015 gram.

_____

Write each number in standard notation. (Example 2)

7. 2×10^{-5}
Hint: Move the decimal left 5 places.

_____

8. 3.582×10^{-6}
Hint: Move the decimal left 6 places.

_____

9. 8.3×10^{-4}

_____

10. 2.97×10^{-2}

_____

11. 9.06×10^{-5}

_____

12. 4×10^{-5}

_____

13. The average length of a dust mite is approximately 0.0001 meter. Write this number in scientific notation. (Example 1)

_____

14. The mass of a proton is about 1.7×10^{-24} gram. Write this number in standard notation. (Example 2)

_____

? ESSENTIAL QUESTION CHECK-IN

15. Describe how to write 0.0000672 in scientific notation.

_____

_____

_____

2.2 Independent Practice

 TEKS 8.2.C

Personal Math Trainer

Online Assessment and Intervention

my.hrw.com

Use the table for problems 16–21. Write the diameter of the fibers in scientific notation.

Average Diameter of Natural Fibers	
Animal	**Fiber Diameter (cm)**
Vicuña	0.0008
Angora rabbit	0.0013
Alpaca	0.00277
Angora goat	0.0045
Llama	0.0035
Orb web spider	0.015

16. Alpaca

_____

17. Angora rabbit

_____

18. Llama

_____

19. Angora goat

_____

20. Orb web spider

_____

21. Vicuña

_____

22. **Make a Conjecture** Which measurement would be least likely to be written in scientific notation: the thickness of a dog hair, the radius of a period on this page, the ounces in a cup of milk? Explain your reasoning.

_____

_____

23. **Multiple Representations** Convert the length 7 centimeters to meters. Compare the numerical values when both numbers are written in scientific notation.

_____

_____

_____

_____

24. **Draw Conclusions** A graphing calculator displays 1.89×10^{12} as 1.89ᴇ12. How do you think it would display 1.89×10^{-12}? What does the ᴇ stand for?

_____

_____

25. **Communicate Mathematical Ideas** When a number is written in scientific notation, how can you tell right away whether or not it is greater than or equal to 1?

_____

_____

_____

26. The volume of a drop of a certain liquid is 0.000047 liter. Write the volume of the drop of liquid in scientific notation.

_____

27. **Justify Reasoning** If you were asked to express the weight in ounces of a ladybug in scientific notation, would the exponent of the 10 be positive or negative? Justify your response.

_____

_____

Physical Science The table shows the length of the radii of several very small or very large items. Complete the table.

	Item	Radius in Meters (Standard Notation)	Radius in Meters (Scientific Notation)
28.	The Moon	1,740,000	
29.	Atom of silver		1.25×10^{-10}
30.	Atlantic wolfish egg	0.0028	
31.	Jupiter		7.149×10^{7}
32.	Atom of aluminum	0.000000000182	
33.	Mars		3.397×10^{6}

34. List the items in the table in order from the smallest to the largest.

_____

_____

 **FOCUS ON HIGHER ORDER THINKING**

35. Analyze Relationships Write the following diameters from least to greatest.

1.5×10^{-2} m 1.2×10^{2} m 5.85×10^{-3} m 2.3×10^{-2} m 9.6×10^{-1} m

_____

_____

36. Critique Reasoning Jerod's friend Al had the following homework problem:

Express 5.6×10^{-7} in standard form.

Al wrote 56,000,000. How can Jerod explain Al's error and how to correct it?

_____

_____

_____

37. Make a Conjecture Two numbers are written in scientific notation. The number with a positive exponent is divided by the number with a negative exponent. Describe the result. Explain your answer.

_____

_____

_____

Work Area

Ready to Go On?

Personal Math Trainer

Online Assessment and Intervention

my.hrw.com

2.1 Scientific Notation with Positive Powers of 10

Write each number in scientific notation.

1. 2,000 _____

2. 91,007,500 _____

3. On average, the Moon's distance from Earth is about 384,400 km.

What is this distance in scientific notation? _____

Write each number in standard notation.

4. 1.0395×10^9 _____

5. 4×10^2 _____

6. The population of Indonesia was about 2.48216×10^8 people in 2011.

What is this number in standard notation? _____

2.2 Scientific Notation with Negative Powers of 10

Write each number in scientific notation.

7. 0.02 _____

8. 0.000701 _____

Write each number in standard notation.

9. 8.9×10^{-5} _____

10. 4.41×10^{-2} _____

Complete the table.

	Name of Biological Structure	Diameter of Structure in Standard Notation	Diameter of Structure in Scientific Notation
11.	Lymphocyte	0.000009 m	
12.	Influenza virus		9.5×10^{-8} m
13.	Neuron (large)	0.000078 m	

? ESSENTIAL QUESTION

14. How is scientific notation used in the real world?

_____

_____

_____

Selected Response

1. Which of the following is the number 90 written in scientific notation?

Ⓐ 90×10^2 Ⓒ 90×10^1

Ⓑ 9×10^2 Ⓓ 9×10^1

2. About 786,700,000 passengers traveled by plane in the United States in 2010. What is this number written in scientific notation?

Ⓐ $7,867 \times 10^5$ passengers

Ⓑ 7.867×10^2 passengers

Ⓒ 7.867×10^8 passengers

Ⓓ 7.867×10^9 passengers

3. In 2011, the population of Mali was about 1.584×10^7 people. What is this number written in standard notation?

Ⓐ 1.584 people

Ⓑ 1,584 people

Ⓒ 15,840,000 people

Ⓓ 158,400,000 people

4. The square root of a number is between 7 and 8. Which could be the number?

Ⓐ 72   Ⓒ 51

Ⓑ 83   Ⓓ 66

5. Pilar is writing a number in scientific notation. The number is greater than ten million and less than one hundred million. Which exponent will Pilar use?

Ⓐ 10   Ⓒ 6

Ⓑ 7   Ⓓ 2

6. Place the numbers in order from least to greatest.
$0.24, 4 \times 10^{-2}, 0.042, 2 \times 10^{-4}, 0.004$

Ⓐ $2 \times 10^{-4}, 4 \times 10^{-2}, 0.004, 0.042, 0.24$

Ⓑ $0.004, 2 \times 10^{-4}, 0.042, 4 \times 10^{-2}, 0.24$

Ⓒ $0.004, 2 \times 10^{-4}, 4 \times 10^{-2}, 0.042, 0.24$

Ⓓ $2 \times 10^{-4}, 0.004, 4 \times 10^{-2}, 0.042, 0.24$

7. Which of the following is the number 1.0085×10^{-4} written in standard notation?

Ⓐ 10,085   Ⓒ 0.00010085

Ⓑ 1.0085   Ⓓ 0.000010085

8. A human hair has a width of about 6.5×10^{-5} meter. What is this width written in standard notation?

Ⓐ 0.00000065 meter

Ⓑ 0.0000065 meter

Ⓒ 0.000065 meter

Ⓓ 0.00065 meter

Gridded Response

9. Write 2.38×10^{-1} in standard form.

MODULE 1 Real Numbers

? ESSENTIAL QUESTION

How can you use real numbers to solve real-world problems?

Key Vocabulary

irrational number (*número irracional*)

perfect square (*cuadrado perfecto*)

principal square root (*raíz cuadrada principal*)

rational number (*número racional*)

real number (*número real*)

repeating decimal (*decimal periódico*)

square root (*raíz cuadrada*)

terminating decimal (*decimal finito*)

EXAMPLE 1

Estimate the value of $\sqrt{5}$, and estimate the position of $\sqrt{5}$ on a number line.

5 is between the perfect squares 4 and 9. $4 < 5 < 9$

Take the square root of each number. $\sqrt{4} < \sqrt{5} < \sqrt{9}$

$\sqrt{5}$ is between 2 and 3. $2 < \sqrt{5} < 3$

$2.2^2 = 4.84$ $2.3^2 = 5.29$

$\sqrt{5}$ is between 2.2 and 2.3.

A good estimate is 2.25.

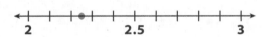

EXAMPLE 2

Write all names that apply to each number.

A $5.\overline{4}$
rational, real

$5.\overline{4}$ is a repeating decimal.

B $\frac{8}{4}$
whole, integer, rational, real

$\frac{8}{4} = 2$

C $\sqrt{13}$
irrational, real

13 is a whole number that is not a perfect square.

EXAMPLE 3

Order 6, 2π, and √38 from least to greatest.

2π is approximately equal to 2×3.14, or 6.28.

$\sqrt{38}$ is approximately 6.15.

$\sqrt{36} < \sqrt{38} < \sqrt{49}$ $6 < \sqrt{38} < 7$ $6.1^2 = 37.21$ $6.2^2 = 38.44$

From least to greatest, the numbers are 6, $\sqrt{38}$, and 2π.

EXERCISES

Find the two square roots of each number. If the number is not a perfect square, approximate the values to the nearest 0.05. (Lesson 1.1)

1. 16 _____

2. $\frac{4}{25}$ _____

3. 225 _____

4. $\frac{1}{49}$ _____

5. $\sqrt{10}$ _____

6. $\sqrt{18}$ _____

Write all names that apply to each number. (Lesson 1.2)

7. $\frac{2}{3}$

_____

8. $-\sqrt{100}$

_____

9. $\frac{15}{5}$

_____

10. $\sqrt{21}$

_____

Compare. Write <, >, or =. (Lesson 1.3)

11. $\sqrt{7} + 5$ ◯ $7 + \sqrt{5}$

12. $6 + \sqrt{8}$ ◯ $\sqrt{6} + 8$

13. $\sqrt{4} - 2$ ◯ $4 - \sqrt{2}$

Order the numbers from least to greatest. (Lesson 1.3)

14. $\sqrt{81}, \frac{72}{7}, 8.9$

_____

15. $\sqrt{7}, 2.55, \frac{7}{3}$

_____

Scientific Notation

ESSENTIAL QUESTION

How can you use scientific notation to solve real-world problems?

EXAMPLE 1

The diameter of Earth at the equator is approximately 12,700 kilometers. Write the diameter of Earth in scientific notation.

Move the decimal point in 12,700 four places to the left: 1.2 7 0 0.

$12{,}700 = 1.27 \times 10^4$

EXAMPLE 2

The diameter of a human hair is approximately 0.00254 centimeters. Write the diameter of a human hair in scientific notation.

Move the decimal point in 0.00254 three places to the right: 0.0 0 2.5 4

$0.00254 = 2.54 \times 10^{-3}$

EXERCISES

Write each number in scientific notation. (Lessons 2.1, 2.2)

1. 3000 _____

2. 0.000015 _____

3. 25,500,000 _____

4. 0.00734 _____

Write each number in standard notation. (Lessons 2.1, 2.2)

5. 5.23×10^4 _____

6. 1.05×10^6 _____

7. 4.7×10^{-1} _____

8. 1.33×10^{-5} _____

Use the information in the table to write each weight in scientific notation. (Lessons 2.1, 2.2)

Animal	ant	butterfly	elephant
Weight (lb)	0.000000661	0.00000625	9900

9. Ant _____

10. Butterfly _____

11. Elephant _____

1. **CAREERS IN MATH** **Astronomer** An astronomer is studying Proxima Centauri, which is the closest star to our Sun. Proxima Centauri is 39,900,000,000,000,000 meters away.

   a. Write this distance in scientific notation.

   _____

   b. Light travels at a speed of 3.0×10^8 m/s (meters per second). How can you use this information to calculate the time in seconds it takes for light from Proxima Centauri to reach Earth? How many seconds does it take? Write your answer in scientific notation.

   _____

   _____

   c. Knowing that 1 year $= 3.1536 \times 10^7$ seconds, how many years does it take for light to travel from Proxima Centauri to Earth? Write your answer in standard notation. Round your answer to two decimal places.

   _____

2. Cory is making a poster of common geometric shapes. He draws a square with a side of length 4^3 cm, an equilateral triangle with a height of $\sqrt{200}$ cm, a circle with a circumference of 8π cm, a rectangle with length $\frac{122}{5}$ cm, and a parallelogram with base 3.14 cm.

   a. Which of these numbers are irrational?

   _____

   b. Write the numbers in this problem in order from least to greatest. Approximate π as 3.14.

   _____

   c. Explain why 3.14 is rational, but π is not.

   _____

   _____

   _____

Selected Response

1. A square on a large calendar has an area of 4220 square millimeters. Between which two integers is the length of one side of the square?

(A) between 20 and 21 millimeters

(B) between 64 and 65 millimeters

(C) between 204 and 205 millimeters

(D) between 649 and 650 millimeters

2. Which of the following numbers is rational but **not** an integer?

(A) −9　　　　(C) 0

(B) −4.3　　　(D) 3

3. Which statement is false?

(A) No integers are irrational numbers.

(B) All whole numbers are integers.

(C) All rational numbers are real numbers.

(D) All integers are whole numbers.

4. Which set best describes the numbers displayed on a telephone keypad?

(A) whole numbers

(B) rational numbers

(C) real numbers

(D) integers

5. In 2011, the population of Laos was about 6.586×10^6 people. What is this number written in standard notation?

(A) 6,586 people

(B) 658,600 people

(C) 6,586,000 people

(D) 65,860,000 people

6. Which of the following is **not** true?

(A) $\sqrt{16} + 4 > \sqrt{4} + 5$

(B) $4\pi > 12$

(C) $\sqrt{18} + 2 < \frac{15}{2}$

(D) $6 - \sqrt{35} < 0$

7. Which number is between $\sqrt{50}$ and $\frac{5\pi}{2}$?

(A) $\frac{22}{3}$　　　　(C) 6

(B) $2\sqrt{8}$　　　　(D) $\pi + 3$

8. What number is indicated on the number line?

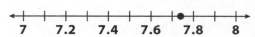

(A) $\pi + 4$

(B) $\frac{152}{20}$

(C) $\sqrt{14} + 4$

(D) $7.\overline{8}$

9. Which of the following is the number 5.03×10^{-5} written in standard form?

(A) 503,000

(B) 50,300,000

(C) 0.00503

(D) 0.0000503

10. In a recent year, about 20,700,000 passengers traveled by train in the United States. What is this number written in scientific notation?

(A) 2.07×10^1 passengers

(B) 2.07×10^4 passengers

(C) 2.07×10^7 passengers

(D) 2.07×10^8 passengers

11. A quarter weighs about 0.025 pounds. What is this weight written in scientific notation?

Ⓐ 2.5×10^{-2} pounds

Ⓑ 2.5×10^{1} pounds

Ⓒ 2.5×10^{-1} pounds

Ⓓ 2.5×10^{2} pounds

12. Which of the following is the number 3.0205×10^{-3} written in standard notation?

Ⓐ 0.00030205   Ⓒ 3.0205

Ⓑ 0.0030205   Ⓓ 3020.5

13. A human fingernail has a thickness of about 4.2×10^{-4} meter. What is this width written in standard notation?

Ⓐ 0.0000042 meter

Ⓑ 0.000042 meter

Ⓒ 0.00042 meter

Ⓓ 0.0042 meter

Gridded Response

14. The square root of a number is −18. What is the other square root?

				•		
⓪	⓪	⓪	⓪		⓪	⓪
①	①	①	①		①	①
②	②	②	②		②	②
③	③	③	③		③	③
④	④	④	④		④	④
⑤	⑤	⑤	⑤		⑤	⑤
⑥	⑥	⑥	⑥		⑥	⑥
⑦	⑦	⑦	⑦		⑦	⑦
⑧	⑧	⑧	⑧		⑧	⑧
⑨	⑨	⑨	⑨		⑨	⑨

Underline key words given in the test question so you know for certain what the question is asking.

15. Jerome is writing a number in scientific notation. The number is greater than one million and less than ten million. What will be the exponent in the number Jerome writes?

			•		
⓪	⓪	⓪	⓪	⓪	⓪
①	①	①	①	①	①
②	②	②	②	②	②
③	③	③	③	③	③
④	④	④	④	④	④
⑤	⑤	⑤	⑤	⑤	⑤
⑥	⑥	⑥	⑥	⑥	⑥
⑦	⑦	⑦	⑦	⑦	⑦
⑧	⑧	⑧	⑧	⑧	⑧
⑨	⑨	⑨	⑨	⑨	⑨

16. Write the number 3.3855×10^{2} in standard notation.

			•		
⓪	⓪	⓪	⓪	⓪	⓪
①	①	①	①	①	①
②	②	②	②	②	②
③	③	③	③	③	③
④	④	④	④	④	④
⑤	⑤	⑤	⑤	⑤	⑤
⑥	⑥	⑥	⑥	⑥	⑥
⑦	⑦	⑦	⑦	⑦	⑦
⑧	⑧	⑧	⑧	⑧	⑧
⑨	⑨	⑨	⑨	⑨	⑨

Proportional and Nonproportional Relationships and Functions

MODULE 3
Proportional Relationships
 **TEKS** 8.4.B, 8.4.C, 8.5.A, 8.5.E

MODULE 4
Nonproportional Relationships
TEKS 8.4.C, 8.5.B, 8.5.F, 8.9

MODULE 5
Writing Linear Equations
 TEKS 8.5.C, 8.5.D, 8.5.I

MODULE 6
Functions
 TEKS 8.4.C, 8.5.A, 8.5.B, 8.5.F, 8.5.G, 8.5.H, 8.5.I

CAREERS IN MATH

Cost Estimator A cost estimator determines the cost of a product or project, which helps businesses decide whether or not to manufacture a product or build a structure. Cost estimators analyze the costs of labor, materials, and use of equipment, among other things. Cost estimators use math when they assemble and analyze data. If you are interested in a career as a cost estimator, you should study these mathematical subjects:
- Algebra
- Trigonometry
- Calculus

Research other careers that require analyzing costs.

Unit 2 Performance Task

At the end of the unit, check out how **cost estimators** use math.

Vocabulary Preview

Use the puzzle to preview key vocabulary from this unit. Unscramble the circled letters within the found words to answer the riddle at the bottom of the page.

```
D I N T F O K F Z Y X I R H L
T I D O N O T N I R A V Z B I
U U R Z I E K N M C J E H Z N
P N X E V T T H W C V W S E E
T A E B C E C E K Q O P D U A
U I V A R T P N M K Q W N Z R
O X G C B O V Q U M Y X P L E
C P E B L K B A J F H L A K Q
J P V S L Q M J R G H R U N U
T E F N I Z B M C I D A X A A
T T O S V D T H W B A D B E T
K O O I I E Y W U O Q T P K I
P G T G L S O J Q R F D I Q O
D T A M H Q T S T A J Q X O N
B I V A R I A T E D A T A Y N
```

- The *y*-coordinate of the point where the graph crosses the *y*-axis. (Lesson 4-2)

- A rule that assigns exactly one output to each input. (Lesson 6-1)

- The result after applying the function machine's rule. (Lesson 6-1)

- A relationship written as $y = kx$, where the data increases or decreases together at a constant rate (2 words). (Lesson 3-4)

- The ratio of change in rise to the corresponding change in run on a graph. (Lesson 3-2)

- A set of data that is made up of two paired variables. (Lesson 5-3)

- An equation whose solutions form a straight line on a coordinate plane. (Lesson 4-1)

Q: How much of the money earned does a professional sports team pay its star athlete?

A: An ___ ___ ___ ___ ___ ___ – ___ ___ ___ ___ ___ ___ ___ ___ !

Proportional Relationships

 ESSENTIAL QUESTION

How can you use proportional relationships to solve real-world problems?

Real-World Video

Speedboats can travel at fast rates while sailboats travel more slowly. If you graphed distance versus time for both types of boats, you could tell by the steepness of the graph which boat was faster.

my.hrw.com

GO DIGITAL
my.hrw.com

my.hrw.com
Go digital with your write-in student edition, accessible on any device.

Math On the Spot
Scan with your smart phone to jump directly to the online edition, video tutor, and more.

Animated Math
Interactively explore key concepts to see how math works.

Personal Math Trainer
Get immediate feedback and help as you work through practice sets.

Are YOU Ready?

Complete these exercises to review skills you will need for this chapter.

Write Fractions as Decimals

EXAMPLE $\dfrac{1.7}{2.5} = ?$ Multiply the numerator and the denominator by a power of 10 so that the denominator is a whole number. $\dfrac{1.7 \times 10}{2.5 \times 10} = \dfrac{17}{25}$

Write the fraction as a division problem.
Write a decimal point and zeros in the dividend.
Place a decimal point in the quotient.
Divide as with whole numbers.

$$\begin{array}{r} 0.68 \\ 25\overline{)17.00} \\ -15\,0 \\ \hline 2\,00 \\ -2\,00 \\ \hline 0 \end{array}$$

Write each fraction as a decimal.

1. $\dfrac{3}{8}$ _____

2. $\dfrac{0.3}{0.4}$ _____

3. $\dfrac{0.13}{0.2}$ _____

4. $\dfrac{0.39}{0.75}$ _____

5. $\dfrac{4}{5}$ _____

6. $\dfrac{0.1}{2}$ _____

7. $\dfrac{3.5}{14}$ _____

8. $\dfrac{7}{14}$ _____

9. $\dfrac{0.3}{10}$ _____

Solve Proportions

EXAMPLE $\dfrac{5}{7} = \dfrac{x}{14}$

$\dfrac{5 \times 2}{7 \times 2} = \dfrac{x}{14}$ $7 \times 2 = 14$, so multiply the numerator and denominator by 2.

$\dfrac{10}{14} = \dfrac{x}{14}$ $5 \times 2 = 10$

$x = 10$

Solve each proportion for x.

10. $\dfrac{20}{18} = \dfrac{10}{x}$ _____

11. $\dfrac{x}{12} = \dfrac{30}{72}$ _____

12. $\dfrac{x}{4} = \dfrac{4}{16}$ _____

13. $\dfrac{11}{x} = \dfrac{132}{120}$ _____

14. $\dfrac{36}{48} = \dfrac{x}{4}$ _____

15. $\dfrac{x}{9} = \dfrac{21}{27}$ _____

16. $\dfrac{24}{16} = \dfrac{x}{2}$ _____

17. $\dfrac{30}{15} = \dfrac{6}{x}$ _____

18. $\dfrac{3}{x} = \dfrac{18}{36}$ _____

Reading Start-Up

Visualize Vocabulary

Use the ✔ words to complete the diagram.

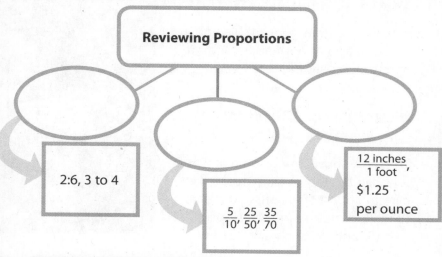

Reviewing Proportions

2:6, 3 to 4

$\frac{5}{10}, \frac{25}{50}, \frac{35}{70}$

$\frac{12 \text{ inches}}{1 \text{ foot}}$,
$1.25 per ounce

Understand Vocabulary

Match the term on the left to the definition on the right.

1. constant of variation

A. A constant ratio of two variables related proportionally.

2. constant of proportionality

B. The nonzero constant in a direct variation.

3. proportional relationship

C. A relationship between two quantities in which the ratio of one quantity to the other quantity is constant.

© Houghton Mifflin Harcourt Publishing Company

Vocabulary

Review Words

constant *(constante)*

✔ equivalent ratios *(razones equivalentes)*

proportion *(proporción)*

rate *(tasa)*

rate of change *(tasa de cambio)*

✔ ratios *(razón)*

✔ unit rates *(tasas unitarias)*

Preview Words

constant of proportionality *(constante de proporcionalidad)*

constant of variation *(constante de variación)*

direct variation *(variación directa)*

proportional relationship *(relación proporcional)*

slope *(pendiente)*

Active Reading

Key-Term Fold Before beginning the module, create a key-term fold to help you learn the vocabulary in this module. Write the highlighted vocabulary words on one side of the flap. Write the definition for each word on the other side of the flap. Use the key-term fold to quiz yourself on the definitions used in this module.

Unpacking the TEKS

Understanding the TEKS and the vocabulary terms in the TEKS will help you know exactly what you are expected to learn in this module.

 TEKS 8.4.C

Use data from a table or graph to determine the rate of change or slope and *y*-intercept in mathematical and real-world problems.

 TEKS 8.5.A

Represent linear proportional situations with tables, graphs, and equations in the form of $y = kx$.

Key Vocabulary

slope *(pendiente)*
A measure of the steepness of a line on a graph; the rise divided by the run.

What It Means to You

You will use data from a table and a graph to apply your understanding of rates to analyzing real-world situations.

UNPACKING EXAMPLE 8.4.C AND 8.5.A

The table shows the volume of water released by Hoover Dam over a certain period of time. Use the data to make a graph. Find the slope of the line and explain what it shows.

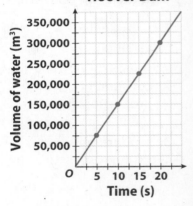

Water Released from Hoover Dam	
Time (s)	Volume of water (m³)
5	75,000
10	150,000
15	225,000
20	300,000

Water Released from Hoover Dam

The slope of the line is 15,000. This means that for every second that passed, 15,000 m³ of water was released from Hoover Dam.

Visit **my.hrw.com** to see all the **TEKS** unpacked.

my.hrw.com

Representing Proportional Relationships

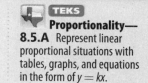
TEKS
Proportionality—
8.5.A Represent linear proportional situations with tables, graphs, and equations in the form of $y = kx$.

? ESSENTIAL QUESTION

How can you use tables, graphs, and equations to represent proportional situations?

EXPLORE ACTIVITY  **TEKS** 8.5.A

Representing Proportional Relationships with Tables

In 1870, the French writer Jules Verne published *20,000 Leagues Under the Sea*, one of the most popular science fiction novels ever written. One definition of a *league* is a unit of measure equaling 3 miles.

A Complete the table.

Distance (leagues)	1	2	6		20,000
Distance (miles)	3			36	

B What relationships do you see among the numbers in the table?

_____

_____

C For each column of the table, find the ratio of the distance in miles to the distance in leagues. Write each ratio in simplest form.

$$\frac{3}{1} = \boxed{} \qquad \frac{\boxed{}}{2} = \boxed{} \qquad \frac{\boxed{}}{6} = \boxed{} \qquad \frac{36}{\boxed{}} = \boxed{} \qquad \frac{\boxed{}}{20,000} = \boxed{}$$

D What do you notice about the ratios? _____

Reflect

1. If you know the distance between two points in leagues, how can you

find the distance in miles? _____

2. If you know the distance between two points in miles, how can you find

the distance in leagues? _____

Representing Proportional Relationships with Equations

The ratio of the distance in miles to the distance in leagues is constant. This relationship is said to be *proportional*. A **proportional relationship** is a relationship between two quantities in which the ratio of one quantity to the other quantity is constant.

A proportional relationship can be described by an equation of the form $y = kx$, where k is a number called the **constant of proportionality**.

Sometimes it is useful to use another form of the equation, $k = \frac{y}{x}$.

EXAMPLE 1

TEKS 8.5.A

Meghan earns $12 an hour at her part-time job. Show that the relationship between the amount she earned and the number of hours she worked is a proportional relationship. Then write an equation for the relationship.

> For every hour Meghan works, she earns $12. So, for 8 hours of work, she earns 8 × $12 = $96.

STEP 1   Make a table relating amount earned to number of hours.

Number of hours	1	2	4	8
Amount earned ($)	12	24	48	96

STEP 2   For each number of hours, write the relationship of the amount earned and the number of hours as a ratio in simplest form.

$\frac{\text{amount earned}}{\text{number of hours}}$ $\frac{12}{1} = 12$ $\frac{24}{2} = 12$ $\frac{48}{4} = 12$ $\frac{96}{8} = 12$

Since the ratios between the two quantities are all equal to 12, the relationship is proportional.

STEP 3   Write an equation.

> First tell what the variables represent.

Let x represent the number of hours.
Let y represent the amount earned.

Use the ratio as the constant of proportionality in the equation $y = kx$.

The equation is $y = 12x$.

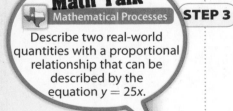

Math Talk
Mathematical Processes

Describe two real-world quantities with a proportional relationship that can be described by the equation $y = 25x$.

YOUR TURN

3. Fifteen bicycles are produced each hour at the Speedy Bike Works. Show that the relationship between the number of bikes produced and the number of hours is a proportional relationship. Then write an equation for the relationship. _____

© Houghton Mifflin Harcourt Publishing Company

Representing Proportional Relationships with Graphs

You can represent a proportional relationship with a graph. The graph will be a line that passes through the origin (0, 0). The graph shows the relationship between distance measured in miles to distance measured in leagues.

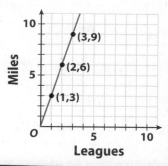

EXAMPLE 2

TEKS 8.5.A

The graph shows the relationship between the weight of an object on the Moon and its weight on Earth. Write an equation for this relationship.

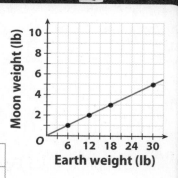

STEP 1 Use the points on the graph to make a table.

Earth weight (lb)	6	12	18	30
Moon weight (lb)	1	2	3	5

STEP 2 Find the constant of proportionality.

$$\frac{\text{Moon weight}}{\text{Earth weight}} \qquad \frac{1}{6} = \frac{1}{6} \qquad \frac{2}{12} = \frac{1}{6} \qquad \frac{3}{18} = \frac{1}{6} \qquad \frac{5}{30} = \frac{1}{6}$$

The constant of proportionality is $\frac{1}{6}$.

STEP 3 Write an equation.

Let x represent weight on Earth.

Let y represent weight on the Moon.

The equation is $y = \frac{1}{6}x$. *Replace k with $\frac{1}{6}$ in $y = kx$.*

YOUR TURN

The graph shows the relationship between the amount of time that a backpacker hikes and the distance traveled.

4. What does the point (5, 6) represent?

_____

5. What is the equation of the relationship?

_____

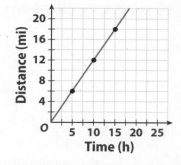

© Houghton Mifflin Harcourt Publishing Company • Image Credits: ©David Epperson/PhotoDisc/Getty Images

1. **Vocabulary** A proportional relationship is a relationship between two quantities in which the ratio of one quantity to the other quantity

   is / is not   constant.

2. **Vocabulary** When writing an equation of a proportional relationship in the form $y = kx$, k is replaced with the _____.

3. Write an equation that describes the proportional relationship between the number of days and the number of weeks in a given length of time. (Explore Activity and Example 1)

   a. Complete the table.

Time (weeks)	1	2	4		10
Time (days)	7			56	

   b. Let x represent _____.

   Let y represent _____.

   The equation that describes the relationship is _____.

Each table or graph represents a proportional relationship. Write an equation that describes the relationship. (Example 1 and Example 2)

4. **Physical Science** The relationship between the numbers of oxygen atoms and hydrogen atoms in water

Oxygen atoms	2	5		120
Hydrogen atoms	4		34	

   _____

5.

   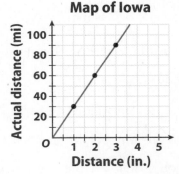

   Map of Iowa

   _____

? ESSENTIAL QUESTION CHECK-IN

6. If you know the equation of a proportional relationship, how can you draw the graph of the equation?

   _____

   _____

3.1 Independent Practice

 **TEKS** 8.5.A

Personal Math Trainer

Online Assessment and Intervention

my.hrw.com

The table shows the relationship between temperatures measured on the Celsius and Fahrenheit scales.

Celsius temperature	0	10	20	30	40	50
Fahrenheit temperature	32	50	68	86	104	122

7. Is the relationship between the temperature scales proportional? Why or why not?

_____

_____

8. Describe the graph of the Celsius-Fahrenheit relationship.

_____

_____

9. Analyze Relationships Ralph opened a savings account with a deposit of $100. Every month after that, he deposited $20 more.

a. Why is the relationship described not proportional?

_____

_____

b. How could the situation be changed to make the situation proportional?

_____

_____

10. Represent Real-World Problems Describe a real-world situation that can be modeled by the equation $y = \frac{1}{20}x$. Be sure to describe what each variable represents.

_____

_____

Look for a Pattern **The variables x and y are related proportionally.**

11. When $x = 8$, $y = 20$. Find y when $x = 42$. _____

12. When $x = 12$, $y = 8$. Find x when $y = 12$. _____

13. The graph shows the relationship between the distance that a snail crawls and the time that it crawls.

Snail Crawling

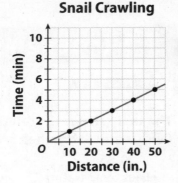

a. Use the points on the graph to make a table.

Distance (in.)					
Time (min)					

b. Write the equation for the relationship and tell what each variable represents.

_____

_____

c. How long does it take the snail to crawl 85 inches? _____

 **FOCUS ON HIGHER ORDER THINKING**

Work Area

14. Communicate Mathematical Ideas Explain why all of the graphs in this lesson show the first quadrant but omit the other three quadrants.

_____

_____

_____

_____

15. Analyze Relationships Complete the table.

Length of side of square	1	2	3	4	5
Perimeter of square					
Area of square					

a. Are the length of the side of a square and the perimeter of the square related proportionally? Why or why not?

_____

_____

b. Are the length of the side of a square and the area of the square related proportionally? Why or why not?

_____

_____

16. Make a Conjecture A table shows a proportional relationship where k is the constant of proportionality. The rows are then switched. How does the new constant of proportionality relate to the original one?

_____

Rate of Change and Slope

TEKS
Proportionality—
8.4.C Use data from a table or graph to determine the rate of change or slope and y-intercept in mathematical and real-world problems.

Math On the Spot
my.hrw.com

ESSENTIAL QUESTION

How do you find a rate of change or a slope?

Investigating Rates of Change

A **rate of change** is a ratio of the amount of change in the output to the amount of change in the input.

 **EXAMPLE 1** **TEKS** 8.4.C

Eve keeps a record of the number of lawns she has mowed and the money she has earned. Tell whether the rates of change are constant or variable.

	Day 1	Day 2	Day 3	Day 4
Number of lawns	1	3	6	8
Amount earned ($)	15	45	90	120

STEP 1 Identify the input and output variables.

Input variable: number of lawns   Output variable: amount earned

STEP 2 Find the rates of change.

Day 1 to Day 2: $\dfrac{\text{change in \$}}{\text{change in lawns}} = \dfrac{45-15}{3-1} = \dfrac{30}{2} = 15$

Day 2 to Day 3: $\dfrac{\text{change in \$}}{\text{change in lawns}} = \dfrac{90-45}{6-3} = \dfrac{45}{3} = 15$

Day 3 to Day 4: $\dfrac{\text{change in \$}}{\text{change in lawns}} = \dfrac{120-90}{8-6} = \dfrac{30}{2} = 15$

The rates of change are constant: $15 per lawn.

Math Talk
Mathematical Processes

Would you expect the rates of change of a car's speed during a drive through a city to be constant or variable? Explain.

YOUR TURN

1. The table shows the approximate height of a football after it is kicked. Tell whether the rates of change are constant or variable.

Find the rates of change:

_____

The rates of change are   **constant / variable**.

Time (s)	Height (ft)
0	0
0.5	18
1.5	31
2	26

Personal Math Trainer
Online Assessment and Intervention
my.hrw.com

Using Graphs to Find Rates of Change

You can also use a graph to find rates of change.

The graph shows the distance Nathan bicycled over time. What is Nathan's rate of change?

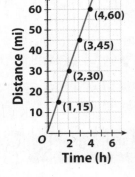

A Find the rate of change from 1 hour to 2 hours.

$$\frac{\text{change in distance}}{\text{change in time}} = \frac{30 - \boxed{}}{2 - 1} = \frac{\boxed{}}{1} = \boxed{} \text{ miles per hour}$$

B Find the rate of change from 1 hour to 4 hours.

$$\frac{\text{change in distance}}{\text{change in time}} = \frac{60 - \boxed{}}{4 - \boxed{}} = \frac{\boxed{}}{\boxed{}} = \boxed{} \text{ miles per hour}$$

C Find the rate of change from 2 hour to 4 hours.

$$\frac{\text{change in distance}}{\text{change in time}} = \frac{60 - \boxed{}}{4 - \boxed{}} = \frac{\boxed{}}{\boxed{}} = \boxed{} \text{ miles per hour}$$

D Recall that the graph of a proportional relationship is a line through the origin. Explain whether the relationship between Nathan's time and distance is a proportional relationship.

_____

_____

Reflect

2. **Make a Conjecture** Does a proportional relationship have a constant rate of change?

_____

3. Does it matter what interval you use when you find the rate of change of a proportional relationship? Explain.

_____

_____

Calculating Slope

When the rate of change of a relationship is constant, every segment of its graph has the same steepness, and the segments together form a line. The constant rate of change is called the *slope* of the line.

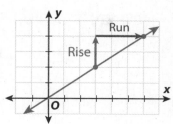

The **slope** of a line is the ratio of the change in *y*-values (rise) for a segment of the graph to the corresponding change in *x*-values (run).

EXAMPLE 2

TEKS 8.4.C

Find the slope of the line.

STEP 1 Choose two points on the line.

STEP 2 Find the change in *y*-values (rise) and the change in *x*-values (run) as you move from one point to the other.

> If you move up or right, the change is positive. If you move down or left, the change is negative.

rise $= +2$ **run** $= -3$

STEP 3 Slope $= \dfrac{\text{rise}}{\text{run}}$

$\qquad = \dfrac{2}{-3}$

$\qquad = -\dfrac{2}{3}$

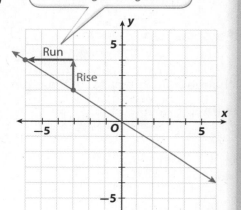

YOUR TURN

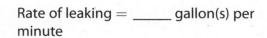

4. The graph shows the rate at which water is leaking from a tank. The slope of the line gives the leaking rate in gallons per minute.

Rise = _____

Run = _____

Rate of leaking = _____ gallon(s) per minute

Leaking tank

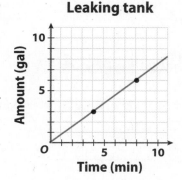

© Houghton Mifflin Harcourt Publishing Company

Tell whether the rates of change are constant or variable. (Example 1)

1. building measurements _____

Feet	3	12	27	75
Yards	1	4	9	25

2. computers sold _____

Week	2	4	9	20
Number Sold	6	12	25	60

3. distance an object falls _____

Distance (ft)	16	64	144	256
Time (s)	1	2	3	4

4. cost of sweaters _____

Number	2	4	7	9
Cost ($)	38	76	133	171

Erica walks to her friend Philip's house. The graph shows Erica's distance from home over time. (Explore Activity)

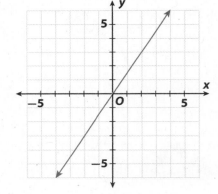

5. Find the rate of change from 1 minute to 2 minutes.

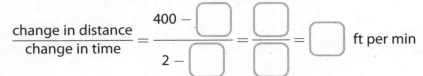

$$\frac{\text{change in distance}}{\text{change in time}} = \frac{400 - \boxed{}}{2 - \boxed{}} = \frac{\boxed{}}{\boxed{}} = \boxed{} \text{ ft per min}$$

6. Find the rate of change from 1 minute to 4 minutes. _____

Find the slope of each line. (Example 2)

7.

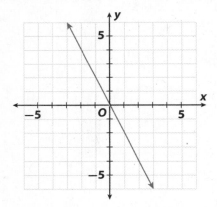

slope = _____

8.

slope = _____

© Houghton Mifflin Harcourt Publishing Company

? ESSENTIAL QUESTION CHECK-IN

9. If you know two points on a line, how can you find the rate of change of the variables being graphed?

_____

_____

_____

3.2 Independent Practice

 8.4.C

Personal Math Trainer

Online Assessment and Intervention

my.hrw.com

10. Rectangle *EFGH* is graphed on a coordinate plane with vertices at *E*(−3, 5), *F*(6, 2), *G*(4, −4), and *H*(−5, −1).

   a. Find the slopes of each side.

   _____

   b. What do you notice about the slopes of opposite sides?

   _____

   c. What do you notice about the slopes of adjacent sides?

   _____

11. A bicyclist started riding at 8:00 A.M. The diagram below shows the distance the bicyclist had traveled at different times. What was the bicyclist's average rate of speed in miles per hour?

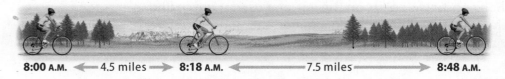

8:00 A.M. ←4.5 miles→ **8:18 A.M.** ←———7.5 miles———→ **8:48 A.M.**

   _____

12. **Multistep** A line passes through (6, 3), (8, 4), and (*n*, −2). Find the value of *n*.

   _____

13. A large container holds 5 gallons of water. It begins leaking at a constant rate. After 10 minutes, the container has 3 gallons of water left.

   a. At what rate is the water leaking?

   _____

   b. After how many minutes will the container be empty?

   _____

14. **Critique Reasoning** Billy found the slope of the line through the points (2, 5) and (−2, −5) using the equation $\frac{2 - (-2)}{5 - (-5)} = \frac{2}{5}$. What mistake did he make?

   _____

   _____

15. Multiple Representations Graph parallelogram *ABCD* on a coordinate plane with vertices at *A*(3, 4), *B*(6, 1), *C*(0, −2), and *D*(−3, 1).

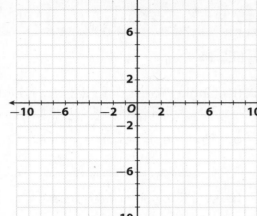

a. Find the slope of each side.

_____

_____

b. What do you notice about the slopes?

_____

_____

c. Draw another parallelogram on the coordinate plane. Do the slopes have the same characteristics?

_____

 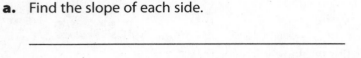

16. Communicate Mathematical Ideas Ben and Phoebe are finding the slope of a line. Ben chose two points on the line and used them to find the slope. Phoebe used two different points to find the slope. Did they get the same answer? Explain.

_____

_____

_____

17. Analyze Relationships Two lines pass through the origin. The lines have slopes that are opposites. Compare and contrast the lines.

_____

_____

_____

_____

18. Reason Abstractly What is the slope of the *x*-axis? Explain.

_____

_____

_____

Work Area

© Houghton Mifflin Harcourt Publishing Company

LESSON 3.3 Interpreting the Unit Rate as Slope

TEKS
Proportionality—
8.4.B Graph proportional relationships, interpreting the unit rate as the slope of the line that models the relationship. *Also 8.4.C*

? ESSENTIAL QUESTION

How do you interpret the unit rate as slope?

 EXPLORE ACTIVITY  **TEKS** 8.4.B, 8.4.C

Relating the Unit Rate to Slope

A rate is a comparison of two quantities that have different units, such as miles and hours. A **unit rate** is a rate in which the second quantity in the comparison is one unit.

A storm is raging on Misty Mountain. The graph shows the constant rate of change of the snow level on the mountain.

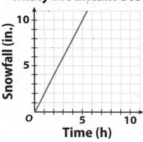

Misty Mountain Storm

A Find the slope of the graph using the points (1, 2) and (5, 10). Remember that the slope is the constant rate of change.

B Find the unit rate of snowfall in inches per hour. Explain your method.

_____

_____

C Compare the slope of the graph and the unit rate of change in the snow level. What do you notice?

_____

D Which point on the graph tells you the slope of the graph and the unit rate of change in the snow level? Explain how you found the point.

_____

_____

_____

_____

Graphing Proportional Relationships

You can use a table and a graph to find the unit rate and slope that describe a real-world proportional relationship. The constant of proportionality for a proportional relationship is the same as the slope.

EXAMPLE 1   **TEKS** 8.4.B, 8.4.C

Every 3 seconds, 4 cubic feet of water pass over a dam. Draw a graph of the situation. Find the unit rate of this proportional relationship.

STEP 1 Make a table.

Time (s)	3	6	9	12	15
Volume (ft³)	4	8	12	16	20

STEP 2 Draw a graph.

STEP 3 Find the slope.

$$\text{slope} = \frac{\text{rise}}{\text{run}} = \frac{8}{6}$$

$$= \frac{4}{3}$$

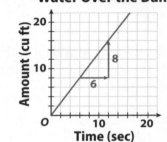

Water Over the Dam

The unit rate of water passing over the dam and the slope of the graph of the relationship are equal, $\frac{4}{3}$ cubic feet per second.

Math Talk
Mathematical Processes

In a proportional relationship, how are the constant of proportionality, the unit rate, and the slope of the graph of the relationship related?

Reflect

1. **What If?** Without referring to the graph, how do you know that the point $\left(1, \frac{4}{3}\right)$ is on the graph?

_____

_____

YOUR TURN

2. Tomas rides his bike at a steady rate of 2 miles every 10 minutes. Graph the situation. Find the unit rate of this proportional relationship.

Tomas's Ride

_____

_____

_____

Using Slopes to Compare Unit Rates

You can compare proportional relationships presented in different ways.

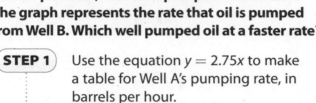

EXAMPLE 2 Real World   **TEKS** 8.4.B, 8.4.C

The equation $y = 2.75x$ represents the rate, in barrels per hour, that oil is pumped from Well A. The graph represents the rate that oil is pumped from Well B. Which well pumped oil at a faster rate?

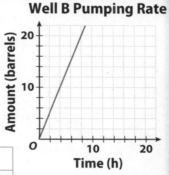

Well B Pumping Rate

STEP 1 Use the equation $y = 2.75x$ to make a table for Well A's pumping rate, in barrels per hour.

Time (h)	1	2	3	4
Quantity (barrels)	2.75	5.5	8.25	11

STEP 2 Use the table to find the slope of the graph of Well A's rate.

slope = unit rate = $\frac{2.75}{1} = \frac{5.5}{2} = \frac{8.25}{3} = \frac{11}{4} =$ **2.75** barrels/hour

STEP 3 Use the graph to find the slope of the graph of Well B's rate.

slope = $\frac{10}{4} =$ **2.5** barrels/hour   slope = $\frac{rise}{run}$

STEP 4 Compare the slopes.

2.75 > 2.5, so Well A's rate, 2.75 barrels/hour, is faster.

Reflect

3. Describe the relationships among the slope of the graph of Well A's rate, the equation representing Well A's rate, and the constant of proportionality.

_____

_____

YOUR TURN

4. The equation $y = 375x$ represents the relationship between x, the time that a plane flies in hours, and y, the distance the plane flies in miles for Plane A. The table represents the relationship for Plane B. Find the slope of the graph for each plane and the plane's rate of speed. Determine which plane is flying at a faster rate of speed.

Time (h)	1	2	3	4
Distance (mi)	425	850	1275	1700

_____

Personal Math Trainer

Online Assessment and Intervention

my.hrw.com

Give the slope of the graph and the unit rate. (Explore Activity and Example 1)

1. Jorge: 5 miles every 6 hours

Jorge

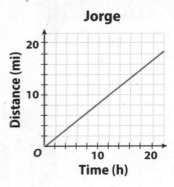

_____

2. Akiko

Time (h)	4	8	12	16
Distance (mi)	5	10	15	20

Akiko

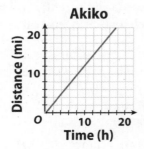

_____

3. The equation $y = 0.5x$ represents the distance Henry hikes in miles over time in hours. The graph represents the rate that Clark hikes. Determine which hiker is faster. Explain. (Example 2)

_____

_____

_____

Clark

Write an equation relating the variables in each table. (Example 2)

4.

Time (x)	1	2	4	6
Distance (y)	15	30	60	80

_____

5.

Time (x)	16	32	48	64
Distance (y)	6	12	18	24

_____

? ESSENTIAL QUESTION CHECK-IN

6. Describe methods you can use to show a proportional relationship between two variables, x and y. For each method, explain how you can find the unit rate and the slope.

_____

_____

_____

_____

3.3 Independent Practice

Personal
Math Trainer

Online
Assessment and
Intervention

my.hrw.com

 **TEKS** 8.4.B, 8.4.C

7. A Canadian goose migrated at a steady rate of 3 miles every 4 minutes.

   a. Fill in the table to describe the relationship.

Time (min)	4	8			20
Distance (mi)			9	12	

   b. Graph the relationship.

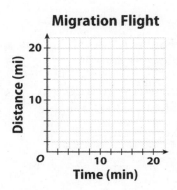

Migration Flight

   c. Find the slope of the graph and describe what it means in the context of this problem.

   _____

   _____

   _____

   _____

8. Vocabulary A unit rate is a rate in which the

   [**first quantity / second quantity**]   in the comparison is one unit.

9. The table and the graph represent the rate at which two machines are bottling milk in gallons per second.

Machine 1

Time (s)	1	2	3	4
Amount (gal)	0.6	1.2	1.8	2.4

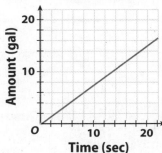

Machine 2

   a. Determine the slope and unit rate of each machine.

   _____

   _____

   b. Determine which machine is working at a faster rate.

   _____

10. Cycling The equation $y = \frac{1}{9}x$ represents the distance y, in kilometers, that Patrick traveled in x minutes while training for the cycling portion of a triathlon. The table shows the distance y Jennifer traveled in x minutes in her training. Who has the faster training rate?

Time (min)	40	64	80	96
Distance (km)	5	8	10	12

_____

_____

_____

 **FOCUS ON HIGHER ORDER THINKING**

Work Area

11. Analyze Relationships There is a proportional relationship between minutes and cost per minute in dollars. The graph passes through the point (1, 4.75). What is the slope of the graph? What is the unit rate? Explain.

_____

_____

_____

12. Draw Conclusions Two cars start at the same time and travel at different constant rates. The graph of the distance in miles given the time in hours for Car A passes through the point (0.5, 27.5), and the graph for Car B passes through the point (4, 240). Which car is traveling faster? Explain.

_____

_____

_____

_____

13. Critical Thinking The table shows the rate at which water is being pumped into a swimming pool.

Time (min)	2	5	7	12
Amount (gal)	36	90	126	216

Use the unit rate and the amount of water pumped after 12 minutes to find how much water will have been pumped into the pool after $13\frac{1}{2}$ minutes. Explain your reasoning.

_____

_____

_____

_____

3.4 Direct Variation

TEKS
Proportionality—
8.5.E Solve problems involving direct variation.

? ESSENTIAL QUESTION

How can you solve problems involving direct variation?

Writing a Direct Variation from a Table

A **direct variation** is a relationship that can be written as $y = kx$, where k is a nonzero constant called the **constant of variation**. The value of k is the same as the constant of proportionality in the equation $\frac{y}{x} = k$. If there is a direct variation between x and y, y *varies directly* with x.

Math On the Spot
my.hrw.com

EXAMPLE 1 Real World    **TEKS** 8.5.E

An amplifier generates sound with an intensity that changes with the power input in a constant ratio. The table shows the relationship between the input signal power in Watts and the resulting sound intensity in Watts per square meter.

Input signal power (W)	2	5	12	19
Output sound intensity (W/m²)	1.5	3.75	9	14.25

Determine whether the data set shows that the sound output intensity varies directly with the input signal power. If so, write an equation that describes the relationship.

STEP 1 Find the ratio $\frac{\text{output sound intensity}}{\text{input signal power}}$.

$\frac{1.5}{2} = 0.75$ $\frac{3.75}{5} = 0.75$ $\frac{9}{12} = 0.75$ $\frac{14.25}{19} = 0.75$

Since the ratios are proportional, the data set shows direct variation. The constant of variation is 0.75.

Math Talk
Mathematical Processes

If you find that the first two ratios in a table of data are equal, does the table definitely show direct variation?

STEP 2 Write the equation.

Let x represent the number of Watts in the amplifier's input signal.

Let y represent the number of Watts per square meter in the amplifier's output.

The ratio 0.75 is the constant of variation. So, $k = 0.75$ in the direct variation equation.

The equation is in the form $y = kx$.

The equation that describes the relationship is $y = 0.75x$.

1. The table shows the widths and lengths of United States flags. Determine whether the data set shows direct variation. If so, write an equation that describes the relationship.

Width (ft)	0.5	1.25	2	4.5	24
Length (ft)	0.95	2.375	3.8	8.55	45.6

Math On the Spot

my.hrw.com

Applying the Graph of a Direct Variation

The graph of a direct variation always passes through the origin and represents a proportional relationship. You can find the equation of a direct variation from a graph and use it to make a prediction.

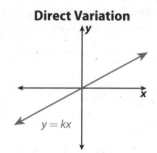

Direct Variation

$y = kx$

Not a Direct Variation

EXAMPLE 2   Problem Solving

TEKS 8.5.E

The minimum amount of time it takes a diver to ascend safely to the surface varies directly with the depth of the diver. How long does it take a diver to ascend safely from a depth of 450 feet?

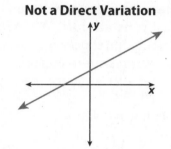

Safe Diving Ascension TIme

Minimum time (min)

Depth (ft)

Analyze Information

The answer is the minimum amount of time it takes a diver to ascend safely from a depth of 450 feet.

Formulate a Plan

Write a direct variation equation. Then use the equation to predict the amount of time it takes to ascend safely from a depth of 450 feet.

Solve

STEP 1 Find the ratio that describes the constant of variation.

$\dfrac{\text{minimum time}}{\text{depth}}$: $\dfrac{2}{60} = \dfrac{3}{90} = \dfrac{4.5}{135} = \dfrac{6}{180} = \dfrac{9}{270}$

Each ratio is equal to $\dfrac{1}{30}$.

STEP 2 Write an equation.

$y = kx$ *y is the time in minutes, and x is the depth in feet.*

$y = \dfrac{1}{30}x$ *Substitute $\dfrac{1}{30}$ for k.*

STEP 3 Predict the time it takes to ascend safely from a depth of 450 feet.

$y = \dfrac{1}{30}(450)$ *Substitute 450 for x in the direct variation equation.*

$y = 15$

The minimum time it takes to ascend safely is 15 minutes.

Math Talk
Mathematical Processes

How many points on the line are solutions to the direct variation equation?

Justify and Evaluate

The graph shows that the minimum amount of time to surface from 90 feet is 3 minutes. So, for a depth five times as deep, it should take five times as long. The answer is reasonable.

Reflect

2. Does the equation $y = \dfrac{3}{2}x - 5$ show a direct variation? Why or why not?

_____

_____

YOUR TURN

3. One brand of motorcycle uses an oil-to-gasoline ratio as shown in the graph. The amount of oil that should be added varies directly with the amount of gasoline. Write a direct variation equation that describes the relationship. Use your equation to determine the amount of oil that should be added to 6.5 gallons of gasoline.

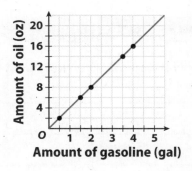

_____

_____

Personal Math Trainer

Online Assessment and Intervention

my.hrw.com

Determine whether the data sets show direct variation. If so, write an equation that describes the relationship. (Example 1)

1.

Resistance (amps)	3	5	6	8
Current (ohms)	4	2.4	2	1.5

_____

2.

Weight (lb)	8	15	28	47
Dosage (mg)	160	300	560	940

_____

3.

Games	20	30	50	160
At-bats	62	93	155	496

_____

4.

Price ($)	4	12	36	60
Sales tax ($)	0.29	0.87	2.61	4.35

_____

5. The number of cups in a measure varies directly as the number of tablespoons. Write a direct variation equation that describes the relationship. Use your equation to determine the number of cups in 56 tablespoons. (Example 2)

_____

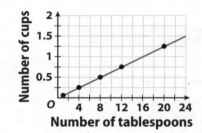

6. The number of calories varies directly with the number of grams of protein. Write a direct variation equation that describes the relationship. Use your equation to determine the number of calories from 25 grams of protein. (Example 2)

_____

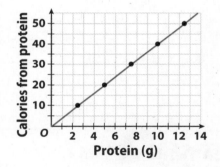

? **ESSENTIAL QUESTION CHECK-IN**

7. How can you solve problems involving direct variation?

_____

_____

_____

3.4 Independent Practice

 8.5.E

Personal Math Trainer

Online Assessment and Intervention

my.hrw.com

8. Vocabulary A _____ is a relationship that can

written be as $y = kx$, where k is a _____.

9. Which equation does NOT represent a direct variation?

Ⓐ $y = \frac{1}{4}x$ Ⓒ $y = 5x + 1$

Ⓑ $y = -4x$ Ⓓ $y = 6x$

10. Environment Mischa bought an energy-efficient washing machine. The amount of water she saves per wash load compared to her old washer is shown in the table.

Number of loads	1	2	5	6
Water (gal)	12	24	60	72

a. Determine whether the relationship is a direct variation. If so, write an equation that describes the relationship.

_____

b. How much water will she save when washing 8 loads?

_____

11. Sandy wants to build a square garden. Complete the table for the different side lengths.

Side length (ft)	1	2	3	5	9
Perimeter (ft)					
Area (ft²)					

a. Does the perimeter of a square vary directly with the side length? If so, write an equation that describes the relationship. Explain your answer.

_____

_____

b. Does the area of a square vary directly with the side length? Why or why not?

_____

_____

c. Sandy decides to build her garden with a side length of 3 feet. The border she buys for the perimeter costs $1.99 for a 1.5 foot piece. The soil she buys covers an area of 3 square feet and costs $4.99 a bag. How much does Sandy spend on border and soil for her garden? Explain.

_____

_____

_____

_____

12. The three-toed sloth is an extremely slow animal. Use the graph to write a direct variation equation for the distance y a sloth will travel in x minutes. How long will it take the sloth to travel 24 feet?

_____

Speed of a Sloth

 **FOCUS ON HIGHER ORDER THINKING**

13. Critique Reasoning Martin is told that a graph includes the points (2, 5) and (4, 10). He says that this is the graph of the direct variation $y = 2.5x$. Do you agree? Explain.

_____

_____

_____

14. Make a Conjecture If you can write a direct variation equation that relates y to x, $y = kx$, then you can write a direct variation equation that relates x to y, $x = k_1y$. Make a conjecture about how the constants of variation are related. Use the table to help you decide.

x	5	10	15	25	40
y	1	2	3	5	8

_____

_____

15. Analyze Relationships One graph of a direct variation equation goes through a point A in Quadrant I that is not at the origin. A second graph of a different direct variation equation goes through a point that is one unit to the right of A. Which direct variation equation has a greater constant of variation? Explain.

_____

_____

Work Area

Ready to Go On?

3.1 Representing Proportional Relationships

1. Find the constant of proportionality for the table of values.

x	2	3	4	5
y	3	4.5	6	7.5

_____

2. Phil is riding his bike. He rides 25 miles in 2 hours, 37.5 miles in 3 hours, and 50 miles in 4 hours. Find the constant of proportionality and write an equation to describe the situation.

_____

3.2 Rate of Change and Slope

Find the slope of each line.

3.

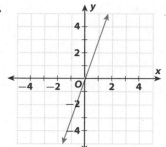

_____

4.

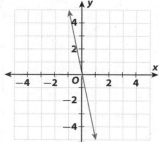

_____

3.3 Interpreting the Unit Rate as Slope

5. What is the slope of the data in

the table? _____

x	13.5	18	22.5	27
y	3	4	5	6

3.4 Direct Variation

6. A wheelchair ramp rises 2.25 feet for every 25 feet of horizontal distance it covers. What is the slope of the ramp? _____

? ESSENTIAL QUESTION

7. What is the relationship among direct variation, lines, rates of change, and slope?

_____

_____

Selected Response

1. Lupe's heart beats 288 times in 4 minutes. Which equation represents the number of times her heart beats per minute?

(A) $y = \frac{1}{288}x$ (C) $y = 72x$

(B) $y = \frac{1}{72}x$ (D) $y = 288x$

2. Prasert earns $9 an hour. Which table represents this proportional relationship?

(A)
Hours	4	6	8
Earnings ($)	36	54	72

(B)
Hours	4	6	8
Earnings ($)	36	45	54

(C)
Hours	2	3	4
Earnings ($)	9	18	27

(D)
Hours	2	3	4
Earnings ($)	18	27	54

3. A factory produces widgets at a constant rate. After 4 hours, 3,120 widgets have been produced. At what rate are the widgets being produced?

(A) 630 widgets per hour

(B) 708 widgets per hour

(C) 780 widgets per hour

(D) 1,365 widgets per hour

4. A full lake begins dropping at a constant rate. After 4 weeks it has dropped 3 feet. What is the unit rate of change in the lake's level compared to its full level?

(A) 0.75 feet per week

(B) 1.33 feet per week

(C) −0.75 feet per week

(D) −1.33 feet per week

5. What is the slope of the line below?

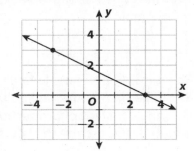

(A) −2   (C) $\frac{1}{2}$

(B) $-\frac{1}{2}$ (D) 2

6. Jim earns $41.25 in 5 hours. Susan earns $30.00 in 4 hours. Pierre's hourly rate is less than Jim's, but more than Susan's. What is his hourly rate?

(A) $6.50   (C) $7.35

(B) $7.75   (D) $8.25

Gridded Response

7. Joelle kept track of her daily reading in the table shown below. What is her fastest daily reading rate in pages per minute?

Day	Monday	Tuesday	Wednesday
Time (Min)	20	40	25
Pages Read	44	70	56

⓪	⓪	⓪	⓪		⓪	⓪
①	①	①	①		①	①
②	②	②	②		②	②
③	③	③	③		③	③
④	④	④	④		④	④
⑤	⑤	⑤	⑤		⑤	⑤
⑥	⑥	⑥	⑥		⑥	⑥
⑦	⑦	⑦	⑦		⑦	⑦
⑧	⑧	⑧	⑧		⑧	⑧
⑨	⑨	⑨	⑨		⑨	⑨

Nonproportional Relationships

MODULE 4

ESSENTIAL QUESTION

How can you use non-proportional relationships to solve real-world problems?

Real-World Video

The distance a car can travel on a tank of gas or a full battery charge in an electric car depends on factors such as fuel capacity and the car's efficiency. This is described by a nonproportional relationship.

my.hrw.com

© Houghton Mifflin Harcourt Publishing Company • Image Credits: ©viappy/Shutterstock

GO DIGITAL

my.hrw.com

my.hrw.com

Go digital with your write-in student edition, accessible on any device.

Math On the Spot

Scan with your smart phone to jump directly to the online edition, video tutor, and more.

Animated Math

Interactively explore key concepts to see how math works.

Personal Math Trainer

Get immediate feedback and help as you work through practice sets.

Are YOU Ready?

Complete these exercises to review skills you will need for this chapter.

Integer Operations

EXAMPLE $-7 - (-4) = -7 + 4$ To subtract an integer, add its opposite.
$|-7| - |4|$ The signs are different, so find the difference
$7 - 4$, or 3 of the absolute values.
$= -3$ Use the sign of the number with the greater absolute value.

Find each difference.

1. $3 - (-5)$ _____

2. $-4 - 5$ _____

3. $6 - 10$ _____

4. $-5 - (-3)$ _____

5. $8 - (-8)$ _____

6. $9 - 5$ _____

7. $-3 - 9$ _____

8. $0 - (-6)$ _____

9. $12 - (-9)$ _____

10. $-6 - (-4)$ _____

11. $-7 - 10$ _____

12. $5 - 14$ _____

Graph Ordered Pairs (First Quadrant)

EXAMPLE

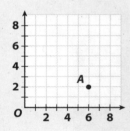

To graph a point at (6, 2), start at the origin.

Move 6 units right.

Then move 2 units up.

Graph point A(6, 2).

Graph each point on the coordinate grid.

13. B (0, 5)

14. C (8, 0)

15. D (5, 7)

16. E (2, 3)

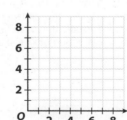

Reading Start-Up

Visualize Vocabulary

Use the ✔ words to complete the diagram. You can put more than one word in each box.

Reviewing Slope

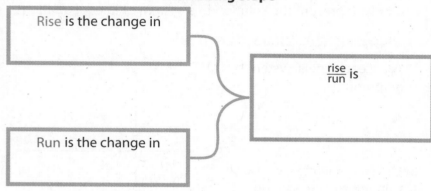

Rise is the change in

Run is the change in

$\frac{rise}{run}$ is

Understand Vocabulary

Complete the sentences using the preview words.

1. Any ordered pair that satisfies all the equations in a system is a

   _____.

2. A _____ is an equation whose solutions form a

   straight line on a coordinate plane.

3. A _____ is a set of two or more equations that

   contain two or more variables.

Vocabulary

Review Words
ordered pair *(par ordenado)*
proportional relationship *(relación proporcional)*
✔ rate of change *(tasa de cambio)*
✔ slope *(pendiente)*
✔ *x*-coordinate *(coordenada x)*
✔ *y*-coordinate *(coordenada y)*

Preview Words
linear equation *(ecuación lineal)*
slope-intercept form of an equation *(forma de pendiente-intersección)*
solution of a system of equations *(solución de un sistema de ecuaciones)*
system of equations *(sistema de ecuaciones)*
y-intercept *(intersección con el eje y)*

Active Reading

Booklet Before beginning the module, create a booklet to help you learn the concepts. Write the main idea of each lesson on each page of the booklet. As you study each lesson, write important details that support the main idea, such as vocabulary and formulas. Refer to your finished booklet as you work on assignments and study for tests.

Unpacking the TEKS

Understanding the TEKS and the vocabulary terms in the TEKS will help you know exactly what you are expected to learn in this module.

Identify and verify the values of x and y that simultaneously satisfy two linear equations in the form $y = mx + b$ from the intersections of the graphed equations.

Key Vocabulary

system of equations
(sistema de ecuaciones)
A set of two or more equations that contain two or more variables.

What It Means to You

You will understand that the points of intersection of two or more graphs represent the solution to a system of linear equations.

UNPACKING EXAMPLE 8.9

Solve each linear system by graphing.

A. $-x = -1 + y$
            $x + y = 1$

The lines coincide, so every solution to one equation is also a solution of the second equation. They system has infinitely many solutions.

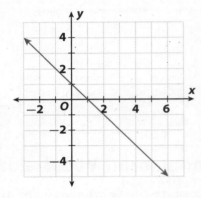

B. $2y + x = 1$
            $y - 2 = x$

The lines intersect at one point, so the solution is $(-1, 1)$.

Verify that the point $(-1, 1)$ is the solution by substituting it in each equation.

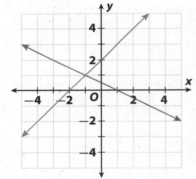

$$2y + x = 1 \qquad y - 2 = x$$
$$2(1) + (-1) = 1 \qquad 1 - 2 = -1$$
$$1 = 1 \qquad -1 = -1$$

Visit **my.hrw.com** to see all the **TEKS** unpacked.

© my.hrw.com

LESSON 4.1 Representing Linear Nonproportional Relationships

TEKS
Proportionality—
8.5.B Represent linear non-proportional situations with tables, graphs, and equations in the form of $y = mx + b$, where $b \neq 0$. Also 8.5.F

? ESSENTIAL QUESTION

How can you use tables, graphs, and equations to represent linear nonproportional situations?

Representing Linear Relationships Using Tables

You can use an equation to describe the relationship between two quantities in a real-world situation. You can use a table to show some values that make the equation true.

EXAMPLE 1 **TEKS** 8.5.B

The equation $y = 3x + 2$ gives the total charge, y, for bowling x games at Baxter Bowling Lanes based on the prices shown. Make a table of values for this situation.

STEP 1 Choose several values for x that make sense in context.

x (number of games)	1	2	3	4
y (total cost in dollars)				

STEP 2 Use the equation $y = 3x + 2$ to find y for each value of x.

x (number of games)	1	2	3	4
y (total cost in dollars)	5	8	11	14

Substitute 1 for x:
$y = 3(1) + 2 = 5$.

YOUR TURN

1. Francisco makes $12 per hour doing part-time work on Saturdays. He spends $4 on transportation to and from work. The equation $y = 12x - 4$ gives his earnings y, after transportation costs, for working x hours. Make a table of values for this situation.

x (number of hours)				
y (earnings in dollars)				

Personal Math Trainer

Online Assessment and Intervention

my.hrw.com

Math On the Spot
my.hrw.com

© Houghton Mifflin Harcourt Publishing Company

Lesson 4.1 **89**

Examining Linear Relationships

Recall that a proportional relationship is a relationship between two quantities in which the ratio of one quantity to the other quantity is constant. The graph of a proportional relationship is a line through the origin. Relationships can have a constant rate of change but not be proportional.

The entrance fee for Mountain World theme park is $20. Visitors purchase additional $2 tickets for rides, games, and food. The equation $y = 2x + 20$ gives the total cost, y, to visit the park, including purchasing x tickets.

STEP 1 Complete the table.

x (number of tickets)	0	2	4	6	8
y (total cost in dollars)	20				

STEP 2 Plot the ordered pairs from the table. Describe the shape of the graph.

_____

STEP 3 Find the rate of change between each point and the next. Is the rate constant?

_____

STEP 4 Calculate $\frac{y}{x}$ for the values in the table. Explain why the relationship between number of tickets and total cost is not proportional.

_____

_____

_____

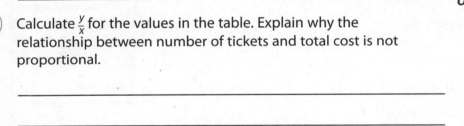

Theme Park Costs

Cost ($)

Number of tickets

Reflect

2. **Analyze Relationships** Would it make sense to add more points to the graph from $x = 0$ to $x = 10$? Would it make sense to connect the points with a line? Explain.

_____

_____

_____

_____

Representing Linear Relationships Using Graphs

A **linear equation** is an equation whose solutions are ordered pairs that form a line when graphed on a coordinate plane. Linear equations can be written in the form $y = mx + b$. When $b \neq 0$, the relationship between x and y is *nonproportional*.

Math On the Spot
my.hrw.com

EXAMPLE 2

TEKS 8.5.B

My Notes

The diameter of a Douglas fir tree is currently 10 inches when measured at chest height. Over the next 50 years, the diameter is expected to increase by an average growth rate of $\frac{2}{5}$ inch per year. The equation $y = \frac{2}{5}x + 10$ gives y, the diameter of the tree in inches, after x years. Draw a graph of the equation. Describe the relationship.

STEP 1 Make a table. Choose several values for x that make sense in context. To make calculations easier, choose multiples of 5.

x (years)	0	10	20	30	50
y (diameter in inches)	10	14	18	22	30

STEP 2 Plot the ordered pairs from the table. Then draw a line connecting the points to represent all the possible solutions.

STEP 3 The relationship is linear but nonproportional. The graph is a line but it does not go through the origin.

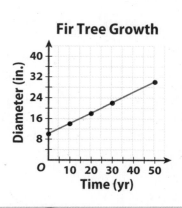

Fir Tree Growth

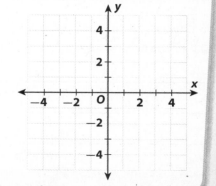

YOUR TURN

3. Make a table and graph the solutions of the equation $y = -2x + 1$.

x	−1	0	1	2
y				

Personal Math Trainer
Online Assessment and Intervention
my.hrw.com

Make a table of values for each equation. (Example 1)

1. $y = 2x + 5$

x	−2	−1	0	1	2
y					

2. $y = \frac{3}{8}x - 5$

x	−8	0	8		
y					

Explain why each relationship is not proportional. (Explore Activity)

3.

x	0	2	4	6	8
y	3	7	11	15	19

First calculate $\frac{y}{x}$ for the values in the table.

_____

_____

_____

_____

4.

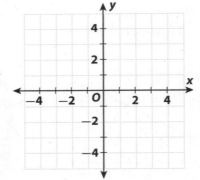

_____

_____

Complete the table for the equation. Then use the table to graph the equation. (Example 2)

5. $y = x - 1$

x	−2	−1	0	1	2
y					

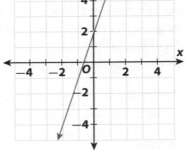

? ESSENTIAL QUESTION CHECK-IN

6. How can you choose values for x when making a table of values representing a real world situation?

_____

_____

_____

4.1 Independent Practice

 **TEKS** 8.5.B, 8.5.F

Personal
Math Trainer

Online
Assessment and
my.hrw.com   Intervention

State whether the graph of each linear relationship is a solid line or a set of unconnected points. Explain your reasoning.

7. The relationship between the number of $4 lunches you buy with a $100 school lunch card and the money remaining on the card

_____

_____

_____

_____

8. The relationship between time and the distance remaining on a 3-mile walk for someone walking at a steady rate of 2 miles per hour

_____

_____

_____

_____

9. Analyze Relationships Simone paid $12 for an initial year's subscription to a magazine. The renewal rate is $8 per year. This situation can be represented by the equation $y = 8x + 12$, where x represents the number of years the subscription is renewed and y represents the total cost.

a. Make a table of values for this situation.

b. Draw a graph to represent the situation.

c. Explain why this relationship is not proportional.

_____

_____

_____

_____

d. Does it make sense to connect the points on the graph with a solid line? Explain.

_____

_____

_____

10. Analyze Relationships A direct variation is a linear relationship because the rate of change is constant (and equal to the constant of variation). What is required of a direct variation relationship that is *not* required of a general linear relationship?

_____

_____

11. Communicate Mathematical Ideas Explain how you can identify a linear non-proportional relationship from a table, a graph, and an equation.

_____

_____

_____

H.O.T. FOCUS ON HIGHER ORDER THINKING

12. Critique Reasoning George observes that for every increase of 1 in the value of *x*, there is an increase of 60 in the corresponding value of *y*. He claims that the relationship represented by the table is proportional. Critique George's reasoning.

x	1	2	3	4	5
y	90	150	210	270	330

_____

_____

_____

_____

13. Make a Conjecture Two parallel lines are graphed on a coordinate plane. How many of the lines could represent proportional relationships? Explain.

_____

_____

_____

_____

_____

© Houghton Mifflin Harcourt Publishing Company

LESSON 4.2 Determining Slope and *y*-intercept

TEKS
Proportionality—
8.4.C Use data from a table or graph to determine the rate of change or slope and *y*-intercept in mathematical and real-world problems.
Also 8.5.B

ESSENTIAL QUESTION

How can you determine the slope and the *y*-intercept of a line?

EXPLORE ACTIVITY 1  TEKS 8.4.C

Investigating Slope and *y*-intercept

The graph of every nonvertical line crosses the *y*-axis. The **y-intercept** is the *y*-coordinate of the point where the graph intersects the *y*-axis. The *x*-coordinate of this point is always 0.

The graph represents the linear equation $y = -\frac{2}{3}x + 4$.

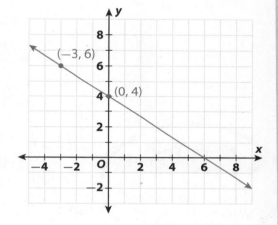

STEP 1 Find the slope of the line using the points (0, 4) and (−3, 6).

$$m = \frac{6 - \boxed{}}{\boxed{} - 0} = \frac{\boxed{}}{\boxed{}} = \boxed{}$$

STEP 2 The line also contains the point (6, 0). What is the slope using (0, 4) and (6, 0)? Using (−3, 6) and (6, 0). What do you notice?

_____

STEP 3 Compare your answers in Steps 1 and 2 with the equation of the graphed line.

_____

_____

STEP 3 Find the value of *y* when *x* = 0 using the equation $y = -\frac{2}{3}x + 4$. Describe the point on the graph that corresponds to this solution.

_____

STEP 5 Compare your answer in Step 3 with the equation of the line.

_____

_____

Determining Rate of Change and Initial Value

The linear equation shown is written in the **slope-intercept form of an equation**. Its graph is a line with **slope m** and **y-intercept b**.

$$y = mx + b$$

slope y-intercept

A linear relationship has a constant rate of change. You can find the **rate of change m** and the **initial value b** for a linear situation from a table of values.

EXAMPLE 1
TEKS 8.4.C

A phone salesperson is paid a minimum weekly salary and a commission for each phone sold, as shown in the table. Confirm that the relationship is linear and give the constant rate of change and the initial value.

STEP 1 Confirm that the rate of change is constant.

$$\frac{\text{change in income}}{\text{change in phones sold}} = \frac{630-480}{20-10} = \frac{150}{10} = 15$$

$$\frac{\text{change in income}}{\text{change in phones sold}} = \frac{780-630}{30-20} = \frac{150}{10} = 15$$

$$\frac{\text{change in income}}{\text{change in phones sold}} = \frac{930-780}{40-30} = \frac{150}{10} = 15$$

Number of Phones Sold	Weekly Income ($)
10	$480
20	$630
30	$780
40	$930

The rate of change is a constant, **15**.

The salesperson receives a $15 commission for each phone sold.

Math Talk
Mathematical Processes
How do you use the rate of change to work backward to find the initial value?

STEP 2 Find the initial value when the number of phones sold is 0.

−10 −10

Number of phones sold	0	10	20
Weekly income ($)	330	480	630

Work backward from $x = 10$ to $x = 0$ to find the initial value.

−150 −150

The initial value is $330. The salesperson receives a salary of $330 each week before commissions.

YOUR TURN

Find the slope and y-intercept of the line represented by each table.

1.

x	2	4	6	8
y	22	32	42	52

_____

2.

x	1	2	3	4
y	8	15	22	29

_____

Deriving the Slope-intercept Form of an Equation

In the following Explore Activity, you will derive the slope-intercept form of an equation.

STEP 1 Let L be a line with slope m and y-intercept b. Circle the point that must be on the line. Justify your choice.

$(b, 0)$ $\qquad$ $(0, b)$ $\qquad$ $(0, m)$ $\qquad$ $(m, 0)$

_____

_____

STEP 2 Recall that slope is the ratio of change in y to change in x. Complete the equation for the slope m of the line using the y-intercept $(0, b)$ and another point (x, y) on the line.

$$m = \frac{y - \boxed{}}{\boxed{} - 0}$$

STEP 3 In an equation of a line, we often want y by itself on one side of the equation. Solve the equation from Step 2 for y.

$$m = \frac{y - b}{x}$$ Simplify the denominator.

$$m \cdot \boxed{} = \frac{y - b}{x} \cdot \boxed{}$$ Multiply both sides of the equation by _____.

$$m \boxed{} = y - b$$

$$mx + \boxed{} = y - b + \boxed{}$$ Add _____ to both sides of the equation.

$$mx + \boxed{} = y$$

$$y = mx + \boxed{}$$ Write the equation with y on the left side.

Reflect

3. **Critical Thinking** Write the equation of a line with slope m that passes through the origin. Explain your reasoning.

_____

_____

_____

Find the slope and y-intercept of the line in each graph. (Explore Activity 1)

1.

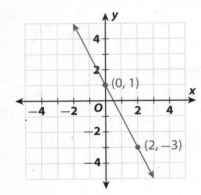

slope m = _____ y-intercept b = _____

2.

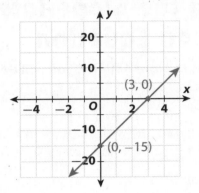

slope m = _____ y-intercept b = _____

3.

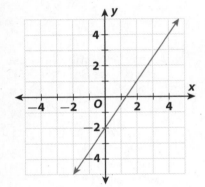

slope m = _____ y-intercept b = _____

4.

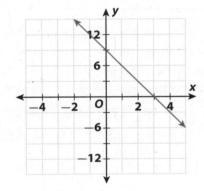

slope m = _____ y-intercept b = _____

Find the slope and y-intercept of the line represented by each table. (Example 1)

5.

x	0	2	4	6	8
y	1	7	13	19	25

slope m = _____ y-intercept b = _____

6.

x	0	5	10	15	20
y	140	120	100	80	60

slope m = _____ y-intercept b = _____

? ESSENTIAL QUESTION CHECK-IN

7. How can you determine the slope and the y-intercept of a line from a graph?

_____

_____

_____

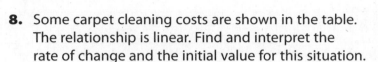

4.2 Independent Practice

 8.4.C, 8.5.B

Personal Math Trainer

Online Assessment and Intervention

my.hrw.com

8. Some carpet cleaning costs are shown in the table. The relationship is linear. Find and interpret the rate of change and the initial value for this situation.

Rooms cleaned	1	2	3	4
Cost ($)	125	175	225	275

_____

_____

_____

9. Make Predictions The total cost to pay for parking at a state park for the day and rent a paddleboat are shown.

a. Find the cost to park for a day and the hourly rate to rent a paddleboat.

_____

b. What will Lin pay if she rents a paddleboat for 3.5 hours and splits the total cost with a friend? Explain.

_____

_____

Number of Hours	Cost ($)
1	$17
2	$29
3	$41
4	$53

10. Multi-Step Raymond's parents will pay for him to take sailboard lessons during the summer. He can take half-hour group lessons or half-hour private lessons. The relationship between cost and number of lessons is linear.

Lessons	1	2	3	4
Group ($)	55	85	115	145
Private ($)	75	125	175	225

a. Find the rate of change and the initial value for the group lessons.

_____

_____

b. Find the rate of change and the initial value for the private lessons.

_____

_____

c. Compare and contrast the rates of change and the initial values.

_____

_____

Vocabulary Explain why each relationship is not linear.

11.

x	1	2	3	4
y	4.5	6.5	8.5	11.5

12.

x	3	5	7	9
y	140	126	110	92

_____

_____

_____

_____

13. Communicate Mathematical Ideas Describe the procedure you performed to derive the slope-intercept form of a linear equation. (Explore Activity 2)

_____

_____

_____

 **FOCUS ON HIGHER ORDER THINKING**

Work Area

14. Critique Reasoning Your teacher asked your class to describe a real-world situation in which a *y*-intercept is 100 and the slope is 5. Your partner gave the following description: *My younger brother originally had 100 small building blocks, but he has lost 5 of them every month since.*

a. What mistake did your partner make?

_____

_____

b. Describe a real-world situation that does match the situation.

_____

_____

15. Justify Reasoning John has a job parking cars. He earns a fixed weekly salary of $300 plus a fee of $5 for each car he parks. His potential earnings for a week are shown in the graph. At what point does John begin to earn more from fees than his fixed salary? Justify your answer.

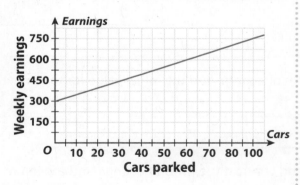

_____

_____

_____

© Houghton Mifflin Harcourt Publishing Company

LESSON 4.3

Graphing Linear Nonproportional Relationships Using Slope and *y*-intercept

TEKS
Proportionality—
8.5.B Represent linear non-proportional situations with tables, graphs, and equations in the form of $y = mx + b$, where $b \neq 0$.

? ESSENTIAL QUESTION

How can you graph a line using the slope and *y*-intercept?

Using Slope-intercept Form to Graph a Line

Recall that $y = mx + b$ is the slope-intercept form of the equation of a line. In this form, it is easy to see the slope *m* and the *y*-intercept *b*. So you can use this form to quickly graph a line by plotting the point $(0, b)$ and using the slope to find a second point.

Math On the Spot
⊙ my.hrw.com

EXAMPLE 1
TEKS 8.5.B

A Graph $y = \frac{2}{3}x - 1$.

STEP 1 The *y*-intercept is $b = -1$. Plot the point that contains the *y*-intercept: $(0, -1)$.

STEP 2 The slope is $m = \frac{2}{3}$. Use the slope to find a second point. From $(0, -1)$, count *up* 2 and *right* 3. The new point is $(3, 1)$.

STEP 3 Draw a line through the points.

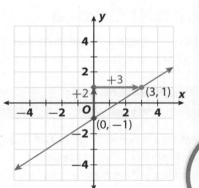

Animated Math
⊙ my.hrw.com

Math Talk
Mathematical Processes

Is a line with a positive slope always steeper than a line with a negative slope? Explain.

B Graph $y = -\frac{5}{2}x + 3$.

STEP 1 The *y*-intercept is $b = 3$. Plot the point that contains the *y*-intercept: $(0, 3)$.

STEP 2 The slope is $m = -\frac{5}{2}$. Use the slope to find a second point. From $(0, 3)$, count *down* 5 and *right* 2, or *up* 5 and *left* 2. The new point is $(2, -2)$ or $(-2, 8)$.

STEP 3 Draw a line through the points.

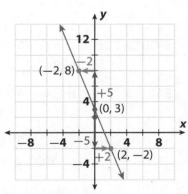

Note that the line passes through all three points: $(-2, 8)$, $(0, 3)$, and $(2, -2)$.

© Houghton Mifflin Harcourt Publishing Company

Reflect

1. Draw Conclusions How can you use the slope of a line to predict the way the line will be slanted? Explain.

_____

_____

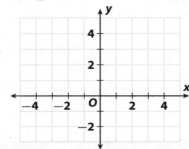

YOUR TURN

Graph each equation.

2. $y = \frac{1}{2}x + 1$

3. $y = -3x + 4$

Analyzing a Graph

Many real-world situations can be represented by linear relationships. You can use graphs of linear relationships to visualize situations and solve problems.

EXAMPLE 2

Real World

TEKS 8.5.B

Ken has a weekly goal for the number of calories he will burn by taking brisk walks. The equation $y = -300x + 2400$ represents the number of calories y Ken has left to burn after x hours of walking.

A Graph the equation $y = -300x + 2400$.

STEP 1 Write the slope as a fraction.

$$m = \frac{-300}{1} = \frac{-600}{2} = \frac{-900}{3}$$

STEP 2 Plot the point for the y-intercept: (0, 2400).

STEP 3 Use the slope to locate a second point.

From (0, 2400), count *down* 900 and *right* 3.

The new point is (3, 1500).

STEP 4 Draw a line through the two points.

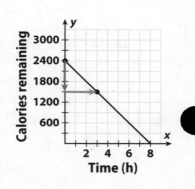

B After how many hours of walking will Ken have 600 calories left to burn? After how many hours will he reach his weekly goal?

STEP 1 Locate 600 calories on the *y*-axis. Read across and down to the *x*-axis.

Ken will have 600 calories left to burn after 6 hours.

STEP 2 Ken will reach his weekly goal when the number of calories left to burn is 0. Because every point on the *x*-axis has a *y*-value of 0, find the point where the line crosses the *x*-axis.

Ken will reach his goal after 8 hours of brisk walking.

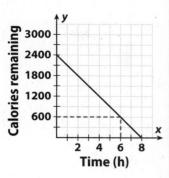

YOUR TURN

What If? Ken decides to modify his exercise plans from Example 2 by slowing the speed at which he walks. The equation for the modified plan is $y = -200x + 2400$.

4. Graph the equation.

5. How does the graph of the new equation compare with the graph in Example 2?

_____

_____

_____

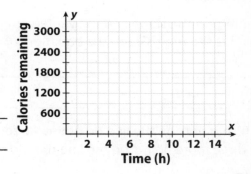

6. Will Ken have to exercise more or less to meet his goal? Explain.

_____

_____

_____

7. Suppose that Ken decides that instead of walking, he will jog, and that jogging burns 600 calories per hour. How do you think that this would change the graph?

_____

_____

_____

Math Talk
Mathematical Processes

What do the slope and the *y*-intercept of the line represent in this situation?

Personal Math Trainer

Online Assessment and Intervention

my.hrw.com

Graph each equation using the slope and the y-intercept. (Example 1)

1. $y = \frac{1}{2}x - 3$

slope = _____ y-intercept = _____

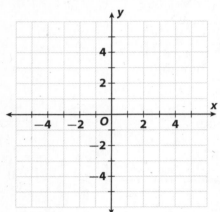

2. $y = -3x + 2$

slope = _____ y-intercept = _____

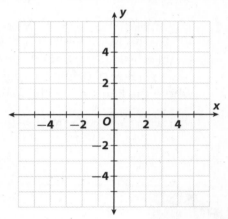

3. A friend gives you two baseball cards for your birthday. Afterward, you begin collecting them. You buy the same number of cards once each week. The equation $y = 4x + 2$ describes the number of cards, y, you have after x weeks. (Example 2)

a. Find and interpret the slope and the y-intercept of the line that represents this situation. Graph the equation $y = 4x + 2$.

_____

_____

b. Discuss which points on the line do not make sense in this situation. Then plot three more points on the line that do make sense.

_____

_____

_____

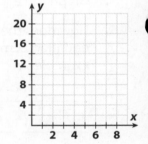

? ESSENTIAL QUESTION CHECK-IN

4. Why might someone choose to use the y-intercept and the slope to graph a line?

_____

_____

_____

_____

4.3 Independent Practice

TEKS 8.5.B

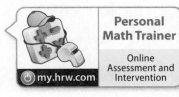

Personal
Math Trainer

Online
Assessment and
Intervention

my.hrw.com

5. **Science** A spring stretches in relation to the weight hanging from it according to the equation $y = 0.75x + 0.25$ where x is the weight in pounds and y is the length of the spring in inches.

   a. Graph the equation.

   b. Interpret the slope and the y-intercept of the line.

   _____

   _____

   _____

   _____

   _____

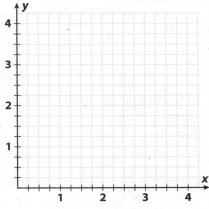

   c. How long will the spring be if a 2-pound weight is hung on it? Will the length double if you double the weight? Explain

   _____

Look for a Pattern **Identify the coordinates of four points on the line with each given slope and y-intercept.**

6. slope = 5, y-intercept = -1

   _____

7. slope = -1, y-intercept = 8

   _____

8. slope = 0.2, y-intercept = 0.3

   _____

9. slope = 1.5, y-intercept = -3

   _____

10. slope = $-\frac{1}{2}$, y-intercept = 4

    _____

11. slope = $\frac{2}{3}$, y-intercept = -5

    _____

12. A music school charges a registration fee in addition to a fee per lesson. Music lessons last 0.5 hour. The equation $y = 40x + 30$ represents the total cost y of x lessons. Find and interpret the slope and y-intercept of the line that represents this situation. Then find four points on the line.

    _____

    _____

13. A public pool charges a membership fee and a fee for each visit. The equation $y = 3x + 50$ represents the cost y for x visits.

a. After locating the y-intercept on the coordinate plane shown, can you move up three gridlines and right one gridline to find a second point? Explain.

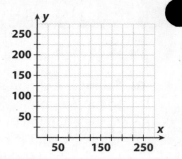

_____

_____

_____

b. Graph the equation $y = 3x + 50$. Then interpret the slope and y-intercept.

_____

_____

c. How many visits to the pool can a member get for $200?

_____

 **FOCUS ON HIGHER ORDER THINKING**

14. Explain the Error A student says that the slope of the line for the equation $y = 20 - 15x$ is 20 and the y-intercept is 15. Find and correct the error.

_____

_____

_____

15. Critical Thinking Suppose you know the slope of a linear relationship and a point that its graph passes through. Can you graph the line even if the point provided does *not* represent the y-intercept? Explain.

_____

_____

_____

16. Make a Conjecture Graph the lines $y = 3x$, $y = 3x - 3$, and $y = 3x + 3$. What do you notice about the lines? Make a conjecture based on your observation.

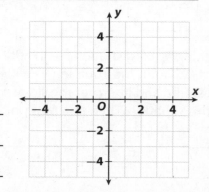

_____

_____

_____

Proportional and Nonproportional Situations

TEKS
Proportionality—
8.5.F Distinguish between proportional and non-proportional situations using tables, graphs, and equations in the form $y = kx$ and $y = mx + b$, where $b \neq 0$.

 ESSENTIAL QUESTION

How can you distinguish between proportional and nonproportional situations?

Distinguish Between Proportional and Nonproportional Situations Using a Graph

If a relationship is nonlinear, it is nonproportional. If it is linear, it may be either proportional or nonproportional. When the graph of the linear relationship contains the origin, the relationship is proportional.

Math On the Spot
my.hrw.com

EXAMPLE 1

TEKS 8.5.F

The graph shows the sales tax charged based on the amount spent at a video game store in a particular city. Does the graph show a linear relationship? Is the relationship proportional or nonproportional?

The graph shows a linear proportional relationship because it is a line that contains the origin.

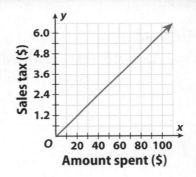

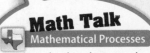
Math Talk
Mathematical Processes
What do the slope and the y-intercept of the graph represent in this situation?

YOUR TURN

Determine if each of the following graphs represents a proportional or nonproportional relationship.

1.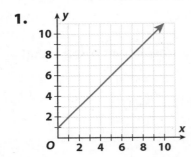

_____

2.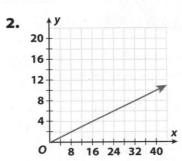

_____

Personal Math Trainer
Online Assessment and Intervention
my.hrw.com

© Houghton Mifflin Harcourt Publishing Company

Distinguish Between Proportional and Nonproportional Situations Using an Equation

If an equation is not a linear equation, it represents a nonproportional relationship. A linear equation of the form $y = mx + b$ may represent either a proportional ($b = 0$) or nonproportional ($b \neq 0$) relationship.

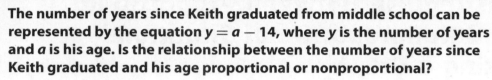

EXAMPLE 2 TEKS 8.5.F

The number of years since Keith graduated from middle school can be represented by the equation $y = a - 14$, where y is the number of years and a is his age. Is the relationship between the number of years since Keith graduated and his age proportional or nonproportional?

$$y = a - 14$$

The equation is in the form $y = mx + b$, with a being used as the variable instead of x. The value of m is 1, and the value of b is -14. Since b is not 0, the relationship between the number of years since Keith graduated and his age is nonproportional.

Reflect

3. **Communicate Mathematical Ideas** In a proportional relationship, the ratio $\frac{y}{x}$ is constant. Show that this ratio is not constant for the equation $y = a - 14$.

_____

_____

4. **What If?** Suppose another equation represents Keith's age in months y given his age in years a. Is this relationship proportional? Explain.

_____

_____

YOUR TURN

Determine if each of the following equations represents a proportional or nonproportional relationship.

5. $d = 65t$

6. $p = 0.1s + 2000$

_____ _____

7. $n = 450 - 3p$

8. $36 = 12d$

_____ _____

Distinguish Between Proportional and Nonproportional Situations Using a Table

If there is not a constant rate of change in the data displayed in a table, then the table represents a nonlinear nonproportional relationship.

A linear relationship represented by a table is a proportional relationship when the quotient of each pair of numbers is constant. Otherwise, the linear relationship is nonproportional.

EXAMPLE 3   TEKS 8.5.F

The values in the table represent the numbers of U.S. dollars three tourists traded for Mexican pesos. The relationship is linear. Is the relationship proportional or nonproportional?

U.S. Dollars Traded	Mexican Pesos Received
130	1,690
255	3,315
505	6,565

$$\frac{1,690}{130} = \frac{169}{13} = 13$$

$$\frac{3,315}{255} = \frac{221}{17} = 13$$

$$\frac{6,565}{505} = \frac{1313}{101} = 13$$

Simplify the ratios to compare the pesos received to the dollars traded.

The ratio of pesos received to dollars traded is constant at 13 Mexican pesos per U.S. dollar. This is a proportional relationship.

Math Talk
Mathematical Processes

How could you confirm that the values in the table have a linear relationship?

YOUR TURN

Determine if the linear relationship represented by each table is a proportional or nonproportional relationship.

9.

x	y
2	30
8	90
14	150

10.

x	y
5	1
40	8
65	13

© Houghton Mifflin Harcourt Publishing Company • Image Credits: ©Jupiter Images/ Hemera Technologies/Getty-Images

Comparing Proportional and Nonproportional Situations

You can use what you have learned about proportional and nonproportional relationships to compare similar real-world situations that are given using different representations.

EXAMPLE 4  TEKS 8.5.F

A **A laser tag league has the choice of two arenas for a tournament. In both cases, x is the number of hours and y is the total charge. Compare and contrast these two situations.**

Math Talk

Mathematical Processes

How might graphing the equation for Arena A help you to compare the situations?

Arena A

$y = 225x$

Arena B

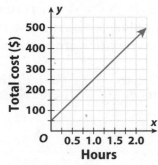

- **Arena A's** equation has the form $y = mx + b$, where $b = 0$. So, Arena A's charges are a proportional relationship. The hourly rate, \$225, is greater than Arena B's, but there is no additional fee.

- **Arena B's** graph is a line that does not include the origin. So, Arena B's charges are a nonproportional relationship. Arena B has a \$50 initial fee but its hourly rate, \$200, is lower.

B **Jessika is remodeling and has the choice of two painters. In both cases, x is the number of hours and y is the total charge. Compare and contrast these two situations.**

Painter A

$y = \$45x$

Painter B

x	0	1	3	4
y	20	55	90	125

Painter A's equation has the form $y = mx + b$, where $b = 0$. So, Painter A's charges are proportional. The hourly rate, \$45, is greater than Painter B's, but there is no additional fee.

Painter B's table is a nonproportional relationship because the ratio of y to x is not constant. Because the table contains the ordered pair (0, 20), Painter B charges an initial fee of \$20, but the hourly rate, \$35, is less than Painter A's.

11. Compare and contrast the following two situations.

Test-Prep Center A	Test-Prep Center B
The cost for Test-Prep Center A is given by $c = 20h$, where c is the cost in dollars and h is the number of hours you attend.	Test-Prep Center B charges $25 per hour to attend, but you have a $100 coupon that you can use to reduce the cost.

_____

_____

_____

_____

_____

Guided Practice

Determine if each relationship is a proportional or nonproportional situation. Explain your reasoning. (Example 1, Example 2, Example 4)

1.

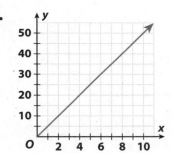

Look at the origin.

_____

_____

2.

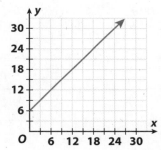

_____

_____

3. $q = 2p + \frac{1}{2}$

Compare the equation with $y = mx + b$.

_____

_____

_____

4. $v = \frac{1}{10} u$

_____

_____

_____

The tables represent linear relationships. Determine if each relationship is a proportional or nonproportional situation. (Example 3, Example 4)

5.

x	y
3	12
9	36
21	84

6.

x	y
22	4
46	8
58	10

Find the quotient of *y* and *x*.

_____   _____

_____   _____

_____   _____

7. The values in the table represent the numbers of households that watched three TV shows and the ratings of the shows. The relationship is linear. Describe the relationship in other ways. (Example 4)

Number of Households that Watched TV Show	TV Show Rating
15,000,000	12
20,000,000	16
25,000,000	20

_____

_____

_____

_____

? ESSENTIAL QUESTION CHECK-IN

8. How are using graphs, equations, and tables similar when distinguishing between proportional and nonproportional situations?

_____

_____

_____

4.4 Independent Practice

 **TEKS** 8.5.F

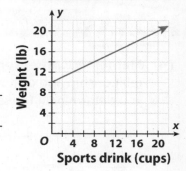
Personal Math Trainer

my.hrw.com Online Assessment and Intervention

9. The graph shows the weight of a cross-country team's beverage cooler based on how much sports drink it contains.

a. Is the relationship proportional or nonproportional? Explain.

_____

_____

b. Identify and interpret the slope and the y-intercept.

_____

_____

For 10-11, tell if the relationship between a rider's height above the first floor and the time since the rider stepped on the elevator or escalator is proportional or nonproportional. Explain.

10. The elevator paused for 10 seconds after you stepped on before beginning to rise at a constant rate of 8 feet per second.

_____

_____

_____

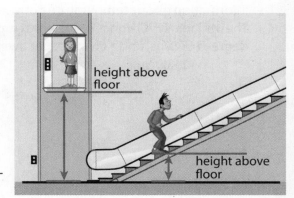
height above floor

height above floor

11. Your height, h, in feet above the first floor on the escalator is given by $h = 0.75t$, where t is the time in seconds.

_____

12. **Analyze Relationships** Compare and contrast the two graphs.

Graph A $y = \frac{1}{3}x$

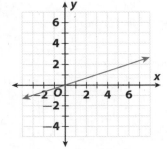

Graph B $y = \sqrt{x}$

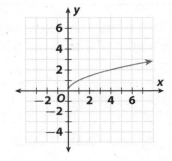

_____

_____

13. Represent Real-World Problems Describe a real-world situation where the relationship is linear and nonproportional.

_____

_____

 **FOCUS ON HIGHER ORDER THINKING**

14. Mathematical Reasoning Suppose you know the slope of a linear relationship and one of the points that its graph passes through. How can you determine if the relationship is proportional or nonproportional?

_____

_____

_____

15. Multiple Representations An entrant at a science fair has included information about temperature conversion in various forms, as shown. The variables F, C, and K represent temperatures in degrees Fahrenheit, degrees Celsius, and Kelvin, respectively.

Equation A

$$F = \frac{9}{5}C + 32$$

Equation B

$$K = C + 273.15$$

Table C	
Degrees Celsius	**kelvins**
8	281.15
15	288.15
36	309.15

a. Is the relationship between kelvins and degrees Celsius proportional? Justify your answer in two different ways.

_____

_____

_____

b. Is the relationship between degrees Celsius and degrees Fahrenheit proportional? Why or why not?

_____

_____

_____

Solving Systems of Linear Equations by Graphing

TEKS Expressions, equations, and relationships—8.9 Identify and verify the values of x and y that simultaneously satisfy two linear equations in the form $y = mx + b$ from the intersections of the graphed equations.

? **ESSENTIAL QUESTION**

How can you solve a system of equations by graphing?

EXPLORE ACTIVITY **TEKS** 8.9

> Slope-intercept form is $y = mx + b$, where m is the slope and b is the y-intercept.

Investigating Systems of Equations

You have learned several ways to graph a linear equation in slope-intercept form. For example, you can use the slope and y-intercept or you can find two points that satisfy the equation and connect them with a line.

A Graph the pair of equations together: $\begin{cases} y = 3x - 2 \\ y = -2x + 3 \end{cases}$

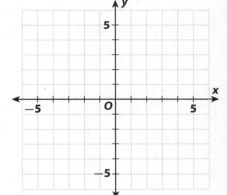

B Explain how to tell whether $(2, -1)$ is a solution of the equation $y = 3x - 2$ without using the graph.

_____

_____

C Explain how to tell whether $(2, -1)$ is a solution of the equation $y = -2x + 3$ without using the graph.

_____

_____

D Explain how to use the graph to tell whether the ordered pair $(2, -1)$ is a solution of either equation.

_____

E Find the point of intersection of the two lines. Check by substitution to determine if it is a solution to both equations.

Point of intersection $\left(\boxed{}, \boxed{} \right)$

$y = 3x - 2$ $y = -2x + 3$

$\boxed{} = 3\boxed{} - 2$ $\boxed{} = -2\boxed{} + 3$

$1 = \boxed{}$ $1 = \boxed{}$

The point of intersection [**is** / **is not**] the solution of both equations.

Solving Systems Graphically

An ordered pair (x, y) is a solution of an equation in two variables if substituting the x- and y-values into the equation results in a true statement. A **system of equations** is a set of equations that have the same variables. An ordered pair is a **solution** of a system of equations if it is a solution of every equation in the system.

Since the graph of an equation represents all ordered pairs that are solutions of the equation, if a point lies on the graphs of two equations, the point is a solution of both equations and is, therefore, a **solution of the system**.

EXAMPLE 1

TEKS 8.9

Solve each system by graphing.

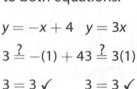

A $\begin{cases} y = -x + 4 \\ y = 3x \end{cases}$

STEP 1 Start by graphing each equation.

STEP 2 Find the point of intersection of the two lines. It appears to be (1, 3). Check by substitution to determine if it is a solution to both equations.

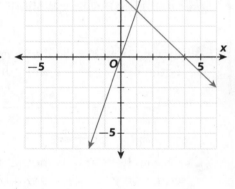

$$y = -x + 4 \quad y = 3x$$

$$3 \overset{?}{=} -(1) + 4 \qquad 3 \overset{?}{=} 3(1)$$

$$3 = 3 \checkmark \qquad 3 = 3 \checkmark$$

The solution of the system is (1, 3).

B $\begin{cases} y = 3x - 3 \\ y = 3(x - 1) \end{cases}$

STEP 1 Start by graphing each equation.

STEP 2 Identify any ordered pairs that are solutions of both equations.

The graphs of the equations are the same line. So, every ordered pair that is a solution of one equation is also a solution of the other equation. The system has infinitely many solutions.

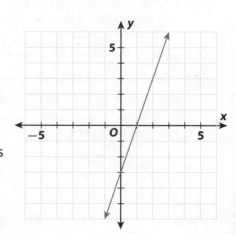

My Notes

Reflect

1. A system of linear equations has infinitely many solutions. Does that mean any ordered pair in the coordinate plane is a solution?

   _____

   _____

2. Can you show algebraically that both equations in part B represent the same line? If so, explain how.

   _____

   _____

   _____

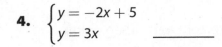

Solve each system by graphing. Check by substitution.

3. $\begin{cases} y = -x + 2 \\ y = -4x - 1 \end{cases}$ _____

   Check:

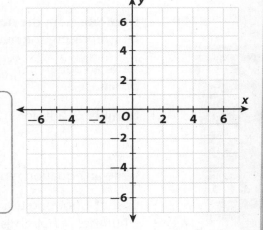

4. $\begin{cases} y = -2x + 5 \\ y = 3x \end{cases}$ _____

   Check:

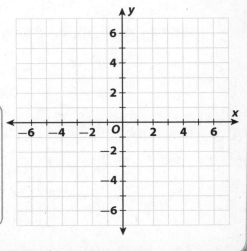

Personal Math Trainer

Online Assessment and Intervention

my.hrw.com

Solving Problems Using Systems of Equations

When using graphs to solve a system of equations, it is best to rewrite both equations in slope-intercept form for ease of graphing.

To write an equation in slope-intercept form starting from $ax + by = c$:

$$ax + by = c$$

$$by = c - ax \qquad \text{Subtract } ax \text{ from both sides.}$$

$$y = \frac{c}{b} - \frac{ax}{b} \qquad \text{Divide both sides by } b.$$

$$y = -\frac{a}{b}x + \frac{c}{b} \qquad \text{Rearrange the equation.}$$

EXAMPLE 2   TEKS 8.9

Keisha and her friends visit the concession stand at a football game. The stand charges $2 for a hot dog and $1 for a drink. The friends buy a total of 8 items for $11. Tell how many hot dogs and how many drinks they bought.

STEP 1 Let x represent the number of hot dogs they bought and let y represent the number of drinks they bought.

Write an equation representing the **number of items they purchased.**

Number of hot dogs	+	Number of drinks	=	Total items
x	+	y	=	8

Write an equation representing the **money spent on the items.**

Cost of 1 hot dog times number of hot dogs	+	Cost of 1 drink times number of drinks	=	Total cost
$2x$	+	$1y$	=	11

STEP 2 Write the equations in slope-intercept form. Then graph.

$$x + y = 8$$
$$y = 8 - x$$
$$y = -x + 8$$

$$2x + 1y = 11$$
$$1y = 11 - 2x$$
$$y = -2x + 11$$

Graph the equations $y = -x + 8$ and $y = -2x + 11$.

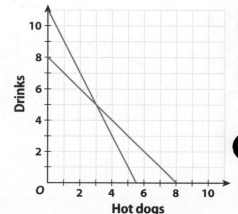

© Houghton Mifflin Harcourt Publishing Company • Image Credits: ©Weronica Ankorhorn/Houghton Mifflin Harcourt

Animated Math — my.hrw.com

STEP 3 Use the graph to identify the solution of the system of equations. Check your answer by substituting the ordered pair into both equations.

Apparent solution: (3, 5)
Check:

$$x + y = 8 \qquad 2x + y = 11$$
$$3 + 5 \overset{?}{=} 8 \qquad 2(3) + 5 \overset{?}{=} 11$$
$$8 = 8 \checkmark \qquad 11 = 11 \checkmark$$

The point (3, 5) is a solution of both equations.

STEP 4 Interpret the solution in the original context.

Keisha and her friends bought 3 hot dogs and 5 drinks.

Reflect

5. Conjecture Why do you think the graph is limited to the first quadrant?

_____

_____

6. During school vacation, Marquis wants to go bowling and to play laser tag. He wants to play 6 total games but needs to figure out how many of each he can play if he spends exactly $20. Each game of bowling is $2 and each game of laser tag is $4.

a. Let x represent the number of games Marquis bowls and let y represent the number of games of laser tag Marquis plays. Write a system of equations that describes the situation. Then write the equations in slope-intercept form.

_____

_____

b. Graph the solutions of both equations.

c. How many games of bowling and how many games of laser tag will Marquis play?

_____

_____

_____

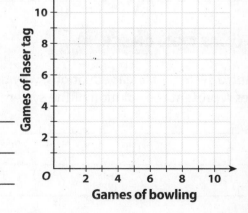

Personal Math Trainer — Online Assessment and Intervention — my.hrw.com

Solve each system by graphing. (Example 1)

1. $\begin{cases} y = 3x - 4 \\ y = x + 2 \end{cases}$ _____

2. $\begin{cases} x - 3y = 2 \\ -3x + 9y = -6 \end{cases}$ _____

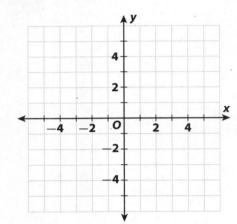

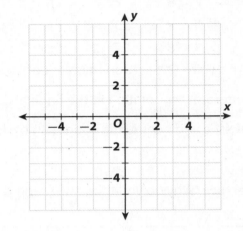

3. **Mrs. Morales wrote a test with 15 questions covering spelling and vocabulary. Spelling questions (x) are worth 5 points and vocabulary questions (y) are worth 10 points. The maximum number of points possible on the test is 100.** (Example 2)

   a. Write an equation in slope-intercept form to represent the number of questions on the test.

   _____

   b. Write an equation in slope-intercept form to represent the total number of points on the test.

   _____

   c. Graph the solutions of both equations.

   d. Use your graph to tell how many of each question type are on the test.

   _____

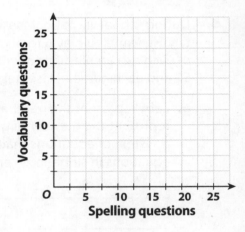

© Houghton Mifflin Harcourt Publishing Company

? ESSENTIAL QUESTION CHECK-IN

4. When you graph a system of linear equations, why does the intersection of the two lines represent the solution of the system?

   _____

   _____

   _____

4.5 Independent Practice

 TEKS 8.9

Personal Math Trainer

Online Assessment and Intervention

my.hrw.com

5. Vocabulary A _____ is a set of equations that have the same variables.

6. Eight friends started a business. They will wear either a baseball cap or a shirt imprinted with their logo while working. They want to spend exactly $36 on the shirts and caps. Shirts cost $6 each and caps cost $3 each.

a. Write a system of equations to describe the situation. Let x represent the number of shirts and let y represent the number of caps.

_____

_____

b. Graph the system to find the solution. Verify the solution. What does it represent?

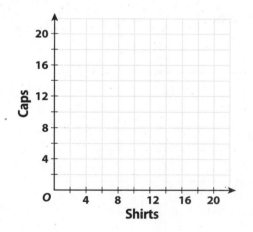

_____

_____

_____

_____

7. Multistep The table shows the cost for bowling at two bowling alleys.

	Shoe Rental Fee	Cost per Game
Bowl-o-Rama	$2.00	$2.50
Bowling Pinz	$4.00	$2.00

a. Write a system of equations, with one equation describing the cost to bowl at Bowl-o-Rama and the other describing the cost to bowl at Bowling Pinz. For each equation, let x represent the number of games played and let y represent the total cost.

_____

_____

b. Graph the system to find the solution. Verify the solution. What does it represent?

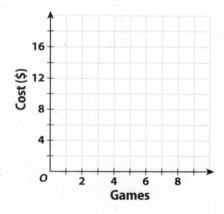

Cost of Bowling

_____

_____

_____

_____

8. Multi-Step Jeremy runs 7 miles per week and increases his distance by 1 mile each week. Tony runs 3 miles per week and increases his distance by 2 miles each week. In how many weeks will Jeremy and Tony be running the same distance? What will that distance be?

_____

9. Critical Thinking Write a real-world situation that could be represented by the system of equations shown below.

$$\begin{cases} y = 4x + 10 \\ y = 3x + 15 \end{cases}$$

_____

_____

_____

 **FOCUS ON HIGHER ORDER THINKING**

10. Multistep The table shows two options provided by a high-speed Internet provider.

	Setup Fee ($)	Cost per Month ($)
Option 1	50	30
Option 2	No setup fee	$40

a. In how many months will the total cost of both options be the same? What will that cost be?

_____

b. If you plan to cancel your Internet service after 9 months, which is the cheaper option? Explain.

_____

_____

_____

11. Draw Conclusions How many solutions does the system formed by $x - y = 3$ and $ay - ax + 3a = 0$ have for a nonzero number a? Explain.

_____

_____

_____

_____

Work Area

Ready to Go On?

Personal Math Trainer
Online Assessment and Intervention
⏻ my.hrw.com

4.1 Representing Linear Nonproportional Relationships

1. Complete the table using the equation $y = 3x + 2$.

x	−1	0	1	2	3
y					

4.2 Determining Slope and *y*-intercept

2. Find the slope and *y*-intercept of the line in the graph.

_____

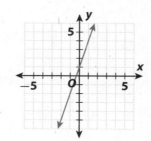

4.3 Graphing Linear Nonproportional Relationships

3. Graph the equation $y = 2x - 3$ using slope and *y*-intercept.

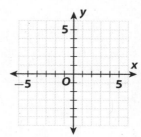

4.4 Proportional and Nonproportional Situations

4. Does the table represent a proportional or a nonproportional linear relationship?

x	1	2	3	4	5
y	4	7	10	13	16

_____

4.5 Solving Systems of Linear Equations by Graphing

5. A school band ordered hats for $3 and large T-shirts for $5. They bought 150 items in all for $590. Graph a system of equations to find how many hats and T-shirts the band ordered. _____

? ESSENTIAL QUESTION

6. How can you identify a linear nonproportional relationship from a table, a graph, and an equation?

_____

_____

Selected Response

1. The table below represents which equation?

x	−1	0	1	2
y	−10	−6	−2	2

(A) $y = -x - 10$

(B) $y = -6x$

(C) $y = 4x - 6$

(D) $y = -4x + 2$

2. The graph of which equation is shown below?

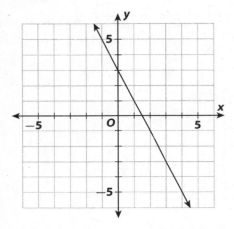

(A) $y = -2x + 3$

(B) $y = -2x + 1.5$

(C) $y = 2x + 3$

(D) $y = 2x + 1.5$

3. The table below represents a linear relationship.

x	2	3	4	5
y	4	7	10	13

What is the y-intercept?

(A) −4   (C) 2

(B) −2   (D) 3

4. Which equation represents a nonproportional relationship?

(A) $y = 3x + 0$

(B) $y = -3x$

(C) $y = 3x + 5$

(D) $y = \frac{1}{3}x$

5. Which statement describes the solution of a system of linear equations for two lines with the same slope and the same y-intercept?

(A) one nonzero solution

(B) infinitely many solutions

(C) no solution

(D) solution of 0

Gridded Response

6. The table shows a proportional relationship. What is the missing y-value?

x	4	10	12
y	6	15	?

				•		
⓪	⓪	⓪	⓪		⓪	⓪
①	①	①	①		①	①
②	②	②	②		②	②
③	③	③	③		③	③
④	④	④	④		④	④
⑤	⑤	⑤	⑤		⑤	⑤
⑥	⑥	⑥	⑥		⑥	⑥
⑦	⑦	⑦	⑦		⑦	⑦
⑧	⑧	⑧	⑧		⑧	⑧
⑨	⑨	⑨	⑨		⑨	⑨

Writing Linear Equations

 ESSENTIAL QUESTION

How can you use linear equations to solve real-world problems?

Real-World Video

Linear equations can be used to describe many situations related to shopping. If a store advertised four books for $32.00, you could write and solve a linear equation to find the price of each book.

🔘 my.hrw.com

GO DIGITAL
my.hrw.com

 my.hrw.com

Go digital with your write-in student edition, accessible on any device.

 Math On the Spot

Scan with your smart phone to jump directly to the online edition, video tutor, and more.

 Animated Math

Interactively explore key concepts to see how math works.

 Personal Math Trainer

Get immediate feedback and help as you work through practice sets.

Are YOU Ready?

Complete these exercises to review skills you will need for this chapter.

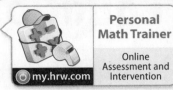

Write Fractions as Decimals

EXAMPLE $\frac{0.5}{0.8} = ?$ Multiply the numerator and the denominator by a power of 10 so that the denominator is a whole number.

$$\frac{0.5 \times 10}{0.8 \times 10} = \frac{5}{8}$$

Write the fraction as a division problem.
Write a decimal point and zeros in the dividend.
Place a decimal point in the quotient.
Divide as with whole numbers.

$$
\begin{array}{r}
0.625 \\
8\overline{)5.000} \\
-48 \\
\hline
20 \\
-16 \\
\hline
40 \\
-40 \\
\hline
0
\end{array}
$$

Write each fraction as a decimal.

1. $\frac{3}{8}$ _____

2. $\frac{0.3}{0.4}$ _____

3. $\frac{0.13}{0.2}$ _____

4. $\frac{0.39}{0.75}$ _____

Inverse Operations

EXAMPLE
$5n = 20$
$\frac{5n}{5} = \frac{20}{5}$
$n = 4$

n is multiplied by 5.
To solve the equation, use the inverse operation, division.

$k + 7 = 9$
$k + 7 - 7 = 9 - 7$
$k = 2$

7 is added to k.
To solve the equation, use the inverse operation, subtraction.

Solve each equation using the inverse operation.

5. $7p = 28$ _____

6. $h - 13 = 5$ _____

7. $\frac{y}{3} = -6$ _____

8. $b + 9 = 21$ _____

9. $c - 8 = -8$ _____

10. $3n = -12$ _____

11. $-16 = m + 7$ _____

12. $\frac{t}{-5} = -5$ _____

Reading Start-Up

© Houghton Mifflin Harcourt Publishing Company

Visualize Vocabulary

Use the ✔ words to complete the diagram. You can put more than one word in each bubble.

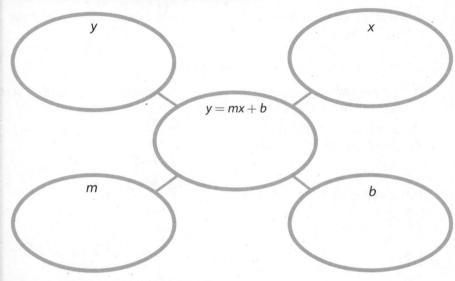

Understand Vocabulary

Complete the sentences using the preview words.

1. A set of data that is made up of two paired variables

   is _____.

2. When the rate of change varies from point to point, the relationship

   is a _____.

Active Reading

Tri-Fold Before beginning the module, create a tri-fold to help you learn the concepts and vocabulary in this module. Fold the paper into three sections. Label the columns "What I Know," "What I Need to Know," and "What I Learned." Complete the first two columns before you read. After studying the module, complete the third column.

MODULE 5

Unpacking the TEKS

Understanding the TEKS and the vocabulary terms in the TEKS will help you know exactly what you are expected to learn in this module.

TEKS 8.5.D

Use a trend line that approximates the linear relationship between bivariate sets of data to make predictions.

Key Vocabulary

bivariate data *(datos bivariados)*
A set of data that is made up of two paired variables.

What It Means to You

You will see how to use a linear relationship between sets of data to make predictions.

UNPACKING EXAMPLE 8.5.D

The graph shows the temperatures in degrees Celsius inside the earth at certain depths in kilometers. Use the graph to find the temperature at 8 km.

You can see that at 8 km, the temperature is 100 °C.

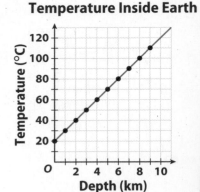

Temperature Inside Earth

TEKS 8.5.I

Write an equation in the form $y = mx + b$ to model a linear relationship between two quantities using verbal, numerical, tabular, and graphical representations.

What It Means to You

You will learn how to write an equation based on a situation that models a linear relationship.

UNPACKING EXAMPLE 8.5.I

In 2006 the fare for a taxicab was an initial charge of $2.50 plus $0.30 per mile. Write an equation in slope-intercept form that can be used to calculate the total fare.

The constant charge is $2.50

The input variable, x, is the number of miles driven. So $0.30x$ is the total for the miles.

The equation for the total fare, y, is

$$y = 0.3x + 2.5$$

Visit **my.hrw.com** to see all the **TEKS** unpacked.

my.hrw.com

Writing Linear Equations from Situations and Graphs

TEKS
Proportionality—
8.5.I Write an equation in the form $y = mx + b$ to model a linear relationship between two quantities using verbal, numerical, tabular, and graphical representations.

? ESSENTIAL QUESTION

How do you write an equation to model a linear relationship given a graph or a description?

EXPLORE ACTIVITY   TEKS 8.5.I

Writing an Equation in Slope-Intercept Form

Greta makes clay mugs and bowls as gifts at the Crafty Studio. She pays a membership fee of $15 a month and an equipment fee of $3.00 an hour to use the potter's wheel, table, and kiln. Write an equation in the form $y = mx + b$ that Greta can use to calculate her monthly costs.

A What is the input variable, x, for this situation?

_____

What is the output variable, y, for this situation?

_____

B During April, Greta does not use the equipment at all. What will be her number of hours (x) for April? _____

What will be her cost (y) for April? _____

What will be the y-intercept, b, in the equation? _____

Math Talk
Mathematical Processes

What change could the studio make that would make a difference to the y-intercept of the equation?

C Greta spends 8 hours in May for a cost of $15 + 8(\$3) =$ _____.

In June, she spends 11 hours for a cost of _____.

From May to June, the change in x-values is _____.

From May to June, the change in y-values is _____.

What will be the slope, m, in the equation? _____

D Use the values for m and b to write an equation for Greta's costs in the form $y = mx + b$: _____

Writing an Equation from a Graph

You can use information presented in a graph to write an equation in slope-intercept form.

EXAMPLE 1 **TEKS** 8.5.I

A video club charges a one-time membership fee plus a rental fee for each DVD borrowed. Use the graph to write an equation in slope-intercept form to represent the amount spent, *y*, on *x* DVD rentals.

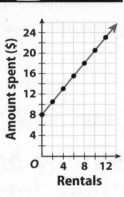

STEP 1 Choose two points on the graph to find the slope.

$m = \dfrac{y_2 - y_1}{x_2 - x_1}$ Use the slope formula.

$m = \dfrac{18 - 8}{8 - 0}$ Substitute (0, 8) for (x_1, y_1) and (8, 18) for (x_2, y_2).

$m = \dfrac{10}{8} = 1.25$ Simplify.

STEP 2 Read the *y*-intercept from the graph.

The *y*-intercept is 8.

STEP 3 Use your slope and *y*-intercept values to write an equation in slope-intercept form.

$y = mx + b$ Slope-intercept form

$y = 1.25x + 8$ Substitute 1.25 for m and 8 for y.

> ## Math Talk
> **Mathematical Processes**
>
> If the graph of an equation is a line that goes through the origin, what is the value of the *y*-intercept?

Reflect

1. What does the value of the slope represent in this context?

   _____

2. Describe the meaning of the *y*-intercept.

   _____

YOUR TURN

3. The cash register subtracts $2.50 from a $25 Coffee Café gift card for every medium coffee the customer buys. Use the graph to write an equation in slope-intercept form to represent this situation.

   _____

Amount on Gift Card

Writing an Equation from a Description

You can use information from a description of a linear relationship to find the slope and *y*-intercept and to write an equation.

EXAMPLE 2 Real World

TEKS 8.5.I

The rent charged for space in an office building is a linear relationship related to the size of the space rented. Write an equation in slope-intercept form for the rent at West Main Street Office Rentals.

West Main St. Office Rentals 🏢
Offices for rent at convenient locations.

Monthly Rates:
600 square feet for **$750**
900 square feet for **$1150**

My Notes

STEP 1 Identify the input and output variables.

The input variable is the square footage of floor space.

The output variable is the monthly rent.

STEP 2 Write the information given in the problem as ordered pairs.

The rent for 600 square feet of floor space is $750: (600, 750)

The rent for 900 square feet of floor space is $1150: (900, 1150)

STEP 3 Find the slope.

$$m = \frac{y_2 - y_1}{x_2 - x_1} = \frac{1150 - 750}{900 - 600} = \frac{400}{300} = \frac{4}{3}$$

STEP 4 Find the *y*-intercept. Use the slope and one of the ordered pairs.

$y = mx + b$ Slope-intercept form

$750 = \frac{4}{3} \cdot 600 + b$ Substitute for *y*, *m*, and *x*.

$750 = 800 + b$ Multiply.

$-50 = b$ Subtract 800 from both sides.

STEP 5 Substitute the slope and *y*-intercept.

$y = mx + b$ Slope-intercept form

$y = \frac{4}{3}x - 50$ Substitute $\frac{4}{3}$ for *m* and -50 for *b*.

Reflect

4. Without graphing, tell whether the graph of this equation rises or falls from left to right. What does the sign of the slope mean in this context?

_____

_____

_____

5. Hari's weekly allowance varies depending on the number of chores he does. He received $16 in allowance the week he did 12 chores, and $14 in allowance the week he did 8 chores. Write an equation for his allowance in slope-intercept form. _____

Guided Practice

1. Li is making beaded necklaces. For each necklace, she uses 27 spacers, plus 5 beads per inch of necklace length. Write an equation to find how many beads Li needs for each necklace. (Explore Activity)

    a. input variable: _____

    b. output variable: _____

    c. equation: _____

2. Kate is planning a trip to the beach. She estimates her average speed to graph her expected progress on the trip. Write an equation in slope-intercept form that represents the situation. (Example 1)

    Choose two points on the graph to find the slope.

    $m = \dfrac{y_2 - y_1}{x_2 - x_1} =$ _____

    Read the y-intercept from the graph: $b =$ _____

    Use your slope and y-intercept values to write an equation in slope-intercept form. _____

Distance to beach (mi) 300 200 100

O 1 2 3 4 5 6
Driving time (h)

3. At 59 °F, crickets chirp at a rate of 76 times per minute, and at 65 °F, they chirp 100 times per minute. Write an equation in slope-intercept form that represents the situation. (Example 2)

    Input variable: _____   Output variable: _____

    $m = \dfrac{y_2 - y_1}{x_2 - x_1} =$ _____

    Substitute in $y = mx + b$: _____ $+ b$; _____ $= b$

    Write an equation in slope-intercept form. _____

? ESSENTIAL QUESTION CHECK-IN

4. Explain what m and b in the equation $y = mx + b$ tell you about the graph of the line with that equation.

    _____

5.1 Independent Practice

 TEKS 8.5.I

Personal Math Trainer

Online Assessment and Intervention

my.hrw.com

5. A dragonfly can beat its wings 30 times per second. Write an equation in slope-intercept form that shows the relationship between flying time in seconds and the number of times the dragonfly beats its wings.

_____

6. A balloon is released from the top of a platform that is 50 meters tall. The balloon rises at the rate of 4 meters per second. Write an equation in slope-intercept form that tells the height of the balloon above the ground after a given number of seconds.

_____

The graph shows a scuba diver's ascent over time.

7. Use the graph to find the slope of the line. Tell what the slope means in this context.

_____

_____

8. Identify the *y*-intercept. Tell what the *y*-intercept means in this context.

_____

9. Write an equation in slope-intercept form that represents the diver's depth over time.

_____

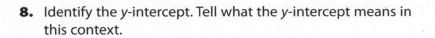

Scuba Diver's Ascent

10. The formula for converting Celsius temperatures to Fahrenheit temperatures is a linear equation. Water freezes at 0 °C, or 32 °F, and it boils at 100 °C, or 212 °F. Find the slope and *y*-intercept for a graph that gives degrees Celsius on the horizontal axis and degrees Fahrenheit on the vertical axis. Then write an equation in slope-intercept form that converts degrees Celsius into degrees Fahrenheit.

_____

_____

11. The cost of renting a sailboat at a lake is $20 per hour plus $12 for lifejackets. Write an equation in slope-intercept form that can be used to calculate the total amount you would pay for using this sailboat.

_____

The graph shows the activity in a savings account.

Amount saved ($)

Months in plan

12. What was the amount of the initial deposit that started this savings account?

_____

13. Find the slope and *y*-intercept of the graphed line.

_____

14. Write an equation in slope-intercept form for the activity in this savings account.

_____

15. Explain the meaning of the slope in this graph.

_____

_____

 **FOCUS ON HIGHER ORDER THINKING**

16. Communicate Mathematical Ideas Explain how you decide which part of a problem will be represented by the variable *x*, and which part will be represented by the variable *y* in a graph of the situation.

_____

_____

_____

_____

17. Represent Real-World Problems Describe what would be true about the rate of change in a situation that could *not* be represented by a graphed line and an equation in the form $y = mx + b$.

_____

_____

_____

18. Draw Conclusions Must *m*, in the equation $y = mx + b$, always be a positive number? Explain.

_____

_____

_____

Work Area

TEKS
Proportionality—
8.5.I Write an equation in the form $y = mx + b$ to model a linear relationship between two quantities using verbal, numerical, tabular, and graphical representations.

 ESSENTIAL QUESTION

How do you write an equation to model a linear relationship given a table?

Graphing from a Table to Write an Equation

You can use information from a table to draw a graph of a linear relationship and to write an equation for the graphed line.

Math On the Spot
⏱ my.hrw.com

 **EXAMPLE 1**  **TEKS** 8.5.I

The table shows the temperature of a fish tank during an experiment. Graph the data, and find the slope and y-intercept from the graph. Then write the equation for the graph in slope-intercept form.

Time (h)	0	1	2	3	4	5
Temperature (°F)	82	80	78	76	74	72

STEP 1 Graph the ordered pairs from the table (time, temperature).

STEP 2 Draw a line through the points.

STEP 3 Choose two points on the graph to find the slope: for example, choose (0, 82) and (1, 80).

$$m = \frac{y_2 - y_1}{x_2 - x_1}$$ *Use the slope formula.*

$$m = \frac{80 - 82}{1 - 0}$$ *Substitute (0, 82) for (x_1, y_1) and (1, 80) for (x_2, y_2).*

$$m = \frac{-2}{1} = -2$$ *Simplify.*

STEP 4 Read the y-intercept from the graph.

$$b = 82$$

STEP 5 Use these slope and y-intercept values to write an equation in slope-intercept form.

$$y = mx + b$$
$$y = -2x + 82$$

Tank Temperature

Math Talk
Mathematical Processes

Which variable in the equation $y = mx + b$ shows the initial temperature of the fish tank at the beginning of the experiment?

YOUR TURN

1. The table shows the volume of water released by Hoover Dam over a certain period of time. Graph the data, and find the slope and *y*-intercept from the graph. Then write the equation for the graph in slope-intercept form.

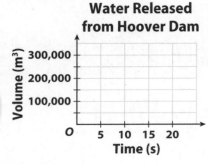

Water Released from Hoover Dam

Water Released from Hoover Dam	
Time (s)	Volume of water (m³)
5	75,000
10	150,000
15	225,000
20	300,000

Math Talk

Mathematical Processes

Which variable in the equation $y = mx + b$ tells you the volume of water released every second from Hoover Dam?

Writing an Equation from a Table

The information from a table can also help you to write the equation that represents a given situation without drawing the graph.

EXAMPLE 2

TEKS 8.5.I

Elizabeth's cell phone plan lets her choose how many minutes are included each month. The table shows the plan's monthly cost *y* for a given number of included minutes *x*. Write an equation in slope-intercept form to represent the situation.

Minutes included, *x*	100	200	300	400	500
Cost of plan ($), *y*	14	20	26	32	38

STEP 1 Notice that the change in cost is the same for each increase of 100 minutes. So, the relationship is linear. Choose any two ordered pairs from the table to find the slope.

$$m = \frac{y_2 - y_1}{x_2 - x_1} = \frac{(20 - 14)}{(200 - 100)} = \frac{6}{100} = 0.06$$

STEP 2 Find the *y*-intercept. Use the slope and any point from the table.

$y = mx + b$ Slope-intercept form

$14 = 0.06 \cdot 100 + b$ Substitute for *y*, *m*, and *x*.

$14 = 6 + b$ Multiply.

$8 = b$ Subtract 6 from both sides.

STEP 3 Substitute the slope and *y*-intercept.

$y = mx + b$ Slope-intercept form

$y = 0.06x + 8$ Substitute 0.06 for *m* and 8 for *b*.

Reflect

2. What is the base price for the cell phone plan, regardless of how many minutes are included? What is the cost per minute? Explain.

_____

_____

_____

_____

_____

3. **What If?** Elizabeth's cell phone company changes the cost of her plan as shown below. Write an equation in slope-intercept form to represent the situation. How did the plan change?

Minutes included, x	100	200	300	400	500
Cost of plan ($), y	30	35	40	45	50

_____

_____

Math Talk
Mathematical Processes

Explain the meaning of the slope and y-intercept of the equation.

YOUR TURN

4. A salesperson receives a weekly salary plus a commission for each computer sold. The table shows the total pay, p, and the number of computers sold, n. Write an equation in slope-intercept form to represent this situation.

Number of computers sold, n	4	6	8	10	12
Total pay ($), p	550	700	850	1000	1150

_____

5. To rent a van, a moving company charges $40.00 plus $0.50 per mile. The table shows the total cost, c, and the number of miles driven, d. Write an equation in slope-intercept form to represent this situation.

Number of miles driven, d	10	20	30	40	50
Total cost ($), c	45	50	55	60	65

_____

Personal Math Trainer

Online Assessment and Intervention

my.hrw.com

© Houghton Mifflin Harcourt Publishing Company

1. Jaime purchased a $20 bus pass. Each time he rides the bus, a certain amount is deducted from the pass. The table shows the amount, *y*, left on his pass after *x* rides. Graph the data, and find the slope and *y*-intercept from the graph. Then write the equation for the graph in slope-intercept form. (Example 1)

Number of rides, *x*	0	4	8	12	16
Amount left on pass ($), *y*	20	15	10	5	0

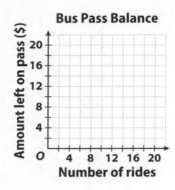

Bus Pass Balance

_____

The table shows the temperature (*y*) at different altitudes (*x*).
This is a linear relationship. (Example 2)

Altitude (ft), *x*	0	2000	4000	6000	8000	10000	12000
Temperature (°F), *y*	59	51	43	35	27	19	11

2. Find the slope for this relationship.

_____

3. Find the *y*-intercept for this relationship.

_____

4. Write an equation in slope-intercept form that represents this relationship.

_____

5. Use your equation to determine the temperature at an altitude of 5000 feet.

_____

? **ESSENTIAL QUESTION CHECK-IN**

6. Describe how you can use the information in a table showing a linear relationship to find the slope and *y*-intercept for the equation.

_____

_____

5.2 Independent Practice

TEKS 8.5.I

Personal Math Trainer

Online Assessment and Intervention

my.hrw.com

7. The table shows the costs of a large cheese pizza with toppings at a local pizzeria. Graph the data, and find the slope and y-intercept from the graph. Then write the equation for the graph in slope-intercept form.

Cost of Large Pizza

Number of toppings, t	0	1	2	3	4	5
Total cost ($), C	8	10	12	14	16	18

_____

8. The table shows how much an air-conditioning repair company charges for different numbers of hours of work. Graph the data, and find the slope and y-intercept from the graph. Then write the equation for the graph in slope-intercept form.

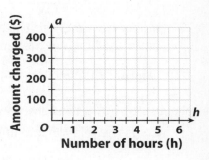

Number of hours (h), t	0	1	2	3	4	5
Amount charged ($), A	50	100	150	200	250	300

_____

9. A friend gave Ms. Morris a gift card for a local car wash. The table shows the linear relationship of how the value left on the card relates to the number of car washes.

Number of car washes, x	0	8	12
Amount left on card ($), y	30	18	12

a. Write an equation that shows the number of dollars left on the card.

_____

b. Explain the meaning of the negative slope in this situation.

_____

_____

c. What is the maximum value of x that makes sense in this context? Explain.

_____

The tables show linear relationships between x and y. Write an equation in slope-intercept form for each relationship.

10.

x	−2	−1	0	2
y	−1	0	1	3

11.

x	−4	1	0	6
y	14	4	6	−6

_____   _____

12. **Finance** Desiree starts a savings account with $125.00. Every month, she deposits $53.50.

a. Complete the table to model the situation.

Month, x					
Amount in Savings ($), y					

b. Write an equation in slope-intercept form that shows how much money Desiree has in her savings account after x months.

_____

c. Use the equation to find how much money Desiree will have in savings after 11 months.

_____

13. Monty documented the amount of rain his farm received on a monthly basis, as shown in the table.

Month, x	1	2	3	4	5
Rainfall (in.), y	5	3	4.5	1	7

a. Is the relationship linear? Why or why not?

_____

_____

b. Can an equation be written to describe the amount of rain? Explain.

_____

 **FOCUS ON HIGHER ORDER THINKING**

Work Area

14. **Analyze Relationships** If you have a table that shows a linear relationship, when can you read the value for b, in $y = mx + b$, directly from the table without drawing a graph or doing any calculations? Explain.

_____

_____

15. **What If?** Jaíme graphed linear data given in the form (cost, number). The y-intercept was 0. Jayla graphed the same data given in the form (number, cost). What was the y-intercept of her graph? Explain.

_____

_____

_____

Linear Relationships and Bivariate Data

TEKS
Proportionality—
8.5.C Contrast bivariate sets of data that suggest a linear relationship with bivariate sets of data that do not suggest a linear relationship from a graphical representation.
Also 8.5.D, 8.5.I.

? ESSENTIAL QUESTION

How can you contrast linear and nonlinear sets of bivariate data?

Finding the Equation of a Linear Relationship

You can use the points on a graph of a linear relationship to write an equation for the relationship. The equation of a linear relationship is $y = mx + b$, where m is the rate of change, or slope, and b is the value of y when x is 0.

Math On the Spot
⏻ my.hrw.com

EXAMPLE 1   TEKS 8.5.I

A handrail runs alongside a stairway. As the horizontal distance from the bottom of the stairway changes, the height of the handrail changes. Show that the relationship is linear, and then find the equation for the relationship.

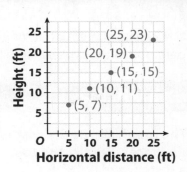

STEP 1   Show that the relationship is linear.

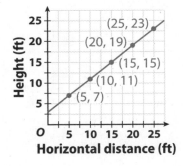

All of the points (5, 7), (10, 11), (15, 15), (20, 19), and (25, 23) lie on the same line, so the relationship is linear.

Animated Math
⏻ my.hrw.com

Math Talk
Mathematical Processes

What does the slope of the equation represent in this situation? What does the y-intercept represent?

STEP 2   Write the equation of the linear relationship.

Choose two points to find the slope.

(5, 7) and (25, 23)

$m = \dfrac{23 - 7}{25 - 5}$

$= \dfrac{16}{20}$

$= 0.8$

Choose a point and use the slope to substitute values for x, y, and m.

$y = mx + b$

$7 = 0.8(5) + b$

$7 = 4 + b$

$3 = b$

The equation of the linear relationship is $y = 0.8x + 3$.

YOUR TURN

Find the equation of each linear relationship.

1.

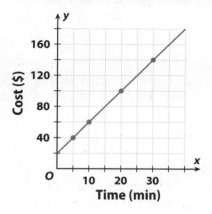

2.

Hours (x)	Number of units (y)
2	480
15	3,600
24	5,760
30	7,200
48	11,520
55	13,200

_____   _____

Making Predictions

You can use an equation of a linear relationship to predict a value between data points that you already know.

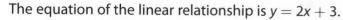

EXAMPLE 2 **TEKS** 8.5.D

The graph shows the cost for taxi rides of different distances. Predict the cost of a taxi ride that covers a distance of 6.5 miles.

STEP 1 Write the equation of the linear relationship.

(2, 7) and (6, 15)   *Select two points.*

$m = \dfrac{15 - 7}{6 - 2}$ *Calculate the rate of change.*

$= \dfrac{8}{4}$ *Simplify.*

$= 2$

$y = mx + b$

$15 = 2(6) + b$ *Fill in values for x, y, and m.*

$15 = 12 + b$ *Simplify.*

$3 = b$ *Solve for b.*

The equation of the linear relationship is $y = 2x + 3$.

You can check your equation using another point on the graph. Try (8, 19). Substituting gives $19 = 2(8) + 3$. The right side simplifies to 19, so $19 = 19$. ✓

STEP 2 Use your equation from Step 1 to predict the cost of a 6.5-mile taxi ride.

$y = 2x + 3$

$y = 2(6.5) + 3$ *Substitute $x = 6.5$.*

Solve for y.

$y = 16$

A taxi ride that covers a distance of 6.5 miles will cost $16.

Reflect

3. **What If?** Suppose a regulation changes the cost of the taxi ride to $1.80 per mile, plus a fee of $4.30. How does the price of the 6.5 mile ride compare to the original price?

_____

_____

4. How can you use a graph of a linear relationship to predict a value for a new input?

_____

_____

_____

5. How can you use a table of linear data to predict a value?

_____

_____

_____

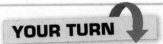 **YOUR TURN**

Paulina's income from a job that pays her a fixed amount per hour is shown in the graph. Use the graph to find the predicted value.

6. Income earned for working 2 hours

_____

7. Income earned for working 3.25 hours

_____

8. Total income earned for working for five 8-hour days all at the standard rate _____

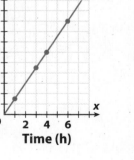

Personal Math Trainer

Online Assessment and Intervention

ⓜ my.hrw.com

Contrasting Linear and Nonlinear Data

Bivariate data is a set of data that is made up of two paired variables. If the relationship between the variables is linear, then the rate of change (slope) is constant. If the graph shows a **nonlinear relationship**, then the rate of change varies between pairs of points.

Andrew has two options in which to invest $200. Option A earns simple interest of 5%, while Option B earns interest of 5% compounded annually. The table shows the amount of the investment for both options over 20 years. Graph the data and describe the differences between the two graphs.

Year, x	Option A Total ($)	Option B Total ($)
0	200.00	200.00
5	250.00	255.26
10	300.00	325.78
15	350.00	415.79
20	400.00	530.66

STEP 1 Graph the data from the table for Options A and B on the same coordinate grid.

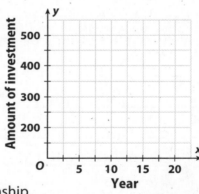

STEP 2 Find the rate of change between pairs of points for Option A and classify the relationship.

Option A	Rate of Change
(0, 200) and (5, 250)	$m = \dfrac{250 - 200}{5 - 0} = $ _____
(5, 250) and (10, 300)	
(10, 300) and (15, 350)	

The rate of change between the data values is _____, so

the graph of Option A shows a _____ relationship.

STEP 3 Find the rate of change between pairs of points for Option B and classify the relationship.

Option B	Rate of Change
(0, 200) and (5, 255.26)	$m = \frac{252.26 - 200}{5 - 0} \approx$ _____
(5, 255.26) and (10, 325.78)	
(10, 325.78) and (15, 415.79)	

The rate of change between the data values is _____,

so the graph of Option B shows a _____ relationship.

Reflect

9. Why are the graphs drawn as lines or curves and not discrete points?

_____

_____

_____

_____

10. Can you determine by viewing the graph if the data have a linear or nonlinear relationship? Explain.

_____

_____

_____

_____

11. Draw Conclusions Find the differences in the account balances to the nearest dollar at 5 year intervals for Option B. How does the length of time that money is in an account affect the advantage that compound interest has over simple interest?

_____

_____

_____

Use the following graphs to find the equation of the linear relationship. (Example 1)

1.

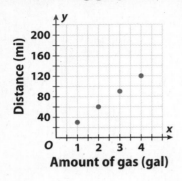

_____

2.

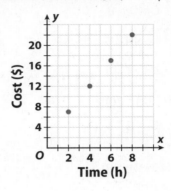

_____

3. The graph shows the relationship between the number of hours a kayak is rented and the total cost of the rental. Write an equation of the relationship. Then use the equation to predict the cost of a rental that lasts 5.5 hours. (Example 2)

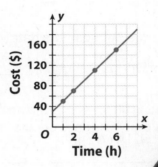

_____

Does each of the following graphs represent a linear relationship? Why or why not? (Explore Activity)

4.

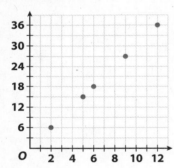

_____

_____

5.

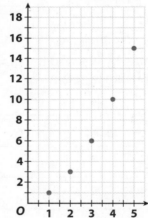

_____

_____

? **ESSENTIAL QUESTION CHECK-IN**

6. How can you tell if a set of bivariate data shows a linear relationship?

_____

_____

5.3 Independent Practice

TEKS 8.5.C, 8.5.D, 8.5.I

Personal Math Trainer

Online Assessment and Intervention

my.hrw.com

Does each of the following tables represent a linear relationship? Why or why not?

7.

Number of boxes	Weight (kg)
3	15
9	45
21	105

8.

Day	Height (cm)
5	30
8	76.8
14	235.2

_____

_____

Explain whether or not you think each relationship is linear.

9. the cost of equal-priced DVDs and the number purchased

_____

10. the height of a person and the person's age

_____

11. the area of a square quilt and its side length

_____

_____

12. the number of miles to the next service station and the number of kilometers

_____

_____

13. Multistep The Mars Rover travels 0.75 feet in 6 seconds. Add the point to the graph. Then determine whether the relationship between distance and time is linear, and if so, predict the distance that the Mars Rover would travel in 1 minute.

_____

_____

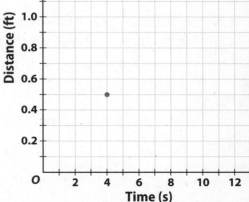

Mars Rover

14. Make a Conjecture Zefram analyzed a linear relationship, found that the slope-intercept equation was $y = 3.5x + 16$, and made a prediction for the value of y for a given value of x. He realized that he made an error calculating the y-intercept and that it was actually 12. Can he just subtract 4 from his prediction if he knows that the slope is correct? Explain.

_____

_____

 **FOCUS ON HIGHER ORDER THINKING**

15. Communicate Mathematical Ideas The table shows a linear relationship. How can you predict the value of y when $x = 6$ without finding the equation of the relationship?

x	y
4	38
8	76
12	114

_____

_____

_____

16. Critique Reasoning Louis says that if the differences between the values of x are constant between all the points on a graph, then the relationship is linear. Do you agree? Explain.

_____

_____

_____

17. Make a Conjecture Suppose you know the slope of a linear relationship and one of the points that its graph passes through. How could you predict another point that falls on the graph of the line?

_____

_____

_____

18. Explain the Error Thomas used (7, 17.5) and (18, 45) from a graph to find the equation of a linear relationship as shown. What was his mistake?

$$m = \frac{45 - 7}{18 - 17.5} = \frac{38}{0.5} = 79$$

$$y = 79x + b$$

$$45 = 79 \cdot 18 + b$$

$$45 = 1422 + b, \text{ so } b = -1377$$

The equation is $y = 79x - 1377$.

_____

Ready to Go On?

5.1 Writing Linear Equations from Situations and Graphs

Write the equation of each line in slope-intercept form.

1.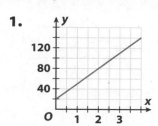

_____

2.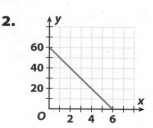

_____

5.2 Writing Linear Equations from a Table

Write the equation of each linear relationship in slope-intercept form.

3.

x	0	100	200	300
y	1.5	36.5	71.5	106.5

_____

4.

x	25	35	45	55
y	94	88	82	76

_____

5.3 Linear Relationships and Bivariate Data

Write the equation of the line that connects each set of data points.

5.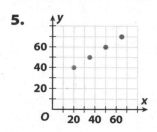

_____

6.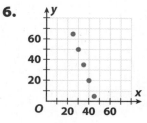

_____

❓ ESSENTIAL QUESTION

7. Write a real-world situation that can be represented by a linear relationship.

_____

_____

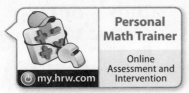
Selected Response

1. An hourglass is turned over with the top part filled with sand. After 3 minutes, there are 855 mm of sand in the top half. After 10 minutes, there are 750 mm of sand in the top half. Which equation represents this situation?

Ⓐ $y = 285x$

Ⓑ $y = -10.5x + 900$

Ⓒ $y = -15x + 900$

Ⓓ $y = 75x$

2. Which graph shows a linear relationship?

Ⓐ
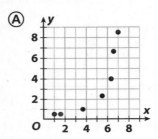

Ⓑ
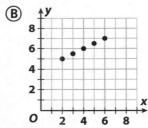

Ⓒ
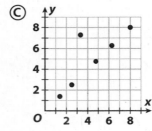

Ⓓ
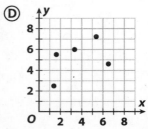

3. What are the slope and y-intercept of the relationship shown in the table?

x	10,000	20,000	30,000
y	2,500	3,000	3,500

Ⓐ slope = 0.05, y-intercept = 1,500

Ⓑ slope = 0.5, y-intercept = 1,500

Ⓒ slope = 0.05, y-intercept = 2,000

Ⓓ slope = 0.5, y-intercept = 2,000

Gridded Response

4. Franklin's faucet was leaking water, so he put a bucket underneath to catch the water. After a while, Franklin started keeping track of how much water was leaking. His data is in the table below.

Hours	2	3	4	5
Gallons	5	6.5	8	9.5

Predict how many gallons of water will have leaked if Franklin hasn't stopped the leak after 14 hours.

				•		
⓪	⓪	⓪	⓪		⓪	⓪
①	①	①	①		①	①
②	②	②	②		②	②
③	③	③	③		③	③
④	④	④	④		④	④
⑤	⑤	⑤	⑤		⑤	⑤
⑥	⑥	⑥	⑥		⑥	⑥
⑦	⑦	⑦	⑦		⑦	⑦
⑧	⑧	⑧	⑧		⑧	⑧
⑨	⑨	⑨	⑨		⑨	⑨

Functions

MODULE 6

ESSENTIAL QUESTION

How can you use functions to solve real-world problems?

Real-World Video

Computerized machines can assist doctors in surgeries such as laser vision correction. Each action the surgeon takes results in one end action by the machine. In math, functions also have a one-in-one-out relationship.

my.hrw.com

GO DIGITAL
my.hrw.com

my.hrw.com

Go digital with your write-in student edition, accessible on any device.

Math On the Spot

Scan with your smart phone to jump directly to the online edition, video tutor, and more.

Animated Math

Interactively explore key concepts to see how math works.

Personal Math Trainer

Get immediate feedback and help as you work through practice sets.

Are YOU Ready?

Complete these exercises to review skills you will need for this chapter.

Evaluate Expressions

EXAMPLE   Evaluate $3x - 5$ for $x = -2$.

$3x - 5 = 3(-2) - 5$ Substitute the given value of x for x.

$\qquad = -6 - 5$ Multiply.

$\qquad = -11$ Subtract.

Evaluate each expression for the given value of x.

1. $2x + 3$ for $x = 3$ _____

2. $-4x + 7$ for $x = -1$ _____

3. $1.5x - 2.5$ for $x = 3$ _____

4. $0.4x + 6.1$ for $x = -5$ _____

5. $\frac{2}{3}x - 12$ for $x = 18$ _____

6. $-\frac{5}{8}x + 10$ for $x = -8$ _____

Connect Words and Equations

EXAMPLE   Erik's earnings equal 9 dollars per hour.

$e =$ earnings; $h =$ hours multiplication

$e = 9 \times h$

Define the variables used in the situation.

Identify the operation involved. "Per" indicates multiplication.

Write the equation.

Define the variables for each situation. Then write an equation.

7. Jana's age plus 5 equals her sister's age.

_____

8. Andrew's class has 3 more students than Lauren's class.

_____

9. The bank is 50 feet shorter than the firehouse.

_____

10. The pencils were divided into 6 groups of 2.

_____

Reading Start-Up

Visualize Vocabulary

Use the ✔ words to complete the diagram. You can put more than one word in each section of the diagram.

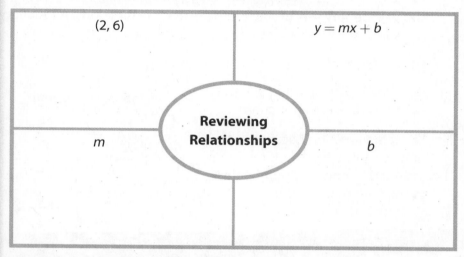

(2, 6)	$y = mx + b$
m	*b*

Reviewing Relationships

Understand Vocabulary

Complete the sentences using the preview words.

1. A rule that assigns exactly one output to each input

   is a _____.

2. The value that is put into a function is the _____.

3. The result after applying the function machine's rule is

   the _____.

© Houghton Mifflin Harcourt Publishing Company

Vocabulary

Review Words
- ✔ bivariate data *(datos bivariados)*
- ✔ linear equation *(ecuación lineal)*
- nonlinear relationship *(relación no lineal)*
- ✔ ordered pair *(par ordenado)*
- proporational relationship *(relación proporcional)*
- ✔ slope *(pendiente)*
- ✔ *x*-coordinate *(coordenada x)*
- ✔ *y*-coordinate *(coordenada y)*
- ✔ *y*-intercept *(intersección con el eje y)*

Preview Words
- function *(función)*
- input *(valor de entrada)*
- linear function *(función lineal)*
- output *(valor de salida)*

Active Reading

Double-Door Fold Create a double-door fold to help you understand the concepts in this module. Label one flap "Proportional Functions" and the other flap "Non-proportional Functions." As you study each lesson, write important ideas under the appropriate flap. Include any sample problems that will help you remember the concepts when you look back at your notes.

Unpacking the TEKS

Understanding the TEKS and the vocabulary terms in the TEKS will help you know exactly what you are expected to learn in this module.

 **TEKS 8.5.G**

Identify functions using sets of ordered pairs, tables, mapping, and graphs.

Key Vocabulary

function *(función)*
An input-output relationship that has exactly one output for each input.

What It Means to You

You will identify sets of ordered pairs that are functions. A function is a rule that assigns exactly one output to each input.

UNPACKING EXAMPLE 8.5.G

Does the following table of inputs/outputs represent a function?

Yes, it is a function because each number in the input column is assigned to only one number in the output column.

Input	Output
14	110
20	130
22	120
30	110

 TEKS 8.5.H

Identify examples of proportional and non-proportional functions that arise from mathematical and real-world problems.

What It Means to You

You will learn to identify and compare functions expressed as equations and tables.

UNPACKING EXAMPLE 8.5.H

A spider descends a 20-foot drainpipe at a rate of 2.5 feet per minute. Another spider descends a drainpipe as shown in the table. Find and compare the rates of change and initial values of the linear functions in terms of the situations they model.

Spider #1: $f(x) = -2.5x + 20$

Spider #2:

Time (min)	0	1	2
Height (ft)	32	29	26

For Spider #1, the rate of change is -2.5, and the initial value is 20. For Spider #2, the rate of change is -3, and the initial value is 32.

Spider #2 started at 32 feet, which is 12 feet higher than Spider #1. Spider #1 is descending at 2.5 feet per minute, which is 0.5 feet per minute slower than Spider #2.

© Houghton Mifflin Harcourt Publishing Company • Image Credits: ©PhotoDisc/Getty Images

Visit **my.hrw.com** to see all the **TEKS** unpacked.

my.hrw.com

Identifying and Representing Functions

TEKS
Proportionality—
8.5.G Identify functions using sets of ordered pairs, tables, mappings, and graphs.

ESSENTIAL QUESTION

How can you identify and represent functions?

EXPLORE ACTIVITY  TEKS 8.5.G

Understanding Relationships

Carlos needs to buy some new pencils from the school supply store at his school. Carlos asks his classmates if they know how much pencils cost. Angela says she bought 2 pencils for $0.50. Paige bought 3 pencils for $0.75, and Spencer bought 4 pencils for $1.00.

Carlos thinks about the rule for the price of a pencil as a machine. When he puts the number of pencils he wants to buy into the machine, the machine applies a rule and tells him the total cost of that number of pencils.

Input  **Output**

	Number of Pencils	Rule	Total Cost
i.	2	?	
ii.	3	?	
iii.	4	?	
iv.	x		
v.	12		

A Use the prices in the problem to fill in total cost in rows **i–iii** of the table.

B Describe any patterns you see. Use your pattern to determine the cost of 1 pencil.

_____

_____

_____

C Use the pattern you identified to write the rule applied by the machine. Write the rule as an algebraic expression and fill in rule column row **iv** of the table.

D Carlos wants to buy 12 pencils. Use your rule to fill in row **v** of the table to show how much Carlos will pay for 12 pencils.

Reflect

1. How did you decide what operation to use in your rule?

_____

_____

2. **What If?** Carlos decides to buy erasers in a package. There are 6 pencil-top erasers in 2 packages of erasers.

    a. Write a rule in words for the number of packages Carlos needs to buy to get *x* erasers. Then write the rule as an algebraic expression.

_____

_____

    b. How many packages does Carlos need to buy to get 18 erasers?

_____

Identifying Functions from Mapping Diagrams

A **function** assigns exactly one output to each input. The value that is put into a function is the **input**. The result is the **output**.

A mapping diagram can be used to represent a relationship between input values and output values. A mapping diagram represents a function if each input value is paired with only one output value.

EXAMPLE 1

 TEKS 8.5.G

Determine whether each relationship is a function.

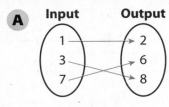

A

Since each input value is paired with only one output value, the relationship is a function.

© Houghton Mifflin Harcourt Publishing Company

Determine whether each relationship is a function.

B 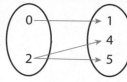 Since 2 is paired with more than one output value (both 4 and 5), the relationship is not a function.

Reflect

3. Is it possible for a function to have more than one input value but only one output value? Provide an illustration to support your answer.

_____

Determine whether each relationship is a function. Explain.

4.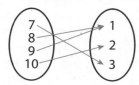

5.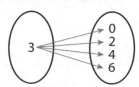

_____

_____

_____

Personal Math Trainer

Online Assessment and Intervention

⊙ my.hrw.com

Math Talk

Mathematical Processes

What is always true about a mapping diagram that represents a function?

Identifying Functions from Tables

Relationships between input values and output values can also be represented using tables. The values in the first column are the input values. The values in the second column are the output values. The relationship represents a function if each input value is paired with only one output value.

Math On the Spot

⊙ my.hrw.com

| **EXAMPLE 2** | | TEKS 8.5.G |

Determine whether each relationship is a function.

A

Input	Output
5	7
10	6
15	15
20	2
25	15

Since 15 is a repeated output value, one output value is paired with two input values. If this occurs in a relationship, the relationship can still be a function.

Since each input value is paired with only one output value, the relationship is a function.

© Houghton Mifflin Harcourt Publishing Company

My Notes

Determine whether each relationship is a function.

B

Input	Output
1	10
5	8
4	6
1	4
7	2

Since 1 is a repeated input value, one input value is paired with two output values. Look back at the rule for functions. Is this relationship a function?

Since the input value 1 is paired with more than one output value (both 10 and 4), the relationship is not a function.

Reflect

6. What is always true about the numbers in the first column of a table that represents a function? Why must this be true?

_____

_____

_____

_____

_____

YOUR TURN

Determine whether each relationship is a function. Explain

7.

Input	Output
53	53
24	24
32	32
17	17
45	45

8.

Input	Output
14	52
8	21
27	16
36	25
8	34

_____

_____

_____

Personal Math Trainer

Online Assessment and Intervention

my.hrw.com

Identifying Functions from Graphs

Graphs can be used to display relationships between two sets of numbers. Each point on a graph represents an ordered pair. The first coordinate in each ordered pair is the input value. The second coordinate is the output value. The graph represents a function if each input value is paired with only one output value.

EXAMPLE 3  TEKS 8.5.G

The graph shows the relationship between the number of hours students spent studying for an exam and the exam grades. Is the relationship represented by the graph a function?

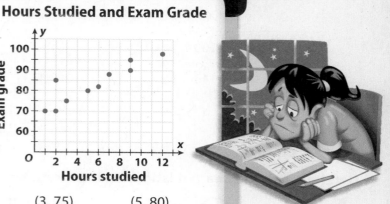

Hours Studied and Exam Grade

The input values are the number of hours spent studying by each student. The output values are the exam grades. The points represent the following ordered pairs:

(1, 70)	(2, 70)	(2, 85)	(3, 75)	(5, 80)
(6, 82)	(7, 88)	(9, 90)	(9, 95)	(12, 98)

Notice that 2 is paired with both 70 and 85, and 9 is paired with both 90 and 95. Therefore, since these input values are paired with more than one output value, the relationship is not a function.

Reflect

9. Many real-world relationships are functions. For example, the amount of money made at a car wash is a function of the number of cars washed. Give another example of a real-world function.

_____

_____

YOUR TURN

10. The graph shows the relationship between the heights and weights of the members of a basketball team. Is the relationship represented by the graph a function? Explain.

_____

_____

_____

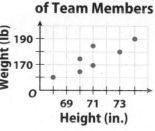

Heights and Weights of Team Members

© Houghton Mifflin Harcourt Publishing Company

Guided Practice

Complete each table. In the row with *x* as the input, write a rule as an algebraic expression for the output. Then complete the last row of the table using the rule. (Explore Activity)

1.

Input	Output
Tickets	Cost ($)
2	40
5	100
7	140
x	
10	

2.

Input	Output
Minutes	Pages
2	1
10	5
20	10
x	
30	

3.

Input	Output
Muffins	Cost ($)
1	2.25
3	6.75
6	13.50
x	
12	

Determine whether each relationship is a function. (Examples 1 and 2)

4.

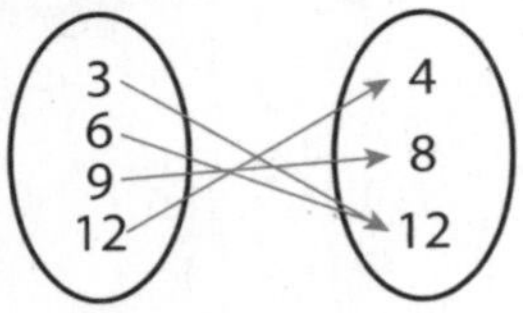

5.

Input	Output
3	20
4	25
5	30
4	35
6	40

6. The graph shows the relationship between the weights of 5 packages and the shipping charge for each package. Is the relationship represented by the graph a function? Explain.

Weights and Shipping Costs

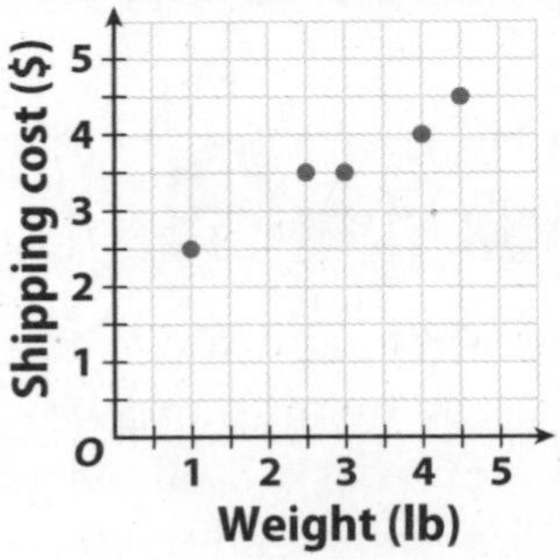

ESSENTIAL QUESTION CHECK-IN

7. What are four different ways of representing functions? How can you tell if a relationship is a function?

6.1 Independent Practice

 TEKS 8.5.G

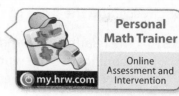

Personal Math Trainer

Online Assessment and Intervention

Determine whether each relationship represented by the ordered pairs is a function. Explain.

8. (2, 2), (3, 1), (5, 7), (8, 0), (9, 1)

_____

_____

_____

9. (0, 4), (5, 1), (2, 8), (6, 3), (5, 9)

_____

_____

_____

10. **Draw Conclusions** Joaquin receives $0.40 per pound for 1 to 99 pounds of aluminum cans he recycles. He receives $0.50 per pound if he recycles more than 100 pounds. Is the amount of money Joaquin receives a function of the weight of the cans he recycles? Explain your reasoning.

_____

_____

_____

11. A biologist tracked the growth of a strain of bacteria, as shown in the graph.

a. Explain why the relationship represented by the graph is a function.

_____

_____

_____

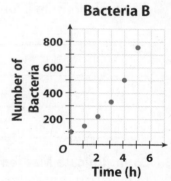

Bacteria B

b. **What If?** Suppose there was the same number of bacteria for two consecutive hours. Would the graph still represent a function? Explain.

_____

12. **Multiple Representations** Give an example of a function in everyday life, and represent it as a graph, a table, and a set of ordered pairs. Describe how you know it is a function.

_____

x				
y				

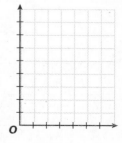

The graph shows the relationship between the weights of six wedges of cheese and the price of each wedge.

Cost of Cheese

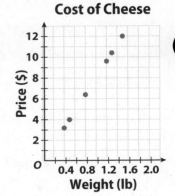

13. Is the relationship represented by the graph a function? Justify your reasoning. Use the words "input" and "output" in your explanation, and connect them to the context represented by the graph.

_____

_____

14. **Analyze Relationships** Suppose the weights and prices of additional wedges of cheese were plotted on the graph. Might that change your answer to question 13? Explain your reasoning.

_____

_____

_____

_____

 FOCUS ON HIGHER ORDER THINKING

Work Area

15. **Justify Reasoning** A mapping diagram represents a relationship that contains three different input values and four different output values. Is the relationship a function? Explain your reasoning.

_____

_____

_____

_____

16. **Communicate Mathematical Ideas** An onion farmer is hiring workers to help harvest the onions. He knows that the number of days it will take to harvest the onions is a function of the number of workers he hires. Explain the use of the word "function" in this context.

_____

_____

_____

_____

_____

_____

TEKS
Proportionality—
8.5.H Identify examples of proportional and non-proportional functions that arise from mathematical and real-world problems. *Also* 8.5.G

? ESSENTIAL QUESTION

What are some characteristics that you can use to describe functions?

EXPLORE ACTIVITY  **TEKS** 8.5.G

Investigating a Constant Rate of Change

The U.S. Department of Agriculture defines heavy rain as rain that falls at a rate of 1.5 centimeters per hour.

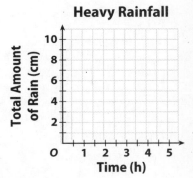

A The table shows the total amount of rain that falls in various amounts of time during a heavy rain. Complete the table.

Time (h)	0	1	2	3	4	5
Total Amount of Rain (cm)	0	1.5				

B Plot the ordered pairs from the table on the coordinate plane at the right.

C How much rain falls in 3.5 hours? _____

D Plot the point corresponding to 3.5 hours of heavy rain.

E What do you notice about all of the points you plotted?

_____

F Is the total amount of rain that falls a function of the number of hours that rain has been falling? Why or why not?

_____

_____

Heavy Rainfall

Reflect

1. Suppose you continued to plot points for times between those in the table, such as 1.2 hours or 4.5 hours. What can you say about the locations of these points?

_____

_____

Graphing Linear Functions

The relationship you investigated in the previous activity can be represented by the equation $y = 1.5x$, where x is the time and y is the total amount of rain. The graph of the relationship is a line, so the equation is a **linear equation**. Since there is exactly one value of y for each value of x, the relationship is a function. It is a **linear function** because its graph is a nonvertical line.

EXAMPLE 1  TEKS 8.5.H

The temperature at dawn was 8 °F and increased steadily 2 °F every hour. The equation $y = 2x + 8$ gives the temperature y after x hours. State whether the relationship between the time and the temperature is proportional or nonproportional. Then graph the function.

Math Talk

Mathematical Processes

Carrie said that for a function to be a linear function, the relationship it represents must be proportional. Do you agree or disagree? Explain.

STEP 1 Compare the equation with the general linear equation $y = mx + b$. $y = 2x + 8$ is in the form $y = mx + b$, with $m = 2$ and $b = 8$. Therefore, the equation is a linear equation. Since $b \neq 0$, the relationship is nonproportional.

STEP 2 Choose several values for the input x. Substitute these values for x in the equation to find the output y.

x	$2x + 8$	y	(x, y)
0	$2(0) + 8$	8	$(0, 8)$
2	$2(2) + 8$	12	$(2, 12)$
4	$2(4) + 8$	16	$(4, 16)$
6	$2(6) + 8$	20	$(6, 20)$

STEP 3 Graph the ordered pairs. Then draw a line through the points to represent the solutions of the function.

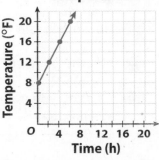

YOUR TURN

2. State whether the relationship between x and y in $y = 0.5x$ is proportional or nonproportional. Then graph the function.

_____

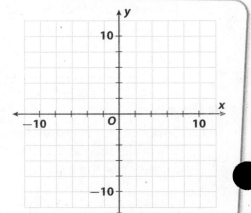

Determining Whether a Function is Linear

The linear equation in Example 1 has the form $y = mx + b$, where m and b are real numbers. Every equation in the form $y = mx + b$ is a linear equation. The linear equations represent linear functions. Equations that cannot be written in this form are not linear equations, and therefore are not linear functions.

Math On the Spot
my.hrw.com

EXAMPLE 2 TEKS 8.5.H

A square tile has a side length of x inches. The equation $y = x^2$ gives the area of the tile in square inches. Determine whether the relationship between x and y is linear and, if so, if it is proportional.

STEP 1 Choose several values for the input x. Substitute these values for x in the equation to find the output y.

x	x^2	y	(x, y)
1	1^2	1	$(1, 1)$
2	2^2	4	$(2, 4)$
3	3^2	9	$(3, 9)$
4	4^2	16	$(4, 16)$

STEP 2 Graph the ordered pairs.

STEP 3 Identify the shape of the graph. The points suggest a curve, not a line. Draw a curve through the points to represent the solutions of the function.

STEP 4 Describe the relationship between x and y.

The graph is not a line so the relationship is not linear.

Only a linear relationship can be proportional, so the relationship is not proportional.

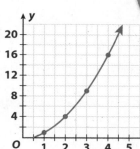

Animated Math
my.hrw.com

Math Talk
Mathematical Processes

How can you use the numbers in the table to decide whether or not the relationship between x and y is linear?

YOUR TURN

3. A soda machine makes $\frac{2}{3}$ gallon of soda every minute. The total amount y that the machine makes in x minutes is given by the equation $y = \frac{2}{3}x$. Determine whether the relationship between x and y is linear and, if so, if it is proportional.

Time (min), x	0	3		9
Amount (gal), y			4	

Making Soda

Personal Math Trainer
Online Assessment and Intervention
my.hrw.com

Plot the ordered pairs from the table. Then graph the function represented by the ordered pairs and tell whether the function is linear or nonlinear. Tell whether the function is proportional. (Examples 1 and 2)

1. $y = 5 - 2x$

Input, x	−1	1	3	5
Output, y				

2. $y = 2 - x^2$

Input, x	−2	−1	0	1	2
Output, y					

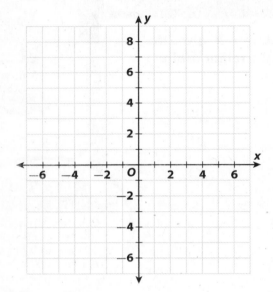

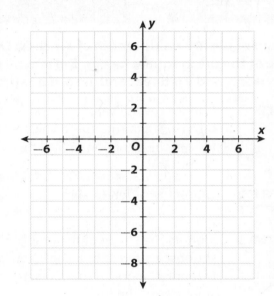

_____

_____

Explain whether each equation is a linear equation. (Example 2)

3. $y = x^2 - 1$

_____

_____

_____

_____

4. $y = 1 - x$

_____

_____

_____

_____

? ESSENTIAL QUESTION CHECK-IN

5. Explain how you can use a table of values, an equation, and a graph to determine whether a function represents a proportional relationship.

_____

_____

_____

6.2 Independent Practice

 **TEKS** 8.5.G, 8.5.H

Personal Math Trainer

Online Assessment and Intervention

my.hrw.com

6. State whether the relationship between x and y in $y = 4x - 5$ is proportional or nonproportional. Then graph the function.

_____

7. The Fortaleza telescope in Brazil is a radio telescope. Its shape can be approximated with the equation $y = 0.013x^2$. Is the relationship between x and y linear? Is it proportional? Explain.

_____

_____

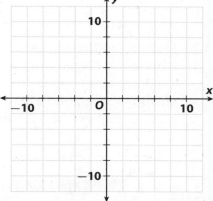

8. Kiley spent $20 on rides and snacks at the state fair. If x is the amount she spent on rides, and y is the amount she spent on snacks, the total amount she spent can be represented by the equation $x + y = 20$. Is the relationship between x and y linear? Is it proportional? Explain.

_____

_____

_____

9. **Represent Real-World Problems** The drill team is buying new uniforms. The table shows y, the total cost in dollars, and x, the number of uniforms purchased.

Number of uniforms, x	1	3	5	9
Total cost ($), y	60	180	300	540

a. Use the data to draw a graph. Is the relationship between x and y linear? Explain.

_____

b. Use your graph to predict the cost of purchasing 12 uniforms.

_____

Drill Team Uniforms

10. Marta, a whale calf in an aquarium, is fed a special milk formula. Her handler uses a graph to track the number of gallons of formula y the calf drinks in x hours. Is the relationship between x and y linear? Is it proportional? Explain.

_____

_____

Marta's Feedings

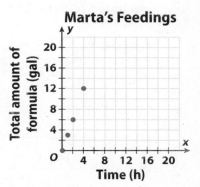

11. Critique Reasoning A student claims that the equation $y = 7$ is not a linear equation because it does not have the form $y = mx + b$. Do you agree or disagree? Why?

_____

_____

_____

12. Make a Prediction Let x represent the number of hours you read a book and y represent the total number of pages you have read. You have already read 70 pages and can read 30 pages per hour. Write an equation relating x hours and y pages you read. Then predict the total number of pages you will have read after another 3 hours.

_____

 **FOCUS ON HIGHER ORDER THINKING**

13. Draw Conclusions Rebecca draws a graph of a real-world relationship that turns out to be a set of unconnected points. Can the relationship be linear? Can it be proportional? Explain your reasoning.

_____

_____

_____

14. Communicate Mathematical Ideas Write a real-world problem involving a proportional relationship. Explain how you know the relationship is proportional.

_____

_____

_____

_____

15. Justify Reasoning Show that the equation $y + 3 = 3(2x + 1)$ is linear and that it represents a proportional relationship between x and y.

_____

_____

_____

_____

_____

Work Area

TEKS
Proportionality—
8.5.I Write an equation in the form $y = mx + b$ to model a linear relationship between two quantities using verbal, numerical, tabular, and graphical representations. *Also 8.4.C, 8.5.A, 8.5.B, 8.5.F, 8.5.H*

? ESSENTIAL QUESTION

How can you use tables, graphs, and equations to compare functions?

Comparing a Table and an Equation

To compare a function written as an equation and another function represented by a table, find the equation for the function in the table.

EXAMPLE 1  **TEKS** 8.5.I

Math On the Spot
my.hrw.com

Josh and Maggie buy MP3 files from different music services. The monthly cost, *y* dollars, for *x* songs is linear. The cost of Josh's service is $y = 0.50x + 10$. The cost of Maggie's service is shown below.

Monthly Cost of MP3s at Maggie's Music Service					
Songs, *x*	5	10	15	20	25
Cost ($), *y*	4.95	9.90	14.85	19.80	24.75

A Write an equation to represent the monthly cost of Maggie's service.

STEP 1 Choose any two ordered pairs from the table to find the slope.

$$m = \frac{y_2 - y_1}{x_2 - x_1} = \frac{9.90 - 4.95}{10 - 5} = \frac{4.95}{5} = 0.99$$

The points (5, 4.95) and (10, 9.90) were used.

STEP 2 Find the *y*-intercept. Use the slope and any point.

$y = mx + b$ *Slope-intercept form.*

$4.95 = 0.99 \cdot 5 + b$ *Substitute for y, m, and x.*

$0 = b$

STEP 3 Substitute the slope and *y*-intercept.

$y = 0.99x + 0$ or $y = 0.99x$ *Substitute 0.99 for m and 0 for y.*

Math Talk
Mathematical Processes
Describe each service's cost in words using the meanings of the slopes and *y*-intercepts.

B Which service is cheaper when 30 songs are downloaded?

Josh's service: Maggie's service:

$y = 0.50 \times 30 + 10$ $y = 0.99 \times 30$

$y = 25$ $y = 29.7$

Josh's service is cheaper.

1. Quentin is choosing between buying books at the bookstore or buying online versions of the books for his tablet. The cost, y dollars, of ordering books online for x books is $y = 6.95x + 1.50$. The cost of buying the books at the bookstore is shown in the table. Which method of buying books is more expensive if Quentin wants to buy 6 books?

Cost of Books at the Bookstore					
Books, x	1	2	3	4	5
Cost ($), y	7.50	15.00	22.50	30.00	37.50

_____

EXPLORE ACTIVITY 1 **TEKS** 8.4.C

Comparing a Table and a Graph

The table and graph show how many words Morgan and Brian typed correctly on a typing test. For both students, the relationship between words typed correctly and time is linear.

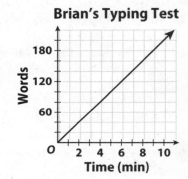

Brian's Typing Test

Morgan's Typing Test					
Time (min)	2	4	6	8	10
Words	30	60	90	120	150

A Find Morgan's unit rate.

_____

B Find Brian's unit rate.

_____

C Which student types more correct words per minute?

_____

Reflect

2. Katie types 17 correct words per minute. Explain how a graph of Katie's test results would compare to Morgan's and Brian's.

_____

_____

Comparing a Graph and a Description

Jamal wants to buy a new game system that costs $200. He does not have enough money to buy it today, so he compares layaway plans at different stores.

The plan at Store A is shown on the graph.

Store B requires an initial payment of $60 and weekly payments of $20 until the balance is paid in full.

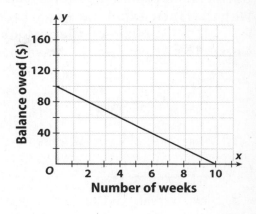

A Write an equation in slope-intercept form for Store A's layaway plan. Let x represent number of weeks and y represent balance owed.

_____

B Write an equation in slope-intercept form for Store B's layaway plan. Let x represent number of weeks and y represent balance owed.

_____

C Sketch a graph of the plan at Store B on the same grid as Store A.

D How can you use the graphs to tell which plan requires the greater down payment? How can you use the equations?

_____

_____

_____

E How can you use the graphs to tell which plan requires the greater weekly payment? How can you use the equations?

_____

_____

_____

F Which plan allows Jamal to pay for the game system faster? Explain.

_____

_____

Doctors have two methods of calculating maximum heart rate. With the first method, maximum heart rate, y, in beats per minute is $y = 220 - x$, where x is the person's age. Maximum heart rate with the second method is shown in the table. (Example 1)

Age, x	20	30	40	50	60
Heart rate (bpm), y	194	187	180	173	166

1. Which method gives the greater maximum heart rate for a 70-year-old?

_____

2. Are heart rate and age proportional or nonproportional for each method?

_____

Aisha runs a tutoring business. With Plan 1, students may choose to pay $15 per hour. With Plan 2, they may follow the plan shown on the graph. (Explore Activity 1 and 2)

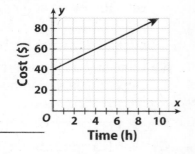

3. Describe the plan shown on the graph.

_____

4. Sketch a graph showing the $15 per hour option.

5. What does the intersection of the two graphs mean?

_____

6. Which plan is cheaper for 10 hours of tutoring?

_____

7. Are cost and time proportional or nonproportional for each plan?

_____

_____

? ESSENTIAL QUESTION CHECK-IN

8. When using tables, graphs, and equations to compare functions, why do you find the equations for tables and graphs?

_____

_____

6.3 Independent Practice

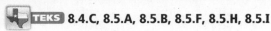 TEKS 8.4.C, 8.5.A, 8.5.B, 8.5.F, 8.5.H, 8.5.I

Personal Math Trainer

Online Assessment and Intervention

The table and graph show the miles driven and gas used for two scooters.

Scooter A

Distance (mi), x	Gas used (gal), y
150	2
300	4
450	6
600	8
750	10

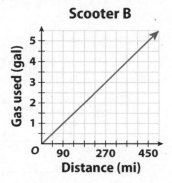

Scooter B

9. Which scooter uses fewer gallons of gas when 1350 miles are driven?

   _____

10. Are gas used and miles proportional or nonproportional for each scooter?

   _____

A cell phone company offers two texting plans to its customers. The monthly cost, y dollars, of one plan is $y = 0.10x + 5$, where x is the number of texts. The cost of the other plan is shown in the table.

Number of texts, x	100	200	300	400	500
Cost ($), y	25	25	30	35	40

11. Which plan is cheaper for under 200 texts? _____

12. The graph of the first plan does not pass through the origin. What does this indicate?

   _____

   _____

13. Brianna wants to buy a digital camera for a photography class. One store offers the camera for $50 down and a payment plan of $20 per month. The payment plan for a second store is described by $y = 15x + 80$, where y is the total cost in dollars and x is the number of months. Which camera is cheaper when the camera is paid off in 12 months? Explain.

   _____

   _____

14. The French club and soccer team are washing cars to earn money. The amount earned, y dollars, for washing x cars is a linear function. Which group makes the most money per car? Explain.

French Club	
Number of cars, x	Amount earned ($), y
2	10
4	20
6	30
8	40
10	50

Soccer Team

_____

_____

_____

H.O.T.   FOCUS ON HIGHER ORDER THINKING

Work Area

15. Draw Conclusions Gym A charges $60 a month plus $5 per visit. The monthly cost at Gym B is represented by $y = 5x + 40$, where x is the number of visits per month. What conclusion can you draw about the monthly costs of the gyms?

_____

_____

_____

16. Justify Reasoning Why will the value of y for the function $y = 5x + 1$ always be greater than that for the function $y = 4x + 2$ when $x > 1$?

_____

_____

_____

17. Analyze Relationships The equations of two functions are $y = -21x + 9$ and $y = -24x + 8$. Which function is changing more quickly? Explain.

_____

_____

_____

_____

Ready to Go On?

6.1 Identifying and Representing Functions

Determine whether each relationship is a function.

1.

x	y
2	0
5	1
8	2
	3

2.

Input, x	Output, y
−1	6
3	5
4	3
6	5

3. (2, 5), (7, 2), (−3, 4), (2, 9), (1, 1)

_____   _____   _____

6.2 Describing Functions

Determine whether each situation is linear or nonlinear, and proportional or nonproportional.

4. Joanna is paid $14 per hour.

5. Alberto started out bench pressing 50 pounds. He then added 5 pounds every week.

_____   _____

6.3 Comparing Functions

6. Which function is changing more quickly? Explain.

_____

_____

_____

Function 1

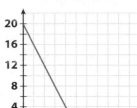

Function 2

Input, x	Output, y
2	11
3	6.5
4	2

ESSENTIAL QUESTION

7. How can you use functions to solve real-world problems?

_____

_____

_____

Selected Response

1. Which table shows a proportional function?

Ⓐ
X	0	5	10
Y	3	15	30

Ⓑ
X	0	5	10
Y	10	20	30

Ⓒ
X	0	5	10
Y	0	50	100

Ⓓ
X	0	5	10
Y	10	5	0

2. Which term does **not** correctly describe the relationship shown in the table?

X	0	2	4
Y	60	120	180

Ⓐ function

Ⓑ linear

Ⓒ proportional

Ⓓ nonproportional

3. The table below shows some input and output values of a function.

Input	4	5	6	7
Output	14	17.5		24.5

What is the missing output value?

Ⓐ 20   Ⓒ 22

Ⓑ 21   Ⓓ 23

4. Which number is not rational?

Ⓐ −7   Ⓒ 0.33

Ⓑ $\sqrt{25}$ Ⓓ $\sqrt{15}$

5. Which of the relationships below is a function?

Ⓐ
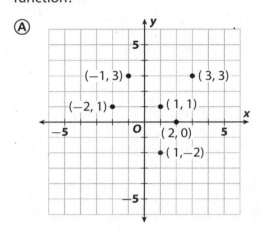

Ⓑ
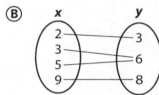

Ⓒ (6, 3), (5, 0), (−1, 2), (0, 7), (−1, 6)

Ⓓ
X	2	3	2	5
Y	5	7	9	11

Gridded Response

6. A dance school charges a registration fee in addition to a fee per lesson. The equation $y = 30x + 25$ represents the total cost y of x lessons. What is the cost per lesson?

				•		
⓪	⓪	⓪	⓪		⓪	⓪
①	①	①	①		①	①
②	②	②	②		②	②
③	③	③	③		③	③
④	④	④	④		④	④
⑤	⑤	⑤	⑤		⑤	⑤
⑥	⑥	⑥	⑥		⑥	⑥
⑦	⑦	⑦	⑦		⑦	⑦
⑧	⑧	⑧	⑧		⑧	⑧
⑨	⑨	⑨	⑨		⑨	⑨

MODULE 3 Proportional Relationships

? ESSENTIAL QUESTION

How can you use proportional relationships to solve real-world problems?

EXAMPLE 1

Write an equation that represents the proportional relationship shown in the graph.

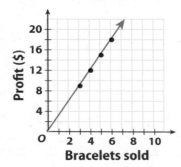

Use the points on the graph to make a table.

Bracelets sold	3	4	5	6
Profit ($)	9	12	15	18

Let x represent the number of bracelets sold.

Let y represent the profit.

The equation is $y = 3x$.

EXAMPLE 2

Find the slope of the line.

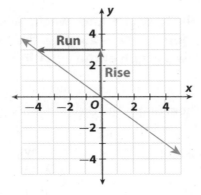

$slope = \dfrac{rise}{run}$

$= \dfrac{3}{-4}$

$= -\dfrac{3}{4}$

EXERCISES

1. The table represents a proportional relationship. Write an equation that describes the relationship. Then graph the relationship represented by the data. (Lessons 3.1, 3.3, 3.4)

Time (x)	6	8	10	12
Distance (y)	3	4	5	6

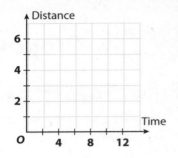

_____

Find the slope and the unit rate represented on each graph.
(Lesson 3.2)

2.

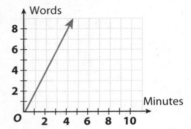

3.

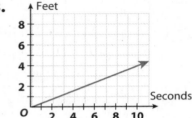

_____ _____

MODULE **4** # Nonproportional Relationships

? ESSENTIAL QUESTION

How can you use nonproportional relationships to solve real-world problems?

EXAMPLE 1

Jai is saving to buy his mother a birthday gift. Each week, he saves $5. He started with $25. The equation $y = 5x + 25$ gives the total Jai has saved, y, after x weeks. Draw a graph of the equation. Then describe the relationship.

Use the equation to make a table. Then, graph the ordered pairs from the table, and draw a line through the points.

x (weeks)	0	1	2	3	4
y (savings in dollars)	25	30	35	40	45

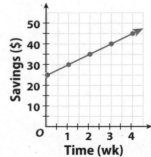

The relationship is linear but nonproportional.

EXAMPLE 2

Graph $y = -\frac{1}{2}x - 2$.

The slope is $\frac{-1}{2}$, or $-\frac{1}{2}$.

The y-intercept is -2.

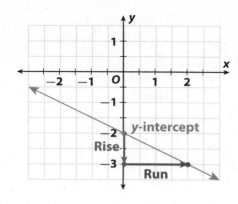

EXAMPLE 3

Solve the system of equations

by graphing: $\begin{cases} y = \frac{3}{4}x - 2 \\ y = -x + 5 \end{cases}$.

The point of intersection appears to be (4, 1). Check by substitution.

$y = \frac{3}{4}x - 2 \qquad y = -x + 5$

$1 = \frac{3}{4}(4) - 2 \quad 1 = -4 + 5$

$1 = 1 \checkmark \qquad 1 = 1 \checkmark$

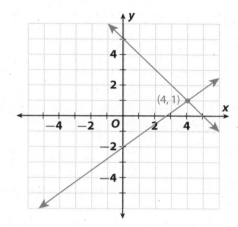

EXERCISES

Complete each table. Explain whether the relationship between x and y is proportional or nonproportional and whether it is linear.

(Lesson 4.1)

1. $y = 10x - 4$

x	0	2		6
y	−4		36	

2. $y = -\frac{3}{2}x$

x	0		2	
y		−1.5		−4.5

_____

_____

3. Find the slope and y-intercept for the linear relationship shown in the table. Graph the line. Is the relationship proportional or nonproportional? (Lessons 4.2, 4.4)

x	−2	−1	0	1
y	0	2	4	6

slope _____

y-intercept _____

The relationship is _____.

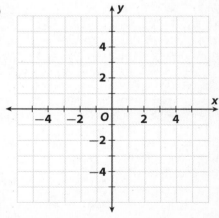

4. Tom's Taxis charges a fixed rate of $4 per ride plus $0.50 per mile. Carla's Cabs does not charge a fixed rate but charges $1.00 per mile. (Lessons 4.3, 4.5)

a. Write an equation that represents the cost of Tom's Taxis. _____

b. Write an equation that represents the cost of Carla's cabs. _____

c. Steve calculated that for the distance he needs to travel, Tom's Taxis will charge the same amount as Carla's Cabs. Graph both equations. How far is Steve going to travel and how much will he pay?

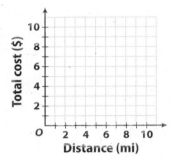

_____

_____

 MODULE 5 # Writing Linear Equations

Key Vocabulary
bivariate data *(datos bivariados)*
nonlinear relationship *(relación no lineal)*

? ESSENTIAL QUESTION

How can you use linear equations to solve real-world problems?

EXAMPLE 1

Jose is renting a backhoe for a construction job. The rental charge for a month is based on the number of days in the month and a set charge per month. In September, which has 30 days, Jose paid $700. In August, which has 31 days, he paid $715. Write an equation in slope-intercept form that represents this situation.

$(x_1, y_1), (x_2, y_2) \rightarrow (30, 700), (31, 715)$	Write the information given as ordered pairs.
$m = \dfrac{y_2 - y_1}{x_2 - x_1} = \dfrac{715 - 700}{31 - 30} = 15$	Find the slope.
$y = mx + b$	Slope-intercept form
$715 = 15(31) + b$	Substitute for y, m, and x to find b.
$250 = b$	Solve for b.
$y = 15x + 250$	Write the equation.

EXAMPLE 2

Determine if the graph shown represents a linear or nonlinear relationship.

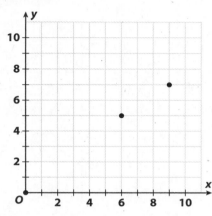

Points	Rate of Change
(0, 0) and (6, 5)	$m = \frac{5-0}{6-0} = \frac{5}{6}$
(6, 5) and (9, 7)	$m = \frac{7-5}{9-6} = \frac{2}{3}$
(0, 0) and (9, 7)	$m = \frac{7-0}{9-0} = \frac{7}{9}$

The rates of change are not constant. The graph represents a nonlinear relationship.

EXERCISES

1. Ms. Thompson is grading math tests. She is giving everyone that took the test a 10-point bonus. Each correct answer is worth 5 points. Write an equation in slope-intercept that represents the scores on the tests. (Lesson 5.1)

_____

The table shows a pay scale based on years of experience. (Lessons 5.1, 5.2)

Experience (yr), x	0	2	4	6	8
Hourly pay ($), y	9	14	19	24	29

2. Find the slope for this relationship. _____

3. Find the *y*-intercept. _____

4. Write an equation in slope-intercept form that represents this relationship. _____

5. Graph the equation, and use it to predict the hourly pay of someone with 10 years of experience.

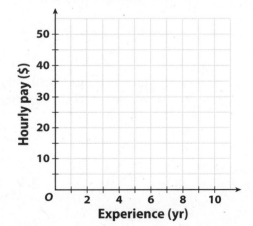

Does each of the following graphs represent a linear relationship? Why or why not? (Lesson 5.3)

6.

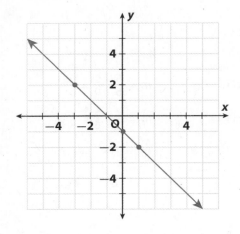

7.

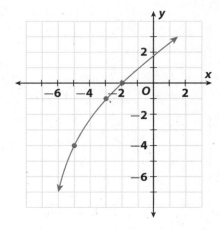

_____

_____

_____

 ESSENTIAL QUESTION

How can you use functions to solve real-world problems?

Key Vocabulary

function *(función)*

input *(valor de entrada)*

linear function *(función lineal)*

output *(valor de salida)*

EXAMPLE 1

Determine whether each relationship is a function.

A

Input	Output
3	10
4	4
5	2
4	0
6	5

The relationship is not a function, because an input, 4, is paired with 2 different outputs, 4 and 0.

B

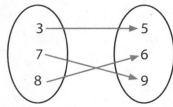

Since each input value is paired with only one output value, the relationship is a function.

EXAMPLE 2

Sally and Louis are on a long-distance bike ride. Sally bikes at a steady rate of 18 miles per hour. The distance y that Sally covers in x hours is given by the equation $y = 18x$. Louis's speed can be found by using the numbers in the table. Who will travel farther in 4 hours and by how much?

Louis's Biking Speed			
Time (h), x	3	5	7
Distance (mi), y	60	100	140

Each distance in the table is 20 times each number of hours. Louis's speed is 20 miles per hour, and his distance covered is represented by $y = 20x$.

Sally's ride:

$y = 18x$

$y = 18(4)$

$y = 72$

Louis's ride:

$y = 20x$

$y = 20(4)$

$y = 80$

Sally will ride 72 miles in 4 hours. Louis will ride 80 miles in 4 hours. Louis will go 8 miles farther in 4 hours.

EXERCISES

Determine whether each relationship is a function. (Lesson 6.1)

1.

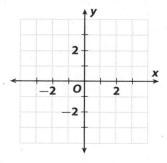

2.

Input	Output
−1	8
0	4
1	8
2	16

_____

_____

Tell whether the function is linear or nonlinear. (Lesson 6.2)

3. $y = 5x + \frac{1}{2}$: _____

4. $y = x^2 + 3$: _____

5. Elaine has a choice of two health club memberships. The first membership option is to pay $500 now and then pay $150 per month. The second option is shown in the table. Elaine plans to go to the club for 12 months. Which option is cheaper? Explain.

Months, x	1	2	3
Total paid ($), y	215	430	645

_____

_____

_____

1. **CAREERS IN MATH** Cost Estimator To make MP3 players, a cost estimator determined it costs a company $1500 per week for overhead and $45 for each MP3 player made.

   a. Define a variable to represent the number of players made. Then write an equation to represent the company's total cost c.

   _____

   b. One week, the company spends $5460 making MP3 players. How many players were made that week? Show your work.

   _____

   _____

   c. If the company sells MP3 players for $120, how much profit would it make if it sold 80 players in one week? Explain how you found your answer.

   _____

   _____

2. A train from Portland, Oregon, to Los Angeles, California, travels at an average speed of 60 miles per hour and covers a distance of 963 miles. Susanna is taking the train from Portland to Los Angeles to see her aunt. She needs to arrive at her aunt's house by 8 p.m. It takes 30 minutes to get from the train station to her aunt's house.

   a. By what time does the train need to leave Portland for Susanna to arrive by 8 p.m.? Explain how you got your answer. As part of your explanation, write a function that you used in your work.

   _____

   _____

   _____

   _____

   b. Susanna does not want to leave Portland later than 10 p.m. or earlier than 6 a.m. Does the train in part **a** meet her requirements? If not, give a new departure time that would allow her to still get to her aunt's house on time, and find the arrival time of that train.

   _____

   _____

   _____

Selected Response

1. Rickie earns $7 an hour babysitting. Which table represents this proportional relationship?

(A)

Hours	4	6	8
Earnings ($)	28	42	56

(B)

Hours	4	6	8
Earnings ($)	28	35	42

(C)

Hours	2	3	4
Earnings ($)	7	14	21

(D)

Hours	2	3	4
Earnings ($)	14	21	42

2. Which of the relationships below is a function?

(A) $(6, 3), (5, 2), (6, 8), (0, 7)$

(B) $(8, 2), (1, 7), (-1, 2), (1, 9)$

(C) $(4, 3), (3, 0), (-1, 3), (2, 7)$

(D) $(7, 1), (0, 0), (6, 2), (0, 4)$

3. Which set best describes the numbers used on the scale for a standard thermometer?

(A) whole numbers

(B) rational numbers

(C) real numbers

(D) integers

4. Which term refers to slope?

(A) rate of change   (C) y-intercept

(B) equation   (D) coordinate

5. The graph of which equation is shown below?

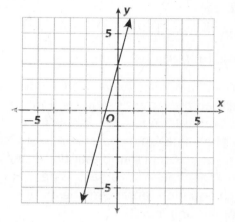

(A) $y = 4x + 3$

(B) $y = -4x - 0.75$

(C) $y = -4x + 3$

(D) $y = 4x - 0.75$

6. Which equation represents a nonproportional relationship?

(A) $y = 5x$ (C) $y = 5x + 3$

(B) $y = -5x$ (D) $y = -\frac{1}{5}x$

7. Which describes the solution of a system of linear equations for two lines with the same slope and the same y-intercepts?

(A) one nonzero solution

(B) infinitely many solutions

(C) no solution

(D) solution of 0

8. Which is 7.0362×10^{-4} written in standard notation?

(A) 0.000070362   (C) 7.0362

(B) 0.00070362   (D) 7036.2

9. Which term does not correctly describe the function shown in the table?

x	0	2	4
y	0	70	140

- (A) relationship
- (B) linear
- (C) proportional
- (D) nonproportional

10. As part of a science experiment, Greta measured the amount of water flowing from Container A to Container B. Container B had half a gallon of water in it to start the experiment. Greta found that the water was flowing at a rate of two gallons per hour. Which equation represents the amount of water in Container B?

- (A) $y = 2x$
- (B) $y = 0.5x$
- (C) $y = 2x + 0.5$
- (D) $y = 0.5x + 2$

Gridded Response

11. A factory produces gaskets at a constant rate. After 6 hours, 4620 gaskets have been produced. How many gaskets does the factory produce per hour?

12. The table below represents a linear relationship.

x	2	3	4	5
y	14	17	20	23

What is the y-intercept?

Estimate your answer before solving the question. Use your estimate to check the reasonableness of your answer.

13. The table below shows some input and output values of a function.

Input	4	5	6	7
Output	18		27	31.5

What number is missing

UNIT 3

Expressions, Equations, and Relationships in Geometry

CAREERS IN MATH

Hydrologist A hydrologist is a scientist who studies and solves water-related issues. A hydrologist might work to prevent or clean up polluted water sources, locate water supplies for urban or rural needs, or control flooding and erosion. A hydrologist uses math to assess water resources and mathematical models to understand water systems, as well as statistics to analyze phenomena such as rainfall patterns. If you are interested in a career as a cost estimator, you should study the following mathematical subjects:

- Algebra
- Trigonometry
- Calculus
- Statistics

Research other careers that require creating and using mathematical models to understand physical phenomena.

Unit 3 Performance Task

At the end of the unit, check out how **hydrologists** use math.

Use the puzzle to preview key vocabulary from this unit. Unscramble the circled letters to answer the riddle at the bottom of the page.

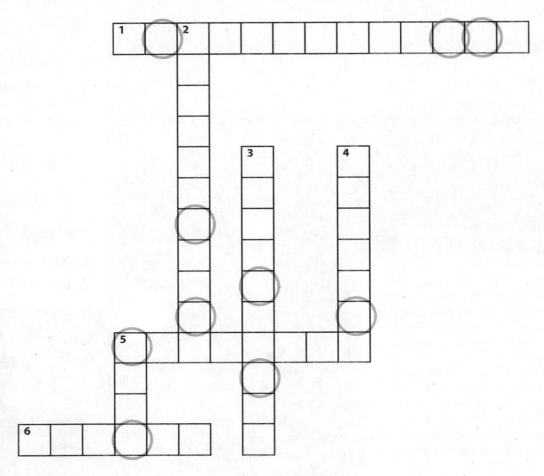

Across

1. The angle formed by two sides of a triangle (2 words) (Lesson 7-2)

5. A three-dimensional figure that has two congruent circular bases. (Lesson 9-1)

6. A three-dimensional figure with all points the same distance from the center. (Lesson 9-3)

Down

2. The line that intersects two or more lines. (Lesson 7-1)

3. The side opposite the right angle in a right triangle. (Lesson 8-1)

4. Figures with the same shape but not necessarily the same size. (Lesson 7-3)

5. A three-dimensional figure that has one vertex and one circular base. (Lesson 9-2)

Q: What do you call an angle that is adorable?

A: ___ ___ ___ ___ ___ ___ ___ ___ ___ ___ ___ ___ !

Angle Relationships in Parallel Lines and Triangles

? ESSENTIAL QUESTION

How can you use angle relationships in parallel lines and triangles to solve real-world problems?

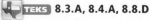

Real-World Video

Many cities are designed on a grid with parallel streets. If another street runs across the parallel lines, it is a transversal. Special relationships exist between parallel lines and transversals.

my.hrw.com

GO DIGITAL
my.hrw.com

my.hrw.com	**Math On the Spot**	**Animated Math**	**Personal Math Trainer**
Go digital with your write-in student edition, accessible on any device.	Scan with your smart phone to jump directly to the online edition, video tutor, and more.	Interactively explore key concepts to see how math works.	Get immediate feedback and help as you work through practice sets.

Are YOU Ready?

Complete these exercises to review skills you will need for this chapter.

Solve Two-Step Equations

EXAMPLE		
	$7x + 9 = 30$	Write the equation.
	$7x + 9 - 9 = 30 - 9$	Subtract 9 from both sides.
	$7x = 21$	Simplify.
	$\frac{7x}{7} = \frac{21}{7}$	Divide both sides by 7.
	$x = 3$	Simplify.

Solve for x.

1. $6x + 10 = 46$ **2.** $7x - 6 = 36$ **3.** $3x + 26 = 59$ **4.** $2x + 5 = -25$

_____

5. $6x - 7 = 41$ **6.** $\frac{1}{2}x + 9 = 30$ **7.** $\frac{1}{3}x - 7 = 15$ **8.** $0.5x - 0.6 = 8.4$

_____

Name Angles

EXAMPLE	
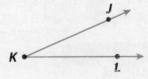	Use three points of an angle, including the vertex, to name the angle. Write the vertex between the other two points: $\angle JKL$ or $\angle LKJ$. You can also use just the vertex letter to name the angle if there is no danger of confusing the angle with another. This is also $\angle K$.

Give two names for the angle formed by the dashed rays.

9. _____   **10.** _____   **11.** _____

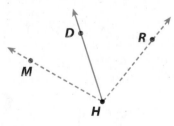 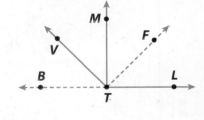

Reading **Start-Up**

Visualize Vocabulary

Use the ✔ words to complete the graphic. You can put more than one word in each section of the triangle.

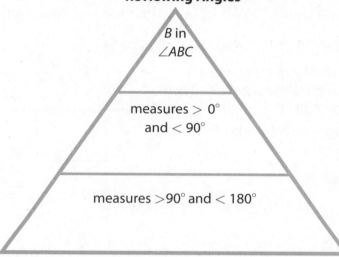

Reviewing Angles

B in
∠*ABC*

measures > 0°
and < 90°

measures >90° and < 180°

Understand Vocabulary

Complete the sentences using preview words.

1. A line that intersects two or more lines is a _____.

2. Figures with the same shape but not necessarily the same size

   are _____.

3. An _____ is an angle formed by one side of the

   triangle and the extension of an adjacent side.

Vocabulary

Review Words
- ✔ acute angle *(ángulo agudo)*
- ✔ angle *(ángulo)*
  congruent *(congruente)*
- ✔ obtuse angle *(ángulo obtuso)*
  parallel lines *(líneas paralelas)*
- ✔ vertex *(vértice)*

Preview Words
  alternate exterior angles *(ángulos alternos externos)*
  alternate interior angles *(ángulos alternos internos)*
  corresponding angles *(ángulos correspondientes (para líneas))*
  exterior angle *(ángulo externo de un polígono)*
  interior angle *(ángulos internos)*
  remote interior angle *(ángulo interno remoto)*
  same-side interior angles *(ángulos internos del mismo lado)*
  similar *(semejantes)*
  transversal *(transversal)*

Active Reading

Pyramid Before beginning the module, create a pyramid to help you organize what you learn. Label each side with one of the lesson titles from this module. As you study each lesson, write important ideas like vocabulary, properties, and formulas on the appropriate side.

© Houghton Mifflin Harcourt Publishing Company

Unpacking the TEKS

Understanding the TEKS and the vocabulary terms in the TEKS will help you know exactly what you are expected to learn in this module.

TEKS 8.8.D

Use informal arguments to establish facts and the angle sum and exterior angle of triangles, the angles created when parallel lines are cut by a transversal, and the angle-angle criterion for similarity of triangles.

Key Vocabulary

transversal *(transversal)*
A line that intersects two or more lines.

What It Means to You

You will learn about the special angle relationships formed when parallel lines are intersected by a third line called a transversal.

UNPACKING EXAMPLE 8.8.D

Which angles formed by the transversal and the parallel lines seem to be congruent?

It appears that the angles below are congruent.

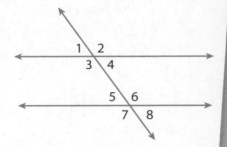

$\angle 1 \cong \angle 4 \cong \angle 5 \cong \angle 8$

$\angle 2 \cong \angle 3 \cong \angle 6 \cong \angle 7$

TEKS 8.8.D

Use informal arguments to establish facts and the angle sum and exterior angle of triangles, the angles created when parallel lines are cut by a transversal, and the angle-angle criterion for similarity of triangles.

What It Means to You

You will use the angle-angle criterion to determine similarity of two triangles.

UNPACKING EXAMPLE 8.8.D

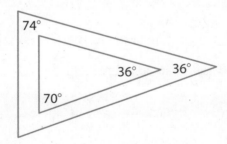

Explain whether the triangles are similar.

$74° + 36° + m\angle 3 = 180°$ 　　　$70° + 36° + m\angle 3 = 180°$

$m\angle 3 = 70°$ 　　　　　　　　$m\angle 3 = 74°$

The three angles in the large triangle are congruent to the three angles in the smaller triangle, so the triangles are similar.

Visit **my.hrw.com** to see all the **TEKS** unpacked.

ⓞ my.hrw.com

Parallel Lines Cut by a Transversal

TEKS
Expressions, equations, and relationships—
8.8.D Use informal arguments to establish facts about ... the angles created when parallel lines are cut by a transversal, ...

? ESSENTIAL QUESTION

What can you conclude about the angles formed by parallel lines that are cut by a transversal?

EXPLORE ACTIVITY 1 TEKS 8.8.D

Parallel Lines and Transversals

A **transversal** is a line that intersects two lines in the same plane at two different points. Transversal *t* and lines *a* and *b* form eight angles.

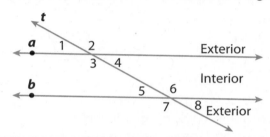

Angle Pairs Formed by a Transversal

Term	Example
Corresponding angles lie on the same side of the transversal *t*, on the same side of lines *a* and *b*.	∠1 and ∠5
Alternate interior angles are nonadjacent angles that lie on opposite sides of the transversal *t*, between lines *a* and *b*.	∠3 and ∠6
Alternate exterior angles lie on opposite sides of the transversal *t*, outside lines *a* and *b*.	∠1 and ∠8
Same-side interior angles lie on the same side of the transversal *t*, between lines *a* and *b*.	∠3 and ∠5

Use geometry software to explore the angles formed when a transversal intersects parallel lines.

A Construct a line and label two points on the line *A* and *B*.

B Create point *C* not on $\overleftrightarrow{AB}$. Then construct a line parallel to $\overleftrightarrow{AB}$ through point *C*. Create another point on this line and label it *D*.

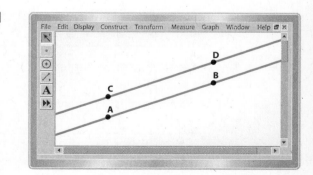

C Create two points outside the two parallel lines and label them *E* and *F*. Construct transversal $\overleftrightarrow{EF}$. Label the points of intersection *G* and *H*.

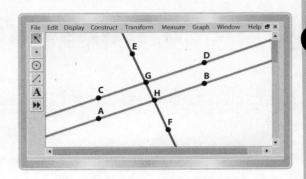

D Measure the angles formed by the parallel lines and the transversal. Write the angle measures in the table below.

E Drag point *E* or point *F* to a different position. Record the new angle measures in the table.

Angle	∠CGE	∠DGE	∠CGH	∠DGH	∠AHG	∠BHG	∠AHF	∠BHF
Measure								
Measure								

Reflect

Make a Conjecture **Identify the pairs of angles in the diagram. Then make a conjecture about their angle measures. Drag a point in the diagram to confirm your conjecture.**

1. corresponding angles

_____

_____

_____

2. alternate interior angles

_____

_____

3. alternate exterior angles

_____

_____

4. same-side interior angles

_____

_____

Justifying Angle Relationships

You can use tracing paper to informally justify your conclusions from the first Explore Activity.

Lines *a* and *b* are parallel. (The black arrows on the diagram indicate parallel lines.)

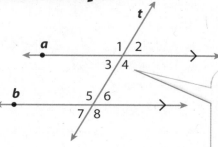

> Recall that vertical angles are the opposite angles formed by two intersecting lines. ∠1 and ∠4 are vertical angles.

A Trace the diagram onto tracing paper.

B Position the tracing paper over the original diagram so that ∠1 on the tracing is over ∠5 on the original diagram. Compare the two angles. Do they appear to be congruent?

_____

_____

C Use the tracing paper to compare all eight angles in the diagram to each other. List all of the congruent angle pairs.

_____

_____

_____

Finding Unknown Angle Measures

You can find any unknown angle measure when two parallel lines are cut by a transversal if you are given at least one other angle measure.

EXAMPLE 1 TEKS 8.8.D

A **Find m∠2 when m∠7 = 125°.**

∠2 is congruent to ∠7 because they are alternate exterior angles.

Therefore, m∠2 = 125°.

B **Find m∠VWZ.**

∠VWZ is supplementary to ∠YVW because they are same-side interior angles.
m∠VWZ + m∠YVW = 180°

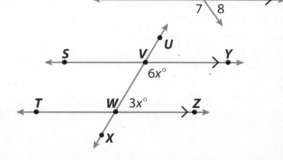

Math On the Spot
⏱ my.hrw.com

Animated Math
⏱ my.hrw.com

From the previous page, m∠*VWZ* + m∠*YVW* = 180°, m∠*VWZ* = 3*x*°, and m∠*YVW* = 6*x*°.

$$m\angle VWZ + m\angle YVW = 180°$$

$$3x° + 6x° = 180°$$ Replace m∠*VWZ* with 3*x*° and m∠*YVW* with 6*x*°.

$$9x = 180$$ Combine like terms.

$$\frac{9x}{9} = \frac{180}{9}$$ Divide both sides by 9.

$$x = 20$$ Simplify.

$$m\angle VWZ = 3x° = (3 \cdot 20)° = 60°$$

YOUR TURN

Find each angle measure.

5. m∠*GDE* = _____

6. m∠*BEF* = _____

7. m∠*CDG* = _____

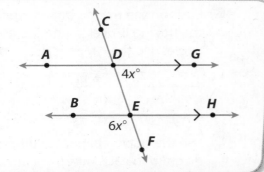

Guided Practice

Use the figure for Exercises 1–4. (Explore Activity 1 and Example 1)

1. ∠*UVY* and _____ are a pair of corresponding angles.

2. ∠*WVY* and ∠*VWT* are _____ angles.

3. Find m∠*SVW*. _____

4. Find m∠*VWT*. _____

5. **Vocabulary** When two parallel lines are cut by a transversal,

_____ angles are supplementary. (Explore Activity 1)

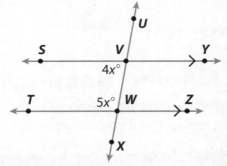

ESSENTIAL QUESTION CHECK-IN

6. What can you conclude about the interior angles formed when two
parallel lines are cut by a transversal?

_____

_____

© Houghton Mifflin Harcourt Publishing Company

7.1 Independent Practice

 TEKS 8.8.D

Personal Math Trainer

Online Assessment and Intervention

my.hrw.com

Vocabulary Use the figure for Exercises 7–10.

7. Name all pairs of corresponding angles.

_____

8. Name both pairs of alternate exterior angles.

_____

9. Name the relationship between ∠3 and ∠6.

_____

10. Name the relationship between ∠4 and ∠6.

_____

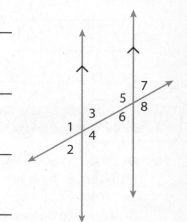

Find each angle measure.

11. m∠AGE when m∠FHD = 30° _____

12. m∠AGH when m∠CHF = 150° _____

13. m∠CHF when m∠BGE = 110° _____

14. m∠CHG when m∠HGA = 120° _____

15. m∠BGH = _____

16. m∠GHD = _____

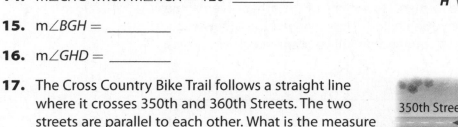

17. The Cross Country Bike Trail follows a straight line where it crosses 350th and 360th Streets. The two streets are parallel to each other. What is the measure of the larger angle formed at the intersection of the bike trail and 360th Street? Explain.

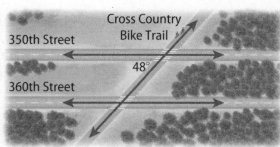

_____

_____

_____

18. **Critical Thinking** How many different angles would be formed by a transversal intersecting three parallel lines? How many different angle measures would there be?

_____

_____

19. Communicate Mathematical Ideas In the diagram at the right, suppose m∠6 = 125°. Explain how to find the measures of each of the other seven numbered angles.

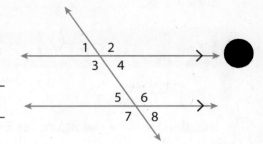

_____

_____

_____

_____

_____

_____

H.O.T. FOCUS ON HIGHER ORDER THINKING

20. Draw Conclusions In a diagram showing two parallel lines cut by a transversal, the measures of two same-side interior angles are both given as 3x°. Without writing and solving an equation, can you determine the measures of both angles? Explain. Then write and solve an equation to find the measures.

_____

_____

_____

21. Make a Conjecture Draw two parallel lines and a transversal. Choose one of the eight angles that are formed. How many of the other seven angles are congruent to the angle you selected? How many of the other seven angles are supplementary to your angle? Will your answer change if you select a different angle?

_____

22. Critique Reasoning In the diagram at the right, ∠2, ∠3, ∠5, and ∠8 are all congruent, and ∠1, ∠4, ∠6, and ∠7 are all congruent. Aiden says that this is enough information to conclude that the diagram shows two parallel lines cut by a transversal. Is he correct? Justify your answer.

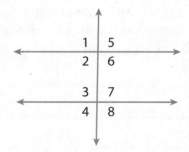

_____

_____

_____

_____

_____

Work Area

Angle Theorems for Triangles

TEKS
Expressions, equations, and relationships—8.8.D Use informal arguments to establish facts about the angle sum and exterior angle of triangles, ...

ESSENTIAL QUESTION

What can you conclude about the measures of the angles of a triangle?

EXPLORE ACTIVITY 1 **TEKS** 8.8.D

Sum of the Angle Measures in a Triangle

There is a special relationship between the measures of the interior angles of a triangle.

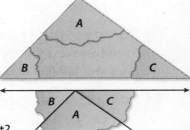

A Draw a triangle and cut it out. Label the angles *A*, *B*, and *C*.

B Tear off each "corner" of the triangle. Each corner includes the vertex of one angle of the triangle.

C Arrange the vertices of the triangle around a point so that none of your corners overlap and there are no gaps between them.

D What do you notice about how the angles fit together around a point?

_____

E What is the measure of a straight angle? _____

F Describe the relationship among the measures of the angles of △*ABC*.

_____

The Triangle Sum Theorem states that for △*ABC*, m∠*A* + m∠*B* + m∠*C* = _____.

Reflect

1. Justify Reasoning Can a triangle have two right angles? Explain.

_____

_____

_____

2. Analyze Relationships Describe the relationship between the two acute angles in a right triangle. Explain your reasoning.

_____

_____

_____

Justifying the Triangle Sum Theorem

You can use your knowledge of parallel lines intersected by a transversal to informally justify the Triangle Sum Theorem.

Follow the steps to informally prove the Triangle Sum Theorem. You should draw each step on your own paper. The figures below are provided for you to check your work.

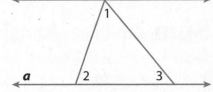

A Draw a triangle and label the angles as ∠1, ∠2, and ∠3 as shown.

B Draw line *a* through the base of the triangle.

C The Parallel Postulate states that through a point not on a line ℓ, there is exactly one line parallel to line ℓ. Draw line *b* parallel to line *a*, through the vertex opposite the base of the triangle.

D Extend each of the non-base sides of the triangle to form transversal *s* and transversal *t*. Transversals *s* and *t* intersect parallel lines *a* and *b*.

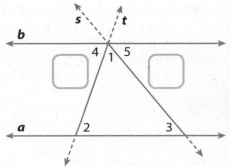

E Label the angles formed by line *b* and the transversals as ∠4 and ∠5.

F Because ∠4 and _____ are alternate interior

angles, they are _____.

Label ∠4 with the number of the angle to which it is congruent.

G Because ∠5 and _____ are alternate interior angles,

they are _____.

Label ∠5 with the number of the angle to which it is congruent.

H The three angles that lie along line *b* at the vertex of the triangle are ∠1, ∠4, and ∠5. Notice that these three angles lie along a line.

So, m∠1 + m∠2 + m∠5 = _____.

Because angles 2 and 4 are congruent and angles 3 and 5 are congruent, you can substitute m∠2 for m∠4 and m∠3 for m∠5 in the equation above.

So, m∠1 + m∠2 + m∠3 = _____.

This shows that the sum of the angle measures in a triangle is

always _____.

Reflect

3. **Analyze Relationships** How can you use the fact that m∠4 + m∠1 + m∠5 = 180° to show that m∠2 + m∠1 + m∠3 = 180°?

_____

_____

_____

Finding Missing Angle Measures in Triangles

If you know the measures of two angles in a triangle, you can use the Triangle Sum Theorem to find the measure of the third angle.

Math On the Spot
my.hrw.com

EXAMPLE 1

TEKS 8.8.D

Find the missing angle measure.

My Notes

STEP 1 Write the Triangle Sum Theorem for this triangle.

$$m\angle D + m\angle E + m\angle F = 180°$$

STEP 2 Substitute the given angle measures.

$$55° + m\angle E + 100° = 180°$$

STEP 3 Solve the equation for m∠E.

$$55° + m\angle E + 100° = 180°$$

$$155° + m\angle E = 180°$$

$$\underline{-155°} \qquad \underline{-155°}$$ Simplify.

$$m\angle E = \quad 25°$$ Subtract 155° from both sides.

So, m∠E = 25°.

YOUR TURN

Find the missing angle measure.

4.

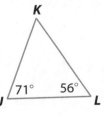

m∠K = _____

5.

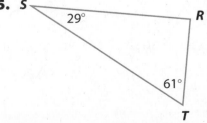

m∠R = _____

Personal Math Trainer
Online Assessment and Intervention
my.hrw.com

Exterior Angles and Remote Interior Angles

An **interior angle** of a triangle is formed by two sides of the triangle. An **exterior angle** is formed by one side of the triangle and the extension of an adjacent side. Each exterior angle has two remote interior angles. A **remote interior angle** is an interior angle that is not adjacent to the exterior angle.

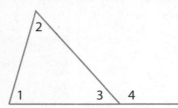

- ∠1, ∠2, and ∠3 are interior angles.

- ∠4 is an exterior angle.

- ∠1 and ∠2 are remote interior angles to ∠4.

There is a special relationship between the measure of an exterior angle and the measures of its remote interior angles.

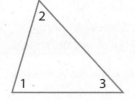

A Extend the base of the triangle and label the exterior angle as ∠4.

B The Triangle Sum Theorem states:

m∠1 + m∠2 + m∠3 = _____.

C ∠3 and ∠4 form a _____,

so m∠3 + m∠4 = _____.

D Use the equations in **B** and **C** to complete the following equation:

m∠1 + m∠2 + _____ = _____ + m∠4

E Use properties of equality to simplify the equation in **D**:

_____

The Exterior Angle Theorem states that the measure of an _____ angle

is equal to the sum of its _____ angles.

Reflect

6. Sketch a triangle and draw all of its exterior angles. How many exterior angles does a triangle have at each vertex?

_____

7. How many total exterior angles does a triangle have?

_____

Using the Exterior Angle Theorem

You can use the Exterior Angle Theorem to find the measures of the interior angles of a triangle.

EXAMPLE 2

TEKS 8.8.D

Find m∠A and m∠B.

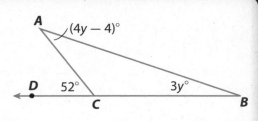

STEP 1 Write the Exterior Angle Theorem as it applies to this triangle.

m∠A + m∠B = m∠ACD

STEP 2 Substitute the given angle measures.

$(4y - 4)° + 3y° = 52°$

STEP 3 Solve the equation for y.

$(4y - 4)° + 3y° = 52°$

$4y° - 4° + 3y° = 52°$	Remove parentheses.
$7y° - 4° = 52°$	Simplify.
$\underline{+4° \qquad +4°}$	Add 4° to both sides.
$7y° = 56°$	Simplify.
$\dfrac{7y°}{7} = \dfrac{56°}{7}$	Divide both sides by 7.
$y = 8$	Simplify.

Math Talk
Mathematical Processes

Describe two ways to find m∠ACB.

STEP 4 Use the value of y to find m∠A and m∠B.

m∠A = 4y − 4   m∠B = 3y
    = 4(8) − 4   = 3(8)
    = 32 − 4   = 24
    = 28

So, m∠A = 28° and m∠B = 24°.

YOUR TURN

8. Find m∠M and m∠N.

m∠M = _____

m∠N = _____

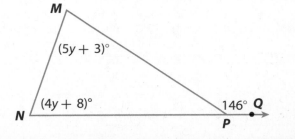

Personal Math Trainer

Online Assessment and Intervention

my.hrw.com

Guided Practice

Find each missing angle measure. (Explore Activity 1 and Example 1)

1.

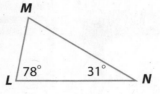

m∠M = _____

2.

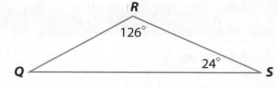

m∠Q = _____

Use the Triangle Sum Theorem to find the measure of each angle in degrees. (Explore Activity 2 and Example 1)

3.

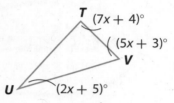

m∠T = _____, m∠U = _____,

m∠V = _____

4.

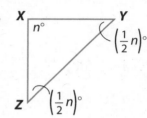

m∠X = _____, m∠Y = _____,

m∠Z = _____

Use the Exterior Angle Theorem to find the measure of each angle in degrees. (Explore Activity 3 and Example 2)

5.

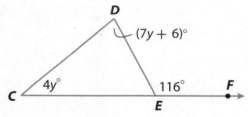

m∠C = _____, m∠D = _____,

m∠DEC = _____

6.

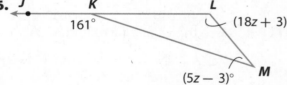

m∠L = _____, m∠M = _____,

m∠LKM = _____

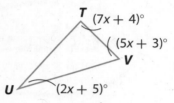

ESSENTIAL QUESTION CHECK-IN

7. Describe the relationships among the measures of the angles of a triangle.

_____

_____

_____

7.2 Independent Practice

TEKS 8.8.D

Find the measure of each angle.

8.

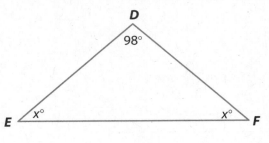

m∠E = _____

m∠F = _____

9.

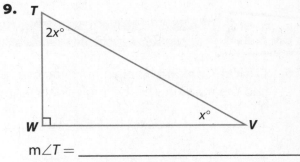

m∠T = _____

m∠V = _____

10.

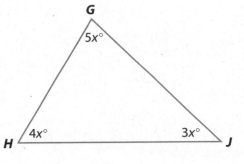

m∠G = _____

m∠H = _____

m∠J = _____

11.

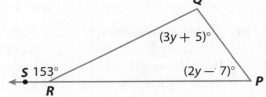

m∠Q = _____

m∠P = _____

m∠QRP = _____

12.

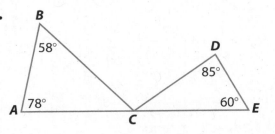

m∠ACB = _____

m∠BCD = _____

m∠DCE = _____

13.

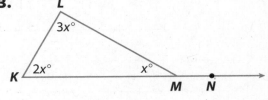

m∠K = _____

m∠L = _____

m∠KML = _____

m∠LMN = _____

14. Multistep The second angle in a triangle is five times as large as the first. The third angle is two-thirds as large as the first. Find the angle measures. _____

15. Analyze Relationships Can a triangle have two obtuse angles? Explain.

_____

_____

_____

_____

Work Area

16. Critical Thinking Explain how you can use the Triangle Sum Theorem to find the measures of the angles of an equilateral triangle.

_____

_____

_____

_____

17. a. Draw Conclusions Find the sum of the measures of the angles in quadrilateral *ABCD*. (Hint: Draw diagonal $\overline{AC}$. How can you use the figures you have formed to find the sum?)

Sum = _____

b. Make a Conjecture Write a "Quadrilateral Sum Theorem." Explain why you think it is true.

_____

_____

_____

_____

_____

_____

18. Communicate Mathematical Ideas Describe two ways that an exterior angle of a triangle is related to one or more of the interior angles.

_____

_____

_____

_____

© Houghton Mifflin Harcourt Publishing Company

Angle-Angle Similarity

TEKS
Expressions, equations, and relationships—8.8.D
Use informal arguments to establish facts about . . . the angle-angle criteria for similarity of triangles. *Also 8.3.A, 8.4.A*

? **ESSENTIAL QUESTION**

How can you determine when two triangles are similar?

EXPLORE ACTIVITY 1  8.8.D

Discovering Angle-Angle Similarity

Similar figures have the same shape but may have different sizes. Two triangles are **similar** if their corresponding angles are congruent and the lengths of their corresponding sides are proportional.

A Use your protractor and a straightedge to draw a triangle. Make one angle measure 45° and another angle measure 60°.

B Compare your triangle to those drawn by your classmates. How are the triangles the same?

_____

How are they different?

_____

C Use the Triangle Sum Theorem to find the measure of the third angle of your triangle.

_____

Reflect

1. If two angles in one triangle are congruent to two angles in another triangle, what do you know about the third pair of angles?

_____

2. **Make a Conjecture** Are two pairs of congruent angles enough information to conclude that two triangles are similar? Explain.

_____

_____

_____

Using the AA Similarity Postulate

Angle-Angle (AA) Similarity Postulate

If two angles of one triangle are congruent to two angles of another triangle, then the triangles are similar.

EXAMPLE 1

 TEKS 8.8.D

Explain whether the triangles are similar.

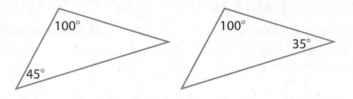

The figure shows only one pair of congruent angles. Find the measure of the third angle in each triangle.

$$45° + 100° + m\angle 3 = 180°$$ $$100° + 35° + m\angle 3 = 180°$$

$$145° + m\angle 3 = 180°$$ $$135° + m\angle 3 = 180°$$

$$145° + m\angle 3 - 145° = 180° - 145°$$ $$135° + m\angle 3 - 135° = 180° - 135°$$

$$m\angle 3 = 35°$$ $$m\angle 3 = 45°$$

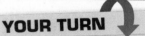

Math Talk
Mathematical Processes

Are all right triangles similar? Why or why not?

Because two angles in one triangle are congruent to two angles in the other triangle, the triangles are similar.

YOUR TURN

3. **Explain whether the triangles are similar.**

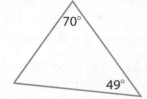

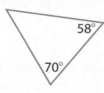

Finding Missing Measures in Similar Triangles

Because corresponding angles are congruent and corresponding sides are proportional in similar triangles, you can use similar triangles to solve real-world problems.

EXAMPLE 2  **TEKS** 8.3.A, 8.8.D

While playing tennis, Matt is 12 meters from the net, which is 0.9 meter high. He needs to hit the ball so that it just clears the net and lands 6 meters beyond the base of the net. At what height should Matt hit the tennis ball?

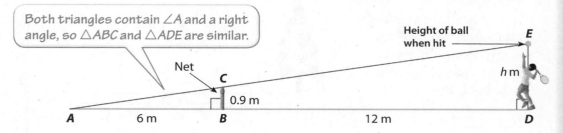

Both triangles contain ∠A and a right angle, so △ABC and △ADE are similar.

Height of ball when hit — E

Net
C
0.9 m
h m

A — 6 m — B — 12 m — D

In similar triangles, corresponding side lengths are proportional.

$$\frac{AD}{AB} = \frac{DE}{BC} \longrightarrow \frac{6+12}{6} = \frac{h}{0.9}$$ Substitute the lengths from the figure.

$$0.9 \times \frac{18}{6} = \frac{h}{0.9} \times 0.9$$ Use properties of equality to get *h* by itself.

$$0.9 \times 3 = h$$ Simplify.

$$2.7 = h$$ Multiply.

Matt should hit the ball at a height of 2.7 meters.

Reflect

4. **What If?** Suppose you set up a proportion so that each ratio compares parts of one triangle, as shown below.

height of △ABC ⟶ $\frac{BC}{AB}$ = $\frac{DE}{AD}$ ⟵ height of △ADE
base of △ABC ⟶ ⟵ base of △ADE

Show that this proportion leads to the same value for *h* as in Example 2.

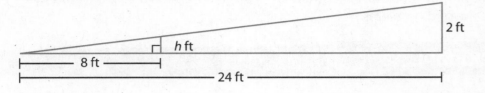

YOUR TURN

5. Rosie is building a wheelchair ramp that is 24 feet long and 2 feet high. She needs to install a vertical support piece 8 feet from the end of the ramp. What is the length of the support piece in inches?

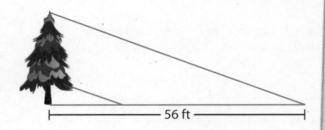

2 ft

h ft

8 ft

24 ft

_____

6. The lower cable meets the tree at a height of 6 feet and extends out 16 feet from the base of the tree. If the triangles are similar, how tall is the tree?

56 ft

_____

EXPLORE ACTIVITY 2 🔲 **TEKS** 8.4.A

Using Similar Triangles to Explain Slope

You can use similar triangles to show that the slope of a line is constant.

A Draw a line ℓ that is not a horizontal line. Label four points on the line as *A*, *B*, *C*, and *D*.

You need to show that the slope between points *A* and *B* is the same as the slope between points *C* and *D*.

B Draw the rise and run for the slope between points A and B. Label the intersection as point E. Draw the rise and run for the slope between points C and D. Label the intersection as point F.

C Write expressions for the slope between A and B and between C and D.

Slope between A and B: $\dfrac{BE}{\boxed{}}$ Slope between C and D: $\dfrac{\boxed{}}{CF}$

D Extend $\overleftrightarrow{AE}$ and $\overleftrightarrow{CF}$ across your drawing. $\overleftrightarrow{AE}$ and $\overleftrightarrow{CF}$ are both horizontal lines, so they are parallel.

Line ℓ is a _____ that intersects parallel lines.

E Complete the following statements:

$\angle BAE$ and _____ are corresponding angles and are _____.

$\angle BEA$ and _____ are right angles and are _____.

F By Angle–Angle Similarity, $\triangle ABE$ and _____ are similar triangles.

G Use the fact that the lengths of corresponding sides of similar

triangles are proportional to complete the following ratios: $\dfrac{BE}{DF} = \dfrac{\boxed{}}{CF}$

H Recall that you can also write the proportion so

that the ratios compare parts of the same triangle: $\dfrac{\boxed{}}{AE} = \dfrac{DF}{\boxed{}}$.

I The proportion you wrote in step **H** shows that the ratios you wrote in **C** are equal. So, the slope of line ℓ is constant.

Reflect

7. What If? Suppose that you label two other points on line ℓ as G and H. Would the slope between these two points be different than the slope you found in the Explore Activity? Explain.

_____

_____

_____

1. Explain whether the triangles are similar. Label the angle measures in the figure. (Explore Activity 1 and Example 1)

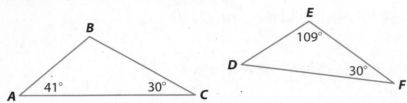

△ABC has angle measures _____ and △DEF has angle

measures _____. Because _____ in one

triangle are congruent to _____ in the other triangle, the

triangles are _____.

2. A flagpole casts a shadow 23.5 feet long. At the same time of day, Mrs. Gilbert, who is 5.5 feet tall, casts a shadow that is 7.5 feet long. How tall in feet is the flagpole? Round your answer to the nearest tenth. (Example 2)

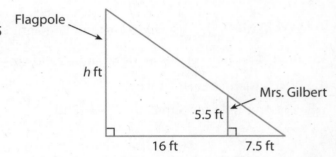

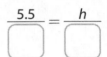

$\dfrac{5.5}{\boxed{}} = \dfrac{h}{\boxed{}}$

$h = $ _____ feet

3. Two transversals intersect two parallel lines as shown. Explain whether △ABC and △DEC are similar. (Example 1)

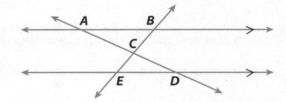

∠BAC and ∠EDC are _____ since they are _____.

∠ABC and ∠DEC are _____ since they are _____.

By _____, △ABC and △DEC are _____.

? ESSENTIAL QUESTION CHECK-IN

4. How can you determine when two triangles are similar?

_____

_____

_____

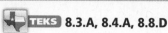

7.3 Independent Practice

TEKS 8.3.A, 8.4.A, 8.8.D

Personal
Math Trainer

Online
Assessment and
Intervention

my.hrw.com

Use the diagrams for Exercises 5–7.

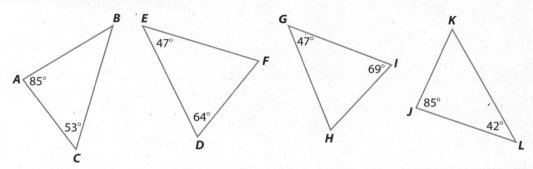

5. Find the missing angle measures in the triangles.

_____

6. Which triangles are similar?

_____

7. **Analyze Relationships** Determine which angles are congruent to the angles in △ABC.

_____

8. **Multistep** A tree casts a shadow that is 20 feet long. Frank is 6 feet tall, and while standing next to the tree he casts a shadow that is 4 feet long.

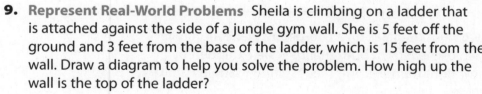

a. How tall is the tree? _____

b. How much taller is the tree than Frank? _____

9. **Represent Real-World Problems** Sheila is climbing on a ladder that is attached against the side of a jungle gym wall. She is 5 feet off the ground and 3 feet from the base of the ladder, which is 15 feet from the wall. Draw a diagram to help you solve the problem. How high up the wall is the top of the ladder? _____

10. **Justify Reasoning** Are two equilateral triangles always similar? Explain.

_____

_____

_____

11. Critique Reasoning Ryan calculated the missing measure in the diagram shown. What was his mistake?

$$\frac{3.4}{6.5} = \frac{h}{19.5}$$

$$19.5 \times \frac{3.4}{6.5} = \frac{h}{19.5} \times 19.5$$

$$\frac{66.3}{6.5} = h$$

$$10.2 \text{ cm} = h$$

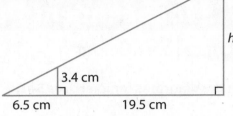

_____

_____

_____

Work Area

12. Communicate Mathematical Ideas For a pair of triangular earrings, how can you tell if they are similar? How can you tell if they are congruent?

_____

_____

_____

13. Critical Thinking When does it make sense to use similar triangles to measure the height and length of objects in real life?

_____

_____

_____

14. Justify Reasoning Two right triangles on a coordinate plane are similar but not congruent. Each of the legs of both triangles are extended by 1 unit, creating two new right triangles. Are the resulting triangles similar? Explain using an example.

_____

_____

_____

_____

Ready to Go On?

Personal Math Trainer

Online Assessment and Intervention

my.hrw.com

7.1 Parallel Lines Cut by a Transversal

In the figure, line $p \parallel$ line q. Find the measure of each angle if $m\angle 8 = 115°$.

1. $m\angle 7 =$ _____

2. $m\angle 6 =$ _____

3. $m\angle 1 =$ _____

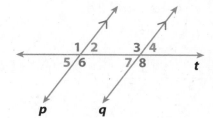

7.2 Angle Theorems for Triangles

Find the measure of each angle.

4. $m\angle A =$ _____

5. $m\angle B =$ _____

6. $m\angle BCA =$ _____

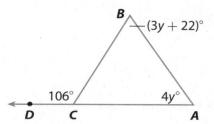

7.3 Angle-Angle Similarity

Triangle *FEG* is similar to triangle *IHJ*. Find the missing values.

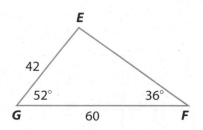 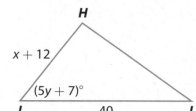

7. $x =$ _____

8. $y =$ _____

9. $m\angle H =$ _____

? ESSENTIAL QUESTION

10. How can you use similar triangles to solve real-world problems?

_____

_____

Personal Math Trainer

Online Assessment and Intervention

my.hrw.com

Selected Response

Use the figure for Exercises 1 and 2.

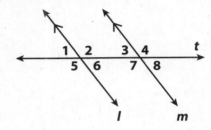

1. Which angle pair is a pair of alternate exterior angles?

Ⓐ ∠5 and ∠6   Ⓒ ∠5 and ∠4

Ⓑ ∠6 and ∠7   Ⓓ ∠5 and ∠2

2. Which of the following angles is **not** congruent to ∠3?

Ⓐ ∠1   Ⓒ ∠6

Ⓑ ∠2   Ⓓ ∠8

3. The measures of the three angles of a triangle are given by $2x + 1$, $3x - 3$, and $9x$. What is the measure of the smallest angle?

Ⓐ 13°   Ⓒ 36°

Ⓑ 27°   Ⓓ 117°

4. Which is a possible measure of ∠DCA in the triangle below?

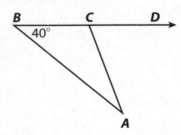

Ⓐ 36°   Ⓒ 40°

Ⓑ 38°   Ⓓ 70°

5. Kaylee wrote in her dinosaur report that the Jurassic period was 1.75×10^8 years ago. According to Kaylee's report, how many years ago was the Jurassic period?

Ⓐ 1,750,000

Ⓑ 17,500,000

Ⓒ 175,000,000

Ⓓ 17,500,000,000

6. Given that y varies directly with x, what is the equation of direct variation if y is 16 when x is 20?

Ⓐ $y = 1\frac{1}{5}x$

Ⓑ $y = \frac{5}{4}x$

Ⓒ $y = \frac{4}{5}x$

Ⓓ $y = 0.6x$

Gridded Response

7. What is the value of h in the triangle below?

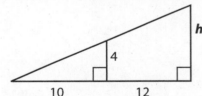

⓪	⓪	⓪	⓪	•	⓪	⓪
①	①	①	①		①	①
②	②	②	②		②	②
③	③	③	③		③	③
④	④	④	④		④	④
⑤	⑤	⑤	⑤		⑤	⑤
⑥	⑥	⑥	⑥		⑥	⑥
⑦	⑦	⑦	⑦		⑦	⑦
⑧	⑧	⑧	⑧		⑧	⑧
⑨	⑨	⑨	⑨		⑨	⑨

The Pythagorean Theorem

ESSENTIAL QUESTION

How can you use the Pythagorean Theorem to solve real-world problems?

Real-World Video

The sizes of televisions are usually described by the length of the diagonal of the screen. To find this length of the diagonal of a rectangle, you can use the Pythagorean Theorem.

my.hrw.com

GO DIGITAL
my.hrw.com

 my.hrw.com
Go digital with your write-in student edition, accessible on any device.

 Math On the Spot
Scan with your smart phone to jump directly to the online edition, video tutor, and more.

 Animated Math
Interactively explore key concepts to see how math works.

 Personal Math Trainer
Get immediate feedback and help as you work through practice sets.

Are YOU Ready?

Complete these exercises to review skills you will need for this chapter.

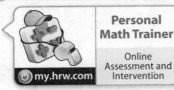

Find the Square of a Number

EXAMPLE Find the square of 2.7.

$$\begin{array}{r} 2.7 \\ \times\, 2.7 \\ \hline 18.9 \\ 54 \\ \hline 7.29 \end{array}$$

Multiply the number by itself.

So, $2.7^2 = 7.29$.

Find the square of each number.

1. 5 _____   **2.** 16 _____   **3.** -11 _____   **4.** $\frac{2}{7}$ _____

Order of Operations

EXAMPLE $\sqrt{(5-2)^2 + (8-4)^2}$ First, operate within parentheses.

$\sqrt{(3)^2 + (4)^2}$ Next, simplify exponents.

$\sqrt{9 + 16}$ Then add and subtract left to right.

$\sqrt{25}$ Finally, take the square root.

5

Evaluate each expression.

5. $\sqrt{(6+2)^2 + (3+3)^2}$ _____   **6.** $\sqrt{(9-4)^2 + (5+7)^2}$ _____

7. $\sqrt{(10-6)^2 + (15-12)^2}$ _____   **8.** $\sqrt{(6+9)^2 + (10-2)^2}$ _____

Simplify Numerical Expressions

EXAMPLE $\frac{1}{2}(2.5)^2(4) = \frac{1}{2}(6.25)(4)$ Simplify the exponent.

$= 12.5$ Multiply from left to right.

Simplify each expression.

9. $5(8)(10)$ _____   **10.** $\frac{1}{2}(6)(12)$ _____   **11.** $\frac{1}{3}(3)(12)$ _____

12. $\frac{1}{2}(8)^2(4)$ _____   **13.** $\frac{1}{4}(10)^2(15)$ _____   **14.** $\frac{1}{3}(9)^2(6)$ _____

Reading Start-Up

Visualize Vocabulary

Use the ✔ words to complete the graphic.

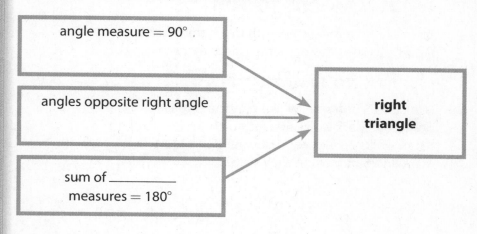

angle measure = 90°

| angles opposite right angle |

| sum of _____ measures = 180° |

right triangle

Vocabulary

Review Words

✔ acute angles *(ángulos agudo)*

✔ angles *(ángulos)*

area *(área)*

ordered pair *(par ordenado)*

✔ right angle *(ángulo recto)*

✔ right triangle *(triángulo recto)*

square root *(raíz cuadrada)*

x-coordinate *(coordenada x)*

y-coordinate *(coordenada y)*

Preview Words

hypotenuse *(hipotenusa)*

legs *(catetos)*

theorem *(teorema)*

vertex *(vértice)*

Understand Vocabulary

Match the term on the left to the correct expression on the right.

1. hypotenuse

2. theorem

3. legs

A. An idea that has been demonstrated as true.

B. The two sides that form the right angle of a right triangle.

C. The side opposite the right angle in a right triangle.

Active Reading

Booklet Before beginning the module, create a booklet to help you learn about the Pythagorean Theorem. Write the main idea of each lesson on each page of the booklet. As you study each lesson, write important details that support the main idea, such as vocabulary and formulas. Refer to your finished booklet as you work on assignments and study for tests.

MODULE 8
Unpacking the TEKS

Understanding the TEKS and the vocabulary terms in the TEKS will help you know exactly what you are expected to learn in this module.

TEKS 8.7.C

Use the Pythagorean Theorem and its converse to solve problems.

Key Vocabulary

Pythagorean Theorem
(Teorema de Pitagóras)
In a right triangle, the square of the length of the hypotenuse is equal to the sum of the squares of the lengths of the legs.

What It Means to You

You will find a missing length in a right triangle, or use side lengths to see whether a triangle is a right triangle.

UNPACKING EXAMPLE 8.7.C

Mark and Sarah start walking at the same point, but Mark walks 50 feet north while Sarah walks 75 feet east. How far apart are Mark and Sarah when they stop?

$$a^2 + b^2 = c^2$$
$$50^2 + 75^2 = c^2$$
$$2500 + 5625 = c^2$$
$$8125 = c^2$$
$$90.1 \approx c$$

50 ft — c — 75 ft

Pythagorean Theorem

Substitute.

Mark and Sarah are approximately 90.1 feet apart.

TEKS 8.7.D

Determine the distance between two points on a coordinate plane using the Pythagorean Theorem.

Key Vocabulary

coordinate plane
(plano cartesiano)
A plane formed by the intersection of a horizontal number line called the *x*-axis and a vertical number lie called the *y*-axis.

Visit **my.hrw.com** to see all the **TEKS** unpacked.

🔴 my.hrw.com

What It Means to You

You can use the Pythagorean Theorem to find the distance between 2 points.

UNPACKING EXAMPLE 8.7.D

Find the distance between points *A* and *B*.

$$(AC)^2 + (BC)^2 = (AB)^2$$
$$(4 - 1)^2 + (6 - 2)^2 = (AB)^2$$
$$3^2 + 4^2 = (AB)^2$$
$$9 + 16 = (AB)^2$$
$$25 = (AB)^2$$
$$5 = AB$$

The distance is 5 units.

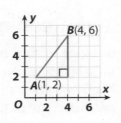

The Pythagorean Theorem

TEKS
Expressions, equations, and relationships—
8.6.C Use models and diagrams to explain the Pythagorean Theorem.
8.7.C Use the Pythagorean Theorem ... to solve problems.

? ESSENTIAL QUESTION

How can you prove the Pythagorean Theorem and use it to solve problems?

EXPLORE ACTIVITY   TEKS 8.6.C

Proving the Pythagorean Theorem

In a right triangle, the two sides that form the right angle are the **legs**. The side opposite the right angle is the **hypotenuse**.

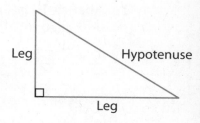

Leg   Hypotenuse

Leg

The Pythagorean Theorem

In a right triangle, the sum of the squares of the lengths of the legs is equal to the square of the length of the hypotenuse.

If a and b are legs and c is the hypotenuse, $a^2 + b^2 = c^2$.

A Draw a right triangle on a piece of paper and cut it out. Make one leg shorter than the other.

B Trace your triangle onto another piece of paper four times, arranging them as shown. For each triangle, label the shorter leg a, the longer leg b, and the hypotenuse c.

C What is the area of the unshaded square?

_____

Label the unshaded square with its area.

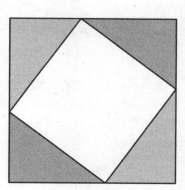

D Trace your original triangle onto a piece of paper four times again, arranging them as shown. Draw a line outlining a larger square that is the same size as the figure you made in **B**.

E What is the area of the unshaded square at the top right of the figure in **D**? at the top left?

_____

Label the unshaded squares with their areas.

F What is the total area of the unshaded regions in **D**?

_____

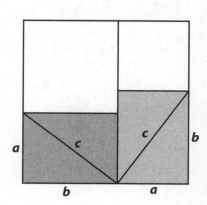

Reflect

1. Explain whether the figures in **B** and **D** have the same area.

_____

2. Explain whether the unshaded regions of the figures in **B** and **D** have the same area.

_____

_____

_____

3. **Analyze Relationships** Write an equation relating the area of the unshaded region in step **B** to the unshaded region in **D**.

_____

Using the Pythagorean Theorem

You can use the Pythagorean Theorem to find the length of a side of a right triangle when you know the lengths of the other two sides.

EXAMPLE 1    TEKS 8.7.C

Find the length of the missing side.

A

7 in.
24 in.

$$a^2 + b^2 = c^2$$

$$24^2 + 7^2 = c^2$$ Substitute into the formula.

$$576 + 49 = c^2$$ Simplify.

$$625 = c^2$$ Add.

$$25 = c$$ Take the square root of both sides.

Math Talk
Mathematical Processes

If you are given the length of the hypotenuse and one leg, does it matter whether you solve for a or b? Explain.

The length of the hypotenuse is 25 inches.

B

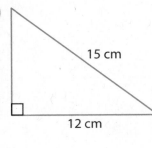
15 cm
12 cm

$$a^2 + b^2 = c^2$$

$$a^2 + 12^2 = 15^2$$ Substitute into the formula.

$$a^2 + 144 = 225$$ Simplify.

$$a^2 = 81$$ Use properties of equality to get a^2 by itself.

$$a = 9$$ Take the square root of both sides.

The length of the leg is 9 centimeters.

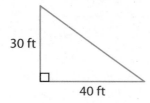
Find the length of the missing side.

4.

30 ft

40 ft

5.

41 in.

40 in.

Pythagorean Theorem in Three Dimensions

You can use the Pythagorean Theorem to solve problems in three dimensions.

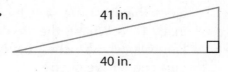

EXAMPLE 2 Real World   TEKS 8.7.C

A box used for shipping narrow copper tubes measures 6 inches by 6 inches by 20 inches. What is the length of the longest tube that will fit in the box, given that the length of the tube must be a whole number of inches?

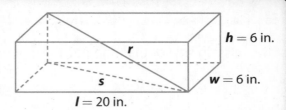

$h = 6$ in.

$w = 6$ in.

$l = 20$ in.

STEP 1 You want to find r, the length from a bottom corner to the opposite top corner. First, find s, the length of the diagonal across the bottom of the box.

$w^2 + l^2 = s^2$

$6^2 + 20^2 = s^2$ Substitute into the formula.

$36 + 400 = s^2$ Simplify.

$436 = s^2$ Add.

STEP 2 Use your expression for s to find r.

$h^2 + s^2 = r^2$

$6^2 + 436 = r^2$ Substitute into the formula.

$472 = r^2$ Add.

$\sqrt{472} = r$ Take the square root of both sides.

$21.7 \approx r$ Use a calculator to round to the nearest tenth.

The length of the longest tube that will fit in the box is 21 inches.

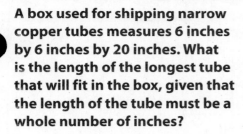

Math Talk
Mathematical Processes

Looking at Step 2, why did the calculations in Step 1 stop before taking the square root of both sides of the final equation?

YOUR TURN

6. Tina ordered a replacement part for her desk. It was shipped in a box that measures 4 in. by 4 in. by 14 in. What is the greatest length in whole inches that the part could have been?

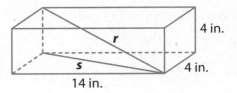

4 in.

4 in.

14 in.

Guided Practice

1. Find the length of the missing side of the triangle. (Explore Activity 1 and Example 1)

$$a^2 + b^2 = c^2 \rightarrow 24^2 + \boxed{} = c^2 \rightarrow \boxed{} = c^2$$

The length of the hypotenuse is $\boxed{}$ feet.

10 ft

24 ft

2. Mr. Woo wants to ship a fishing rod that is 42 inches long to his son. He has a box with the dimensions shown. (Example 2)

h = 10 in.

w = 10 in.

l = 40 in.

   a. Find the square of the length of the diagonal across the bottom of the box.

   _____

   b. Find the length from a bottom corner to the opposite top corner to the nearest tenth. Will the fishing rod fit?

   _____

? ESSENTIAL QUESTION CHECK-IN

3. Use a model or a diagram to help you state the Pythagorean Theorem and tell how you can use it to solve problems.

   _____

   _____

   _____

   _____

8.1 Independent Practice

TEKS 8.6.C, 8.7.C

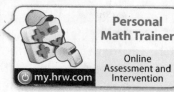

Personal Math Trainer

Online Assessment and Intervention

my.hrw.com

Find the length of the missing side of each triangle. Round your answers to the nearest tenth.

4.

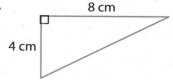

8 cm

4 cm

_____

5.

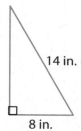

14 in.

8 in.

_____

6. The diagonal of a rectangular big-screen TV screen measures 152 cm. The length measures 132 cm. What is the height of the screen? _____

7. Dylan has a square piece of metal that measures 10 inches on each side. He cuts the metal along the diagonal, forming two right triangles. What is the length of the hypotenuse of each right triangle to the nearest tenth of an inch? _____

8. **Represent Real-World Problems** A painter has a 24-foot ladder that he is using to paint a house. For safety reasons, the ladder must be placed at least 8 feet from the base of the side of the house. To the nearest tenth of a foot, how high can the ladder safely reach? _____

9. What is the longest flagpole (in whole feet) that could be shipped in a box that measures 2 ft by 2 ft by 12 ft? _____

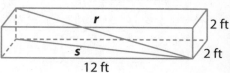

r

s

12 ft

2 ft

2 ft

10. **Sports** American football fields measure 100 yards long between the end zones, and are $53\frac{1}{3}$ yards wide. Is the length of the diagonal across this field more or less than 120 yards? Explain.

_____

11. **Justify Reasoning** A tree struck by lightning broke at a point 12 ft above the ground as shown. What was the height of the tree to the nearest tenth of a foot? Explain your reasoning.

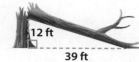

12 ft

39 ft

_____

_____

_____

12. Multistep Main Street and Washington Avenue meet at a right angle. A large park begins at this corner. Usually Joe walks 1.2 miles along Main Street and then 0.9 miles up Washington Avenue to get to school. Today he walked in a straight path across the park and returned home along the same path. What is the difference in distance between Joe's round trip today and his usual round trip? Explain.

_____

_____

_____

13. Analyze Relationships An isosceles right triangle is a right triangle with congruent legs. If the length of each leg is represented by x, what algebraic expression can be used to represent the length of the hypotenuse? Explain your reasoning.

_____

_____

14. Persevere in Problem Solving A square hamburger is centered on a circular bun. Both the bun and the burger have an area of 16 square inches.

a. How far, to the nearest hundredth of an inch, does each corner of the burger stick out from the bun? Explain.

_____

_____

_____

_____

_____

b. How far does each bun stick out from the center of each side of the burger?

_____

c. Are the distances in part **a** and part **b** equal? If not, which sticks out more, the burger or the bun? Explain.

_____

_____

_____

Converse of the Pythagorean Theorem

TEKS
Expressions, equations, and relationships—
8.7.C Use the Pythagorean Theorem and its converse to solve problems.

? ESSENTIAL QUESTION

How can you test the converse of the Pythagorean Theorem and use it to solve problems?

EXPLORE ACTIVITY  **TEKS 8.7.C**

Testing the Converse of the Pythagorean Theorem

The Pythagorean Theorem states that if a triangle is a right triangle, then $a^2 + b^2 = c^2$.

The *converse* of the Pythagorean Theorem states that if $a^2 + b^2 = c^2$, then the triangle is a right triangle.

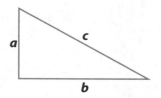

Decide whether the converse of the Pythagorean Theorem is true.

A Verify that the following sets of lengths make the equation $a^2 + b^2 = c^2$ true. Record your results in the table.

a	b	c	Is $a^2 + b^2 = c^2$ true?	Makes a right triangle?
3	4	5		
5	12	13		
7	24	25		
8	15	17		
20	21	29		

B For each set of lengths in the table, cut strips of grid paper with a width of one square and lengths that correspond to the values of a, b, and c.

C For each set of lengths, use the strips of grid paper to try to form a right triangle. An example using the first set of lengths is shown. Record your findings in the table.

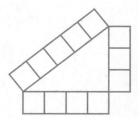

Reflect

1. Draw Conclusions Based on your observations, explain whether you think the converse of the Pythagorean Theorem is true.

_____

_____

Identifying a Right Triangle

The converse of the Pythagorean Theorem gives you a way to tell if a triangle is a right triangle when you know the side lengths.

EXAMPLE 1

 **TEKS** 8.7.C

Tell whether each triangle with the given side lengths is a right triangle.

A 9 inches, 40 inches, and 41 inches

Let $a = 9$, $b = 40$, and $c = 41$.

$$a^2 + b^2 = c^2$$

$$9^2 + 40^2 \overset{?}{=} 41^2 \qquad \text{Substitute into the formula.}$$

$$81 + 1600 \overset{?}{=} 1681 \qquad \text{Simpify.}$$

$$1681 = 1681 \qquad \text{Add.}$$

Since $9^2 + 40^2 = 41^2$, the triangle is a right triangle by the converse of the Pythagorean Theorem.

B 8 meters, 10 meters, and 12 meters

Let $a = 8$, $b = 10$, and $c = 12$.

$$a^2 + b^2 = c^2$$

$$8^2 + 10^2 \overset{?}{=} 12^2 \qquad \text{Substitute into the formula.}$$

$$64 + 100 \overset{?}{=} 144 \qquad \text{Simpify.}$$

$$164 \neq 144 \qquad \text{Add.}$$

Since $8^2 + 10^2 \neq 12^2$, the triangle is not a right triangle by the converse of the Pythagorean Theorem.

YOUR TURN

Tell whether each triangle with the given side lengths is a right triangle.

2. 14 cm, 23 cm, and 25 cm

_____

3. 16 in., 30 in., and 34 in.

_____

4. 27 ft, 36 ft, 45 ft

_____

5. 11 mm, 18 mm, 21 mm

_____

Using the Converse of the Pythagorean Theorem

You can use the converse of the Pythagorean Theorem to solve real-world problems.

EXAMPLE 2 Real World

 TEKS 8.7.C

Katya is buying edging for a triangular flower garden she plans to build in her backyard. If the lengths of the three pieces of edging that she purchases are 13 feet, 10 feet, and 7 feet, will the flower garden be in the shape of a right triangle?

Use the converse of the Pythagorean Theorem. Remember to use the longest length for c.

Let $a = 7$, $b = 10$, and $c = 13$.

$$a^2 + b^2 = c^2$$

$7^2 + 10^2 \overset{?}{=} 13^2$ Substitute into the formula.

$49 + 100 \overset{?}{=} 169$ Simpify.

$149 \neq 169$ Add.

Since $7^2 + 10^2 \neq 13^2$, the garden will not be in the shape of a right triangle.

> **Math Talk**
> Mathematical Processes
>
> To what length, to the nearest tenth, can Katya trim the longest piece of edging to form a right triangle?

YOUR TURN

6. A blueprint for a new triangular playground shows that the sides measure 480 ft, 140 ft, and 500 ft. Is the playground in the shape of a right triangle? Explain.

_____

_____

7. A triangular piece of glass has sides that measure 18 in., 19 in., and 25 in. Is the piece of glass in the shape of a right triangle? Explain.

_____

8. A corner of a fenced yard forms a right angle. Can you place a 12 foot long board across the corner to form a right triangle for which the leg lengths are whole numbers? Explain.

_____

_____

Personal
Math Trainer

Online Assessment
and Intervention

my.hrw.com

1. Lashandra used grid paper to construct the triangle shown. (Explore Activity)

   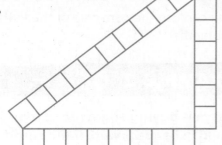

   a. What are the lengths of the sides of Lashandra's triangle?

   _____units, _____units, _____units

   b. Use the converse of the Pythagorean Theorem
      to determine whether the triangle is a right triangle.

   $$a^2 + b^2 = c^2$$

   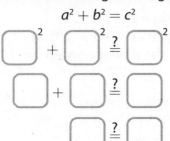

   The triangle that Lashandra constructed | is / is not | a right triangle.

2. A triangle has side lengths 9 cm, 12 cm, and 16 cm. Tell whether the triangle
   is a right triangle. (Example 1)

   Let $a = $ _____, $b = $ _____, and $c = $ _____.

   $$a^2 + b^2 = c^2$$

   By the converse of the Pythagorean Theorem, the triangle | is / is not |
   a right triangle.

3. The marketing team at a new electronics company is designing a logo that
   contains a circle and a triangle. On one design, the triangle's side lengths are
   2.5 in., 6 in., and 6.5 in. Is the triangle a right triangle? Explain. (Example 2)

   _____

4. How can you use the converse of the Pythagorean Theorem
   to tell if a triangle is a right triangle?

   _____

   _____

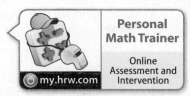

8.2 Independent Practice

 TEKS 8.7.C

Personal Math Trainer

Online Assessment and Intervention

my.hrw.com

Tell whether each triangle with the given side lengths is a right triangle.

5. 11 cm, 60 cm, 61 cm

_____

6. 5 ft, 12 ft, 15 ft

_____

7. 9 in., 15 in., 17 in.

_____

8. 15 m, 36 m, 39 m

_____

9. 20 mm, 30 mm, 40 mm

_____

10. 20 cm, 48 cm, 52 cm

_____

11. 18.5 ft, 6 ft, 17.5 ft

_____

12. 2 mi, 1.5 mi, 2.5 mi

_____

13. 35 in., 45 in., 55 in.

_____

14. 25 cm, 14 cm, 23 cm

_____

15. The emblem on a college banner consists of the face of a tiger inside a triangle. The lengths of the sides of the triangle are 13 cm, 14 cm, and 15 cm. Is the triangle a right triangle? Explain.

_____

16. Kerry has a large triangular piece of fabric that she wants to attach to the ceiling in her bedroom. The sides of the piece of fabric measure 4.8 ft, 6.4 ft, and 8 ft. Is the fabric in the shape of a right triangle? Explain.

_____

17. A mosaic consists of triangular tiles. The smallest tiles have side lengths 6 cm, 10 cm, and 12 cm. Are these tiles in the shape of right triangles? Explain.

_____

18. **History** In ancient Egypt, surveyors made right angles by stretching a rope with evenly spaced knots as shown. Explain why the rope forms a right angle.

_____

_____

_____

19. Justify Reasoning Yoshi has two identical triangular boards as shown. Can he use these two boards to form a rectangle? Explain.

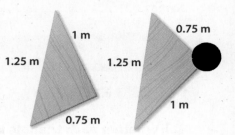

_____

_____

_____

20. Critique Reasoning Shoshanna says that a triangle with side lengths 17 m, 8 m, and 15 m is not a right triangle because $17^2 + 8^2 = 353$, $15^2 = 225$, and $353 \neq 225$. Is she correct? Explain.

_____

_____

 FOCUS ON HIGHER ORDER THINKING

21. Make a Conjecture Diondre says that he can take any right triangle and make a new right triangle just by doubling the side lengths. Is Diondre's conjecture true? Test his conjecture using three different right triangles.

_____

_____

_____

_____

22. Draw Conclusions A diagonal of a parallelogram measures 37 inches. The sides measure 35 inches and 1 foot. Is the parallelogram a rectangle? Explain your reasoning.

_____

_____

_____

23. Represent Real-World Problems A soccer coach is marking the lines for a soccer field on a large recreation field. The dimensions of the field are to be 90 yards by 48 yards. Describe a procedure she could use to confirm that the sides of the field meet at right angles.

_____

_____

_____

TEKS
Expressions, equations, and relationships—
8.7.D Determine the distance between two points on a coordinate plane using the Pythagorean Theorem.

? **ESSENTIAL QUESTION**

How can you use the Pythagorean Theorem to find the distance between two points on a coordinate plane?

Pythagorean Theorem in the Coordinate Plane

EXAMPLE 1  **TEKS** 8.7.D

Math On the Spot
my.hrw.com

The figure shows a right triangle. Approximate the length of the hypotenuse to the nearest tenth without using a calculator.

STEP 1 Find the length of each leg.

The length of the vertical leg is 4 units.

The length of the horizontal leg is 2 units.

STEP 2 Let $a = 4$ and $b = 2$. Let c represent the length of the hypotenuse. Use the Pythagorean Theorem to find c.

$$a^2 + b^2 = c^2$$

$$4^2 + 2^2 = c^2 \quad \text{Substitute into the formula.}$$

$$20 = c^2 \quad \text{Add.}$$

$$\sqrt{20} = c \quad \text{Take the square root of both sides.}$$

STEP 3 Approximate $\sqrt{20}$ by finding perfect squares close to 20.

$\sqrt{20}$ is between $\sqrt{16}$ and $\sqrt{25}$, or $\sqrt{16} < \sqrt{20} < \sqrt{25}$.

Simplifying gives $4 < \sqrt{20} < 5$.

Since 20 is about halfway between 16 and 25, $\sqrt{20}$ is about halfway between 4 and 5. So, $\sqrt{20} \approx 4.5$.

The hypotenuse is about 4.5 units long.

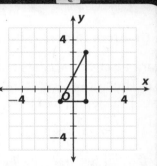

YOUR TURN

1. Approximate the length of the hypotenuse to the nearest tenth without using a calculator.

_____

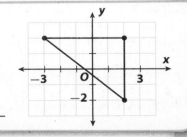
Personal Math Trainer
Online Assessment and Intervention
my.hrw.com

Finding the Distance Between Any Two Points

The Pythagorean Theorem can be used to find the distance between any two points (x_1, y_1) and (x_2, y_2) in the coordinate plane. The resulting expression is called the Distance Formula.

> **Distance Formula**
>
> In a coordinate plane, the distance d between two points (x_1, y_1) and (x_2, y_2) is
> $$d = \sqrt{(x_2 - x_1)^2 + (y_2 - y_1)^2}.$$

Use the Pythagorean Theorem to derive the Distance Formula.

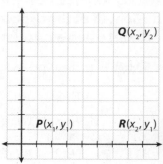

A To find the distance between points P and Q, draw segment $\overline{PQ}$ and label its length d. Then draw horizontal segment $\overline{PR}$ and vertical segment $\overline{QR}$. Label the lengths of these segments a and b. Triangle

PQR is a _____ triangle, with hypotenuse _____.

B Since $\overline{PR}$ is a horizontal segment, its length, a, is the difference

between its x-coordinates. Therefore, $a = x_2 -$ _____.

C Since $\overline{QR}$ is a vertical segment, its length, b, is the difference between

its y-coordinates. Therefore, $b = y_2 -$ _____.

D Use the Pythagorean Theorem to find d, the length of segment $\overline{PQ}$. Substitute the expressions from **B** and **C** for a and b.

$d^2 = a^2 + b^2$

$d = \sqrt{a^2 + b^2}$

$d = \sqrt{\left(\boxed{} - \boxed{}\right)^2 + \left(\boxed{} - \boxed{}\right)^2}$

Math Talk
Mathematical Processes

What do $x_2 - x_1$ and $y_2 - y_1$ represent in terms of the Pythagorean Theorem?

Reflect

2. Why are the coordinates of point R the ordered pair (x_2, y_1)?

_____

_____

_____

Finding the Distance Between Two Points

The Pythagorean Theorem can be used to find the distance between two points in a real-world situation. You can do this by using a coordinate grid that overlays a diagram of the real-world situation.

Math On the Spot
my.hrw.com

EXAMPLE 2 Real World    TEKS 8.7.D

Francesca wants to find the distance between her house on one side of a lake and the beach on the other side. She marks off a third point forming a right triangle, as shown. The distances in the diagram are measured in meters.

Use the Pythagorean Theorem to find the straight-line distance from Francesca's house to the beach.

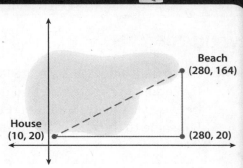

House
(10, 20)

Beach
(280, 164)

(280, 20)

STEP 1 Find the length of the horizontal leg.

The length of the horizontal leg is the absolute value of the difference between the x-coordinates of the points (280, 20) and (10, 20).

$$|280 - 10| = 270$$

The length of the horizontal leg is 270 meters.

STEP 2 Find the length of the vertical leg.

The length of the vertical leg is the absolute value of the difference between the y-coordinates of the points (280, 164) and (280, 20).

$$|164 - 20| = 144$$

The length of the vertical leg is 144 meters.

STEP 3 Let $a = 270$ and $b = 144$. Let c represent the length of the hypotenuse. Use the Pythagorean Theorem to find c.

$$a^2 + b^2 = c^2$$

$270^2 + 144^2 = c^2$ Substitute into the formula.

$72{,}900 + 20{,}736 = c^2$ Simplify.

$93{,}636 = c^2$ Add.

$\sqrt{93{,}636} = c$ Take the square root of both sides.

$306 = c$ Simplify.

The distance from Francesca's house to the beach is 306 meters.

> **Math Talk**
> Mathematical Processes
>
> Why is it necessary to take the absolute value of the coordinates when finding the length of a segment?

Reflect

3. Show how you could use the Distance Formula to find the distance from Francesca's house to the beach.

_____

_____

_____

YOUR TURN

4. Camp Sunshine is also on the lake. Use the Pythagorean Theorem to find the distance between Francesca's house and Camp Sunshine to the nearest tenth of a meter.

_____

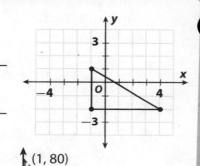

Camp Sunshine (200, 120)

House (10, 20)   (200, 20)

Guided Practice

1. Approximate the length of the hypotenuse of the right triangle to the nearest tenth without using a calculator. (Example 1)   _____

2. Find the distance between the points (3, 7) and (15, 12) on the coordinate plane. (Explore Activity) _____

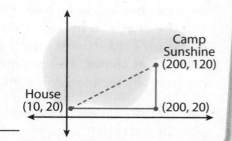

3. A plane leaves an airport and flies due north. Two minutes later, a second plane leaves the same airport flying due east. The flight plan shows the coordinates of the two planes 10 minutes later. The distances in the graph are measured in miles. Use the Pythagorean Theorem to find the distance shown between the two planes.

(Example 2) _____

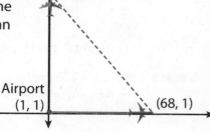

(1, 80)

Airport (1, 1)   (68, 1)

? ESSENTIAL QUESTION CHECK-IN

4. Describe two ways to find the distance between two points on a coordinate plane.

_____

_____

_____

8.3 Independent Practice

 TEKS 8.7.D

Personal
Math Trainer

Online
Assessment and
Intervention

my.hrw.com

5. A metal worker traced a triangular piece of sheet metal on a coordinate plane, as shown. The units represent inches. What is the length of the longest side of the metal triangle? Approximate the length to the nearest tenth of an inch without using a calculator.

_____

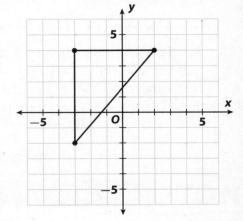

6. When a coordinate grid is superimposed on a map of Harrisburg, the high school is located at (17, 21) and the town park is located at (28, 13). If each unit represents 1 mile, how many miles apart are the high school and the town park? Round your answer to the nearest tenth.

_____

7. The coordinates of the vertices of a rectangle are given by $R(-3, -4)$, $E(-3, 4)$, $C(4, 4)$, and $T(4, -4)$. Plot these points on the coordinate plane at the right and connect them to draw the rectangle. Then connect points E and T to form diagonal $\overline{ET}$.

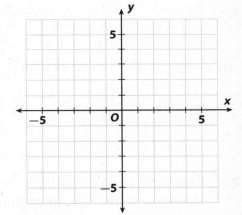

a. Use the Pythagorean Theorem to find the exact length of $\overline{ET}$.

_____

b. How can you use the Distance Formula to find the length of $\overline{ET}$? Show that the Distance Formula gives the same answer.

_____

_____

_____

_____

_____

8. Multistep The locations of three ships are represented on a coordinate grid by the following points: $P(-2, 5)$, $Q(-7, -5)$, and $R(2, -3)$. Which ships are farthest apart?

_____

9. Make a Conjecture Find as many points as you can that are 5 units from the origin. Make a conjecture about the shape formed if all the points 5 units from the origin were connected.

_____

_____

_____

10. Justify Reasoning The graph shows the location of a motion detector that has a maximum range of 34 feet. A peacock at point *P* displays its tail feathers. Will the motion detector sense this motion? Explain.

_____

_____

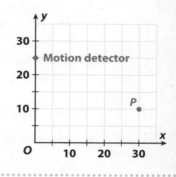

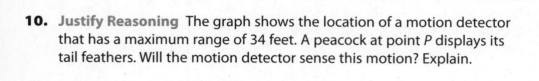
FOCUS ON HIGHER ORDER THINKING

11. Persevere in Problem Solving One leg of an isosceles right triangle has endpoints (1, 1) and (6, 1). The other leg passes through the point (6, 2). Draw the triangle on the coordinate plane below. Then show how you can use the Distance Formula to find the length of the hypotenuse. Round your answer to the nearest tenth.

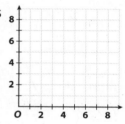

_____

_____

_____

12. Represent Real-World Problems The figure shows a representation of a football field. The units represent yards. A sports analyst marks the locations of the football from where it was thrown (point *A*) and where it was caught (point *B*). Explain how you can use the Pythagorean Theorem to find the distance the ball was thrown. Then find the distance.

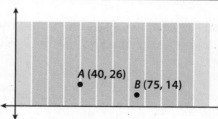

_____

_____

_____

_____

_____

Ready to Go On?

8.1 The Pythagorean Theorem

Find the length of the missing side.

1.

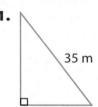

35 m

21 m

_____

2.

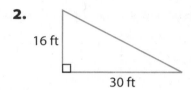

16 ft

30 ft

_____

8.2 Converse of the Pythagorean Theorem

Tell whether each triangle with the given side lengths is a right triangle.

3. 11, 60, 61 _____

4. 9, 37, 40 _____

5. 15, 35, 38 _____

6. 28, 45, 53 _____

7. Keelie has a triangular-shaped card. The lengths of its sides are 4.5 cm, 6 cm, and 7.5 cm. Is the card a right triangle? _____

8.3 Distance Between Two Points

Find the distance between the given points. Round to the nearest tenth.

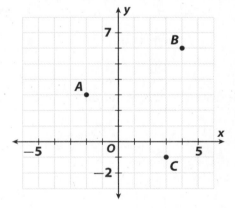

8. *A* and *B* _____

9. *B* and *C* _____

10. *A* and *C* _____

? **ESSENTIAL QUESTION**

11. How can you use the Pythagorean Theorem to solve real-world problems?

_____

_____

_____

Texas Test Prep

Personal Math Trainer

Online Assessment and Intervention

my.hrw.com

Selected Response

1. What is the missing length of the side?

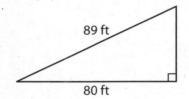

89 ft
80 ft

- (A) 9 ft
- (C) 39 ft
- (B) 30 ft
- (D) 120 ft

2. Which relation does **not** represent a function?

- (A) (0, 8), (3, 8), (1, 6)
- (B) (4, 2), (6, 1), (8, 9)
- (C) (1, 20), (2, 23), (9, 26)
- (D) (0, 3), (2, 3), (2, 0)

3. Two sides of a right triangle have lengths of 72 cm and 97 cm. The third side is **not** the hypotenuse. How long is the third side?

- (A) 25 cm
- (C) 65 cm
- (B) 45 cm
- (D) 121 cm

4. What is the distance between point *F* and point *G*?

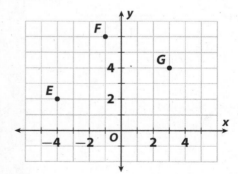

- (A) 4.5 units
- (C) 7.3 units
- (B) 5 units
- (D) 20 units

5. A flagpole is 53 feet tall. A rope is tied to the top of the flagpole and secured to the ground 28 feet from the base of the flagpole. What is the length of the rope?

- (A) 25 feet
- (C) 53 feet
- (B) 45 feet
- (D) 60 feet

6. Which set of lengths are **not** the side lengths of a right triangle?

- (A) 36, 77, 85
- (C) 27, 120, 123
- (B) 20, 99, 101
- (D) 24, 33, 42

7. Which is an irrational number?

- (A) 5.4
- (C) −13
- (B) $\sqrt{7}$
- (D) $\frac{2}{9}$

8. A triangle has one right angle. What could the measures of the other two angles be?

- (A) 25° and 65°
- (C) 55° and 125°
- (B) 30° and 15°
- (D) 90° and 100°

Gridded Response

9. A right triangle has legs that measure 1.5 centimeters and 2 centimeters. What is the length of the hypotenuse in centimeters?

				•		
⓪	⓪	⓪	⓪		⓪	⓪
①	①	①	①		①	①
②	②	②	②		②	②
③	③	③	③		③	③
④	④	④	④		④	④
⑤	⑤	⑤	⑤		⑤	⑤
⑥	⑥	⑥	⑥		⑥	⑥
⑦	⑦	⑦	⑦		⑦	⑦
⑧	⑧	⑧	⑧		⑧	⑧
⑨	⑨	⑨	⑨		⑨	⑨

Volume

ESSENTIAL QUESTION

How can you use volume to solve real-world problems?

Real-World Video

Many foods are in the shape of cylinders, cones, and spheres. To find out how much of the food you are eating, you can use formulas for volume.

ⓞ my.hrw.com

GO DIGITAL
my.hrw.com

my.hrw.com

Go digital with your write-in student edition, accessible on any device.

Math On the Spot

Scan with your smart phone to jump directly to the online edition, video tutor, and more.

Animated Math

Interactively explore key concepts to see how math works.

Personal Math Trainer

Get immediate feedback and help as you work through practice sets.

Are YOU Ready?

Complete these exercises to review skills you will need for this chapter.

 Personal Math Trainer

Online Assessment and Intervention

my.hrw.com

Exponents

EXAMPLE $6^3 = 6 \times 6 \times 6$ Multiply the base (6) by itself the number of times indicated by the exponent (3).

$= 36 \times 6$ Find the product of the first two terms.

$= 216$ Find the product of all the terms.

Evaluate each exponential expression.

1. 11^2 _____   **2.** 2^5 _____   **3.** $\left(\frac{1}{5}\right)^3$ _____   **4.** $(0.3)^2$ _____

5. 2.1^3 _____   **6.** 0.1^3 _____   **7.** $\left(\frac{9.6}{3}\right)^2$ _____   **8.** 100^3 _____

Round Decimals

EXAMPLE   Round 43.2685 to the underlined place.

$43.2685 \rightarrow 43.27$

The digit to be rounded: 6
The digit to its right is 8.
8 is *5 or greater,* so round *up.*
The rounded number is 43.27.

Round to the underlined place.

9. 2.3<u>7</u>4 _____   **10.** 12<u>6</u>.399 _____   **11.** 13.<u>9</u>577 _____   **12.** 42.6<u>9</u>0 _____

13. 134.<u>9</u>5 _____   **14.** 2.<u>0</u>486 _____   **15.** 63.6<u>3</u>52 _____   **16.** 98.<u>9</u>499 _____

Simplify Numerical Expressions

EXAMPLE $\frac{1}{3} (3.14) (4)^2 (3) = \frac{1}{3} (3.14) (16) (3)$ Simplify the exponent.

$= 50.24$ Multiply from left to right.

Simplify each expression.

17. $3.14 (5)^2 (10)$ _____   **18.** $\frac{1}{3} (3.14) (3)^2 (5)$ _____   **19.** $\frac{4}{3} (3.14) (3)^3$ _____

20. $\frac{4}{3} (3.14) (6)^3$ _____   **21.** $3.14 (4)^2 (9)$ _____   **22.** $\frac{1}{3} (3.14) (9)^2 \left(\frac{2}{3}\right)$ _____

Reading Start-Up

Visualize Vocabulary

Use the ✔ words to complete the empty columns in the chart. You may use words more than once.

Shape	Distance Around	Attributes	Associated Review Words
circle		r, d	
square		90° corner, sides	
rectangle		90° corner, sides	

Vocabulary

Review Words

area *(área)*

base *(base, en numeración)*

✔ circumference *(circunferencia)*

✔ diameter *(diámetro)*

height *(altura)*

✔ length *(longitud)*

✔ perimeter *(perímetro)*

✔ radius *(radio)*

✔ right angle *(ángulo recto)*

✔ width *(ancho)*

Preview Words

cone *(cono)*

cylinder *(cilindro)*

sphere *(esfera)*

Understand Vocabulary

Complete the sentences using the preview words.

1. A three-dimensional figure that has one vertex and one circular base is a _____.

2. A three-dimensional figure with all points the same distance from the center is a _____.

3. A three-dimensional figure that has two congruent circular bases is a _____.

Active Reading

Three-Panel Flip Chart Before beginning the module, create a three-panel flip chart to help you organize what you learn. Label each flap with one of the lesson titles from this module. As you study each lesson, write important ideas like vocabulary, properties, and formulas under the appropriate flap.

Unpacking the TEKS

Understanding the TEKS and the vocabulary terms in the TEKS will help you know exactly what you are expected to learn in this module.

© Houghton Mifflin Harcourt Publishing Company

TEKS 8.6.A

Describe the volume formula $V = Bh$ of a cylinder in terms of its base and its height.

Key Vocabulary

formula *(fórmula)*
A rule showing relationships among quantities.

volume *(volumen)*
The number of cubic units needed to fill a given space.

cylinder *(cilindro)*
A three-dimensional figure with two parallel, congruent circular bases connected by a curved lateral surface.

What It Means to You

You will learn the formula for the volume of a cylinder.

UNPACKING EXAMPLE 8.6.A

The Asano Taiko Company of Japan built the world's largest drum in 2000. The drum's diameter is 4.8 meters, and its height is 4.95 meters. Estimate the volume of the drum.

$$d = 4.8 \approx 5$$
$$h = 4.95 \approx 5$$
$$r = \frac{d}{2} = \frac{5}{2} = 2.5$$

Volume of a cylinder.

$$V = (\pi r^2)h$$

Use 3 for π.

$$= (3)(2.5)^2 \cdot 5$$
$$= (3)(6.25)(5)$$
$$= 18.75 \cdot 5$$
$$= 93.75$$
$$\approx 94$$

The volume of the drum is approximately 94 m³.

TEKS 8.7.A

Solve problems involving the volume of cylinders, cones, and spheres.

Key Vocabulary

cone *(cono)*
A three-dimensional figure with one vertex and one circular base.

What It Means to You

You will learn the formula for the volume of a cone.

UNPACKING EXAMPLE 8.7.A

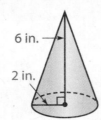

6 in.

2 in.

Find the volume of the cone. Use 3.14 for π.

$$B = \pi(2^2) = 4\pi \text{ in}^2$$
$$V = \frac{1}{3} \cdot 4\pi \cdot 6$$
$$V = 8\pi$$
$$\approx 25.1 \text{ in}^3$$

$V = \frac{1}{3}Bh$

Use 3.14 for π.

The volume of the cone is approximately 25.1 in³.

Visit **my.hrw.com** to see all the **TEKS** unpacked.

 my.hrw.com

TEKS
Expressions, equations, and relationships—8.6.A
Describe the volume formula $V = Bh$ of a cylinder in terms of its base area and height.
8.7.A Solve problems involving the volume of cylinders.

? **ESSENTIAL QUESTION**

How do you find the volume of a cylinder?

EXPLORE ACTIVITY  **TEKS** 8.6.A

Modeling the Volume of a Cylinder

A **cylinder** is a three-dimensional figure that has two congruent circular bases that lie in parallel planes. The volume of any three-dimensional figure is the number of cubic units needed to fill the space taken up by the solid figure.

One cube represents one cubic unit of volume. You can develop the formula for the volume of a cylinder using an empty soup can or other cylindrical container. First, remove one of the bases.

A Arrange centimeter cubes in a single layer at the bottom of the cylinder. Fit as many cubes into the layer as possible. How many cubes are in this layer?

_____

B To find how many layers of cubes fit in the cylinder, make a stack of cubes along the inside of the cylinder. How many layers fit in the cylinder?

_____

C How can you use what you know to find the approximate number of cubes that would fit in the cylinder?

_____

_____

Reflect

1. **Make a Conjecture** Suppose you know the area of the base of a cylinder and the height of the cylinder. How can you find the cylinder's volume?

_____

2. Let the area of the base of a cylinder be B and the height of the cylinder be h. Write a formula for the cylinder's volume V. _____

Finding the Volume of a Cylinder Using a Formula

Finding volumes of cylinders is similar to finding volumes of prisms. You find the volume V of both a prism and a cylinder by multiplying the height h by the area of the base B, so $V = Bh$.

The base of a cylinder is a circle, so for a cylinder, $B = \pi r^2$.

Volume of a Cylinder

The volume V of a cylinder with radius r is the area of the base B times the height h.

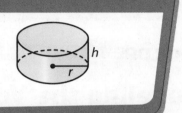

$V = Bh$ or $V = \pi r^2 h$

EXAMPLE 1   **TEKS** 8.7.A

Find the volume of each cylinder. Round your answers to the nearest tenth if necessary. Use 3.14 for π.

A

10 in.

3 in.

$V = \pi r^2 h$

$\approx 3.14 \cdot 3^2 \cdot 10$ Substitute.

$\approx 3.14 \cdot 9 \cdot 10$ Simplify.

≈ 282.6 Multiply.

The volume is about 282.6 in³.

B   6.4 cm   13 cm

Since the diameter is 6.4 cm, the radius is 3.2 cm.

> Recall that the diameter of a circle is twice the radius, so $2r = d$ and $r = \frac{d}{2}$.

$V = \pi r^2 h$

$\approx 3.14 \cdot 3.2^2 \cdot 13$ Substitute.

$\approx 3.14 \cdot 10.24 \cdot 13$ Simplify.

≈ 418 Multiply.

The volume is about 418 cm³.

My Notes

Reflect

3. **What If?** If you want a formula for the volume of a cylinder that involves the diameter d instead of the radius r, how can you rewrite it?

_____

© Houghton Mifflin Harcourt Publishing Company

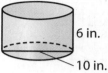

Find the volume of each cylinder. Round your answers to the nearest tenth if necessary. Use 3.14 for π.

4.

6 in.

10 in.

_____

5.

4 ft

12 ft

_____

Finding the Volume of a Cylinder in a Real-World Context

The Longhorn Band at the University of Texas at Austin has one of the world's largest bass drums, known as Big Bertha.

EXAMPLE 2 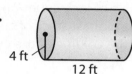   TEKS 8.7.A

Big Bertha has a diameter of 8 feet and is 4.5 feet deep. Find the volume of the drum to the nearest tenth. Use 3.14 for π.

STEP 1 Find the radius of the drum.

$$r = \frac{d}{2} = \frac{8}{2} = 4 \text{ ft}$$

STEP 2 Find the volume of the drum.

$$V = \pi r^2 h$$

$\approx 3.14 \cdot 4^2 \cdot 4.5$ Substitute.

$\approx 3.14 \cdot 16 \cdot 4.5$ Simplify the exponent.

≈ 226.08 Multiply.

The volume of the drum is about 226.1 ft³.

YOUR TURN

6. A drum company advertises a snare drum that is 4 inches high and 12 inches in diameter. Find the volume of the drum to the nearest tenth. Use 3.14 for π.

_____

1. Vocabulary Describe the bases of a cylinder. (Explore Activity)

_____

2. Figure 1 shows a view from above of inch cubes on the bottom of a cylinder. Figure 2 shows the highest stack of cubes that will fit inside the cylinder. Estimate the volume of the cylinder. Explain your reasoning. (Explore Activity)

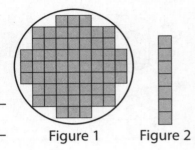

Figure 1   Figure 2

_____

_____

_____

3. Find the volume of the cylinder to the nearest tenth. Use 3.14 for π. (Example 1)

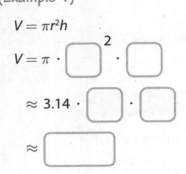

$V = \pi r^2 h$

$V = \pi \cdot \boxed{}^2 \cdot \boxed{}$

$\approx 3.14 \cdot \boxed{} \cdot \boxed{}$

$\approx \boxed{}$

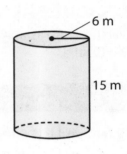

6 m

15 m

The volume of the cylinder is approximately _____ m³.

4. A Japanese odaiko is a very large drum that is made by hollowing out a section of a tree trunk. A museum in Takayama City hold three odaikos of similar size carved from a single tree trunk. The largest measures about 2.7 meters in both diameter and length, and weighs about 4.5 metric tons. Using the volume formula for a cylinder, approximate the volume of the drum to the nearest tenth. (Example 2)

The radius of the drum is about _____ m.

The volume of the drum is about _____ m³.

? ESSENTIAL QUESTION CHECK-IN

5. How do you find the volume of a cylinder? Describe which measurements of a cylinder you need to know.

_____

_____

_____

9.1 Independent Practice

 **TEKS** 8.6.A, 8.7.A

Find the volume of each figure. Round your answers to the nearest tenth if necessary. Use 3.14 for π.

6.
1.5 cm
11 cm

_____

7.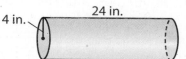
4 in.
24 in.

_____

8.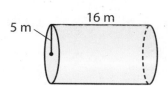
5 m
16 m

_____

9.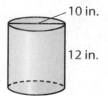
10 in.
12 in.

_____

10. A cylinder has a radius of 4 centimeters and a height of 40 centimeters.

_____

11. A cylinder has a radius of 8 meters and a height of 4 meters.

_____

Round your answer to the nearest tenth, if necessary. Use 3.14 for π.

12. The cylindrical Giant Ocean Tank at the New England Aquarium in Boston is 24 feet deep and has a radius of 18.8 feet. Find the volume of the tank.

_____

13. A standard-size bass drum has a diameter of 22 inches and is 18 inches deep. Find the volume of this drum.

_____

14. Grain is stored in cylindrical structures called silos. Find the volume of a silo with a diameter of 11.1 feet and a height of 20 feet.

_____

15. The Frank Erwin Center, or "The Drum," at the University of Texas in Austin can be approximated by a cylinder that is 120 meters in diameter and 30 meters in height. Find its volume.

_____

16. A barrel of crude oil contains about 5.61 cubic feet of oil. How many barrels of oil are contained in 1 mile (5280 feet) of a pipeline that has an inside diameter of 6 inches and is completely filled with oil? How much is "1 mile" of oil in this pipeline worth at a price of $100 per barrel?

_____

17. A pan for baking French bread is shaped like half a cylinder. It is 12 inches long and 3.5 inches in diameter. What is the volume of uncooked dough that would fill this pan?

_____

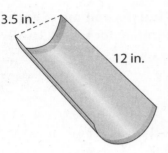

3.5 in.

12 in.

 **FOCUS ON HIGHER ORDER THINKING**

18. What's the Error? A student said the volume of a cylinder with a 3-inch diameter is two times the volume of a cylinder with the same height and a 1.5-inch radius. What is the error?

_____

_____

_____

19. Communicate Mathematical Ideas Explain how you can find the height of a cylinder if you know the diameter and the volume. Include an example with your explanation.

_____

_____

_____

_____

_____

_____

20. Analyze Relationships Cylinder A has a radius of 6 centimeters. Cylinder B has the same height and a radius half as long as cylinder A. What fraction of the volume of cylinder A is the volume of cylinder B? Explain.

_____

_____

_____

_____

Work Area

TEKS
Expressions, equations, and relationships—8.6.B
Model the relationship between the volume of a cylinder and a cone . . . and connect that relationship to the formulas.
8.7.A Solve problems involving the volume of cones.

? ESSENTIAL QUESTION

How do you find the volume of a cone?

EXPLORE ACTIVITY  **TEKS** 8.6.B

Modeling the Volume of a Cone

A **cone** is a three-dimensional figure that has one vertex and one circular base.

To explore the volume of a cone, Sandi does an experiment with a cone and a cylinder that have congruent bases and heights. She fills the cone with popcorn kernels and then pours the kernels into the cylinder. She repeats this until the cylinder is full.

Sandi finds that it takes 3 cones to fill the volume of the cylinder.

STEP 1 What is the formula for the volume V of a cylinder with base area B and height h? _____

STEP 2 What is the area of the base of the cone? _____

STEP 3 Sandi found that, when the bases and height are the same,

_____ times $V_{cone} = V_{cylinder}$.

STEP 4 How does the volume of the cone compare to the volume of the cylinder?

Volume of the cone: $V_{cone} = \dfrac{\square}{\square} \cdot V_{cylinder}$

Reflect

1. Use the conclusion from this experiment to write a formula for the volume of a cone in terms of the height and the radius. Explain.

_____

2. How are the formulas for the volume of a cone and a prism similar?

_____

Finding the Volume of a Cone Using a Formula

The formulas for the volume of a prism and the volume of a cylinder are the same: multiply the height h by the area of the base B, so $V = Bh$.

In the **Explore Activity**, you saw that the volume of a cone is one third the volume of a cylinder with the same base and height.

Volume of a Cone

The volume V of a cone with radius r is one third the area of the base B times the height h. $V = \frac{1}{3}Bh$ or $V = \frac{1}{3}\pi r^2 h$	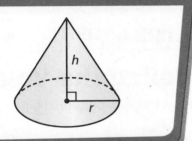

EXAMPLE 1

 TEKS 8.7.A

Find the volume of each cone. Round your answers to the nearest tenth. Use 3.14 for π.

A

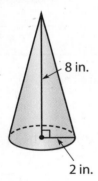
8 in.
2 in.

$V = \frac{1}{3}\pi r^2 h$

$\approx \frac{1}{3} \cdot 3.14 \cdot 2^2 \cdot 8$ Substitute.

$\approx \frac{1}{3} \cdot 3.14 \cdot 4 \cdot 8$ Simplify.

≈ 33.5 Multiply.

The volume is about 33.5 in³.

B Since the diameter is 8 ft, the radius is 4 ft.

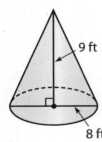
9 ft
8 ft

$V = \frac{1}{3}\pi r^2 h$

$\approx \frac{1}{3} \cdot 3.14 \cdot 4^2 \cdot 9$ Substitute.

$\approx \frac{1}{3} \cdot 3.14 \cdot 16 \cdot 9$ Simplify.

≈ 150.7 Multiply.

The volume is about 150.7 ft³.

Reflect

3. How can you rewrite the formula for the volume of a cone using the diameter d instead of the radius r? _____

Personal Math Trainer

Online Assessment and Intervention

my.hrw.com

YOUR TURN

Find the volume of each cone. Round your answers to the nearest tenth. Use 3.14 for π.

4.

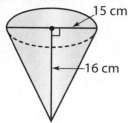

15 cm

16 cm

5.

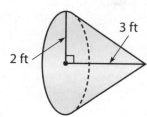

3 ft

2 ft

_____   _____

Finding the Volume of a Volcano

The mountain created by a volcano is often cone–shaped.

EXAMPLE 2 Real World   TEKS 8.7.A

For her geography project, Karen built a clay model of a volcano in the shape of a cone. Her model has a diameter of 12 inches and a height of 8 inches. Find the volume of clay in her model to the nearest tenth. Use 3.14 for π.

STEP 1 Find the radius.

$r = \frac{12}{2} = 6$ in.

STEP 2 Find the volume of clay.

$V = \frac{1}{3}\pi r^2 h$

$\approx \frac{1}{3} \cdot 3.14 \cdot 6^2 \cdot 8$ Substitute.

$\approx \frac{1}{3} \cdot 3.14 \cdot 36 \cdot 8$ Simplify.

≈ 301.44 Multiply.

The volume of the clay is about 301.4 in³.

YOUR TURN

6. The cone of the volcano Parícutin in Mexico had a height of 410 meters and a diameter of 424 meters. Approximate the volume of the cone.

_____

Math On the Spot

my.hrw.com

Personal Math Trainer

Online Assessment and Intervention

my.hrw.com

1. The area of the base of a cylinder is 45 square inches and its height is 10 inches. A cone has the same area for its base and the same height. What is the volume of the cone? (Explore Activity)

$$V_{cylinder} = Bh = \boxed{} \cdot \boxed{} = \boxed{}$$

$$V_{cone} = \frac{1}{3} V_{cylinder}$$

$$= \frac{1}{3} \boxed{}$$

$$= \boxed{}$$

The volume of the cone is _____ in³.

2. A cone and a cylinder have congruent height and bases. The volume of the cone is 18 m³. What is the volume of the cylinder? Explain. (Explore Activity)

_____

_____

_____

_____

_____

Find the volume of each cone. Round your answer to the nearest tenth if necessary. Use 3.14 for π. (Example 1)

3.

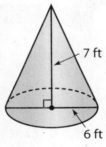

7 ft

6 ft

_____

4.

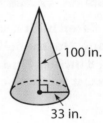

100 in.

33 in.

_____

5. Gretchen made a paper cone to hold a gift for a friend. The paper cone was 15 inches high and had a radius of 3 inches. Find the volume of the paper cone to the nearest tenth. Use 3.14 for π. (Example 2)

_____

6. A cone-shaped building is commonly used to store sand. What would be the volume of a cone-shaped building with a diameter of 50 meters and a height of 20 meters? Round your answer to the nearest tenth. Use 3.14 for π. (Example 2)

_____

? ESSENTIAL QUESTION CHECK-IN

7. How do you find the volume of a cone? For help, use the model in the Explore Activity.

_____

_____

 **9.2 Independent Practice**

TEKS 8.6.B, 8.7.A

Find the volume of each cone. Round your answers to the nearest tenth if necessary. Use 3.14 for π.

8.

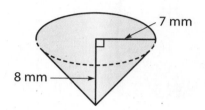

7 mm

8 mm

_____

9.

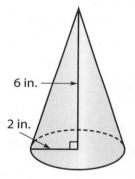

6 in.

2 in.

_____

10. A cone has a diameter of 6 centimeters and a height of 11.5 centimeters.

_____

11. A cone has a radius of 3 meters and a height of 10 meters.

_____

Round your answers to the nearest tenth if necessary. Use 3.14 for π.

12. Antonio is making mini waffle cones. Each waffle cone is 3 inches high and has a radius of $\frac{3}{4}$ inch. What is the volume of a waffle cone?

_____

13. A snack bar sells popcorn in cone-shaped containers. One container has a diameter of 8 inches and a height of 10 inches. How many cubic inches of popcorn does the container hold?

_____

14. A volcanic cone has a diameter of 300 meters and a height of 150 meters. What is the volume of the cone?

_____

15. **Multistep** Orange traffic cones come in a variety of sizes. Approximate the volume, in cubic inches, of a traffic cone that has a height of 2 feet and a diameter of 10 inches. Use 3.14 for π.

_____

Find the missing measure for each cone. Round your answers to the nearest tenth if necessary. Use 3.14 for π.

16. radius = _____

height = 6 in.

volume = 100.48 in³

17. diameter = 6 cm

height = _____

volume = 56.52 cm³

18. The diameter of a cone-shaped container is 4 inches, and its height is 6 inches. How much greater is the volume of a cylinder-shaped container with the same diameter and height? Round your answer to the nearest hundredth. Use 3.14 for π.

_____

Work Area

19. Alex wants to know the volume of sand in an hourglass. When all the sand is in the bottom, he stands a ruler up beside the hourglass and estimates the height of the cone of sand.

   a. What else does he need to measure to find the volume of sand?

   _____

   _____

   b. **Make a Conjecture** If the volume of sand is increasing at a constant rate, is the height increasing at a constant rate? Explain.

   _____

   _____

   _____

20. **Problem Solving** The diameter of a cone is x cm, the height is 18 cm, and the volume is 301.44 cm³. What is x? Use 3.14 for π.

_____

21. **Analyze Relationships** A cone has a radius of 1 foot and a height of 2 feet. How many cones of liquid would it take to fill a cylinder with a diameter of 2 feet and a height of 2 feet? Explain.

_____

_____

_____

22. **Critique Reasoning** Herb knows that the volume of a cone is one third that of a cylinder with the same base and height. He reasons that a cone with the same height as a given cylinder but 3 times the radius should therefore have the same volume as the cylinder, since $\frac{1}{3} \cdot 3 = 1$. Is Herb correct? Explain.

_____

_____

_____

_____

_____

9.3 Volume of Spheres

TEKS
Expressions, equations, and relationships—
8.7.A Solve problems involving the volume of spheres.

ESSENTIAL QUESTION

How do you find the volume of a sphere?

EXPLORE ACTIVITY  **TEKS** 8.7.A

Modeling the Volume of a Sphere

A **sphere** is a three-dimensional figure with all points the same distance from the center. The **radius** of a sphere is the distance from the center to any point on the sphere.

You have seen that a cone fills $\frac{1}{3}$ of a cylinder of the same radius and height h. If you were to do a similar experiment with a sphere of the same radius, you would find that a sphere fills $\frac{2}{3}$ of the cylinder. The cylinder's height is equal to twice the radius of the sphere.

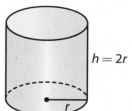 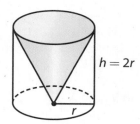 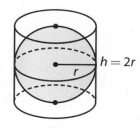

STEP 1 Write the formula $V = Bh$ for each shape. Use $B = \pi r^2$ and substitute the fractions you know for the cone and sphere.

Cylinder	Cone	Sphere
$V = \pi r^2 h$	$V = \frac{1}{3}\pi r^2 h$	$V = \frac{2}{3}\pi r^2 h$

STEP 2 Notice that a sphere always has a height equal to twice the radius. Substitute $2r$ for h. $\qquad V = \frac{2}{3}\pi r^2(2r)$

STEP 3 Simplify this formula for the volume of a sphere. $\quad V = \boxed{}\,\pi r^3$

Reflect

1. **Analyze Relationships** A cone has a radius of r and a height of $2r$. A sphere has a radius of r. Compare the volume of the sphere and cone.

_____

_____

_____

Finding the Volume of a Sphere Using a Formula

The Explore Activity illustrates a formula for the volume of a sphere with radius r.

Volume of a Sphere	
The volume V of a sphere is $\frac{4}{3}\pi$ times the cube of the radius r.	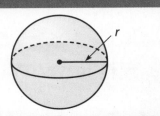
$V = \frac{4}{3}\pi r^3$	

EXAMPLE 1

TEKS 8.7.A

Find the volume of each sphere. Round your answers to the nearest tenth if necessary. Use 3.14 for π.

A

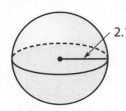

2.1 cm

$V = \frac{4}{3}\pi r^3$

$\approx \frac{4}{3} \cdot 3.14 \cdot 2.1^3$ Substitute.

$\approx \frac{4}{3} \cdot 3.14 \cdot 9.26$ Simplify.

≈ 38.8 Multiply.

The volume is about 38.8 cm³.

B

7 cm

Since the diameter is 7 cm, the radius is 3.5 cm.

$V = \frac{4}{3}\pi r^3$

$\approx \frac{4}{3} \cdot 3.14 \cdot 3.5^3$ Substitute.

$\approx \frac{4}{3} \cdot 3.14 \cdot 42.9$ Simplify.

≈ 179.6 Multiply.

The volume is about 179.6 cm³.

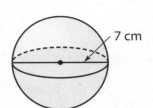

YOUR TURN

Find the volume of each sphere. Round your answers to the nearest tenth. Use 3.14 for π.

2. A sphere has a radius of 10 centimeters. _____

3. A sphere has a diameter of 3.4 meters. _____

Finding the Volume of a Sphere in a Real-World Context

Many sports, including golf and tennis, use a ball that is spherical in shape.

EXAMPLE 2 🌐 TEKS 8.7.A

Soccer balls come in several different sizes. One soccer ball has a diameter of 22 centimeters. What is the volume of this soccer ball? Round your answer to the nearest tenth. Use 3.14 for π.

STEP 1 Find the radius.

$$r = \frac{d}{2} = 11 \text{ cm}$$

STEP 2 Find the volume of the soccer ball.

$$V = \frac{4}{3}\pi r^3$$
$$\approx \frac{4}{3} \cdot 3.14 \cdot 11^3 \qquad \text{Substitute.}$$
$$\approx \frac{4}{3} \cdot 3.14 \cdot 1331 \qquad \text{Simplify.}$$
$$\approx 5572.4533 \qquad \text{Multiply.}$$

The volume of the soccer ball is about 5572.5 cm³.

Reflect

4. What is the volume of the soccer ball in terms of π, to the nearest whole number multiple? Explain your answer.

_____

_____

5. **Analyze Relationships** The diameter of a basketball is about 1.1 times that of a soccer ball. The diameter of a tennis ball is about 0.3 times that of a soccer ball. How do the volumes of these balls compare to that of a soccer ball? Explain.

_____

_____

_____

 **YOUR TURN**

6. Val measures the diameter of a ball as 12 inches. How many cubic inches of air does this ball hold, to the nearest tenth? Use 3.14 for π.

_____

 **Personal Math Trainer**

Online Assessment and Intervention

⏻ my.hrw.com

1. **Vocabulary** A sphere is a three-dimensional figure with all points

   _____ from the center. (Explore Activity)

2. **Vocabulary** The _____ is the distance from the center
   of a sphere to a point on the sphere. (Explore Activity)

**Find the volume of each sphere. Round your answers to the nearest tenth
if necessary. Use 3.14 for π.** (Example 1)

3.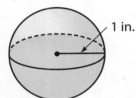
1 in.

_____

4.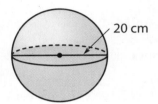
20 cm

_____

5. A sphere has a radius of 1.5 feet. _____

6. A sphere has a diameter of 2 yards. _____

7. A baseball has a diameter of 2.9 inches. Find the volume of the baseball. Round
   your answer to the nearest tenth if necessary. Use 3.14 for π. (Example 2)   _____

8. A basketball has a radius of 4.7 inches. What is its volume to the nearest
   cubic inch. Use 3.14 for π. (Example 2)   _____

9. A company is deciding whether to package a ball
   in a cubic box or a cylindrical box. In either case,
   the ball will touch the bottom, top, and sides.
   (Explore Activity)

   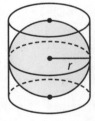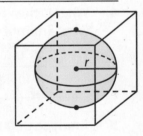

   a. What portion of the space inside the cylindrical
      box is empty? Explain.

      _____

   b. Find an expression for the volume of the box. _____

   c. About what portion of the space inside the cubic box is empty? Explain.

      _____

      _____

? ESSENTIAL QUESTION CHECK-IN

10. Explain the steps you use to find the volume of a sphere.

    _____

9.3 Independent Practice

 8.7.A

Personal Math Trainer

Online Assessment and Intervention

my.hrw.com

Find the volume of each sphere. Round your answers to the nearest tenth if necessary. Use 3.14 for π.

11. radius of 3.1 meters _____

12. diameter of 18 inches _____

13. $r = 6$ in. _____

14. $d = 36$ m _____

15.

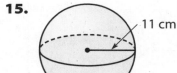

11 cm

_____

16.

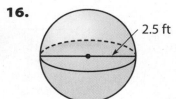

2.5 ft

_____

The eggs of birds and other animals come in many different shapes and sizes. Eggs often have a shape that is nearly spherical. When this is true, you can use the formula for a sphere to find their volume.

17. The green turtle lays eggs that are approximately spherical with an average diameter of 4.5 centimeters. Each turtle lays an average of 113 eggs at one time. Find the total volume of these eggs, to the nearest cubic centimeter.

_____

18. Hummingbirds lay eggs that are nearly spherical and about 1 centimeter in diameter. Find the volume of an egg. Round your answer to the nearest tenth.

_____

19. Fossilized spherical eggs of dinosaurs called titanosaurid sauropods were found in Patagonia. These eggs were 15 centimeters in diameter. Find the volume of an egg. Round your answer to the nearest tenth.

_____

20. **Persevere in Problem Solving** An ostrich egg has about the same volume as a sphere with a diameter of 5 inches. If the eggshell is about $\frac{1}{12}$ inch thick, find the volume of just the shell, not including the interior of the egg. Round your answer to the nearest tenth.

_____

21. **Multistep** Write the steps you would use to find a formula for the volume of the figure at right. Then write the formula.

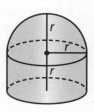

_____

_____

_____

_____

_____

_____

_____

_____

_____

22. Critical Thinking Explain what happens to the volume of a sphere if you double the radius.

_____

23. Multistep A cylindrical can of tennis balls holds a stack of three balls so that they touch the can at the top, bottom, and sides. The radius of each ball is 1.25 inches. Find the volume inside the can that is not taken up by the three tennis balls.

_____

 **FOCUS ON HIGHER ORDER THINKING**

24. Critique Reasoning A sphere has a radius of 4 inches, and a cube-shaped box has an edge length of 7.5 inches. J.D. says the box has a greater volume, so the sphere will fit in the box. Is he correct? Explain.

_____

_____

_____

25. Critical Thinking Which would hold the most water: a bowl in the shape of a hemisphere with radius r, a cylindrical glass with radius r and height r, or a cone-shaped drinking cup with radius r and height r? Explain.

_____

_____

_____

26. Analyze Relationships Hari has models of a sphere, a cylinder, and a cone. The sphere's diameter and the cylinder's height are the same, $2r$. The cylinder has radius r. The cone has diameter $2r$ and height $2r$. Compare the volumes of the cone and the sphere to the volume of the cylinder.

_____

_____

_____

27. A spherical helium balloon that is 8 feet in diameter can lift about 17 pounds. What does the diameter of a balloon need to be to lift a person who weighs 136 pounds? Explain.

_____

_____

_____

Ready to Go On?

Personal
Math Trainer

Online Assessment
and Intervention

my.hrw.com

9.1 Volume of Cylinders

Find the volume of each cylinder. Round your answers to the nearest tenth if necessary. Use 3.14 for π.

1. 6 ft

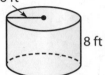

8 ft

_____

2. A can of juice has a radius of 4 inches and a height of 7 inches. What is the volume of the can?

_____

9.2 Volume of Cones

Find the volume of each cone. Round your answers to the nearest tenth if necessary. Use 3.14 for π.

3.

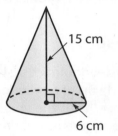

15 cm

6 cm _____

4.

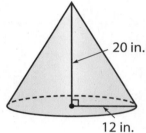

20 in.

12 in. _____

9.3 Volume of Spheres

Find the volume of each sphere. Round your answers to the nearest tenth if necessary. Use 3.14 for π.

5.

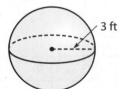

3 ft

_____

6.

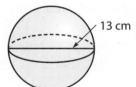

13 cm

_____

? ESSENTIAL QUESTION

7. What measurements do you need to know to find the volume of a cylinder? a cone? a sphere?

_____

_____

MODULE 9 MIXED REVIEW

Texas Test Prep

Personal
Math Trainer
Online
Assessment and
Intervention

my.hrw.com

Selected Response

1. The bed of a longbed pickup truck measures 4 feet by 8 feet. Which is the length of the longest thin metal bar that will lie flat in the bed?

  Ⓐ 11 ft 3 in.   Ⓒ 8 ft 11 in.

  Ⓑ 10 ft. 0 in.   Ⓓ 8 ft 9 in.

2. Using 3.14 for π, what is the volume of the cylinder below to the nearest tenth?

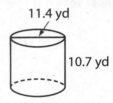

11.4 yd

10.7 yd

  Ⓐ 102 cubic yards

  Ⓑ 347.6 cubic yards

  Ⓒ 1,091.6 cubic yards

  Ⓓ 4,366.4 cubic yards

3. Rhett made mini waffle cones for a birthday party. Each waffle cone was 3.5 inches high and had a radius of 0.8 inches. What is the volume of each cone to the nearest hundredth?

  Ⓐ 1.70 cubic inches

  Ⓑ 2.24 cubic inches

  Ⓒ 2.34 cubic inches

  Ⓓ 8.79 cubic inches

4. Using 3.14 for π, what is the volume to the nearest tenth of a cone that has a height of 17 meters and a base with a radius of 6 meters?

  Ⓐ 204 cubic meters

  Ⓑ 640.6 cubic meters

  Ⓒ 2,562.2 cubic meters

  Ⓓ 10,249 cubic meters

5. Using 3.14 for π, what is the volume of the sphere to the nearest tenth?

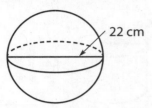

22 cm

  Ⓐ 4180 cubic centimeters

  Ⓑ 5572.5 cubic centimeters

  Ⓒ 33,434.7 cubic centimeters

  Ⓓ 44,579.6 cubic centimeters

Gridded Response

6. A diagram of a deodorant container is shown. It is made up of a cylinder and half of a sphere. What is the volume of the whole container to the nearest tenth cubic centimeter? Use 3.14 for π.

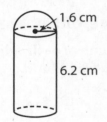

1.6 cm

6.2 cm

⓪	⓪	⓪	⓪	•	⓪	⓪
①	①	①	①		①	①
②	②	②	②		②	②
③	③	③	③		③	③
④	④	④	④		④	④
⑤	⑤	⑤	⑤		⑤	⑤
⑥	⑥	⑥	⑥		⑥	⑥
⑦	⑦	⑦	⑦		⑦	⑦
⑧	⑧	⑧	⑧		⑧	⑧
⑨	⑨	⑨	⑨		⑨	⑨

Surface Area

MODULE

10

ESSENTIAL QUESTION

How can you use surface area to solve real-world problems?

LESSON 10.1
Surface Area of Prisms
 TEKS 8.7.B

LESSON 10.2
Surface Area of Cylinders
TEKS 8.7.B

Real-World Video

Buildings in cities across the world are designed in the shape of prisms, cylinders, and composite three-dimensional figures. To find the amount of glass needed for a building, you could find its surface area.

my.hrw.com

GO DIGITAL
my.hrw.com

my.hrw.com

Go digital with your write-in student edition, accessible on any device.

Math On the Spot

Scan with your smart phone to jump directly to the online edition, video tutor, and more.

Animated Math

Interactively explore key concepts to see how math works.

Personal Math Trainer

Get immediate feedback and help as you work through practice sets.

Are YOU Ready?

Complete these exercises to review skills you will need for this chapter.

Personal Math Trainer

Online Assessment and Intervention

my.hrw.com

Area of Squares, Rectangles, and Triangles

EXAMPLE

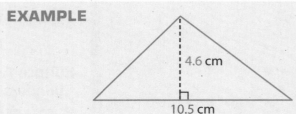

4.6 cm

10.5 cm

The area of a square is the length of a side squared.
The area of a rectangle is the length times the width.
The area of a triangle with base b and height h is $\frac{1}{2}bh$.

$$A = \frac{1}{2}(10.5)(4.6)$$
$$= 24.15 \text{ cm}^2$$

Find the area of each figure.

1. square with side lengths of

   9.3 cm _____

2. triangle with base 14 in. and height

   7 in. _____

3. rectangle with length $2\frac{1}{2}$ ft and width

   $1\frac{1}{2}$ ft _____

4. triangle with base 6.4 m and height

   3.8 m _____

Area of Circles

EXAMPLE

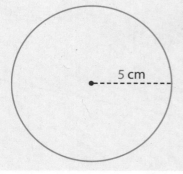

5 cm

$$A = \pi r^2$$
Using 3.14 for π, $A = 3.14(5)^2$
$$= 78.5 \text{ cm}^2$$

Find the area of each circle. Use 3.14 for π.

5. $r = 18$ in. _____

6. $r = 7.5$ m _____

7. $r = 2\frac{1}{2}$ ft _____

Reading Start-Up

Visualize Vocabulary

Use the ✔ words to complete the chart.

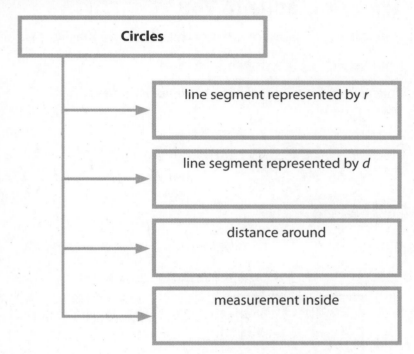

Circles

→ line segment represented by *r*

→ line segment represented by *d*

→ distance around

→ measurement inside

Understand Vocabulary

Complete the sentences using the review words.

1. A three-dimensional figure in which six faces are

   rectangles is a _____.

2. An individual surface of a solid object is a _____.

Active Reading

Tri-Fold Before beginning the module, create a tri-fold to help you learn the concepts and vocabulary in this module. Fold the paper into three sections. Label the columns "What I Know," "What I Need to Know," and "What I Learned." Complete the first two columns before you read. After studying the module, complete the third column.

Unpacking the TEKS

Understanding the TEKS and the vocabulary terms in the TEKS will help you know exactly what you are expected to learn in this module.

TEKS 8.7.B

Use previous knowledge of surface area to make connections to the formulas for lateral and total surface area and determine solutions for problems involving rectangular prisms, triangular prisms, and cylinders.

Key Vocabulary

surface area *(área total)*
The sum of the areas for the surfaces of a three-dimensional figure.

What It Means to You

You will find the surface areas of three-dimensional figures.

UNPACKING EXAMPLE 8.7.B

Julie is wrapping a present for a friend. Find the surface area of the box.

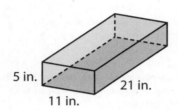

Draw a net to help you see each face of the prism. Use the formula $A = \ell w$ to find the area of each face.

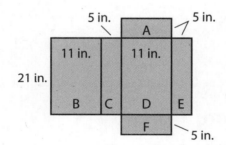

A: $A = 11 \times 5 = 55$
B: $A = 21 \times 11 = 231$
C: $A = 21 \times 5 = 105$
D: $A = 21 \times 11 = 231$
E: $A = 21 \times 5 = 105$
F: $A = 11 \times 5 = 55$

$S = 55 + 231 + 105 + 231 + 105 + 55 = 782$
The surface area is 782 in².

© Houghton Mifflin Harcourt Publishing Company

TEKS
Expressions, equations, and relationships—8.7.B
... make connections to the formulas for lateral and total surface area and determine solutions for problems involving prisms ...

 ESSENTIAL QUESTION

How do you find the surface area of a prism?

EXPLORE ACTIVITY  **TEKS** 8.7.B

Modeling the Surface Area of a Prism

The **surface area** of a three-dimensional figure is the sum of the areas of all of its surfaces. You can use a net to help you explore formulas related to the surface area of a prism.

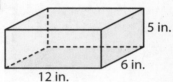

A net for a CD storage box made of balsa wood is shown.

A The front and _____ have the same area.

$A = lh = $ ____ · ____ = ____ square inches

B The left side and _____ have the same area.

$A = wh = $ _____ · _____ = _____ square inches

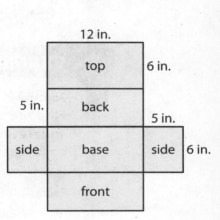

C The *lateral faces* of a prism are parallelograms that connect the bases. The *lateral area* (L) of a prism is the sum of the areas of its lateral faces. Find the lateral area of Ethan's box.

$L = 2 \cdot $ _____ $+ 2 \cdot $ _____ = _____ square inches

D Find the perimeter (P) of the base of the box.

$P = $ _____ + _____ + _____ + _____ = _____ inches

E Multiply the perimeter of the base by the height.

$Ph = $ _____ · _____ = _____ square inches

F What do you notice about your answers in parts C and E?

G The top and _____ have the same base area (B).

$B = lw = $ _____ · _____ = _____ square inches

H Add the lateral area to the area of the two bases to find the total surface area (S).

$S = 2B + L = 2 \cdot $ _____ + _____ = _____ square inches

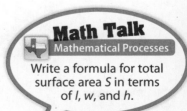
Math Talk
Mathematical Processes
Write a formula for total surface area S in terms of l, w, and h.

Surface Area of a Rectangular Prism

Lateral and Total Surface Area of a Prism

The lateral area *L* of a prism is the perimeter *P* of the base times the height *h* of the prism. $L = Ph$	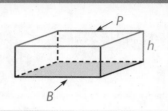
The total surface area *S* of a prism is twice the area of a base *B* plus the lateral area *L*. $S = 2B + L$ or $S = 2B + Ph$	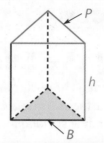

EXAMPLE 1 *Problem Solving*   🔲 TEKS 8.7.B

Joanna is wrapping a present in the box shown. Find the amount of wrapping paper in square inches that Joanna needs, not counting overlap.

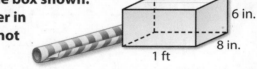

6 in.
8 in.
1 ft

 Analyze Information

What are you asked to find?

   You need to find the total surface area of the box.

List the **important information**.

   The length of the box is 1 foot.   The width of the box is 8 inches.

            The height of the box is 6 inches.

 Formulate a Plan

Change 1 foot to 12 inches. Then find the area and perimeter of a base of the box, and substitute into the formula for the surface area of a prism.

Solve

Area of Base: $B = l \cdot w = 12 \cdot 8 = 96$

Perimeter of Base: $P = 2l + 2w = 2(12) + 2(8) = 40$

$S = 2B + Ph$ *Total surface area of a prism*

$S = 2(96) + (40)(6)$ *Substitute: B = 96, P = 40, and h = 6.*

$S = 192 + 240 = 432$ *Simplify.*

The total surface area of the box is 432 square inches.

Math Talk
Mathematical Processes

Is it possible to wrap the box with a 30-inch by 20-inch piece of wrapping paper? Explain.

Animated Math

⏱ my.hrw.com

© Houghton Mifflin Harcourt Publishing Company

You can also find the area of the front, top, and side, and multiply each by 2 to find the surface area.

Front: $12 \cdot 6 = 72$ Top: $12 \cdot 8 = 96$ Side: $8 \cdot 6 = 48$

   $2 \cdot 72 = 144$ $2 \cdot 96 = 192$ $2 \cdot 48 = 96$

$S = 144 + 192 + 96 = 432$ square inches, so the answer is correct.

YOUR TURN

1. Sara is lining the bottom and lateral faces of a drawer with liner paper. The dimensions of the inside of the drawer are 1 yard, 20 inches, and 9 inches. What is the total area in square inches being covered?

_____

Personal Math Trainer

Online Assessment and Intervention

⏱ my.hrw.com

Surface Area of a Triangular Prism

When you find the total surface area of a triangular prism, don't confuse the base and height of the triangular base with the base and height of the prism.

Math On the Spot

⏱ my.hrw.com

 EXAMPLE 2 Real World  TEKS 8.7.B

Kevin is painting a block in the shape of a triangular prism. What is the surface area of the block?

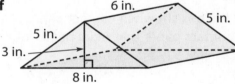

6 in.
5 in.
5 in.
3 in.
8 in.

STEP 1 Find the area of a base.

$B = \frac{1}{2}bh$ Area of a triangle

$B = \frac{1}{2}(8)(3) = 12$ Substitute.

STEP 2 Find the perimeter of a base.

$P = 8 + 5 + 5 = 18$ Perimeter of a triangle

STEP 3 Use the formula for surface area.

$S = 2B + Ph$

$S = 2(12) + (18)(6)$ Substitute: $B = 12$, $P = 18$, and $h = 6$

$S = 24 + 108 = 132$

The surface area of the triangular prism is 132 cm^2.

YOUR TURN

Find the lateral area and total surface area of each prism.

2.

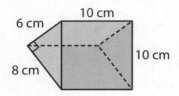

10 cm
6 cm
10 cm
8 cm

_____

3.

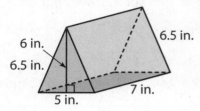

6.5 in.
6 in.
6.5 in.
7 in.
5 in.

_____

Guided Practice

Find the lateral area and total surface area of each prism. (Example 1)

1.

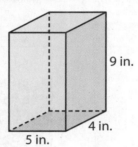

9 in.
4 in.
5 in.

_____

2.

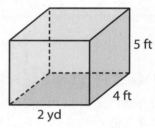

5 ft
4 ft
2 yd

_____

3. Akira plans to cover the box shown in contact paper. Find the amount of contact paper that Akira needs, not counting overlap. (Example 1)

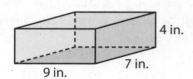

4 in.
9 in.
7 in.

_____

4. A gift box is in the shape of a triangular prism. How much cardboard is needed to construct the box, not counting overlap? (Example 2)

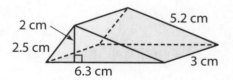

2 cm
2.5 cm
5.2 cm
3 cm
6.3 cm

_____

❓ ESSENTIAL QUESTION CHECK-IN

5. What are two ways that you can find the surface area of a prism?

_____

_____

10.1 Independent Practice

TEKS 8.7.B

Personal Math Trainer

Online Assessment and Intervention

my.hrw.com

Find the lateral and total surface area of each prism. Round to the nearest tenth if necessary.

6.
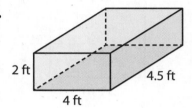
2 ft   4.5 ft   4 ft

_____

7.
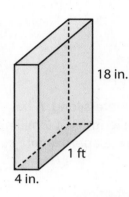
18 in.   1 ft   4 in.

_____

8.
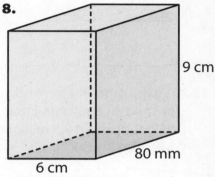
9 cm   80 mm   6 cm

_____

9.
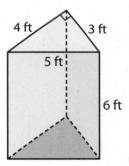
4 ft   3 ft   5 ft   6 ft

_____

10.
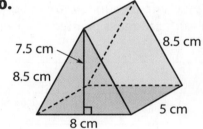
7.5 cm   8.5 cm   8.5 cm   5 cm   8 cm

_____

11.
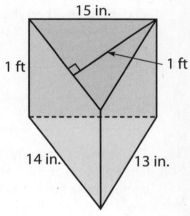
15 in.   1 ft   1 ft   14 in.   13 in.

_____

12. The bases of a prism are right triangles with side lengths 6 meters, 8 meters, and 10 meters. The height of the prism is 3 meters. What is the lateral area of the prism? What is the total surface area?   _____

13. A rectangular prism has a length of 8 inches and a width of 7 inches. The lateral area is 150 square inches. What is the height of the prism?   _____

14. Multiple Representations Write a formula for the total surface area of a cube in terms of its edge length x. Explain your reasoning.

_____

_____

15. Multistep Matt bought a tent without a floor. Estimate the surface area of the tent in square feet.

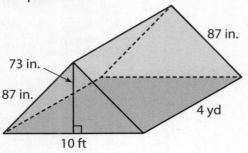

87 in.

73 in.

87 in.

4 yd

10 ft

_____

16. Multistep Keeshawn is building a box with a lid out of plywood with the dimensions shown. Plywood costs $0.50 per square foot. Find the cost of the plywood Keeshawn needs for the box.

_____

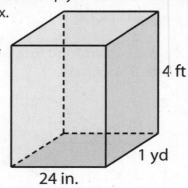

4 ft

1 yd

24 in.

17. A glass prism on a chandelier is 75 millimeters long. A base of the prism is an equilateral triangle with side lengths of 9 millimeters and a height of about 7.8 millimeters. What is the approximate surface area of the prism?

_____

 **FOCUS ON HIGHER ORDER THINKING**

18. Problem Solving A cube with an edge length of 4 inches is painted on all of its sides. Then the cube is cut into 64 cubes with an edge length of 1 inch. What percent of the total surface area is painted? Explain.

_____

_____

_____

19. Problem Solving The base of a triangular prism is a right triangle whose legs are 7 cm and 24 cm. The height of the prism is 30 cm. What is the lateral area of the prism? Explain how you found your answer.

_____

_____

_____

20. Communicate Mathematical Ideas Explain how to find the surface area of the composite figure. Then find its surface area.

_____

_____

_____

_____

_____

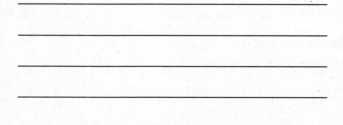

1 in.

2 in.

2 in.

2 in.

4 in.

3 in.

3 in.

Work Area

10.2 Surface Area of Cylinders

TEKS
Expressions, equations, and relationships—8.7.B
... make connections to the formulas for lateral and total surface area and determine solutions for problems involving ... cylinders.

? **ESSENTIAL QUESTION**

How do you find the surface area of a cylinder?

EXPLORE ACTIVITY **TEKS** 8.7.B

Modeling the Surface Area of a Cylinder

Just as you did with a prism, you can use a net to help you find a formula for the surface area of a cylinder.

The lateral area of a cylinder is the area of the curved surface that connects the two bases. The net shows that the lateral surface is a rectangle.

$C = 2\pi r$

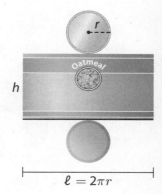

$\ell = 2\pi r$

Use the diagram of the oatmeal container and its net.

A Imagine unrolling the container's lateral surface to form a rectangle.

What dimension of the cylinder matches the rectangle's *length*? _____

What dimension of the cylinder matches the rectangle's *height*? _____

B Express the lateral area of a cylinder in words and as a formula using the given variables.

Lateral area = Area of one _____ = Length · Height

$L =$ _____ (C = circumference, h = height)

$L =$ _____ (r = radius, h = height)

> The formula for the circumference of a circle is $C = 2\pi r$.

C Express the total surface area of a cylinder in words and as a formula using the given variables.

Total surface area = Area of two _____ + Area of one _____

$S =$ _____ (B = base area, C = circumference, h = height)

$S =$ _____ (r = radius, h = height)

> The formula for the area of a circle is $A = \pi r^2$.

Reflect

1. **Communicate Mathematical Ideas** How is the process for finding lateral and total surface area of a cylinder like the process for a prism?

_____

_____

Finding the Surface Area of a Cylinder

The total surface area of a cylinder is the area of the bases plus the lateral area.

Lateral and Total Surface Area of a Cylinder

The lateral area L of a cylinder with height h and radius r is the circumference of the base times the height.

$$L = Ch \quad \text{or} \quad L = 2\pi rh$$

The total surface area S of a cylinder with height h and radius r is twice the area of a base B plus the lateral area L.

$$S = 2B + L \quad \text{or} \quad S = 2\pi r^2 + 2\pi rh$$

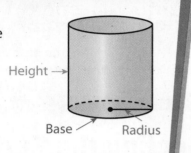

Height →
Base
Radius

My Notes

EXAMPLE 1

TEKS 8.7.B

Find the lateral and total surface area of the cylinder to the nearest tenth. Use 3.14 for π.

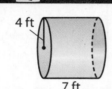

4 ft

7 ft

STEP 1   Find the lateral area.

$L = 2\pi rh$ Use the formula for the lateral area of a cylinder.

$\approx 2(3.14)(4)(7)$ Substitute.

≈ 175.84 Simplify.

The lateral area is about 175.8 square feet.

STEP 2   Find the total surface area.

$S = 2\pi r^2 + L$ Use the formula for the total surface area of a cylinder.

$\approx 2(3.14)(4^2) + 175.84$ Substitute.

$\approx 100.48 + 175.84$ Simplify.

≈ 276.32 Add.

The total surface area of the cylinder is about 276.3 square feet.

YOUR TURN

Find the lateral and total surface area of each cylinder. Round your answers to the nearest tenth. Use 3.14 for π.

2.
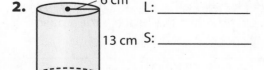
6 cm

13 cm

L: _____

S: _____

3. 7 ft
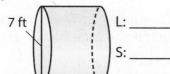

5 ft

L: _____

S: _____

© Houghton Mifflin Harcourt Publishing Company

Finding the Surface Area of a Cylinder in a Real-World Situation

You can find many examples of cylinders in your kitchen.

EXAMPLE 2 Real World    TEKS 8.7.B

The can shown is 11 inches high and has a diameter of 9 inches. How many square inches of paper are needed for the label? How many square inches of metal are needed to make the entire can? Round your answers to the nearest whole number. Use 3.14 for π.

STEP 1 Find the radius of the base.

$d = 9$ in., so $r = 4.5$ in.   *The radius is half of the diameter.*

STEP 2 To find the area of the label, find the lateral area.

$L = 2\pi rh$ *Use the formula for the lateral area of a cylinder.*

$\approx 2(3.14)(4.5)(11)$ *Substitute.*

≈ 310.86 *Multiply.*

It takes about 311 square inches of paper to make the label.

STEP 3 To find the amount of metal, find the total surface area.

$S = 2\pi r^2 + 2\pi rh$ *Use the formula for the total surface area of a cylinder.*

$\approx 2(3.14)(4.5^2) + 2(3.14)(4.5)(11)$ *Substitute.*

$\approx 127.17 + 310.86$ *Simplify.*

≈ 438.03 *Add.*

It takes about 438 square inches of metal to make the can.

© Houghton Mifflin Harcourt Publishing Company

YOUR TURN

4. How many square inches of cardboard are needed for the lateral area of the raisin container shown? What is the total surface area of the container? Round your answers to the nearest tenth. Use 3.14 for π.

_____

Personal Math Trainer

Online Assessment and Intervention

⏻ my.hrw.com

1. Draw a net of the cylinder. Label the radius and the height. Then find the lateral area and total surface area. Round your answers to the nearest tenth. Use 3.14 for π. (Explore Activity and Example 1)

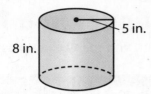

Find the circumference of the circle. Use 3.14 for π.

$C = 2\pi r \approx 2 \cdot 3.14 \cdot$ _____ $\approx$ _____ inches

The lateral area is the circumference times the height of the can.

$L \approx 31.4 \cdot$ _____ $\approx$ _____ in²

Find the area of two bases. Use 3.14 for π.

$2B = 2\pi r^2 \approx 2(3.14)$ (_____) $\approx$ _____ in²

Add the area of the bases and the lateral area.

$S \approx$ _____ + _____ $\approx$ _____ in²

2. A can of tuna fish has a height of 1 inch and a diameter of 3 inches. How many square inches of paper are needed for the label? How many square inches of metal are needed to make the can including the top and bottom? Round your answers to the nearest whole number. Use 3.14 for π. (Example 2)

It takes about _____ square inches of paper to make the label.

It takes about _____ square inches of metal to make the can.

? ESSENTIAL QUESTION CHECK-IN

3. How do you find the total surface area of a cylinder?

_____

_____

_____

10.2 Independent Practice

 TEKS 8.7.B

Personal
Math Trainer

Online
Assessment and
Intervention

my.hrw.com

Find the lateral and total surface area of each cylinder. Round your answers to the nearest tenth. Use 3.14 for π.

4.

16 in.

8 in.

_____

5. 3 in.

8.5 in.

_____

6.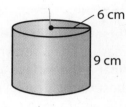

6 cm

9 cm

_____

7. A container of bread crumbs has a radius of 4 inches and a height of 8 inches.

_____

8. A rain barrel has a diameter of 18 inches and a height of 3 feet.

_____

9. A drum has a diameter of 14 inches and a height of 5.5 inches.

_____

10. Multistep A pipe is 25 inches long and has a diameter of 5 inches. What is the lateral area of the pipe to the nearest tenth? Use 3.14 for π.

_____

11. Multistep A size D battery has a diameter of 32 millimeters and a length of 5.6 centimeters. What is the lateral area of the battery to the nearest square centimeter? Use 3.14 for π.

_____

12. What If? Carol is designing an oatmeal container. Her first design is a rectangular prism with a height of 12 inches, a width of 8 inches, and a depth of 3 inches.

a. What is the total surface area of the container to the nearest square inch? Use 3.14 for π.

_____

b. Carol wants to redesign the package as a cylinder with the same total surface area as the prism in part **a**. If the radius of the cylinder is 2 inches, what is the height of the cylinder? Round your answer to the nearest square inch. Use 3.14 for π.

_____

13. Vocabulary How do the lateral and total surface area of a cylinder differ?

_____

_____

14. Multiple Representations The formula for the total surface area of a cylinder is $S = 2\pi r^2 + 2\pi rh$. Explain how you could use the Distributive Property to write the formula another way.

_____

_____

15. Persevere in Problem Solving The treasure chest shown is a composite figure. What is the surface area of the treasure chest to the nearest square foot? Explain how you found your answer.

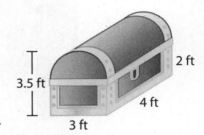

3.5 ft

2 ft

4 ft

3 ft

_____

_____

_____

_____

_____

16. Analyze Relationships A square prism has the same height as the cylinder shown. The perimeter of the prism's base equals the circumference of the cylinder's base.

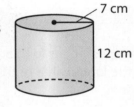

7 cm

12 cm

a. Find the side length of the prism's base to the nearest centimeter. _____

b. Which figure has the greater lateral area? Which has the greater total surface area? Which has the greater volume? Explain.

_____

_____

_____

17. Communicate Mathematical Ideas A cylinder has a circumference of 16π inches and its height is half the radius of the cylinder. What is the total surface area of the cylinder? Give your answer in terms of π. Explain how you found your answer.

_____

_____

_____

_____

Ready to Go On?

10.1 Surface Area of Prisms

Find the lateral and total surface area of each prism. Round your answers to the nearest tenth if necessary.

1.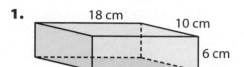
18 cm   10 cm   6 cm

_____

2.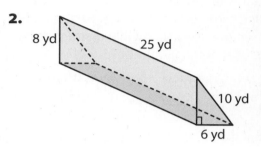
8 yd   25 yd   10 yd   6 yd

_____

3.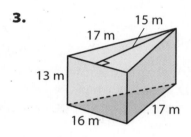
15 m   17 m   13 m   16 m   17 m

_____

4.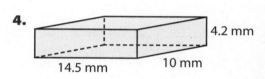
4.2 mm   14.5 mm   10 mm

_____

10.2 Surface Area of Cylinders

Find the lateral and total surface area of each cylinder. Round your answers to the nearest tenth if necessary. Use 3.14 for π.

5.
18 yd   14 yd

_____

6.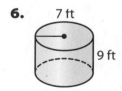
7 ft   9 ft

_____

? **ESSENTIAL QUESTION**

7. How can finding surface area help you solve packaging problems?

_____

_____

Selected Response

1. Grain is stored in cylindrical structures called silos. Which is the best estimate for the volume of a silo with a diameter of 12.3 feet and a height of 25 feet?

Ⓐ 450 cubic feet   Ⓒ 2970 cubic feet

Ⓑ 900 cubic feet   Ⓓ 10,800 cubic feet

2. What is the side length of a cube that has a total surface area of 384 square inches?

Ⓐ 6 inches   Ⓒ 8 inches

Ⓑ 7 inches   Ⓓ 9 inches

3. A block of cheese is shown in the shape of the triangular prism below.

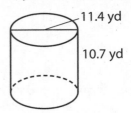

What is the total surface area of the block of cheese?

Ⓐ 120 in²   Ⓒ 510 in²

Ⓑ 494 in²   Ⓓ 640 in²

4. Using 3.14 for π, what is the lateral surface area of the cylinder to the nearest unit?

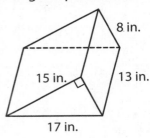

Ⓐ 122 yd²   Ⓒ 383 yd²

Ⓑ 204 yd²   Ⓓ 587 yd²

5. The net of a cylinder is shown.

What is the total surface area of the cylinder represented by the net?

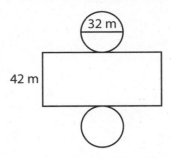

Ⓐ 1607.7 m²   Ⓒ 4220.2 m²

Ⓑ 1856 m²   Ⓓ 5827.8 m²

6. A cylinder has a circumference of 12π cm and a height that is half the radius. What is the total surface area of the cylinder?

Ⓐ 36π cm²   Ⓒ 108π cm²

Ⓑ 72π cm²   Ⓓ 144π cm²

Gridded Response

7. A rectangular prism has a length of 4 feet, a width of 1 yard, and a height of 3 inches. What is the total surface area of the prism to the nearest tenth of a square foot?

				•		
⓪	⓪	⓪	⓪		⓪	⓪
①	①	①	①		①	①
②	②	②	②		②	②
③	③	③	③		③	③
④	④	④	④		④	④
⑤	⑤	⑤	⑤		⑤	⑤
⑥	⑥	⑥	⑥		⑥	⑥
⑦	⑦	⑦	⑦		⑦	⑦
⑧	⑧	⑧	⑧		⑧	⑧
⑨	⑨	⑨	⑨		⑨	⑨

Angle Relationships in Parallel Lines and Triangles

Key Vocabulary

alternate exterior angles *(ángulos alternos externos)*

alternate interior angles *(ángulos alternos internos)*

corresponding angles *(ángulos correspondientes (para líneas))*

exterior angle *(ángulo externo de un polígono)*

interior angle *(ángulos internos)*

remote interior angle *(ángulo interno remoto)*

same-side interior angles *(ángulos internos del mismo lado)*

similar *(semejantes)*

transversal *(transversal)*

? ESSENTIAL QUESTION

How can you solve real-world problems that involve angle relationships in parallel lines and triangles?

EXAMPLE 1

Find each angle measure when m∠6 = 81°.

A m∠5 = 180° − 81° = 99°

5 and 6 are supplementary angles.

B m∠1 = 99°

1 and 5 are corresponding angles.

C m∠3 = 180° − 81° = 99°

3 and 6 are same-side interior angles.

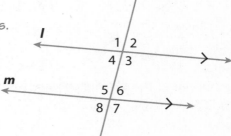

EXAMPLE 2

Are the triangles similar? Explain your answer.

$y = 180° - (67° + 35°)$

$y = 78°$

$x = 180° - (67° + 67°)$

$x = 46°$

The triangles are not similar, because they do not have 2 or more pairs of corresponding congruent angles.

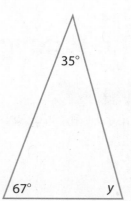
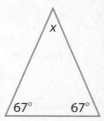

EXERCISES

1. If m∠GHA = 76°, find the measures of the given angles. (Lesson 7.1)

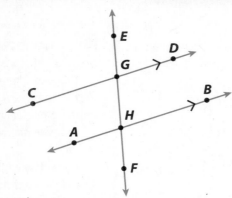

m∠EGC = _____

m∠EGD = _____

m∠BHF = _____

m∠HGD = _____

2. Find the measure of the missing angles. (Lesson 7.2)

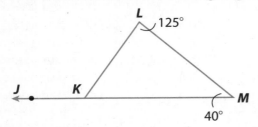

m∠JKM = _____

m∠LKM = _____

3. Is the larger triangle similar to the smaller triangle? Explain your answer. (Lesson 7.3)

_____

_____

4. Find the value of x and y in the figure. (Lesson 7.3)

_____

MODULE 8   # The Pythagorean Theorem

Key Vocabulary

hypotenuse *(hipotenusa)*

legs *(catetos)*

Pythagorean Theorem
(teorema de Pitágoras)

? ESSENTIAL QUESTION

How can you use the Pythagorean Theorem to solve real-world problems?

EXAMPLE 1

Find the missing side length.
Round your answer to the nearest tenth.

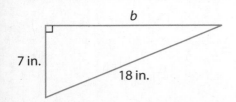

$$a^2 + b^2 = c^2$$

$$7^2 + b^2 = 18^2$$

$$49 + b^2 = 324$$

$$b^2 = 275$$

$$b = \sqrt{275} \approx 16.6$$

The length of the leg is about 16.6 inches.

EXAMPLE 2

Thomas drew a diagram to represent the location of his house, the school, and his friend Manuel's house. What is the distance from the school to Manuel's house? Round your answer to the nearest tenth.

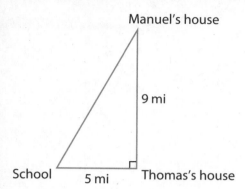

Manuel's house

9 mi

School   5 mi   Thomas's house

$a^2 + b^2 = c^2$

$5^2 + 9^2 = c^2$

$25 + 81 = c^2$

$c^2 = 106$

$c = \sqrt{106} \approx 10.3$

The distance from the school to Manuel's house is about 10.3 miles.

EXERCISES

Find the missing side lengths. Round your answers to the nearest hundredth. (Lesson 8.1)

1.

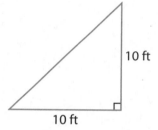

10 ft

10 ft

_____

2.

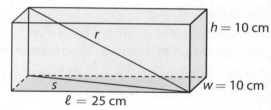

$h = 10$ cm

r

s

$w = 10$ cm

$\ell = 25$ cm

_____

_____

3. Hye Sun has a modern coffee table whose top is a triangle with the following side lengths: 8 feet, 3 feet, and 5 feet. Is Hye Sun's coffee table top a right triangle? (Lesson 8.2)

_____

4. Find the length of each side of triangle *ABC*. If necessary, round your answers to the nearest hundredth. (Lesson 8.3)

$\overline{AB}$ _____

$\overline{BC}$ _____

$\overline{AC}$ _____

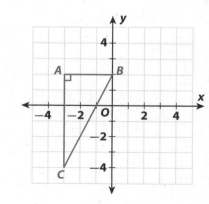

? **ESSENTIAL QUESTION**

How can you solve real-world problems that involve volume?

EXAMPLE 1

Find the volume of the cistern. Round your answer to the nearest hundredth.

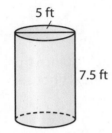

5 ft

7.5 ft

$V = \pi r^2 h$

$\approx 3.14 \cdot 2.5^2 \cdot 7.5$

$\approx 3.14 \cdot 6.25 \cdot 7.5$

≈ 147.19

The cistern has a volume of approximately 147.19 cubic feet.

EXAMPLE 2

Find the volume of a sphere with a radius of 3.7 cm. Write your answer in terms of π and to the nearest hundredth.

$V = \frac{4}{3}\pi r^3$

$\approx \frac{4}{3} \cdot \pi \cdot 3.7^3$

$\approx \frac{4}{3} \cdot \pi \cdot 50.653$

$\approx 67.54\pi$

$V = \frac{4}{3}\pi r^3$

$\approx \frac{4}{3} \cdot 3.14 \cdot 3.7^3$

$\approx \frac{4}{3} \cdot 3.14 \cdot 50.653$

≈ 212.07

The volume of the sphere is approximately 67.54π cm³, or 212.07 cm³.

EXERCISES

Find the volume of each figure. Round your answers to the nearest hundredth. (Lessons 9.1, 9.2, 9.3)

1.

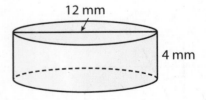

12 mm

4 mm

2.

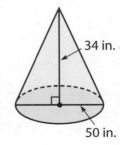

34 in.

50 in.

_____   _____

3. Find the volume of a ball with a radius of 1.68 inches. _____

Key Vocabulary
surface area (*área total*)

? ESSENTIAL QUESTION

How can you solve real-world problems that involve surface area?

EXAMPLE 1

Kris wants to buy decorative paper to cover her new storage chest. The chest is a rectangular prism with a height of 3 feet, a width of 2 feet, and a length of 4.5 feet. How much paper will Kris need if she does not cover the top and bottom of the chest? How much paper will she need to cover the entire chest?

$L = Ph$

$= 13(3)$ $P = 2l + 2w$

$= 39$

$S = 2B + Ph$

$= 2(4.5)(2) + 13(3)$ $B = \ell w$

$= 57$

Kris will need 39 square feet of paper to cover the lateral faces of the chest and 57 square feet to cover the entire chest.

EXAMPLE 2

Find the lateral and total surface area of the cylinder. Round your answer to the nearest hundredth.

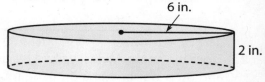

6 in.

2 in.

$L = 2\pi rh$

$\approx 2(3.14)(6)(2)$

$= 76.36$

$S = 2\pi r^2 + 2\pi rh$

$= 2(3.14)(6^2) + 2(3.14)(6)(2)$

$= 301.44$

The lateral area is 76.36 in². The total surface area is 301.44 in².

EXERCISES

Find the lateral and total surface area of each figure. If necessary, round your answers to the nearest hundredth. (Lessons 10.1, 10.2)

1. 5 ft

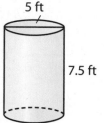

7.5 ft

2. 8.5 ft

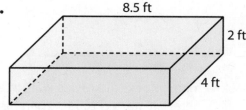

2 ft

4 ft

_____   _____

3. A cylindrical water tower has a height of 50 meters and a radius of 20 meters.   _____

Unit 3 Performance Tasks

1. **CAREERS IN MATH** | **Hydrologist** A hydrologist needs to estimate the mass of water in an underground aquifer, which is roughly cylindrical in shape. The diameter of the aquifer is 65 meters, and its depth is 8 meters. One cubic meter of water has a mass of about 1000 kilograms.

   a. The aquifer is completely filled with water. What is the total mass of the water in the aquifer? Explain how you found your answer. Use 3.14 for π and round your answer to the nearest kilogram.

   _____

   _____

   _____

   b. Another cylindrical aquifer has a diameter of 70 meters and a depth of 9 meters. The mass of the water in it is 27×10^7 kilograms. Is the aquifer totally filled with water? Explain your reasoning.

   _____

   _____

   _____

2. From his home, Myles walked his dog north 5 blocks, east 2 blocks, and then stopped at a drinking fountain. He then walked north 3 more blocks and east 4 more blocks. It started to rain so he cut through a field and walked straight home.

   a. Draw a diagram of his path.

   b. How many blocks did Myles walk in all? How much longer was his walk before it started to rain than his walk home?

   _____

UNIT 4

Equations and Inequalities

MODULE 11

Equations and Inequalities with the Variable on Both Sides

 TEKS 8.8.A, 8.8.B, 8.8.C

CAREERS IN MATH

Hydraulic Engineer A hydraulic engineer specializes in the behavior of fluids, mainly water. A hydraulic engineer applies the mathematics of fluid dynamics to the collection, transport, measurement, and regulation of water and other fluids.

If you are interested in a career in hydraulic engineering, you should study the following mathematical subjects:
- Algebra
- Geometry
- Trigonometry
- Probability and Statistics
- Calculus

Research other careers that require the understanding of the mathematics of fluid dynamics.

Unit 4 Performance Task

At the end of the unit, check out how **hydraulic engineers** use math.

Use the puzzle to preview key vocabulary from this unit. Unscramble the circled letters to answer the riddle at the bottom of the page.

1. **FIACALRONT INFEOCIECTF**

2. **LCMADEI CINETFOEFIC**

3. **UQAOTENI**

4. **ROPWE**

5. **TINELQUYAI**

1. A number that is multiplied by the variable in an algebraic expression, where the number is a fraction. (Lesson 11.2)

2. A number that is multiplied by the variable in an algebraic expression, where the number is a decimal. (Lesson 11.2)

3. A mathematical statement that two expressions are equal. (Lesson 11.1)

4. A number that is formed by repeated multiplication of the same factor. Multiply this to remove decimals from an unsolved equation. (Lesson 11.2)

5. A statement that two expressions are not equal. (Lesson 11.3)

Q: What is the best time to divide a half dollar between two people?

A: at a __ __ __ __ __ __ __ __ __ __ __!

Equations and Inequalities with the Variable on Both Sides

? ESSENTIAL QUESTION

How can you use equations and inequalities with variables on both sides to solve real-world problems?

Real-World Video

 my.hrw.com

Some employees earn commission plus their salary when they make a sale. There may be options about their pay structure. They can find the best option by solving an equation with variables on both sides.

GO DIGITAL
my.hrw.com

my.hrw.com

Go digital with your write-in student edition, accessible on any device.

Math On the Spot

Scan with your smart phone to jump directly to the online edition, video tutor, and more.

Animated Math

Interactively explore key concepts to see how math works.

Personal Math Trainer

Get immediate feedback and help as you work through practice sets.

Are YOU Ready?

Complete these exercises to review skills you will need for this module.

Find Common Denominators

EXAMPLE Find the LCD of 3, 5, and 10.

3: 3, 6, 9, 12, 15, 18, 21, 24, 27, 30,…
5: 5, 10, 15, 20, 25, 30, 35,…
10: 10, 20, 30, 40, 50,…

List the multiples of each number. Choose the least multiple the lists have in common.
LCD(3, 5, 10) = 30

Find the LCD.

1. 8, 12 _____   **2.** 9, 12 _____   **3.** 15, 20 _____   **4.** 8, 10 _____

Multiply Decimals by Powers of 10

EXAMPLE 3.719×100

$3.719 \times 100 = 371.9$

Count the zeros in 100: 2 zeros
Move the decimal point 2 places to the right.

Find the product.

5. 0.683×100 **6.** $9.15 \times 1{,}000$ **7.** 0.005×100 **8.** $1{,}000 \times 1{,}000$

_____   _____   _____   _____

Connect Words and Equations

EXAMPLE Two times a number decreased by 5 is −6.

Two times x decreased by 5 is −6.

$2x - 5$ is −6

$2x - 5 = -6$

Represent the unknown with a variable.
Times means multiplication.
Decreased by means subtraction.
Place the equal sign.

Write an algebraic equation for the sentence.

9. The difference between three times a number and 7 is 14. _____

10. The quotient of five times a number and 7 is no more than 10. _____

11. 14 less than 3 times a number is 5 more than half of the number.   _____

Reading Start-Up

Visualize Vocabulary

Use the ✔ words to complete the bubble map. You may put more than one word in each oval.

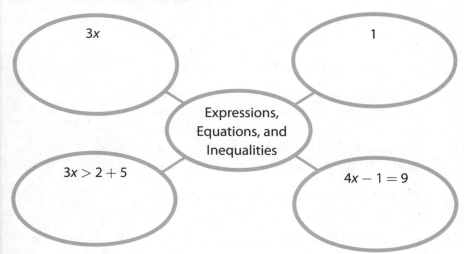

$3x$

1

Expressions, Equations, and Inequalities

$3x > 2 + 5$

$4x - 1 = 9$

Understand Vocabulary

Complete the sentences using the review words.

1. A value of the variable that makes an equation true is a _____.

2. The set of all whole numbers and their opposites are _____.

3. An _____ is an expression that contains at least one variable.

Active Reading

Layered Book Before beginning the module, create a layered book to help you learn the concepts in this module. At the top of the first flap, write the title of the book, "Equations and Inequalities with Variables on Both Sides." Then label each flap with one of the lesson titles in this module. As you study each lesson, write important ideas, such as vocabulary and formulas, under the appropriate flap.

Unpacking the TEKS

Understanding the TEKS and the vocabulary terms in the TEKS will help you know exactly what you are expected to learn in this module.

 **TEKS 8.8.A**

Write one-variable equations or inequalities with variables on both sides that represent problems using rational number coefficients and constants.

Key Vocabulary

coefficient *(coeficiente)*
The number that is multiplied by the variable in an algebraic expression.

constant *(constante)*
A value that does not change.

inequality *(desigualdad)*
A mathematical sentence that shows the relationship between quantities that are not equal.

What It Means to You

You will learn to write an equation that represents a situation, such as comparing costs in a real-world situation.

UNPACKING EXAMPLE 8.8.A

At Work It Out, a gym membership is $50 per month. At Get Fit, the initiation fee is $100 and membership is $30 per month. Write an equation to find the number of months for which the total cost is the same.

The cost of a membership at Work It Out for x months is represented by $50x$.

The cost of a membership at Get Fit for x months is represented by $100 + 30x$.

Total cost at Work It Out	=	Total cost at Get Fit
$50x$	=	$100 + 30x$

 TEKS 8.8.C

Model and solve one-variable equations with variables on both sides of the equal sign that represent mathematical and real-world problems using rational number coefficients and constants.

Key Vocabulary

rational number *(número racional)*
A number that can be expressed as the ratio of two integers.

What It Means to You

You can write and solve an equation that has a variable on both sides of the equal sign.

UNPACKING EXAMPLE 8.8.C

Yellow Taxi has no pickup fee but charges $0.25 per mile. AAA Taxi charges $3 for pickup and $0.15 per mile. Find the number of miles for which the cost of the two taxis is the same.

$$0.25x = 3 + 0.15x$$
$$100(0.25x) = 100(3) + 100(0.15x)$$
$$25x = 300 + 15x$$
$$10x = 300$$
$$x = 30$$

The cost is the same for 30 miles.

Visit **my.hrw.com** to see all the **TEKS** unpacked.

my.hrw.com

© Houghton Mifflin Harcourt Publishing Company • Image Credits: ©SW Productions/Getty Images

LESSON 11.1
Equations with the Variable on Both Sides

TEKS
Expressions, equations, and relationships—8.8.A Write one-variable equations or inequalities with variables on both sides that represent problems using rational number coefficients and constants. *Also 8.8.B, 8.8.C*

? ESSENTIAL QUESTION

How can you represent and solve equations with the variable on both sides?

EXPLORE ACTIVITY **TEKS** 8.8.C

Modeling an Equation with a Variable on Both Sides

Algebra tiles can model equations with a variable on both sides.

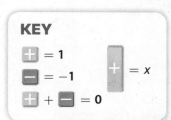

KEY

Use algebra tiles to model and solve $x + 5 = 3x - 1$.

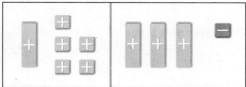

Model $x + 5$ on the left side of the mat and $3x - 1$ on the right side.
Remember that $3x - 1$ is the same as

$3x +$ _____ .

Remove one x-tile from both sides. This

represents subtracting _____ from both sides of the equation.

Math Talk
Mathematical Processes

Why is a positive unit tile added to both sides in the third step?

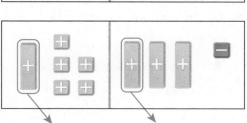

Place one +1-tile on both sides. This

represents adding _____ to both sides of the equation. Remove zero pairs.

Separate each side into 2 equal groups.

One x-tile is equivalent to _____ +1-tiles.

The solution is _____ = _____ .

Reflect

1. How can you check the solution to $x + 5 = 3x - 1$ using algebra tiles?

_____

_____

Solving an Equation with the Variable on Both Sides

Equations with the variable on both sides can be used to compare costs of real-world situations. To solve these equations, use inverse operations to get the variable terms on one side of the equation.

EXAMPLE 1  **TEKS** 8.8.A, 8.8.C

Andy's Rental Car charges an initial fee of $20 plus an additional $30 per day to rent a car. Buddy's Rental Car charges an initial fee of $36 plus an additional $28 per day. For what number of days is the total cost charged by the companies the same?

 STEP 1 Write an expression representing the total cost of renting a car from Andy's Rental Car.

$$\text{Initial fee} \quad + \quad \text{Cost for } x \text{ days}$$
$$20 \quad + \quad 30x$$

 STEP 2 Write an expression representing the total cost of renting a car from Buddy's Rental Car.

$$\text{Initial fee} \quad + \quad \text{Cost for } x \text{ days}$$
$$36 \quad + \quad 28x$$

 STEP 3 Write an equation that can be solved to find the number of days for which the total cost charged by the companies would be the same.

$$\text{Total cost at Andy's} \quad = \quad \text{Total cost at Buddy's}$$
$$20 + 30x \quad = \quad 36 + 28x$$

 STEP 4 Solve the equation for x.

$$
\begin{aligned}
20 + 30x &= 36 + 28x && \text{Write the equation.}\\
-28x &\quad\quad -28x && \text{Subtract } 28x \text{ from both sides.}\\
20 + 2x &= 36\\
-20 &\quad\quad -20 && \text{Subtract 20 from both sides.}\\
2x &= 16\\
\frac{2x}{2} &= \frac{16}{2} && \text{Divide both sides by 2.}\\
x &= 8
\end{aligned}
$$

The total cost is the same if the rental is for 8 days.

Math Talk
Mathematical Processes

When is it more economical to rent from Andy's Rental Car? When is it more economical to rent from Buddy's?

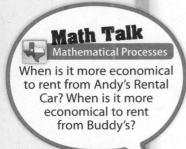

2. A water tank holds 256 gallons but is leaking at a rate of 3 gallons per week. A second water tank holds 384 gallons but is leaking at a rate of 5 gallons per week. After how many weeks will the amount of water in the two tanks be the same?

_____

Writing a Real-World Situation from an Equation

As shown in Example 1, an equation with the variable on both sides can be used to represent a real-world situation. You can reverse this process by writing a real-world situation for a given equation.

Math On the Spot

my.hrw.com

EXAMPLE 2  **TEKS** 8.8.B

Write a real-world situation that could be modeled by the equation $150 + 25x = 55x$.

My Notes

STEP 1 The left side of the equation consists of a constant plus a variable term. It could represent the total cost for doing a job where there is an initial fee plus an hourly charge.

STEP 2 The right side of the equation consists of a variable term. It could represent the cost for doing the same job based on an hourly charge only.

STEP 3 The equation $150 + 25x = 55x$ could be represented by this situation: A handyman charges \$150 plus \$25 per hour for house painting. A painter charges \$55 per hour. How many hours would a job have to take for the handyman's fee and the painter's fee to be the same?

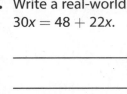
3. Write a real-world situation that could be modeled by the equation $30x = 48 + 22x$.

_____

_____

_____

_____

Guided Practice

Use algebra tiles to model and solve each equation (Explore Activity)

1. $x + 4 = -x - 4$ _____

2. $2 - 3x = -x - 8$ _____

3. At Silver Gym, membership is $25 per month, and personal training sessions are $30 each. At Fit Factor, membership is $65 per month, and personal training sessions are $20 each. In one month, how many personal training sessions would Sarah have to buy to make the total cost at the two gyms equal? (Example 1)

_____

4. Write a real-world situation that could be modeled by the equation $120 + 25x = 45x$. (Example 2)

_____

_____

_____

_____

5. Write a real-world situation that could be modeled by the equation $100 - 6x = 160 - 10x$. (Example 2)

_____

_____

_____

_____

_____

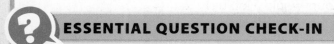 **ESSENTIAL QUESTION CHECK-IN**

6. How can you solve an equation with a variable on both sides?

_____

_____

_____

_____

_____

11.1 Independent Practice

TEKS 8.8.A, 8.8.B, 8.8.C

Personal
Math Trainer

Online
Assessment and
Intervention

my.hrw.com

**Derrick's
Dog Sitting**

$12 plus
$5 per hour

**Darlene's
Dog Sitting**

$18 plus
$3 per hour

7. Derrick' Dog Sitting and Darlene's Dog Sitting are competing for new business. The companies ran the ads shown.

   a. Write and solve an equation to find the number of hours for which the total cost will be the same for the two services.

      _____

   b. **Analyze Relationships** Which dog sitting service is more economical to use if you need 5 hours of service? Explain.

      _____

      _____

8. Country Carpets charges $22 per square yard for carpeting, and an additional installation fee of $100. City Carpets charges $25 per square yard for the same carpeting, and an additional installation fee of $70.

   a. Write and solve an equation to find the number of square yards of carpeting for which the total cost charged by the two companies will be the same.

      _____

   b. **Justify Reasoning** Mr. Shu wants to hire one of the two carpet companies to install carpeting in his basement. Is he more likely to hire Country Carpets or City Carpets? Explain your reasoning.

      _____

      _____

      _____

      _____

Write an equation to represent each relationship. Then solve the equation.

9. Two less than 3 times a number is the same as the number plus 10.

      _____

10. A number increased by 4 is the same as 19 minus 2 times the number.

      _____

11. Twenty less than 8 times a number is the same as 15 more than the number.

      _____

12. The charges for an international call made using the calling card for two phone companies are shown in the table.

Phone Company	Charges
Company A	35¢ plus 3¢ per minute
Company B	45¢ plus 2¢ per minute

a. What is the length of a phone call that would cost the same no matter which company is used?

_____

b. **Analyze Relationships** When is it better to use the card from Company B?

_____

_____

 **FOCUS ON HIGHER ORDER THINKING**

Work Area

13. **Draw Conclusions** Liam is setting up folding chairs for a meeting. If he arranges the chairs in 9 rows of the same length, he has 3 chairs left over. If he arranges the chairs in 7 rows of that same length, he has 19 left over. How many chairs does Liam have?

_____

14. **Explain the Error** Rent-A-Tent rents party tents for a flat fee of $365 plus $125 a day. Capital Rentals rents party tents for a flat fee of $250 plus $175 a day. Delia wrote the following equation to find the number of days for which the total cost charged by the two companies would be the same:

$$365x + 125 = 250x + 175$$

Find and explain the error in Delia's work. Then write the correct equation.

_____

_____

_____

_____

15. **Persevere in Problem Solving** Lilliana is training for a marathon. She runs the same distance every day for a week. On Monday, Wednesday, and Friday, she runs 3 laps on a running trail and then runs 6 more miles. On Tuesday and Sunday, she runs 5 laps on the trail and then runs 2 more miles. On Saturday, she just runs laps. How many laps does Lilliana run on Saturday?

_____

TEKS
Expressions, equations, and relationships—8.8.A Write one-variable equations ... with variables on both sides... using rational number coefficients and constants. *Also 8.8.B, 8.8.C*

? ESSENTIAL QUESTION

How can you solve equations with rational number coefficients and constants?

Solving an Equation that Involves Fractions

To solve an equation with the variable on both sides that involves fractions, start by eliminating the fractions from the equation.

Math On the Spot
my.hrw.com

EXAMPLE 1 ⬤ TEKS 8.8.C

Solve $\frac{7}{10}n + \frac{3}{2} = \frac{3}{5}n + 2$.

STEP 1 Determine the least common multiple of the denominators: LCM(**10, 5, 2**) = 10

$$10 = 10 \times 1$$
$$= 5 \times 2$$
$$= 2 \times 5$$

STEP 2 Multiply both sides of the equation by the LCM.

$$10\left(\frac{7}{10}n + \frac{3}{2}\right) = 10\left(\frac{3}{5}n + 2\right)$$

$$\overset{1}{10}\left(\frac{7}{\underset{1}{10}}n\right) + \overset{5}{10}\left(\frac{3}{\underset{1}{2}}\right) = \overset{2}{10}\left(\frac{3}{\underset{1}{5}}n\right) + 10(2)$$

$$7n + 15 = 6n + 20$$

STEP 3 Use inverse operations to solve the equation.

$$
\begin{array}{rcl}
7n + 15 & = & 6n + 20 \\
-15 & & -15 \\
\hline
7n & = & 6n + 5 \\
-6n & & -6n \\
\hline
n & = & 5 \\
\end{array}
$$

Subtract 15 from both sides.

Subtract 6n from both sides.

Math Talk
Mathematical Processes

The constant on the right side, 2, is not a fraction. Why do you still need to multiply it by the LCM, 10?

Reflect

1. What is the advantage of multiplying both sides of the equation by the least common multiple of the denominators in the first step?

_____

2. **What If?** What happens in the first step if you multiply both sides by a common multiple of the denominators that is not the LCM?

_____

_____

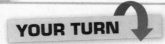

Solve.

3. $\frac{1}{7}k - 6 = \frac{3}{7}k + 4$ _____   **4.** $\frac{5}{6}y + 1 = -\frac{1}{2}y + \frac{1}{4}$ _____

Solving an Equation that Involves Decimals

Solving an equation with the variable on both sides that involves decimals is similar to solving an equation with fractions. But instead of first multiplying both sides by the LCM, multiply by a power of 10 to eliminate the decimals.

EXAMPLE 2    **TEKS** 8.8.A, 8.8.C

Javier walks from his house to the zoo at a constant rate. After walking 0.75 mile, he meets his brother, Raul, and they continue walking at the same constant rate. When they arrive at the zoo, Javier has walked for 0.5 hour and Raul has walked for 0.2 hour. What is the rate in miles per hour at which the brothers walked to the zoo?

STEP 1   Write an equation for the distance from the brothers' house to the zoo, using the fact that distance equals rate times time. Let $r =$ the brothers' walking rate.

$$\underbrace{0.2r + 0.75}_{\text{distance to zoo}} = \underbrace{0.5r}_{\text{distance to zoo}}$$

STEP 2   Multiply both sides of the equation by $10^2 = 100$.

> Multiplying by 100 clears the equation of decimals. Multiplying by 10 does not: $10 \times 0.75 = 7.5$.

$$100(0.2r) + 100(0.75) = 100(0.5r)$$
$$20r + 75 = 50r$$

STEP 3   Use inverse operations to solve the equation.

$$\begin{array}{rl} 20r + 75 = & 50r \\ \underline{-20r} & \underline{-20r} \\ 75 = & 30r \end{array}$$ *Write the equation.*
      Subtract 20r from both sides.

$$\frac{75}{30} = \frac{30r}{30}$$ *Divide both sides by 30.*

$$2.5 = r$$

So, the brothers' constant rate of speed was 2.5 miles per hour.

© Houghton Mifflin Harcourt Publishing Company

11.2 Independent Practice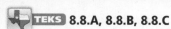

TEKS 8.8.A, 8.8.B, 8.8.C

Personal Math Trainer

Online Assessment and Intervention

my.hrw.com

10. Members of the Wide Waters Club pay $105 per summer season, plus $9.50 each time they rent a boat. Nonmembers must pay $14.75 each time they rent a boat. How many times would a member and a non-member have to rent a boat in order to pay the same amount?

_____

11. Margo can purchase tile at a store for $0.79 per tile and rent a tile saw for $24. At another store she can borrow the tile saw for free if she buys tiles there for $1.19 per tile. How many tiles must she buy for the cost to be the same at both stores?

_____

12. The charges for two shuttle services are shown in the table. Find the number of miles for which the cost of both shuttles is the same.

	Pickup Charge ($)	Charge per Mile ($)
Easy Ride	10	0.10
Best	0	0.35

_____

13. Multistep Rapid Rental Car charges a $40 rental fee, $15 for gas, and $0.25 per mile driven. For the same car, Capital Cars charges $45 for rental and gas and $0.35 per mile.

a. For how many miles is the rental cost at both companies the same?

_____

b. What is that cost?

_____

14. Write an equation with the solution $x = 20$. The equation should have the variable on both sides, a fractional coefficient on the left side, and a fraction anywhere on the right side.

_____

15. Write an equation with the solution $x = 25$. The equation should have the variable on both sides, a decimal coefficient on the left side, and a decimal anywhere on the right side. One of the decimals should be written in tenths, the other in hundredths.

_____

16. Geometry The perimeters of the rectangles shown are equal. What is the perimeter of each rectangle?

$n + 0.1$

$n + 0.6$

n

$2n$

_____

17. Analyze Relationships The formula $F = 1.8C + 32$ gives the temperature in degrees Fahrenheit (F) for a given temperature in degrees Celsius (C). There is one temperature for which the number of degrees Fahrenheit is equal to the number of degrees Celsius. Write an equation you can solve to find that temperature and then use it to find the temperature.

18. Explain the Error Agustin solved an equation as shown. What error did Agustin make? What is the correct answer?

_____

_____

_____

_____

$$\frac{1}{3}x - 4 = \frac{3}{4}x + 1$$
$$12\left(\frac{1}{3}x\right) - 4 = 12\left(\frac{3}{4}x\right)$$
$$4x - 4 = 9x + 1$$
$$-5 = 5x$$
$$x = -1$$

 **FOCUS ON HIGHER ORDER THINKING**

19. Draw Conclusions Solve the equation $\frac{1}{2}x - 5 + \frac{2}{3}x = \frac{7}{6}x + 4$. Explain your results.

_____

_____

_____

_____

20. Look for a Pattern Describe the pattern in the equation. Then solve the equation.

$$0.3x + 0.03x + 0.003x + 0.0003x + \ldots = 3$$

_____

_____

_____

_____

21. Critique Reasoning Jared wanted to find three consecutive even integers whose sum was 4 times the first of those integers. He let k represent the first integer, then wrote and solved this equation: $k + (k + 1) + (k + 2) = 4k$. Did he get the correct answer? Explain.

_____

_____

_____

_____

_____

Work Area

TEKS
Expressions, equations, and relationships—8.8.A
Write one-variable equations or inequalities with variables on both sides that represent problems using rational number coefficients and constants. *Also 8.8.B*

ESSENTIAL QUESTION

How can you use inequalities to represent real-world problems?

EXPLORE ACTIVITY **TEKS** 8.8.A

Modeling a Real-World Situation with an Inequality

Many real-world situations can be modeled by inequalities. Some phrases that indicate an inequality are "less than," "greater than," "no more than," and "at least."

Super-Clean house cleaning company charges a fee of $384 to power wash a house plus $2 per linear foot. Power Bright charges $6 per linear foot, but no flat fee. Write an inequality that can be solved to find the number of linear feet a house must have to make the total cost charged by Super-Clean less than the cost charged by Power Bright.

A Translate from words into symbols.

Let *l* represent the number of _____ of the house.

Super-Clean fee	plus	$2 per linear foot	times	number of linear feet	is less than	Power Bright's charge per linear foot	times	number of linear feet
☐	☐	☐	☐	☐	☐	☐	☐	☐

B Write the inequality.

_____

Reflect

1. How did you decide which inequality symbol to use?

_____

_____

_____

Writing an Inequality for a Real-World Situation

Once you have modeled a real-world situation with an inequality, you can solve the inequality to answer the question posed by the situation. Use inverse operations to get the variable terms on one side of the inequality and the constant terms on the other side. Recall that if you multiply or divide both sides by a negative number, you need to reverse the inequality symbol.

My Notes

EXAMPLE 1    TEKS 8.8.A

A yellow hot-air balloon is 100 feet off the ground and rising at a rate of 8 feet per second. An orange hot-air balloon is 160 feet off the ground and rising at a rate of 5 feet per second. After how long will the yellow balloon be higher than the orange balloon?

STEP 1 Write an expression representing the height of the yellow balloon.

Current height (ft)	+	Number of feet it rises in s seconds
100	+	$8s$

> Let s represent the number of seconds the balloons are rising.

STEP 2 Write an expression representing the height of the orange balloon.

Current height (ft)	+	Number of feet it rises in s seconds
160	+	$5s$

STEP 3 Write an inequality that can be solved to find the number of seconds it will take for the height of the yellow balloon to be greater than the height of the orange balloon.

Height of yellow balloon	>	Height of orange balloon
$100 + 8s$	>	$160 + 5s$

STEP 4 Solve the inequality for s.

$$100 + 8s > 160 + 5s$$
$$\underline{-5s \qquad\qquad -5s}$$ Subtract 5s from both sides.
$$100 + 3s > 160$$
$$\underline{-100 \qquad\qquad -100}$$ Subtract 100 from both sides.
$$3s > 60$$
$$\frac{3s}{3} > \frac{60}{3}$$ Divide both sides by 3.
$$s > 20$$

The yellow balloon will be higher than the orange balloon after 20 seconds.

2. The temperature in Amarillo is 74°F and is increasing at a rate of 2°F per hour. In Houston, it is 68°F and increasing 4°F per hour. Write and solve an inequality to find how long it will take for the temperature in Houston to exceed the temperature in Amarillo.

_____

Writing a Real-World Situation from an Inequality

As shown in Example 1, inequalities with the variable on both sides can be used to represent real-world situations. You can reverse this process by writing a real-world situation for a given inequality.

EXAMPLE 2   TEKS 8.8.B

Write a real-world situation that can be modeled by the inequality $50 - 3d < 30 - 2d$.

Each side of the inequality consists of a constant with a variable term subtracted from it.

This side can represent a lunch account that begins with $50 and has $3 taken out each day.

This side can represent a lunch account that begins with $30 and has $2 taken out each day.

$$50 - 3d \quad < \quad 30 - 2d$$

The inequality symbol is <, so find when the balance in the first account is *less than* the balance in the second account.

The inequality $50 - 3d < 30 - 2d$ can represent this situation: Joe has $50 in his lunch account and spends $3 each day. Renee has $30 in her lunch account and spends $2 each day. After how many days will the balance in Joe's account be less than the balance in Renee's account?

YOUR TURN

3. Write a real-world situation that can be modeled by the inequality $46h > 84 + 25h$.

_____

_____

_____

1. *The Daily Record* charges a fee of $525 plus $75 per week to run an ad. *The Chronicle* charges $150 per week. (Explore Activity and Example 1)

    a. Write an inequality that can be solved to find the number of weeks an ad must run to make the total cost of running an ad in *The Daily Record* less than the cost in *The Chronicle*.

    _____

    b. Solve your inequality.

    _____

2. The inventory report at Jacob's Office Supplies shows that there are 150 packages of pencils and 120 packages of markers. If the store sells 7 packages of pencils each day and 5 packages of markers each day, write and solve an inequality to find in how many days the number of packages of pencils will be fewer than the number of packages of markers. (Example 1)

    _____

3. Write a real-world situation that can be modeled by the inequality $834 + 14s > 978 - 10s$. Then solve the inequality. (Example 2)

    _____

    _____

    _____

    _____

    _____

    _____

? ESSENTIAL QUESTION CHECK-IN

4. How can you use inequalities to represent real-world problems?

    _____

    _____

    _____

    _____

11.3 Independent Practice

TEKS 8.8.A, 8.8.B

Personal Math Trainer

Online Assessment and Intervention

my.hrw.com

5. The school band is selling pizzas for $7 each to raise money for new uniforms. The supplier charges $100 plus $4 per pizza.

a. Write an inequality that can be solved to find the number of pizzas the band members must sell to make a profit.

_____

b. Solve your inequality.

_____

6. Nadia was offered a job selling ads for a magazine. She must agree to one of the following payment options:

Choice A $110 for each ad she sells

Choice B   A weekly salary of $150, plus $85 for each ad she sells

Write and solve an inequality to determine the number of ads Nadia would need to sell per week in order for Choice A to be the better choice.

_____

7. Represent Real-World Problems Write a real-world situation that can be modeled by the inequality $20x > 30 + 15x$.

_____

_____

_____

_____

_____

Write an inequality to represent each relationship. Then solve your inequality.

8. Ten less than five times a number is less than six times the number decreased by eight.

_____

9. The sum of a number and twenty is greater than four times the number decreased by one.

_____

10. Bob's Bagels offers pre-paid cards and has the specials shown. Carol has a $50 card she uses to buy coffee and a bagel each week. Diego has a $60 card he uses to buy tea and a breakfast sandwich each week. Write and solve an inequality to find the number of weeks in which the balance on Carol's card will be greater than the balance on Diego's card.

_____

 **FOCUS ON HIGHER ORDER THINKING**

11. **Critique Reasoning** Ahmad and Cameron solved the same inequality but got different answers. One of the solutions is incorrect. Find and correct the error.

Ahmad's Solution

$$28 - 7x < 40 - 3x$$
$$\underline{+ 7x \qquad\quad + 7x}$$
$$28 < 40 + 4x$$
$$\underline{- 40 \quad - 40}$$
$$-12 < \qquad 4x$$
$$\frac{-12}{4} < \frac{4x}{4}$$
$$-3 < x$$

Cameron's Solution

$$28 - 7x < 40 - 3x$$
$$\underline{+ 3x \qquad\quad + 3x}$$
$$28 - 4x < 40$$
$$\underline{- 28 \qquad - 28}$$
$$-4x < 12$$
$$\frac{-4x}{-4} < \frac{12}{-4}$$
$$x < -3$$

_____

_____

_____

12. **Represent Real-World Problems** Meena sells apple pies at the farmer's market. She charges $12 for each pie. It costs her $5 to make each pie, and there is a $35 fee she must pay each week to have a booth at the market.

a. Write and solve an inequality to find the number of pies Meena must sell each week in order to make a profit.

_____

b. **What If?** Suppose the fee to have a booth at the farmer's market increases to $40. Will the new fee increase the number of pies Meena will have to sell in order to make a profit? Explain your reasoning.

_____

_____

_____

_____

Work Area

Inequalities with Rational Numbers

TEKS
Expressions, equations, and relationships—8.8.A
Write one-variable equations or inequalities with variables on both sides . . . using rational number coefficients and constants. *Also 8.8.B*

? ESSENTIAL QUESTION

How can you use inequalities with rational number coefficients and constants to represent real-world problems?

Modeling with an Inequality that Involves Fractions

If an inequality contains fractions, you can to multiply both sides by the least common multiple of the denominators to clear the fractions.

Math On the Spot
⏱ my.hrw.com

EXAMPLE 1    **TEKS** 8.8.A

Write an inequality to represent the relationship "Twice a number plus four is greater than two thirds of the number". Then solve your inequality.

STEP 1   Write an inequality.

Twice a number	plus	four	is greater than	two thirds of the number.
$2x$	$+$	4	$>$	$\frac{2}{3}x$

An inequality is $2x + 4 > \frac{2}{3}x$.

STEP 2   Multiply both sides of the inequality by the LCM, 3.

$$3(2x) + 3(4) > 3\left(\frac{2}{3}x\right)$$

$$6x + 12 > \overset{1}{3}\left(\frac{2}{3}\underset{1}{x}\right)$$

$$6x + 12 > 2x$$

STEP 3   Use inverse operations to solve the inequality.

$$
\begin{array}{rcl}
6x + 12 & > & 2x \\
-6x & & -6x \\
\hline
12 & > & -4x \\
\frac{12}{-4} & < & \frac{-4x}{-4} \\
-3 & < & x
\end{array}
$$

Subtract 6x from both sides.

Divide both sides by −4, reversing the direction of the inequality symbol.

Math Talk
Mathematical Processes

What could you do differently in Step 3 so you would not have to reverse the inequality symbol?

YOUR TURN

1. Write an inequality to represent the relationship "Three-fourths of a number is greater than five less than the number." Then solve your inequality. _____

Personal Math Trainer
Online Assessment and Intervention
⏱ my.hrw.com

Modeling with an Inequality that Involves Decimals

To solve an inequality with the variable on both sides that involves decimals, multiply both sides by a power of 10 to eliminate the decimals.

EXAMPLE 2 Real World    **TEKS** 8.8.A, 8.8.C

Two water tanks hold 28.62 gallons and 31.2 gallons of water. The larger tank is leaking at a rate of 0.12 gallon per hour. The smaller tank is leaking at a rate of 0.08 gallon per hour. After how many hours will there be less water in the larger tank than in the smaller tank?

STEP 1 Write an inequality. Let h represent the number of hours.

amount in larger tank < amount in smaller tank

$$31.2 - 0.12h < 28.62 - 0.08h$$

STEP 2 Multiply both sides of the inequality by $10^2 = 100$.

$$100(31.2) - 100(0.12h) < 100(28.62) - 100(0.08h)$$

$$3{,}120 - 12h < 2{,}862 - 8h$$

STEP 3 Use inverse operations to solve the inequality.

$$
\begin{array}{rcl}
3{,}120 - 12h & < & 2{,}862 - 8h \\
- 2{,}862 & & - 2{,}862 \\
\hline
258 - 12h & < & -8h \\
+ 12h & & + 12h \\
\hline
258 & < & 4h \\
\dfrac{258}{4} & < & \dfrac{4h}{4} \\
64.5 & < & h
\end{array}
$$

Subtract 2,862 from both sides.

Add 12h to both sides.

Divide both sides by 4.

So, after 64.5 hours, there will be less water in the larger tank.

Reflect

2. In Step 2, why do you multiply both sides by 100 rather than by 10?

_____

_____

YOUR TURN

3. Bamboo Plant A is 1.2 meters tall and growing at a rate of 0.45 meter per day. Bamboo Plant B is 0.85 meter tall and growing 0.5 meter per day. After how many days will Plant B be taller than Plant A? _____

Writing a Real-World Situation from an Inequality

By studying the way that a given inequality is constructed, you can write a real-world situation that the inequality models. The table gives phrases you can use for the symbols that appear in inequalities.

Symbol	$<$	$>$	$\leq$	$\geq$
Phrases	less than; fewer than	greater than; more than	less than or equal to; at most; no more than; a maximum of	greater than or equal to; at least; no less than; a minimum of

EXAMPLE 3

TEKS 8.8.B

Write a real-world situation that can be modeled by the inequality $11.25x - 20 \geq 10.75x - 12.5$.

My Notes

Each side of the inequality consists of a variable term with a constant subtracted from it. The left side must exceed or be equal to the right side.

The numbers 11.25 and 10.75 can represent hourly wages at two jobs.

$$11.25x - 20 \qquad \geq \qquad 10.75x - 12.5$$

The numbers 20 and 12.5 can represent fixed amounts of money being subtracted.

The inequality $11.25x - 20 \geq 10.75x - 12.5$ can represent this situation: Ryan earns $11.25 per hour. His transit cost to and from work is $20 per week. Tony earns $10.75 per hour. His weekly transit cost is $12.50. After how many hours of work in a week do Ryan's earnings minus transit cost exceed Tony's earnings minus transit cost?

4. Write a real-world problem that can be modeled by the inequality $-10 - \frac{1}{4}x > 20 - \frac{1}{2}x$.

_____

_____

_____

_____

Personal Math Trainer

Online Assessment and Intervention

my.hrw.com

Write an inequality to represent each relationship. Then solve your inequality. (Example 1)

1. Three fourths of a number is less than six plus the number.

_____

2. One fifth of a number added to eleven is greater than three fourths of the number.

_____

3. Ian wants to promote his band on the Internet. Site A offers website hosting for $4.95 per month with a $49.95 startup fee. Site B offers website hosting for $9.95 per month with no startup fee. Write and solve an inequality to determine how many months Ian could have his website on Site B and still keep his total cost less than on Site A. (Example 2)

_____

4. Write a real-world problem that can be modeled by the inequality $10x > 5.5x + 31.5$. (Example 3)

_____

_____

_____

_____

_____

? ESSENTIAL QUESTION CHECK-IN

5. How can you use inequalities with rational number coefficients and constants to represent real-world problems?

_____

_____

_____

_____

11.4 Independent Practice

TEKS 8.8.A, 8.8.B

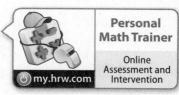

Personal Math Trainer

Online Assessment and Intervention

my.hrw.com

6. Rugs Emporium installs carpet for $80 plus $9.50 per square yard of carpet. Carpets-4-U charges $120 for installation and $7.50 per square yard of carpet. Write and solve an inequality to find the number of square yards of carpet for which Rugs Emporium charges more than Carpets-4-U.

_____

7. Billie needs to have her refrigerator repaired. She contacts two appliance repair companies and is given the rates shown in the table. Write and solve an inequality to find the number of hours for which Ace's charge is less than or the same as Acme's charge.

	Flat Fee Charge ($)	Charge per Hour ($)
Acme Repair	49	22.50
Ace Repair	0	34.75

_____

8. Write an inequality with the solution $x < 12$. The inequality should have the variable on both sides, a decimal coefficient of the variable on the left side, and a decimal anywhere on the right side. One of the decimals should be written in tenths, the other in hundredths.

_____

9. Write an inequality with the solution $x \geq 4$. The inequality should have the variable on both sides, a fractional coefficient of the variable on the left side, and a fraction anywhere on the right side.

_____

10. Multistep According to the Triangle Inequality, the length of the longest side of a triangle must be less than the sum of the lengths of the other two sides. The two shortest sides of a triangle measure $\frac{3}{10}$ and $x + \frac{1}{5}$, and the longest side measures $\frac{3}{2}x$.

a. Write an inequality that uses the Triangle Inequality to relate the three sides.

_____

b. For what values of x is the Triangle Inequality true for this triangle?

_____

11. José and Maris work for different car dealerships. José earns a monthly salary of $3,500 plus a 6% commission on sales. Maris earns a monthly salary of $4,000 plus a 4% commission on sales. Above what value of sales are José's monthly earnings more than those of Maris?

_____

12. Multistep Consider the figures shown.

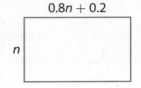

    a. Write an expression for the perimeter of each figure.

    _____

    _____

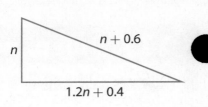

    b. For what values of n will the rectangle have a greater perimeter than the triangle?

    _____

 **FOCUS ON HIGHER ORDER THINKING**

13. Draw Conclusions The inequality $y < \frac{2}{3}x + 5$ represents all points on the coordinate plane that are below the line $y = \frac{2}{3}x + 5$.

    a. If you substitute the x- and y-values of the point (6, 11) into the inequality, do you get a true statement? What does this mean?

    _____

    b. If $y = 2\frac{1}{2}$, what are the possible values of x? What does this mean?

    _____

    _____

    _____

14. Communicate Mathematical Ideas Describe what you can do when solving an inequality to assure that the coefficient of the variable term will be positive.

_____

_____

_____

15. Make a Conjecture For what values of x is the absolute value of x less than or equal to 1.5? (*Hint*: Substitute numbers into the inequality $|x| \leq 1.5$ and see which numbers make the inequality true.) Choose three other positive numbers and answer the question using those numbers. Make a conjecture about when the absolute value of x is less than or equal to a given positive number a.

_____

_____

_____

_____

© Houghton Mifflin Harcourt Publishing Company

Equations and Inequalities with the Variable on Both Sides

? ESSENTIAL QUESTION

How can you use equations and inequalities with variables on both sides to solve real-world problems?

EXAMPLE 1

A tutor gives students a choice of how to pay: a base rate of $20 plus $8 per hour, or a set rate of $13 per hour. Find the number of hours of tutoring for which the cost is the same for either choice.

Plan 1 cost: $20 + 8x$ Plan 2 cost: $13x$

$20 + 8x = \ 13x$	*Write the equation.*
$\underline{\ -8x \quad\ -8x}$	*Subtract 8x from both sides.*
$\quad\ 20 = 5x$	*Divide both sides by 5.*
$\quad\ \ x = 4$	

The cost is the same for 4 hours of tutoring.

EXAMPLE 2

Solve $0.6y - 12.3 < 7.4 - 1.9y$.

$0.6y - 12.3 < 7.4 - 1.9y$	*Write the inequality.*
$10(0.6y) - 10(12.3) < 10(7.4) - 10(1.9y)$	*Multiply both sides by 10.*
$6y - 123 < \quad 74 - 19y$	
$\underline{+123 \quad\ +123}$	*Add 123 to both sides.*
$6y < \quad 197 - 19y$	
$\underline{+19y \qquad\qquad +19y}$	*Add 19y to both sides.*
$25y < \qquad\qquad 197$	
$y < \qquad\qquad 7.88$	*Divide both sides by 25.*

EXERCISES

Solve. (Lessons 11.1, 11.2, 11.3, 11.4)

1. $13 - 6y = 8y$

2. $\frac{1}{5}x + 5 = 19 - \frac{1}{2}x$

3. $7.3t + 22 \leq 2.1t - 22.2$

4. $7 - 45z < 5z + 13$

5. $1.4 + \frac{2}{5}e \geq \frac{3}{15}e - 0.8$

6. $0.75x - 6.5 = -0.5 - 0.25x$

7. Write a real-world situation that could be modeled by the equation $650 + 10m = 60m + 400$. (Lesson 11.1)

_____

_____

_____

_____

8. John is trying to decide which carpeting company to use to put carpet in his living room. Carla's Carpeting charges $45 plus $5.50 per square foot. Fred's Flooring charges $195 plus $4.25 per square foot. For what size room is Carla's Carpeting cheaper than Fred's Flooring? (Lesson 11.3)

_____

Unit 4 Performance Tasks

1. **CAREERS IN MATH** **Hydraulic Engineer** A hydraulic engineer is studying the pressure in a particular fluid. The pressure is equal to the atmospheric pressure 101 kN/m plus 8 kN/m for every meter below the surface, where kN/m is kilonewtons per meter, a unit of pressure.

a. Write an expression for the pressure at a depth of d_1 meters below the liquid surface. _____

b. Write and solve an equation to find the depth at which the pressure is 200 kN/m.

_____

c. The hydraulic engineer alters the density of the fluid so that the pressure at depth d_2 below the surface is atmospheric pressure 101 kN/m plus 9 kN/m for every meter below the surface. Write an expression for the pressure at depth d_2. _____

d. If the pressure at depth d_1 in the first fluid is equal to the pressure at depth d_2 in the second fluid, what is the relationship between d_1 and d_2? Explain how you found your answer.

_____

_____

_____

Transformational Geometry

MODULE 12
Transformations and Congruence
TEKS 8.10.A, 8.10.C

MODULE 13
Dilations, Similarity, and Proportionality
TEKS 8.3.A, 8.3.B, 8.3.C, 8.10.A, 8.10.B, 8.10.D

CAREERS IN MATH

Contractor A contractor is engaged in the construction, repair, and dismantling of structures such as buildings, bridges, and roads. Contractors use math when researching and implementing building codes, making measurements and scaling models, and in financial management.

If you are interested in a career as a contractor, you should study the following mathematical subjects:
- Business Math
- Geometry
- Algebra
- Trigonometry

Research other careers that require the use of business math and scaling.

Unit 5 Performance Task

At the end of the unit, check out how **contractors** use math.

Vocabulary Preview

Use the puzzle to preview key vocabulary from this unit. Unscramble the circled letters within found words to answer the riddle at the bottom of the page.

```
W  T  C  F  V  A  F  I  L  I  T  U  G  N  S
M  U  J  L  O  C  Z  H  B  R  S  D  E  O  W
F  E  Q  V  H  B  T  E  A  N  T  P  X  I  A
M  Y  J  G  B  O  G  N  P  K  G  G  B  T  Q
N  X  L  H  A  A  S  E  V  Z  R  U  B  C  W
L  O  X  D  M  L  A  G  R  H  H  L  R  U  A
G  P  I  I  A  E  M  X  K  V  A  K  X  D  K
B  D  E  T  N  E  M  E  G  R  A  L  N  E  A
W  R  I  E  C  A  N  R  E  Y  M  A  T  R  P
P  O  G  L  K  E  R  O  T  A  T  I  O  N  R
N  Z  Y  E  A  C  L  R  O  V  Z  S  P  I  U
U  Y  T  J  N  T  Q  F  N  B  X  G  G  C  J
O  N  E  R  Z  I  I  P  E  I  Y  F  A  B  W
I  F  V  U  C  M  S  O  G  R  P  Q  K  B  W
C  Q  T  U  I  C  C  U  N  L  N  T  L  D  Y
```

The input of a transformation. (Lesson 12.1)

A transformation that flips a figure across a line. (Lesson 12.2)

A transformation that slides a figure along a straight line. (Lesson 12.1)

A transformation that turns a figure around a given point. (Lesson 12.3)

The product of a figure made larger by dilation. (Lesson 13.1)

The product of a figure made smaller by dilation. (Lesson 13.1)

Scaled replicas that change the size but not the shape of a figure. (Lesson 13.1)

Q: What do you call an angle that's broken?

A: A ___ ___ ___ ___ ___ ___ ___ ___ ___ ___!

Transformations and Congruence

ESSENTIAL QUESTION

How can you use transformations and congruence to solve real-world problems?

Real-World Video

When a marching band lines up and marches across the field, they are modeling a translation. As they march, they maintain size and orientation. A translation is one type of transformation.

my.hrw.com

GO DIGITAL

my.hrw.com

my.hrw.com

Go digital with your write-in student edition, accessible on any device.

Math On the Spot

Scan with your smart phone to jump directly to the online edition, video tutor, and more.

 Animated Math

Interactively explore key concepts to see how math works.

Personal Math Trainer

Get immediate feedback and help as you work through practice sets.

Are YOU Ready?

Complete these exercises to review skills you will need for this module.

Integer Operations

EXAMPLE

$-3 - (-6) = -3 + 6$

$= |-3| - |6|$

$= 3$

To subtract an integer, add its opposite. The signs are different, so find the difference of the absolute values: $6 - 3 = 3$. Use the sign of the number with the greater absolute value.

Find each difference.

1. $5 - (-9)$ _____

2. $-6 - 8$ _____

3. $2 - 9$ _____

4. $-10 - (-6)$ _____

5. $3 - (-11)$ _____

6. $12 - 7$ _____

7. $-4 - 11$ _____

8. $0 - (-12)$ _____

Measure Angles

EXAMPLE

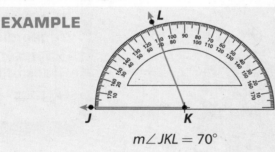

$m\angle JKL = 70°$

Place the center point of the protractor on the angle's vertex.

Align one ray with the base of the protractor.

Read the angle measure where the other ray intersects the semicircle.

Use a protractor to measure each angle.

9.

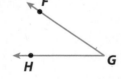

10.

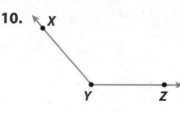

11.

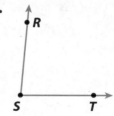

_____ _____ _____

Reading Start-Up

© Houghton Mifflin Harcourt Publishing Company

Visualize Vocabulary

Use the ✔ words to complete the graphic organizer. You will put one word in each oval.

Types of Quadrilaterals

A quadrilateral in which all sides are congruent and opposite sides are parallel.

A quadrilateral in which opposite sides are parallel and congruent.

A quadrilateral in which two sides are parallel.

Vocabulary

Review Words

coordinate plane *(plano cartesiano)*

✔ parallelogram *(paralelogramo)*

quadrilateral *(cuadrilátero)*

✔ rhombus *(rombo)*

✔ trapezoid *(trapecio)*

Preview Words

center of rotation *(centro de rotación)*

image *(imagen)*

line of reflection *(línea de reflexión)*

preimage *(imagen original)*

reflection *(reflexión)*

rotation *(rotación)*

transformation *(transformación)*

translation *(traslación)*

Understand Vocabulary

Match the term on the left to the correct expression on the right.

1. transformation

A. A function that describes a change in the position, size, or shape of a figure.

2. reflection

B. A function that slides a figure along a straight line.

3. translation

C. A transformation that flips a figure across a line.

Active Reading

Booklet Before beginning the module, create a booklet to help you learn the concepts in this module. Write the main idea of each lesson on each page of the booklet. As you study each lesson, write important details that support the main idea, such as vocabulary and formulas. Refer to your finished booklet as you work on assignments and study for tests.

Unpacking the TEKS

Understanding the TEKS and the vocabulary terms in the TEKS will help you know exactly what you are expected to learn in this module.

© Houghton Mifflin Harcourt Publishing Company

TEKS 8.10.A

Generalize the properties of orientation and congruence of rotations, reflections, translations, and dilations of two-dimensional shapes on a coordinate plane.

What It Means to You

You will identify a rotation, a reflection, and a translation, and understand that the image has the same shape and size as the preimage.

UNPACKING EXAMPLE 8.10.A

The figure shows triangle *ABC* and its image after three different transformations. Identify and describe the translation, the reflection, and the rotation of triangle *ABC*.

Figure 1 is a translation 4 units down. Figure 2 is a reflection across the *y*-axis. Figure 3 is a rotation of 180°.

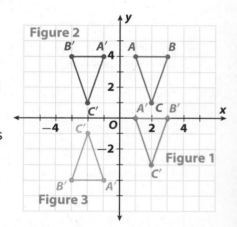

TEKS 8.10.C

Explain the effect of translations, reflections over the *x*- or *y*-axis, and rotations limited to 90°, 180°, 270°, and 360° as applied to two-dimensional shapes on a coordinate plane using an algebraic representation.

What It Means to You

You can use an algebraic representation to translate, reflect, or rotate a two-dimensional figure.

UNPACKING EXAMPLE 8.10.C

Rectangle *RSTU* with vertices $(-4, -1)$, $(-1, 1)$, $(-1, -3)$, and $(-4, -3)$ is reflected across the *y*-axis. Find the coordinates of the image.

The rule to reflect across the *y*-axis is to change the sign of the *x*-coordinate.

Coordinates	Reflect across the y-axis $(-x, y)$	Coordinates of image
$(-4, 1)$, $(-1, 1)$, $(-1, -3)$, $(-4, -3)$	$(-(-4), 1)$, $(-(-1), 1)$, $(-(-1), -3)$, $(-(-4), -3)$	$(4, -1)$, $(1, 1)$, $(1, -3)$, $(4, -3)$

The coordinates of the image are $(4, 1)$, $(1, 1)$, $(1, -3)$, and $(4, -3)$.

Visit **my.hrw.com** to see all the **TEKS** unpacked.

my.hrw.com

LESSON
12.1

Properties of Translations

TEKS
Two-dimensional shapes—8.10.A
Generalize the properties of orientation and congruence of ... translations...of two-dimensional shapes on a coordinate plane.

? ESSENTIAL QUESTION

How do you describe the properties of orientation and congruence of translations?

EXPLORE ACTIVITY 1  TEKS 8.10.A

Exploring Translations

You learned that a function is a rule that assigns exactly one output to each input. A **transformation** is a function that describes a change in the position, size, or shape of a figure. The input of a transformation is the **preimage**, and the output of a transformation is the **image**.

A **translation** is a transformation that slides a figure along a straight line. The image has the same size and shape as the preimage.

The triangle shown on the grid is the preimage (input). The arrow shows the motion of a translation and how point A is translated to point A′.

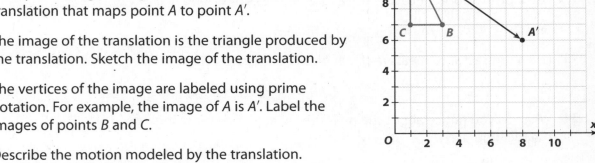

A Trace triangle *ABC* onto a piece of paper. Cut out your traced triangle.

B Slide your triangle along the arrow to model the translation that maps point *A* to point *A′*.

C The image of the translation is the triangle produced by the translation. Sketch the image of the translation.

D The vertices of the image are labeled using prime notation. For example, the image of *A* is *A′*. Label the images of points *B* and *C*.

E Describe the motion modeled by the translation.

Move _____ units right and _____ units down.

F Check that the motion you described in part **E** is the same motion that maps point *A* onto *A′*, point *B* onto *B′*, and point *C* onto *C′*.

Reflect

1. How is the orientation of the triangle affected by the translation?

_____

Properties of Translations

Use trapezoid *TRAP* to investigate the properties of translations.

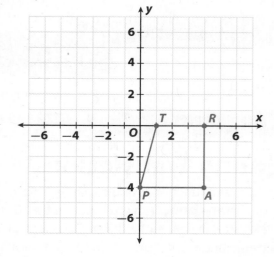

A Trace the trapezoid onto a piece of paper. Cut out your traced trapezoid.

B Place your trapezoid on top of the trapezoid in the figure. Then translate your trapezoid 5 units to the left and 3 units up. Sketch the image of the translation by tracing your trapezoid in this new location. Label the vertices of the image T', R', A', and P'.

C Use a ruler to measure the sides of trapezoid *TRAP* in centimeters.

$TR =$ _____ $RA =$ _____ $AP =$ _____ $TP =$ _____

D Use a ruler to measure the sides of trapezoid $T'R'A'P'$ in centimeters.

$T'R' =$ _____ $R'A' =$ _____ $A'P' =$ _____ $T'P' =$ _____

E What do you notice about the lengths of corresponding sides of the two figures?

_____

F Use a protractor to measure the angles of trapezoid *TRAP*.

$m\angle T =$ _____ $m\angle R =$ _____ $m\angle A =$ _____ $m\angle P =$ _____

G Use a protractor to measure the angles of trapezoid $T'R'A'P'$.

$m\angle T' =$ _____ $m\angle R' =$ _____ $m\angle A' =$ _____ $m\angle P' =$ _____

H What do you notice about the measures of corresponding angles of the two figures?

_____

I Which sides of trapezoid *TRAP* are parallel? How do you know?

_____

Which sides of trapezoid $T'R'A'P'$ are parallel? _____

What do you notice? _____

_____

Reflect

2. Make a Conjecture Use your results from parts **E**, **H**, and **I** to make a conjecture about translations.

_____

_____

3. What can you say about translations and congruence?

_____

_____

Graphing Translations

To translate a figure in the coordinate plane, translate each of its vertices. Then connect the vertices to form the image.

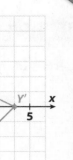

Math On the Spot
my.hrw.com

EXAMPLE 1

TEKS 8.10.A

The figure shows triangle *XYZ*. Graph the image of the triangle after a translation of 4 units to the right and 1 unit up.

> **STEP 1** Translate point *X*.
>
> Count right 4 units and up 1 unit and plot point *X'*.
>
> **STEP 2** Translate point *Y*.
>
> Count right 4 units and up 1 unit and plot point *Y'*.
>
> **STEP 3** Translate point *Z*.
>
> Count right 4 units and up 1 unit and plot point *Z'*.
>
> **STEP 4** Connect *X'*, *Y'*, and *Z'* to form triangle *X'Y'Z'*.

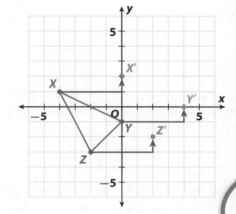

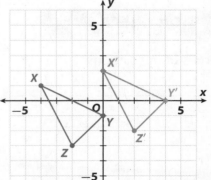

Each vertex is moved 4 units right and 1 unit up.

Math Talk
Mathematical Processes

Is the image congruent to the preimage? How do you know?

YOUR TURN

4. The figure shows parallelogram *ABCD*. Graph the image of the parallelogram after a translation of 5 units to the left and 2 units down.

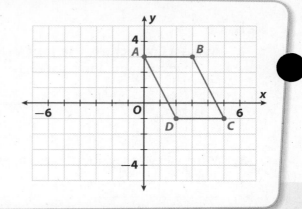

Guided Practice

1. **Vocabulary** A _____ is a change in the position, size, or shape of a figure.

2. **Vocabulary** When you perform a transformation of a figure on the coordinate plane, the input of the transformation is called the _____, and the output of the transformation is called the _____.

3. Joni translates a right triangle 2 units down and 4 units to the right. How does the orientation of the image of the triangle compare with the orientation of the preimage? (Explore Activity 1)

   _____

4. Rashid drew rectangle *PQRS* on a coordinate plane. He then translated the rectangle 3 units up and 3 units to the left and labeled the image *P'Q'R'S'*. How do rectangle *PQRS* and rectangle *P'Q'R'S'* compare? (Explore Activity 2)

   _____

5. The figure shows trapezoid *WXYZ*. Graph the image of the trapezoid after a translation of 4 units up and 2 units to the left. (Example 1)

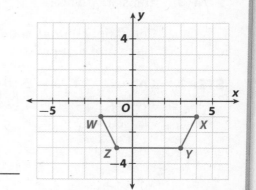

? ESSENTIAL QUESTION CHECK-IN

6. What are the properties of translations?

   _____

   _____

12.1 Independent Practice

TEKS 8.10.A

Personal Math Trainer

Online Assessment and Intervention

my.hrw.com

7. The figure shows triangle *DEF*.

   a. Graph the image of the triangle after the translation that maps point *D* to point *D'*.

   b. How would you describe the translation?

   _____

   _____

   c. How does the image of triangle *DEF* compare with the preimage?

   _____

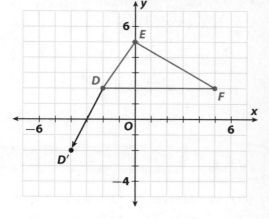

8. a. Graph quadrilateral *KLMN* with vertices *K*(−3, 2), *L*(2, 2), *M*(0, −3), and *N*(−4, 0) on the coordinate grid.

   b. On the same coordinate grid, graph the image of quadrilateral *KLMN* after a translation of 3 units to the right and 4 units up.

   c. Which side of the image is congruent to side $\overline{LM}$?

   _____

   Name three other pairs of congruent sides.

   _____

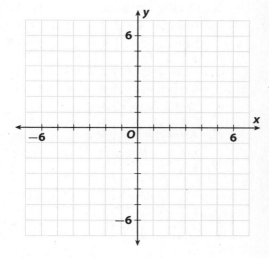

Draw the image of the figure after each translation.

9. 4 units left and 2 units down

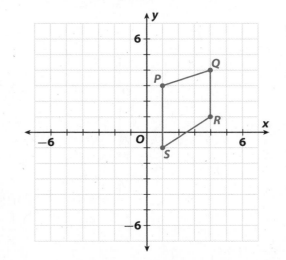

10. 5 units right and 3 units up

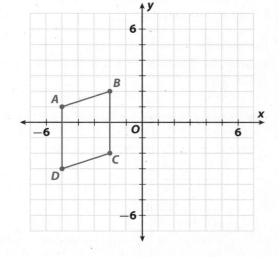

11. The figure shows the ascent of a hot air balloon. How would you describe the translation?

_____

_____

12. Critical Thinking Is it possible that the orientation of a figure could change after it is translated? Explain.

_____

_____

_____

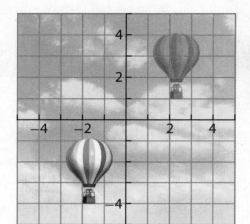

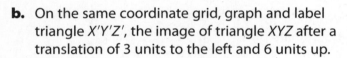

FOCUS ON HIGHER ORDER THINKING

13. a. Multistep Graph triangle *XYZ* with vertices *X*(−2, −5), *Y*(2, −2), and *Z*(4, −4) on the coordinate grid.

b. On the same coordinate grid, graph and label triangle *X′Y′Z′*, the image of triangle *XYZ* after a translation of 3 units to the left and 6 units up.

c. Now graph and label triangle *X″Y″Z″*, the image of triangle *X′Y′Z′* after a translation of 1 unit to the left and 2 units down.

d. Analyze Relationships How would you describe the translation that maps triangle *XYZ* onto triangle *X″Y″Z″*?

_____

_____

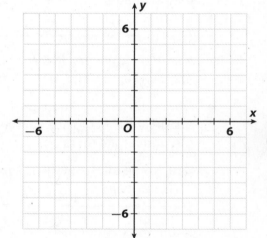

14. Critical Thinking The figure shows rectangle *P′Q′R′S′*, the image of rectangle *PQRS* after a translation of 5 units to the right and 7 units up. Graph and label the preimage *PQRS*.

15. Communicate Mathematical Ideas Explain why the image of a figure after a translation is congruent to its preimage.

_____

_____

_____

_____

_____

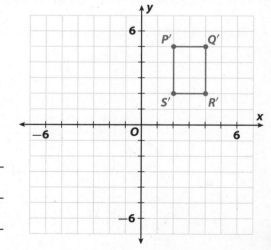

Properties of Reflections

TEKS
Two-dimensional
shapes—8.10.A
Generalize the properties
of orientation and congruence
of... reflections... of two-
dimensional shapes on a
coordinate plane.

ESSENTIAL QUESTION

How do you describe the properties of orientation and
congruence of reflections?

EXPLORE ACTIVITY 1  **TEKS** 8.10.A

Exploring Reflections

A **reflection** is a transformation that flips a figure across a line.
The line is called the **line of reflection**. Each point and its image
are the same distance from the line of reflection.

**The triangle shown on the grid is the preimage. You will
explore reflections across the x- and y-axes.**

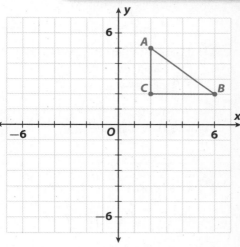

A Trace triangle ABC and the x- and y-axes onto a piece of
paper.

B Fold your paper along the x-axis and trace the image of
the triangle on the opposite side of the x-axis. Unfold your
paper and label the vertices of the image A', B', and C'.

C What is the line of reflection for this transformation?

_____

D Find the perpendicular distance from each point to the
line of reflection.

Point A _____   Point B _____   Point C _____

E Find the perpendicular distance from each point to the line of reflection.

Point A' _____   Point B' _____   Point C' _____

F What do you notice about the distances you found in **D** and **E**?

_____

Reflect

1. Fold your paper from **A** along the y-axis and trace the image of
triangle ABC on the opposite side. Label the vertices of the image
A'', B'', and C''. What is the line of reflection for this transformation? _____

2. How does each image in your drawings compare with its preimage?

_____

Properties of Reflections

Use trapezoid *TRAP* to investigate the properties of reflections.

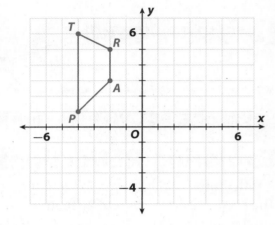

A Trace the trapezoid onto a piece of paper. Cut out your traced trapezoid.

B Place your trapezoid on top of the trapezoid in the figure. Then reflect your trapezoid across the *y*-axis. Sketch the image of the reflection by tracing your trapezoid in this new location. Label the vertices of the image *T′*, *R′*, *A′*, and *P′*.

C Use a ruler to measure the sides of trapezoid *TRAP* in centimeters.

$TR =$ _____ $RA =$ _____ $AP =$ _____ $TP =$ _____

D Use a ruler to measure the sides of trapezoid *T′R′A′P′* in centimeters.

$T′R′ =$ _____ $R′A′ =$ _____ $A′P′ =$ _____ $T′P′ =$ _____

E What do you notice about the lengths of corresponding sides of the two figures?

_____

F Use a protractor to measure the angles of trapezoid *TRAP*.

$m\angle T =$ _____ $m\angle R =$ _____ $m\angle A =$ _____ $m\angle P =$ _____

G Use a protractor to measure the angles of trapezoid *T′R′A′P′*.

$m\angle T′ =$ _____ $m\angle R′ =$ _____ $m\angle A′ =$ _____ $m\angle P′ =$ _____

H What do you notice about the measures of corresponding angles of the two figures?

_____

I Which sides of trapezoid *TRAP* are parallel? _____

Which sides of trapezoid *T′R′A′P′* are parallel? _____
What do you notice?

_____

_____

Reflect

3. **Make a Conjecture** Use your results from **E**, **H**, and **I** to make a conjecture about reflections.

_____

_____

_____

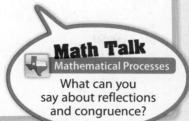
Math Talk
Mathematical Processes
What can you say about reflections and congruence?

Graphing Reflections

To reflect a figure across a line of reflection, reflect each of its vertices. Then connect the vertices to form the image. Remember that each point and its image are the same distance from the line of reflection.

Math On the Spot
my.hrw.com

EXAMPLE 1

TEKS 8.10.A

The figure shows triangle *XYZ*. Graph the image of the triangle after a reflection across the *x*-axis.

My Notes

STEP 1 Reflect point *X*.

Point *X* is 3 units below the *x*-axis. Count 3 units above the *x*-axis and plot point *X'*.

STEP 2 Reflect point *Y*.

Point *Y* is 1 unit below the *x*-axis. Count 1 unit above the *x*-axis and plot point *Y'*.

STEP 3 Reflect point *Z*.

Point *Z* is 5 units below the *x*-axis. Count 5 units above the *x*-axis and plot point *Z'*.

STEP 4 Connect *X'*, *Y'*, and *Z'* to form triangle *X'Y'Z'*.

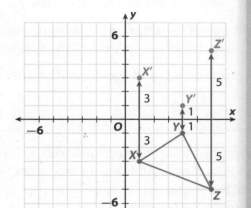

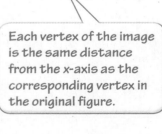
Each vertex of the image is the same distance from the *x*-axis as the corresponding vertex in the original figure.

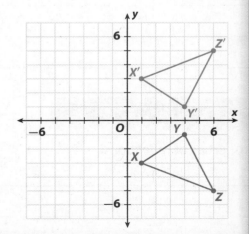

YOUR TURN

4. The figure shows pentagon *ABCDE*. Graph the image of the pentagon after a reflection across the *y*-axis.

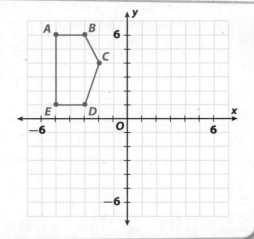

Guided Practice

1. **Vocabulary** A reflection is a transformation that flips a figure across

   a line called the _____.

2. The figure shows trapezoid *ABCD*. (Explore Activities 1 and 2 and Example 1)

   a. Graph the image of the trapezoid after a reflection across the *x*-axis. Label the vertices of the image.

   b. How do trapezoid *ABCD* and trapezoid *A′B′C′D′* compare?

   _____

   c. **What If?** Suppose you reflected trapezoid *ABCD* across the *y*-axis. How would the orientation of the image of the trapezoid compare with the orientation of the preimage?

   _____

   _____

   _____

   _____

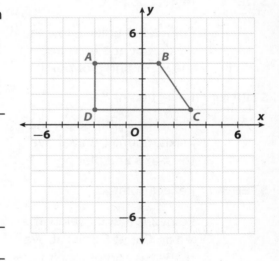

? ESSENTIAL QUESTION CHECK-IN

3. What are the properties of reflections?

   _____

   _____

12.2 Independent Practice

 TEKS 8.10.A

Personal Math Trainer

Online Assessment and Intervention

my.hrw.com

The graph shows four right triangles. Use the graph for Exercises 4–7.

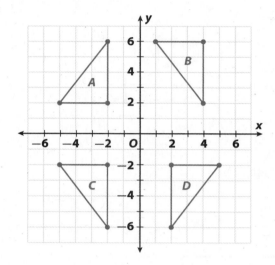

4. Which two triangles are reflections of each other across the *x*-axis?

_____

5. For which two triangles is the line of reflection the *y*-axis?

_____

6. Which triangle is a translation of triangle *C*? How would you describe the translation?

_____

_____

7. Which triangles are congruent? How do you know?

_____

_____

_____

_____

_____

8. a. Graph quadrilateral *WXYZ* with vertices *W*(−2, −2), *X*(3, 1), *Y*(5, −1), and *Z*(4, −6) on the coordinate grid.

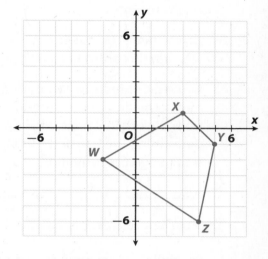

b. On the same coordinate grid, graph quadrilateral *W′X′Y′Z′*, the image of quadrilateral *WXYZ* after a reflection across the *x*-axis.

c. Which side of the image is congruent to side $\overline{YZ}$?

_____

Name three other pairs of congruent sides.

_____

_____

d. Which angle of the image is congruent to ∠*X*?

_____

Name three other pairs of congruent angles.

_____

_____

9. Critical Thinking Is it possible that the image of a point after a reflection could be the same point as the preimage? Explain.

_____

_____

 **FOCUS ON HIGHER ORDER THINKING**

10. a. Graph the image of the figure shown after a reflection across the *y*-axis.

b. On the same coordinate grid, graph the image of the figure you drew in part **a** after a reflection across the *x*-axis.

c. **Make a Conjecture** What other sequence of transformations would produce the same final image from the original preimage? Check your answer by performing the transformations. Then make a conjecture that generalizes your findings.

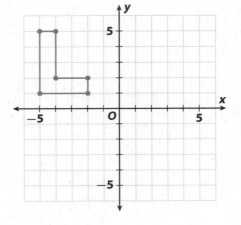

_____

_____

_____

_____

_____

_____

11. a. Graph triangle *DEF* with vertices *D*(2, 6), *E*(5, 6), and *F*(5, 1) on the coordinate grid.

b. Next graph triangle *D′E′F′*, the image of triangle *DEF* after a reflection across the *y*-axis.

c. On the same coordinate grid, graph triangle *D″E″F″*, the image of triangle *D′E′F′* after a translation of 7 units down and 2 units to the right.

d. **Analyze Relationships** Find a different sequence of transformations that will transform triangle *DEF* to triangle *D″E″F″*.

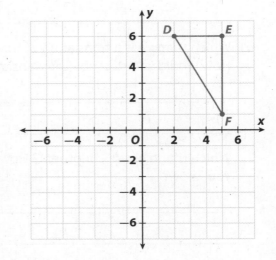

_____

_____

_____

_____

LESSON 12.3 Properties of Rotations

TEKS
Two-dimensional shapes—8.10.A
Generalize the properties of orientation and congruence of rotations... of two-dimensional shapes on a coordinate plane.

? **ESSENTIAL QUESTION**

How do you describe the properties of orientation and congruence of rotations?

EXPLORE ACTIVITY 1 **TEKS** 8.10.A

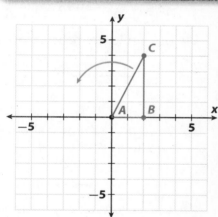

Exploring Rotations

A **rotation** is a transformation that turns a figure around a given point called the **center of rotation**. The image has the same size and shape as the preimage.

The triangle shown on the grid is the preimage. You will use the origin as the center of rotation.

A Trace triangle *ABC* onto a piece of paper. Cut out your traced triangle.

B Rotate your triangle 90° counterclockwise about the origin. The side of the triangle that lies along the *x*-axis should now lie along the *y*-axis.

C Sketch the image of the rotation. Label the images of points *A*, *B*, and *C* as *A′*, *B′*, and *C′*.

D Describe the motion modeled by the rotation.

Rotate _____ degrees _____ about the origin.

E Check that the motion you described in **D** is the same motion that maps point *A* onto *A′*, point *B* onto *B′*, and point *C* onto *C′*.

Reflect

1. **Communicate Mathematical Ideas** How are the size and the orientation of the triangle affected by the rotation?

_____

_____

_____

2. Rotate triangle *ABC* 90° clockwise about the origin. Sketch the result on the coordinate grid above. Label the image vertices *A″*, *B″*, and *C″*.

© Houghton Mifflin Harcourt Publishing Company • Image Credits: ©IKO/Fotolia

Lesson 12.3 **345**

Properties of Rotations

Use trapezoid *TRAP* to investigate the properties of rotations.

A Trace the trapezoid onto a piece of paper. Include the portion of the *x*- and *y*-axes bordering the third quadrant. Cut out your tracing.

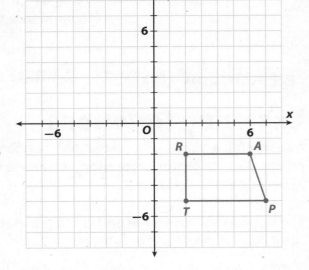

B Place your trapezoid and axes on top of those in the figure. Then use the axes to help rotate your trapezoid 180° counterclockwise about the origin. Sketch the image of the rotation of your trapezoid in this new location. Label the vertices of the image *T′*, *R′*, *A′*, and *P′*.

C Use a ruler to measure the sides of trapezoid *TRAP* in centimeters.

$TR =$ _____ $RA =$ _____

$AP =$ _____ $TP =$ _____

D Use a ruler to measure the sides of trapezoid *T′R′A′P′* in centimeters.

$T′R′ =$ _____ $R′A′ =$ _____

$A′P′ =$ _____ $T′P′ =$ _____

E What do you notice about the lengths of corresponding sides of the two figures?

_____

F Use a protractor to measure the angles of trapezoid *TRAP*.

$m\angle T =$ _____ $m\angle R =$ _____ $m\angle A =$ _____ $m\angle P =$ _____

G Use a protractor to measure the angles of trapezoid *T′R′A′P′*.

$m\angle T′ =$ _____ $m\angle R′ =$ _____ $m\angle A′ =$ _____ $m\angle P′ =$ _____

H What do you notice about the measures of corresponding angles of the two figures?

_____

I Which sides of trapezoid *TRAP* are parallel? _____

Which sides of trapezoid *T′R′A′P′* are parallel? _____

What do you notice? _____

_____

Reflect

3. **Make a Conjecture** Use your results from **E**, **H**, and **I** to make a conjecture about rotations.

_____

_____

4. Place your tracing back in its original position. Then perform a 180° _clockwise_ rotation about the origin. Compare the result.

_____

_____

Graphing Rotations

To rotate a figure in the coordinate plane, rotate each of its vertices. Then connect the vertices to form the image.

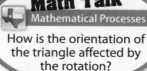
EXAMPLE 1

 TEKS 8.10.A

The figure shows triangle _ABC_. Graph the image of triangle _ABC_ after a rotation of 90° clockwise.

STEP 1 Rotate the figure clockwise from the _y_-axis to the _x_-axis. Point _A_ will still be at (0, 0).

Point _B_ is 2 units to the left of the _y_-axis, so point _B′_ is 2 units above the _x_-axis.

Point _C_ is 2 units to the right of the _y_-axis, so point _C′_ is 2 units below the _x_-axis.

Animated Math
my.hrw.com

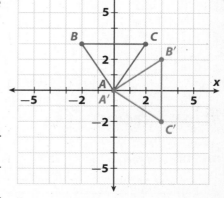

STEP 2 Connect _A′_, _B′_, and _C′_ to form the image triangle _A′B′C′_.

Math Talk
Mathematical Processes

How is the orientation of the triangle affected by the rotation?

Reflect

5. Is the image congruent to the preimage? How do you know?

_____

_____

_____

_____

YOUR TURN

Graph the image of quadrilateral *ABCD* after each rotation.

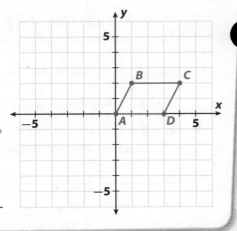

6. 180°

7. 270° clockwise

8. Find the coordinates of Point *C* after a 90° counterclockwise rotation followed by a 180° rotation.

_____

Guided Practice

1. **Vocabulary** A rotation is a transformation that turns a figure around a given _____ called the center of rotation.

Siobhan rotates a right triangle 90° counterclockwise about the origin.

2. How does the orientation of the image of the triangle compare with the orientation of the preimage? (Explore Activity 1)

_____

3. Is the image of the triangle congruent to the preimage? (Explore Activity 2)

_____

Draw the image of the figure after the given rotation about the origin. (Example 1)

4. 90° counterclockwise

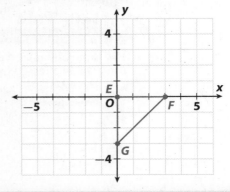

5. 180°

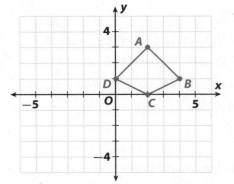

? ESSENTIAL QUESTION CHECK-IN

6. What are the properties of rotations?

_____

12.3 Independent Practice

TEKS 8.10.A

Personal Math Trainer

Online Assessment and Intervention

my.hrw.com

7. The figure shows triangle *ABC* and a rotation of the triangle about the origin.

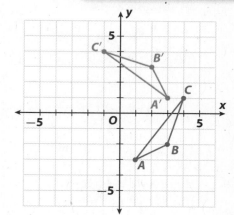

   a. How would you describe the rotation?

   _____

   _____

   b. What are the coordinates of the image?

   _____ , _____ , _____

8. The graph shows a figure and its image after a transformation.

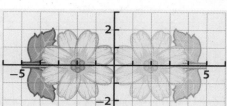

   a. How would you describe this as a rotation?

   _____

   _____

   b. Can you describe this as a transformation other than a rotation? Explain.

   _____

   _____

9. What type of rotation will preserve the orientation of the H-shaped figure in the grid?

   _____

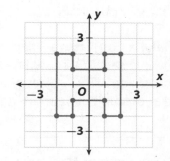

10. A point with coordinates $(-2, -3)$ is rotated 90° clockwise about the origin. What are the coordinates of its image?

    _____

Complete the table with rotations of 180° or less. Include the direction of rotation for rotations of less than 180°.

	Shape in quadrant	Image in quadrant	Rotation
11.	I	IV	
12.	III	I	
13.	IV	III	

Draw the image of the figure after the given rotation about the origin.

14. 180°

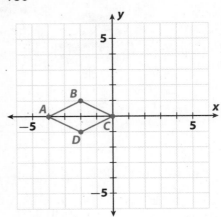

15. 270° counterclockwise

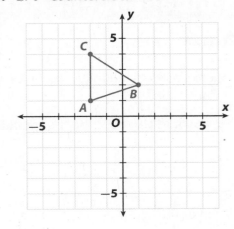

16. Is there a rotation for which the orientation of the image is always the same as that of the preimage? If so, what?

_____

FOCUS ON HIGHER ORDER THINKING

17. Problem Solving Lucas is playing a game where he has to rotate a figure for it to fit in an open space. Every time he clicks a button, the figure rotates 90 degrees clockwise. How many times does he need to click the button so that each figure returns to its original orientation?

Figure A _____

Figure B _____

Figure C _____

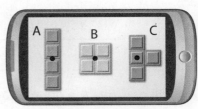

18. Make a Conjecture Triangle *ABC* is reflected across the *y*-axis to form the image *A'B'C'*. Triangle *A'B'C'* is then reflected across the *x*-axis to form the image *A"B"C"*. What type of rotation can be used to describe the relationship between triangle *A"B"C"* and triangle *ABC*?

_____

19. Communicate Mathematical Ideas Point *A* is on the *y*-axis. Describe all possible locations of image *A'* for rotations of 90°, 180°, and 270°. Include the origin as a possible location for *A*.

_____

_____

_____

_____

Work Area

12.4 Algebraic Representations of Transformations

TEKS
Two-dimensional shapes—8.10.C Explain the effect of translations, reflections over the x- or y-axis, and rotations limited to 90°, 180°, 270°, and 360° as applied to two-dimensional shapes on a coordinate plane using an algebraic representation.

? ESSENTIAL QUESTION

How can you describe the effect of a translation, rotation, or reflection on coordinates using an algebraic representation?

Algebraic Representations of Translations

The rules shown in the table describe how coordinates change when a figure is translated up, down, right, and left on the coordinate plane.

Math On the Spot
⏻ my.hrw.com

Translations	
Right a units	Add a to the x-coordinate: $(x, y) \rightarrow (x + a, y)$
Left a units	Subtract a from the x-coordinate: $(x, y) \rightarrow (x - a, y)$
Up b units	Add b to the y-coordinate: $(x, y) \rightarrow (x, y + b)$
Down b units	Subtract b from the y-coordinate: $(x, y) \rightarrow (x, y - b)$

EXAMPLE 1

TEKS 8.10.C

Triangle *XYZ* has vertices *X*(0, 0), *Y*(2, 3), and *Z*(4, −1). Find the vertices of triangle *X'Y'Z'* after a translation of 3 units to the right and 1 unit down. Then graph the triangle and its image.

> Add 3 to the x-coordinate of each vertex and subtract 1 from the y-coordinate of each vertex.

STEP 1 Apply the rule to find the vertices of the image.

Vertices of △*XYZ*	Rule: $(x + 3, y − 1)$	Vertices of △*X' Y' Z'*
$X(0, 0)$	$(0 + 3, 0 − 1)$	$X'(3, −1)$
$Y(2, 3)$	$(2 + 3, 3 − 1)$	$Y'(5, 2)$
$Z(4, −1)$	$(4 + 3, −1 − 1)$	$Z'(7, −2)$

STEP 2 Graph triangle *XYZ* and its image.

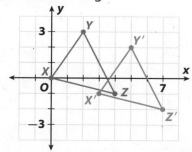

Math Talk
Mathematical Processes

When you translate a figure to the left or right, which coordinate do you change?

1. A rectangle has vertices at (0, −2), (0, 3), (3, −2), and (3, 3). What are the coordinates of the vertices of the image after the translation $(x, y) \rightarrow (x − 6, y − 3)$? Describe the translation.

_____

_____

Algebraic Representations of Reflections

The signs of the coordinates of a figure change when the figure is reflected across the x-axis and y-axis. The table shows the rules for changing the signs of the coordinates after a reflection.

Reflections	
Across the x-axis	Multiply each y-coordinate by −1: $(x, y) \rightarrow (x, −y)$
Across the y-axis	Multiply each x-coordinate by −1: $(x, y) \rightarrow (−x, y)$

EXAMPLE 2

 TEKS 8.10.C

My Notes

Rectangle *RSTU* has vertices *R*(−4, −1), *S*(−1, −1), *T*(−1, −3), and *U*(−4, −3). Find the vertices of rectangle *R′S′T′U′* after a reflection across the y-axis. Then graph the rectangle and its image.

> Multiply the x-coordinate of each vertex by −1.

STEP 1 Apply the rule to find the vertices of the image.

Vertices of *RSTU*	Rule: $(−1 \cdot x, y)$	Vertices of *R′S′T′U′*
R(−4, −1)	(−1 · (−4), − 1)	*R′*(4, −1)
S(−1, −1)	(−1 · (−1), − 1)	*S′*(1, −1)
T(−1, −3)	(−1 · (−1), − 3)	*T′*(1, −3)
U(−4, −3)	(−1 · (−4), − 3)	*U′*(4, −3)

STEP 2 Graph rectangle *RSTU* and its image.

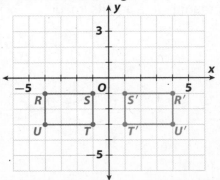

YOUR TURN

2. Triangle *ABC* has vertices *A*(−2, 6), *B*(0, 5), and *C*(3, −1). Find the vertices of triangle *A'B'C'* after a reflection across the *x*-axis.

_____

Algebraic Representations of Rotations

When points are rotated about the origin, the coordinates of the image can be found using the rules shown in the table.

Rotations	
90° clockwise	Multiply each *x*-coordinate by −1; then switch the *x*- and *y*-coordinates: $(x, y) \rightarrow (y, -x)$
90° counterclockwise	Multiply each *y*-coordinate by −1; then switch the *x*- and *y*-coordinates: $(x, y) \rightarrow (-y, x)$
180°	Multiply both coordinates by −1: $(x, y) \rightarrow (-x, -y)$

EXAMPLE 3

 **TEKS** 8.10.C

Quadrilateral *ABCD* has vertices at *A*(−4, 2), *B*(−3, 4), *C*(2, 3), and *D*(0, 0). Find the vertices of quadrilateral *A'B'C'D'* after a 90° clockwise rotation. Then graph the quadrilateral and its image.

STEP 1 Apply the rule to find the vertices of the image.

> Multiply the *x*-coordinate of each vertex by −1, and then switch the *x*- and *y*-coordinates.

Vertices of *ABCD*	Rule: $(y, -x)$	Vertices of *A'B'C'D'*
A(−4, 2)	(2, −1 · (−4))	*A'*(2, 4)
B(−3, 4)	(4, −1 · (−3))	*B'*(4, 3)
C(2, 3)	(3, −1 · 2)	*C'*(3, −2)
D(0, 0)	(0, −1 · 0)	*D'*(0, 0)

STEP 2 Graph the quadrilateral and its image.

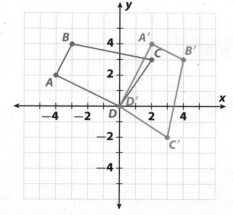

Math Talk
Mathematical Processes

Explain how to use the 90° rotation rule to develop a rule for a 360° rotation.

Reflect

3. **Communicate Mathematical Ideas** How would you find the vertices of an image if a figure were rotated 270° clockwise? Explain.

_____

_____

_____

Personal Math Trainer

Online Assessment and Intervention

⏱ my.hrw.com

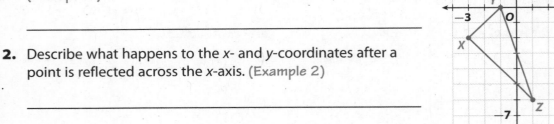

YOUR TURN

4. A triangle has vertices at $J(-2, -4)$, $K(1, 5)$, and $L(2, 2)$. What are the coordinates of the vertices of the image after the triangle is rotated 90° counterclockwise?

_____

Guided Practice

1. Triangle XYZ has vertices $X(-3, -2)$, $Y(-1, 0)$, and $Z(1, -6)$. Find the vertices of triangle $X'Y'Z'$ after a translation of 6 units to the right. Then graph the triangle and its image. (Example 1)

   _____

2. Describe what happens to the x- and y-coordinates after a point is reflected across the x-axis. (Example 2)

   _____

   _____

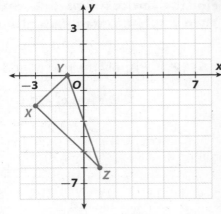

3. Use the rule $(x, y) \rightarrow (y, -x)$ to graph the image of the triangle at right. Then describe the transformation. (Example 3)

   _____

? ESSENTIAL QUESTION CHECK-IN

4. How do the x- and y-coordinates change when a figure is translated right a units and down b units?

   _____

   _____

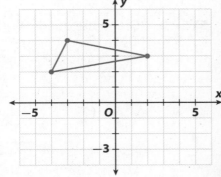

12.4 Independent Practice

 TEKS 10.8C

Personal Math Trainer

Online Assessment and Intervention

my.hrw.com

Write an algebraic rule to describe each transformation. Then describe the transformation.

5.

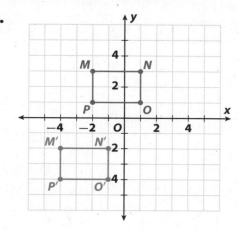

_____

_____

6.

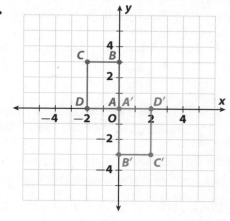

_____

_____

7. Triangle *XYZ* has vertices *X*(6, −2.3), *Y*(7.5, 5), and *Z*(8, 4). When translated, *X*′ has coordinates (2.8, −1.3). Write a rule to describe this transformation. Then find the coordinates of *Y*′ and *Z*′.

_____

8. Point *L* has coordinates (3, −5). The coordinates of point *L*′ after a reflection are (−3, −5). Without graphing, tell which axis point *L* was reflected across. Explain your answer.

_____

_____

_____

9. Use the rule (*x*, *y*) → (*x* − 2, *y* − 4) to graph the image of the rectangle. Then describe the transformation.

_____

_____

10. Parallelogram *ABCD* has vertices *A*(−2, −5$\frac{1}{2}$), *B*(−4, −5$\frac{1}{2}$), *C*(−3, −2), and *D*(−1, −2). Find the vertices of parallelogram *A*′*B*′*C*′*D*′ after a translation of 2$\frac{1}{2}$ units down.

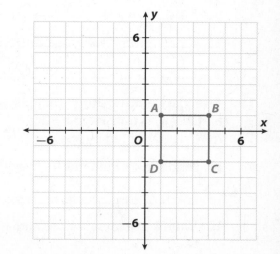

_____

_____

11. Alexandra drew the logo shown on half-inch graph paper. Write a rule that describes the translation Alexandra used to create the shadow on the letter A.

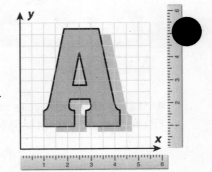

_____

12. Kite *KLMN* has vertices at *K*(1, 3), *L*(2, 4), *M*(3, 3), and *N*(2, 0). After the kite is rotated, *K'* has coordinates (−3, 1). Describe the rotation, and include a rule in your description. Then find the coordinates of *L'*, *M'*, and *N'*.

_____

_____

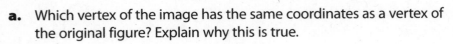

FOCUS ON HIGHER ORDER THINKING

13. Make a Conjecture Graph the triangle with vertices (−3, 4), (3, 4), and (−5, −5). Use the transformation (*y*, *x*) to graph its image.

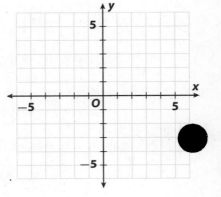

a. Which vertex of the image has the same coordinates as a vertex of the original figure? Explain why this is true.

_____

_____

b. What is the equation of a line through the origin and this point?

_____

c. Describe the transformation of the triangle.

_____

14. Critical Thinking Mitchell says the point (0, 0) does not change when reflected across the *x*- or *y*-axis or when rotated about the origin. Do you agree with Mitchell? Explain why or why not.

_____

_____

_____

15. Analyze Relationships Triangle *ABC* with vertices *A*(−2, −2), *B*(−3, 1), and *C*(1, 1) is translated by $(x, y) \rightarrow (x − 1, y + 3)$. Then the image, triangle *A'B'C'*, is translated by $(x, y) \rightarrow (x + 4, y − 1)$, resulting in *A''B''C''*.

a. Find the coordinates for the vertices of triangle *A''B''C''*.

_____

b. Write a rule for one translation that maps triangle *ABC* to triangle *A''B''C''*.

_____

Work Area

Ready to Go On?

Personal
Math Trainer
Online Assessment
and Intervention
my.hrw.com

12.1–12.3 Properties of Translations, Reflections, and Rotations

Use the graph for Exercises 1–2.

1. Graph the image of triangle *ABC* after a translation of 6 units to the right and 4 units down. Label the vertices of the image *A′*, *B′*, and *C′*.

2. On the same coordinate grid, graph the image of triangle *ABC* after a reflection across the *y*-axis. Label the vertices of the image *A″*, *B″*, and *C″*.

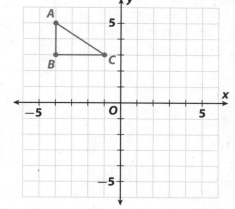

3. Graph the image of trapezoid *HIJK* after it is rotated 180° about the origin. Label the vertices of the image. Find the vertices if the trapezoid *HIJK* is rotated 360°.

_____

4. **Vocabulary** Translations, reflections, and rotations produce a figure that is

_____ to the original figure.

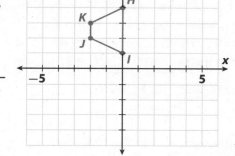

12.4 Algebraic Representations of Transformations

5. A triangle has vertices at (2, 3), (−2, 2), and (−3, 5). What are the coordinates of the vertices of the image after the translation $(x, y) \rightarrow (x + 4, y - 3)$? Describe the transformation.

_____

_____

ESSENTIAL QUESTION

6. How can you use transformations to solve real-world problems?

_____

_____

MODULE 12 MIXED REVIEW

Texas Test Prep

Personal
Math Trainer

Online
Assessment and
Intervention

my.hrw.com

Selected Response

1. What would be the orientation of the figure L after a translation of 8 units to the right and 3 units up?

Ⓐ

Ⓒ

Ⓑ

Ⓓ

2. A straw has a diameter of 0.6 cm and a length of 19.5 cm. What is the surface area of the straw to the nearest tenth? Use 3.14 for π.

Ⓐ 5.5 cm²   Ⓒ 36.7 cm²

Ⓑ 11.7 cm²   Ⓓ 37.3 cm²

3. In what quadrant would the triangle be located after a rotation of 270° clockwise about the origin?

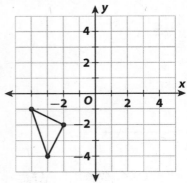

Ⓐ I   Ⓒ III

Ⓑ II   Ⓓ IV

4. Which rational number is greater than $-3\frac{1}{3}$ but less than $-\frac{4}{5}$?

Ⓐ −0.4   Ⓒ −0.19

Ⓑ $-\frac{9}{7}$ Ⓓ $-\frac{22}{5}$

5. Which of the following is **not** true of a trapezoid that has been reflected across the x-axis?

Ⓐ The new trapezoid is the same size as the original trapezoid.

Ⓑ The new trapezoid is the same shape as the original trapezoid.

Ⓒ The new trapezoid is in the same orientation as the original trapezoid.

Ⓓ The x-coordinates of the new trapezoid are the same as the x-coordinates of the original trapezoid.

6. A triangle with coordinates (6, 4), (2, −1), and (−3, 5) is translated 4 units left and rotated 180° about the origin. What are the coordinates of its image?

Ⓐ (2, 4), (−2, −1), (−7, 5)

Ⓑ (4, 6), (−1, 2), (5, −3)

Ⓒ (4, −2), (−1, 2), (5, 7)

Ⓓ (4, 2), (−1, −2), (5, −7)

Gridded Response

7. Solve the equation $3y + 17 = -2y + 25$ for y.

				•		
⓪	⓪	⓪	⓪		⓪	⓪
①	①	①	①		①	①
②	②	②	②		②	②
③	③	③	③		③	③
④	④	④	④		④	④
⑤	⑤	⑤	⑤		⑤	⑤
⑥	⑥	⑥	⑥		⑥	⑥
⑦	⑦	⑦	⑦		⑦	⑦
⑧	⑧	⑧	⑧		⑧	⑧
⑨	⑨	⑨	⑨		⑨	⑨

Dilations, Similarity, and Proportionality

ESSENTIAL QUESTION

How can you use dilations, similarity, and proportionality to solve real-world problems?

Real-World Video

To plan a mural, the artist first makes a smaller drawing showing what the mural will look like. Then the image is enlarged by a scale factor on the mural canvas. This enlargement is called a dilation.

my.hrw.com

GO DIGITAL
my.hrw.com

my.hrw.com

Go digital with your write-in student edition, accessible on any device.

Math On the Spot

Scan with your smart phone to jump directly to the online edition, video tutor, and more.

Animated Math

Interactively explore key concepts to see how math works.

Personal Math Trainer

Get immediate feedback and help as you work through practice sets.

Are YOU Ready?

Complete these exercises to review skills you will need for this module.

Simplify Ratios

EXAMPLE $\frac{35}{21} = \frac{35 \div 7}{21 \div 7}$

$= \frac{5}{3}$

To write a ratio in simplest form, find the greatest common factor of the numerator and denominator. Divide the numerator and denominator by the GCF.

Write each ratio in simplest form.

1. $\frac{6}{15}$ _____

2. $\frac{8}{20}$ _____

3. $\frac{30}{18}$ _____

4. $\frac{36}{30}$ _____

Find Perimeter

EXAMPLE

8 in.

3 in.

Find the sum of the lengths of the sides.

$P = 8 + 3 + 8 + 3 = 22$ in.

Find the perimeter.

5. square with sides of 8.9 cm _____

6. rectangle with length $5\frac{1}{2}$ ft and width $2\frac{3}{4}$ ft _____

7. equilateral triangle with sides of $8\frac{3}{8}$ in. _____

Area of Squares, Rectangles, Triangles

EXAMPLE

18 cm

14 cm

$A = bh$

$A = 18 \times 14$

$= 252$ cm²

Use the formula for the area of a rectangle.
Substitute for the variables.
Multiply.

Find the area.

8. Square with sides of 6.5 cm: _____

9. Triangle with base 10 in. and height 6 in.: _____

10. Rectangle with length $3\frac{1}{2}$ ft and width $2\frac{1}{2}$ ft: _____

Reading Start-Up

© Houghton Mifflin Harcourt Publishing Company

Vocabulary

Review Words

coordinate plane *(plano cartesiano)*

image *(imagen)*

✔ origin *(origen)*

preimage *(imagen original)*

✔ quadrants *(cuadrante)*

ratio *(razón)*

scale *(escala)*

✔ x-axis *(eje x)*

✔ y-axis *(eje y)*

Preview Words

center of dilation *(centro de dilatación)*

dilation *(dilatación)*

enlargement *(agrandamiento)*

reduction *(reducción)*

scale factor *(factor de escala)*

Visualize Vocabulary

Use the ✔ words to complete the graphic organizer.
You will put one word in each rectangle.

The four regions on a coordinate plane.		The point where the axes intersect to form the coordinate plane.
	Reviewing the Coordinate Plane	
The horizontal axis of a coordinate plane.		The vertical axis of a coordinate plane.

Understand Vocabulary

Complete the sentences using the review words.

1. A figure larger than the original, produced through dilation, is

an _____.

2. A figure smaller than the original, produced through dilation, is

a _____.

Active Reading

Key-Term Fold Before beginning the module, create a key-term fold to help you learn the vocabulary in this module. Write the highlighted vocabulary words on one side of the flap. Write the definition for each word on the other side of the flap. Use the key-term fold to quiz yourself on the definitions used in this module.

Unpacking the TEKS

Understanding the TEKS and the vocabulary terms in the TEKS will help you know exactly what you are expected to learn in this module.

TEKS 8.3.C

Use an algebraic representation to explain the effect of a given positive rational scale factor applied to two-dimensional figures on a coordinate plane with the origin as the center of dilation.

Key Vocabulary

scale factor *(factor de escala)*
The ratio used to enlarge or reduce similar figures.

What It Means to You

You will use an algebraic representation to describe a dilation.

UNPACKING EXAMPLE 8.3.C

The blue square *ABCD* is the preimage. Write two algebraic representations, one for the dilation to the green square and one for the dilation to the purple square.

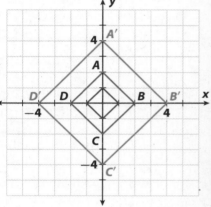

The coordinates of the vertices of the original image are multiplied by 2 for the green square.

Green square: $(x, y) \rightarrow (2x, 2y)$

The coordinates of the vertices of the original image are multiplied by $\frac{1}{2}$ for the purple square.

Purple square: $(x, y) \rightarrow \left(\frac{1}{2}x, \frac{1}{2}y\right)$

TEKS 8.10.D

Model the effect on linear and area measurements of dilated two-dimensional shapes.

Key Vocabulary

similar shapes *(formas)*
Figures with the same shape but not necessarily the same size.

What It Means to You

You can find the effect of a dilation on the perimeter and area of a figure.

UNPACKING EXAMPLE 8.10.D

The length of the side of a square is 3 inches. If the square is dilated by a scale factor of 5, what are the perimeter and the area of the new square?

The length of a side of the original square is 3 inches. The length of a side of the dilated square is 5 · 3, or 15 inches.

Original Square	**Dilated square**
Perimeter: $4(3) = 12$ in.	Perimeter: $4(15) = 60$ in.
Area: $3^2 = 9$ in^2	Area: $15^2 = 225$ in^2

Visit **my.hrw.com** to see all the **TEKS** unpacked.

my.hrw.com

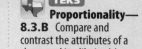

TEKS
Proportionality—
8.3.B Compare and contrast the attributes of a shape and its dilation(s) on a coordinate plane. *Also 8.3.A, 8.10.A, 8.10.B*

ESSENTIAL QUESTION

How do you describe the properties of dilations?

EXPLORE ACTIVITY 1  **TEKS** 8.3.A, 8.10.A

Exploring Dilations

The missions that placed 12 astronauts on the moon were controlled at the Johnson Space Center in Houston. The toy models at the right are scaled-down replicas of the Saturn V rocket that powered the moon flights. Each replica is a transformation called a **dilation**. Unlike the other transformations you have studied—translations, rotations, and reflections—dilations change the size (but not the shape) of a figure.

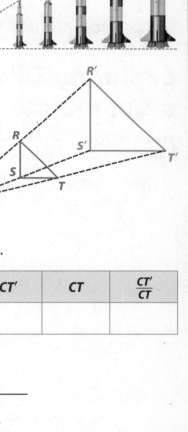

Center of dilation

Every dilation has a fixed point called the **center of dilation** located where the lines connecting corresponding parts of figures intersect.

Triangle *R′S′T′* is a dilation of triangle *RST*. Point *C* is the center of dilation.

A Use a ruler to measure segments $\overline{CR}$, $\overline{CR'}$, $\overline{CS}$, $\overline{CS'}$, $\overline{CT}$, and $\overline{CT'}$ to the nearest millimeter. Record the measurements and ratios in the table.

CR′	CR	$\frac{CR'}{CR}$	CS′	CS	$\frac{CS'}{CS}$	CT′	CT	$\frac{CT'}{CT}$

B Write a conjecture based on the ratios in the table.

_____

C Measure and record the corresponding side lengths of the triangles.

R′S′	RS	$\frac{R'S'}{RS}$	S′T′	ST	$\frac{S'T'}{ST}$	R′T′	RT	$\frac{R'T'}{RT}$

D Write a conjecture based on the ratios in the table.

_____

E Measure the corresponding angles and describe your results.

_____

Reflect

1. Are triangles *RST* and *R'S'T'* similar? Why or why not?

_____

_____

2. Compare the orientation of a figure with the orientation of its dilation.

_____

_____

EXPLORE ACTIVITY 2  **TEKS** 8.3.B

Exploring Dilations on a Coordinate Plane

In this activity you will explore how the coordinates of a figure on a coordinate plane are affected by a dilation.

A Complete the table. Record the *x*- and *y*-coordinates of the points in the two figures and the ratios of the *x*-coordinates and the *y*-coordinates.

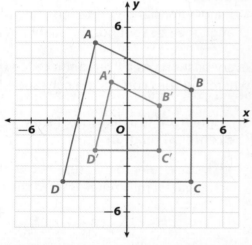

Vertex	x	y	Vertex	x	y	Ratio of x-coordinates (A'B'C'D' ÷ ABCD)	Ratio of y-coordinates (A'B'C'D' ÷ ABCD)
A'			A				
B'			B				
C'			C				
D'			D				

B Write a conjecture about the ratios of the coordinates of a dilation image to the coordinates of the original figure.

_____

_____

Reflect

3. In Explore Activity 1, triangle *R'S'T'* was larger than triangle *RST*. How is the relationship between quadrilateral *A'B'C'D'* and quadrilateral *ABCD* different?

_____

Math Talk
Mathematical Processes

How are dilations different from the other transformations you have learned about?

Finding a Scale Factor

As you have seen in the two activities, a dilation can produce a larger figure (an **enlargement**) or a smaller figure (a **reduction**). The **scale factor** describes how much the figure is enlarged or reduced. The scale factor is the ratio of a length of the image to the corresponding length on the original figure.

In Explore Activity 1, the side lengths of triangle *R'S'T'* were twice the length of those of triangle *RST*, so the scale factor was 2. In Explore Activity 2, the side lengths of quadrilateral *A'B'C'D'* were half those of quadrilateral *ABCD*, so the scale factor was 0.5.

EXAMPLE 1   TEKS 8.3.B

An art supply store sells several sizes of drawing triangles. All are dilations of a single basic triangle. The basic triangle and one of its dilations are shown on the grid. Find the scale factor of the dilation.

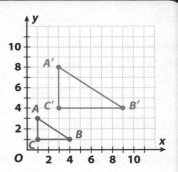

STEP 1 Use the coordinates to find the lengths of the sides of each triangle.

Triangle *ABC*: $AC = 2$ $CB = 3$

Triangle *A'B'C'*: $A'C' = 4$ $C'B' = 6$

Since the scale factor is the same for all corresponding sides, you can record just two pairs of side lengths. Use one pair as a check on the other.

STEP 2 Find the ratios of the corresponding sides.

$\dfrac{A'C'}{AC} = \dfrac{4}{2} = 2$ $\dfrac{C'B'}{CB} = \dfrac{6}{3} = 2$

The scale factor of the dilation is 2.

Reflect

4. Is the dilation an enlargement or a reduction? How can you tell?

_____

_____

YOUR TURN

5. Find the scale factor of the dilation.

_____

_____

Math Talk

Mathematical Processes

Which scale factors lead to enlargements? Which scale factors lead to reductions?

Guided Practice

Use triangles *ABC* and *A'B'C'* for 1–5. (Explore Activities 1 and 2, Example 1)

1. For each pair of corresponding vertices, find the ratio of the *x*-coordinates and the ratio of the *y*-coordinates.

   ratio of *x*-coordinates = _____

   ratio of *y*-coordinates = _____

2. I know that triangle *A'B'C'* is a dilation of triangle *ABC* because the ratios of the corresponding

   x-coordinates are _____ and the ratios of the

   corresponding *y*-coordinates are _____.

3. The ratio of the lengths of the corresponding sides of triangle *A'B'C'* and

   triangle *ABC* equals _____.

4. The corresponding angles of triangle *ABC* and triangle *A'B'C'*

   are _____.

5. The scale factor of the dilation is _____.

❓ ESSENTIAL QUESTION CHECK-IN

6. How can you find the scale factor of a dilation?

   _____

   _____

13.1 Independent Practice

 TEKS 8.3.A, 8.10.A, 8.3.B, 8.10.B

Personal Math Trainer

Online Assessment and Intervention

my.hrw.com

For 7–11, tell whether one figure is a dilation of the other or not. Explain your reasoning.

7. Quadrilateral *MNPQ* has side lengths of 15 mm, 24 mm, 21 mm, and 18 mm. Quadrilateral *M'N'P'Q'* has side lengths of 5 mm, 8 mm, 7 mm, and 4 mm.

_____

_____

_____

8. Triangle *RST* has angles measuring 38° and 75°. Triangle *R'S'T'* has angles measuring 67° and 38°.

_____

_____

_____

_____

9. Two triangles, Triangle 1 and Triangle 2, are similar.

_____

_____

10. Quadrilateral *MNPQ* is the same shape but a different size than quadrilateral *M'N'P'Q*.

_____

_____

_____

_____

_____

11. On a coordinate plane, triangle *UVW* has coordinates *U*(20, −12), *V*(8, 6), and *W*(−24, −4). Triangle *U'V'W'* has coordinates *U'*(15, −9), *V'*(6, 4.5), and *W'*(−18, −3).

_____

_____

_____

_____

_____

_____

_____

Complete the table by writing "same" or "changed" to compare the image with the original figure in the given transformation.

Image Compared to Original Figure			
	Orientation	**Size**	**Shape**
12. Translation			
13. Reflection			
14. Rotation			
15. Dilation			

16. Describe the image of a dilation with a scale factor of 1.

_____

_____

Identify the scale factor used in each dilation.

17.

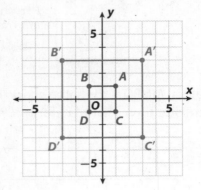

_____

18.

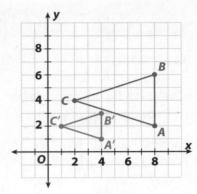

_____

![H.O.T.] **FOCUS ON HIGHER ORDER THINKING**

Work Area

19. Critical Thinking Explain how you can find the center of dilation of a triangle and its dilation.

_____

_____

_____

20. Make a Conjecture

a. A square on the coordinate plane has vertices at (−2, 2), (2, 2), (2, −2), and (−2, −2). A dilation of the square has vertices at (−4, 4), (4, 4), (4, −4), and (−4, −4). Find the scale factor and the perimeter of each square.

_____

_____

b. A square on the coordinate plane has vertices at (−3, 3), (3, 3), (3, −3), and (−3, −3). A dilation of the square has vertices at (−6, 6), (6, 6), (6, −6), and (−6, −6). Find the scale factor and the perimeter of each square.

_____

_____

c. Make a conjecture about the relationship of the scale factor to the perimeter of a square and its image.

_____

_____

TEKS
Proportionality—
8.3.C Use an algebraic representation to explain the effect of a given positive rational scale factor applied to two-dimensional figures on a coordinate plane with the origin as the center of dilation. *Also 8.3.B, 8.10.D*

 ESSENTIAL QUESTION

How can you describe the effect of a dilation on coordinates using an algebraic representation?

Graphing Enlargements

When a dilation in the coordinate plane has the origin as the center of dilation, you can find points on the dilated image by multiplying the x- and y-coordinates of the original figure by the scale factor. For scale factor k, the algebraic representation of the dilation is (x, y) → (kx, ky). For enlargements, k > 1.

The figure shown on the grid is the preimage. The center of dilation is the origin.

A List the coordinates of the vertices of the preimage in the first column of the table.

Preimage (x, y)	Image (3x, 3y)
(2, 2)	(6, 6)

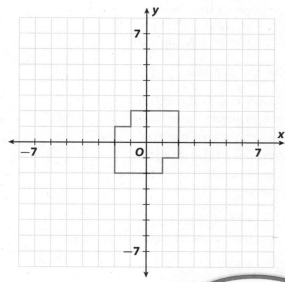

B What is the scale factor for the dilation? _____

C Apply the dilation to the preimage and write the coordinates of the vertices of the image in the second column of the table.

D Sketch the image after the dilation on the coordinate grid.

Math Talk
Mathematical Processes

What effect would the dilation (x, y) → (4x, 4y) have on the radius of a circle?

© Houghton Mifflin Harcourt Publishing Company

Reflect

1. How does the dilation affect the length of line segments?

_____

_____

2. How does the dilation affect angle measures?

_____

EXPLORE ACTIVITY 2  TEKS 8.3.C

Graphing Reductions

For scale factors between 0 and 1, the image is smaller than the preimage. This is called a reduction.

The arrow shown is the preimage. The center of dilation is the origin.

A List the coordinates of the vertices of the preimage in the first column of the table.

B What is the scale factor for the dilation? _____

C Apply the dilation to the preimage and write the coordinates of the vertices of the image in the second column of the table.

Preimage (x, y)	Image $\left(\frac{1}{2}x, \frac{1}{2}y\right)$

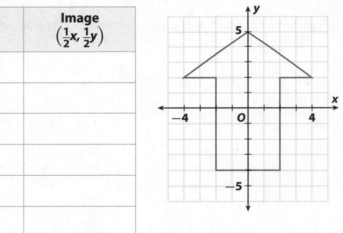

D Sketch the image after the dilation on the coordinate grid.

Reflect

3. How does the dilation affect the length of line segments?

_____

4. How would a dilation with scale factor 1 affect the preimage?

_____

Center of Dilation Outside the Image

The center of dilation can be inside *or* outside the original image and the dilated image. The center of dilation can be anywhere on the coordinate plane as long as the lines that connect each pair of corresponding vertices between the original and dilated image intersect at the center of dilation.

EXAMPLE 1

TEKS 8.3.C

Graph the image of △ABC after a dilation with the origin as its center and a scale factor of 3. What are the vertices of the image?

STEP 1 Multiply each coordinate of the vertices of △ABC by 3 to find the vertices of the dilated image.

$$\triangle ABC \ (x, y) \rightarrow (3x, 3y) \ \triangle A'B'C'$$

$$A(1, 1) \rightarrow A'(1 \cdot 3, 1 \cdot 3) \rightarrow A'(3, 3)$$

$$B(3, 1) \rightarrow B'(3 \cdot 3, 1 \cdot 3) \rightarrow B'(9, 3)$$

$$C(1, 3) \rightarrow C'(1 \cdot 3, 3 \cdot 3) \rightarrow C'(3, 9)$$

The vertices of the dilated image are $A'(3, 3)$, $B'(9, 3)$, and $C'(3, 9)$.

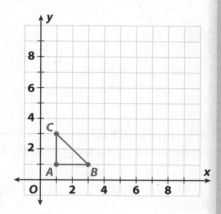

STEP 2 Graph the dilated image.

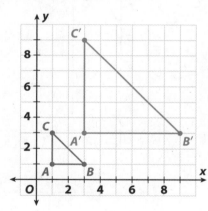

Math Talk
Mathematical Processes

Describe how you can check graphically that you have drawn the image triangle correctly.

YOUR TURN

5. Graph the image of △XYZ after a dilation with a scale factor of $\frac{1}{3}$ and the origin as its center. Then write an algebraic rule to describe the dilation.

_____

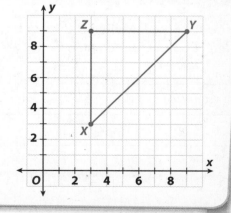

© Houghton Mifflin Harcourt Publishing Company

1. The grid shows a diamond-shaped preimage. Write the coordinates of the vertices of the preimage in the first column of the table. Then apply the dilation $(x, y) \rightarrow \left(\frac{3}{2}x, \frac{3}{2}y\right)$ and write the coordinates of the vertices of the image in the second column. Sketch the image of the figure after the dilation. (Explore Activities 1 and 2)

Preimage	Image
(2, 0)	(3, 0)

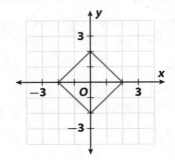

Graph the image of each figure after a dilation with the origin as its center and the given scale factor. Then write an algebraic rule to describe the dilation. (Example 1)

2. scale factor of 1.5

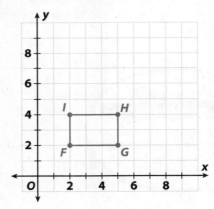

_____

3. scale factor of $\frac{1}{3}$

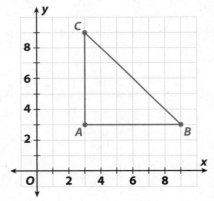

_____

? ESSENTIAL QUESTION CHECK-IN

4. A dilation of $(x, y) \rightarrow (kx, ky)$ when $0 < k < 1$ has what effect on the figure? What is the effect on the figure when $k > 1$?

_____

_____

_____

13.2 Independent Practice

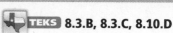

TEKS 8.3.B, 8.3.C, 8.10.D

Personal Math Trainer

Online Assessment and Intervention

my.hrw.com

5. The blue square is the preimage. Write two algebraic representations, one for the dilation to the green square and one for the dilation to the purple square.

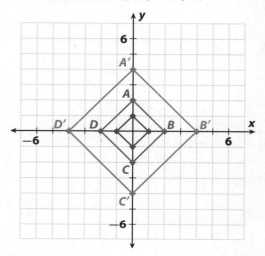

_____

_____

6. Critical Thinking A triangle has vertices $A(-5, -4)$, $B(2, 6)$, and $C(4, -3)$. The center of dilation is the origin and $(x, y) \rightarrow (3x, 3y)$. What are the vertices of the dilated image?

_____

_____

7. Critical Thinking $M'N'O'P'$ has vertices at $M'(3, 4)$, $N'(6, 4)$, $O'(6, 7)$, and $P'(3, 7)$. The center of dilation is the origin. $MNOP$ has vertices at $M(4.5, 6)$, $N(9, 6)$, $O'(9, 10.5)$, and $P'(4.5, 10.5)$. What is the algebraic representation of this dilation?

_____

_____

8. Critical Thinking A dilation with center $(0,0)$ and scale factor k is applied to a polygon. What dilation can you apply to the image to return it to the original preimage?

_____

_____

9. Represent Real-World Problems The blueprints for a new house are scaled so that $\frac{1}{4}$ inch equals 1 foot. The blueprint is the preimage and the house is the dilated image. The blueprints are plotted on a coordinate plane.

a. What is the scale factor in terms of inches to inches?

_____

b. One inch on the blueprint represents how many inches in the actual house? How many feet?

_____

c. Write the algebraic representation of the dilation from the blueprint to the house.

_____

d. A rectangular room has coordinates $Q(2, 2)$, $R(7, 2)$, $S(7, 5)$, and $T(2, 5)$ on the blueprint. The homeowner wants this room to be 25% larger. What are the coordinates of the new room?

_____

_____

e. What are the dimensions of the new room, in inches, on the blueprint? What will the dimensions of the new room be, in feet, in the new house?

_____

_____

_____

_____

10. Write the algebraic representation of the dilation shown.

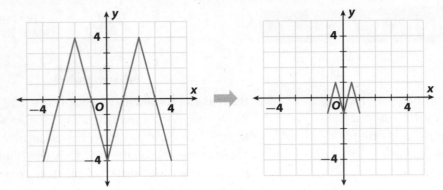

_____

Work Area

11. Critique Reasoning The set for a school play needs a replica of a historic building painted on a backdrop that is 20 feet long and 16 feet high. The actual building measures 400 feet long and 320 feet high. A stage crewmember writes $(x, y) \rightarrow \left(\frac{1}{12}x, \frac{1}{12}y\right)$ to represent the dilation. Is the crewmember's calculation correct if the painted replica is to cover the entire backdrop? Explain.

_____

_____

12. Communicate Mathematical Ideas Explain what each of these algebraic transformations does to a figure.

a. $(x, y) \rightarrow (y, -x)$ _____

b. $(x, y) \rightarrow (-x, -y)$ _____

c. $(x, y) \rightarrow (x, 2y)$ _____

_____

d. $(x, y) \rightarrow \left(\frac{2}{3}x, y\right)$ _____

_____

e. $(x, y) \rightarrow (0.5x, 1.5y)$ _____

_____

13. Communicate Mathematical Ideas Triangle *ABC* has coordinates *A*(1, 5), *B*(−2, 1), and *C*(−2, 4). Sketch triangle *ABC* and *A′B′C′* for the dilation $(x, y) \rightarrow (-2x, -2y)$. What is the effect of a negative scale factor?

_____

_____

TEKS
Two-dimensional shapes—8.10.D Model the effect on linear and area measurements of dilated two-dimensional shapes.
Also 8.3.B, 8.10.A, 8.10.B

? **ESSENTIAL QUESTION**

How do you describe the effects of dilation on linear and area measurements?

EXPLORE ACTIVITY 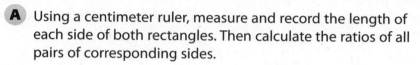 **TEKS** 8.10.D

Exploring Dilations and Measurement

The blue rectangle is a dilation (enlargement) of the green rectangle.

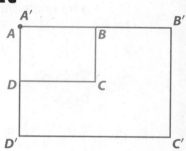

A Using a centimeter ruler, measure and record the length of each side of both rectangles. Then calculate the ratios of all pairs of corresponding sides.

$AB =$ _____ $BC =$ _____ $CD =$ _____ $DA =$ _____

$A'B' =$ _____ $B'C' =$ _____ $C'D' =$ _____ $D'A' =$ _____

$\dfrac{A'B'}{AB} =$ _____ $\dfrac{B'C'}{BC} =$ _____ $\dfrac{C'D'}{CD} =$ _____ $\dfrac{D'A'}{DA} =$ _____

What is true about the ratios that you calculated?

_____

What scale factor was used to dilate the green rectangle
to the blue rectangle?   _____

How are the side lengths of the blue rectangle related to the
side lengths of the green rectangle?

_____

B What is the perimeter of the green rectangle? _____

What is the perimeter of the blue rectangle? _____

How is the perimeter of the blue rectangle related to the perimeter
of the green rectangle?

_____

_____

_____

C What is the area of the green rectangle? _____

What is the area of the blue rectangle? _____

How is the area of the blue rectangle related to the area of the green rectangle?

_____

_____

Reflect

1. **Make a Conjecture** The perimeter and area of two shapes before and after dilation are given. How are the perimeter and area of a dilated figure related to the perimeter and area of the original figure?

	Perimeter	Area
Original	8	4
Dilation	16	16

Scale factor = 2

	Perimeter	Area
Original	30	54
Dilation	5	1.5

Scale factor = $\frac{1}{6}$

_____

_____

_____

_____

Math On the Spot
my.hrw.com

Animated Math
my.hrw.com

Problem-Solving Application

Understanding how dilations affect the linear and area measurements of shapes will enable you to solve many real-world problems.

EXAMPLE 1 Problem Solving   TEKS 8.3.B

A souvenir shop sells standard-sized decks of cards and mini-decks of cards. A card in the standard deck is a rectangle that has a length of 3.5 inches and a width of 2.5 inches. The perimeter of a card in the mini-deck is 6 inches. What is the area of a card in the mini-deck?

Analyze Information

I need to find the area of a mini-card. I know the length and width of a standard card and the perimeter of a mini-card.

Formulate a Plan

Since the mini-card is a dilation of the standard card, the figures are similar. Find the perimeter of the standard card, and use that to find the scale factor. Then use the scale factor to find the area of the mini-card.

Solve

STEP 1 Find the perimeter of the standard card.

$$P_s = 2l + 2w$$

$$P_s = 2(3.5) + 2(2.5)$$

$$P_s = 12 \text{ in.}$$

STEP 2 Find the scale factor.

$$P_m = P_s \cdot k$$

$$6 = 12 \cdot k$$

$$\frac{1}{2} = k$$

Multiply the perimeter of the standard card by the scale factor to get the perimeter of the mini-card.

STEP 3 Find the area of the standard card.

$$A_s = l_s \cdot w_s$$

$$A_s = 3.5 \cdot 2.5$$

$$A_s = 8.75 \text{ in}^2$$

Use the formula for the area of a rectangle.

STEP 4 Find the area of the mini-card.

$$A_m = A_s \cdot k^2$$

$$A_m = 8.75 \cdot \left(\frac{1}{2}\right)^2$$

$$A_m = 8.75 \cdot \frac{1}{4}$$

$$A_m = 2.1875 \text{ in}^2$$

Multiply the area of the standard card by the scale factor squared to get the area of the mini-card.

The area of the mini card is about 2.2 square inches.

Justify and Evaluate

To find the area of the mini-card, find its length and width by multiplying the dimensions of the standard card by the scale factor. The length of the mini card is $l_s \cdot \frac{1}{2} = 3.5 \cdot \frac{1}{2} = 1.75$ in., and the width is $w_s \cdot \frac{1}{2} = 2.5 \cdot \frac{1}{2} = 1.25$ in. So, $A_m = l_m \cdot w_m = 1.75 \cdot 1.25 = 2.1875$ in². The answer is correct.

YOUR TURN

2. Johnson Middle School is selling mouse pads that are replicas of a student's award-winning artwork. The rectangular mouse pads are dilated from the original artwork and have a length of 9 inches and a width of 8 inches. The perimeter of the original artwork is 136 inches. What is the area of the original artwork?

_____

Guided Practice

Find the perimeter and area of the image after dilating the figures shown with the given scale factor. (Explore Activity and Example 1)

1. Scale factor = 5

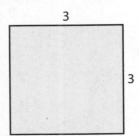

3

3

$P = 12$ $A = 9$

$P' = $ _____ $A' = $ _____

2. Scale factor = $\frac{3}{4}$

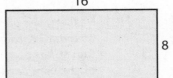

16

8

$P = 48$ $A = 128$

$P' = $ _____ $A' = $ _____

A group of friends is roping off a soccer field in a back yard. A full-size soccer field is a rectangle with a length of 100 yards and a width of 60 yards. To fit the field in the back yard, the group needs to reduce the size of the field so its perimeter is 128 yards. (Example 1)

3. What is the perimeter of the full-size soccer field? _____

4. What is the scale factor of the dilation? _____

5. What is the area of the soccer field in the back yard? _____

? ESSENTIAL QUESTION CHECK-IN

6. When a rectangle is dilated, how do the perimeter and area of the rectangle change?

_____

_____

_____

_____

13.3 Independent Practice

TEKS 8.3.B, 8.10.A, 8.10.B, 8.10.D

Personal Math Trainer

Online Assessment and Intervention

my.hrw.com

7. When you make a photocopy of an image, is the photocopy a dilation? What is the scale factor? How do the perimeter and area change?

_____

_____

8. Problem Solving The universally accepted film size for movies has a width of 35 millimeters. If you want to project a movie onto a square sheet that has an area of 100 square meters, what is the scale factor that is needed for the projection of the movie? Explain.

_____

_____

_____

9. The perimeter of a square is 48 centimeters. If the square is dilated by a scale factor of 0.75, what is the length of each side of the new square?

_____

10. The screen of an eReader has a length of 8 inches and a width of 6 inches. Can the page content from an atlas that measures 19 inches by 12 inches be replicated in the eReader? If not, propose a solution to move the atlas content into the eReader format.

_____

_____

_____

_____

11. Represent Real-World Problems There are 64 squares on a chessboard. Each square on a tournament chessboard measures 2.25 × 2.25 inches. A travel chessboard is a dilated replica of the tournament chessboard using a scale factor of $\frac{1}{3}$.

a. What is the size of each square on the travel chessboard? _____

b. How long is each side of the travel board? _____

c. How much table space do you need to play on the travel chessboard?

_____

12. Draw Conclusions The legs of a right triangle are 3 units and 4 units long. Another right triangle is dilated from this triangle using a scale factor of 3. What are the side lengths and the perimeter of the dilated triangle?

_____

_____

_____

 **FOCUS ON HIGHER ORDER THINKING**

13. Critique Reasoning Rectangle $W'X'Y'Z'$ below is a dilation of rectangle $WXYZ$. A student calculated the area of rectangle $W'X'Y'Z'$ to be 36 square units. Do you agree with this student's calculation? If not, explain and correct the mistake.

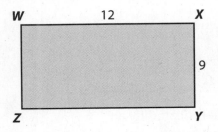
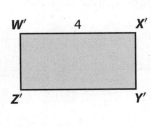

_____

_____

_____

_____

_____

14. Multistep Rectangle $A'B'C'D'$ is a dilation of rectangle $ABCD$, and the scale factor is 2. The perimeter of $ABCD$ is 18 mm. The area of $ABCD$ is 20 mm².

a. Write an equation for, and calculate, the perimeter of $A'B'C'D'$.

_____

_____

b. Write an equation for, and calculate, the area of $A'B'C'D'$.

_____

_____

c. The side lengths of both rectangles are whole numbers of millimeters. What are the side lengths of $ABCD$ and $A'B'C'D'$?

_____

Ready to Go On?

Personal Math Trainer

Online Assessment and Intervention

my.hrw.com

13.1 Properties of Dilations

Determine whether one figure is a dilation of the other. Justify your answer.

1. Triangle *XYZ* has angles measuring 54° and 29°. Triangle *X'Y'Z'* has angles measuring 29° and 92°.

_____

2. Quadrilateral *DEFG* has sides measuring 16 m, 28 m, 24 m, and 20 m. Quadrilateral *D'E'F'G'* has sides measuring 20 m, 35 m, 30 m, and 25 m.

_____

_____

13.2 Algebraic Representations of Dilations

Dilate each figure with the origin as the center of dilation.

3. $(x, y) \rightarrow (0.8x, 0.8y)$

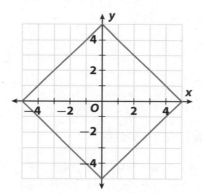

4. $(x, y) \rightarrow (2.5x, 2.5y)$

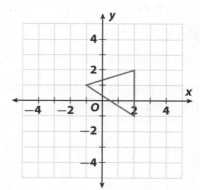

13.3 Dilations and Measurement

5. A rectangle with length 8 cm and width 5 cm is dilated by a scale factor of 3. What are the perimeter and area of the image? _____

? ESSENTIAL QUESTION

6. How can you use dilations to solve real-world problems?

_____

_____

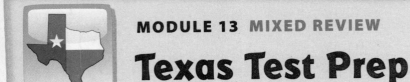

Selected Response

1. Quadrilateral *HIJK* has sides measuring 12 cm, 26 cm, 14 cm, and 30 cm. Which could be the side lengths of a dilation of *HIJK*?

  Ⓐ 24 cm, 50 cm, 28 cm, 60 cm

  Ⓑ 6 cm, 15 cm, 7 cm, 15 cm

  Ⓒ 18 cm, 39 cm, 21 cm, 45 cm

  Ⓓ 30 cm, 78 cm, 35 cm, 75 cm

2. A rectangle has vertices (6, 4), (2, 4), (6, −2), and (2, −2). What are the coordinates of the vertices of the image after a dilation with the origin as its center and a scale factor of 2.5?

  Ⓐ (9, 6), (3, 6), (9, −3), (3, −3)

  Ⓑ (3, 2), (1, 2), (3, −1), (1, −1)

  Ⓒ (12, 8), (4, 8), (12, −4), (4, −4)

  Ⓓ (15, 10), (5, 10), (15, −5), (5, −5)

3. Which represents the dilation shown where the black figure is the preimage?

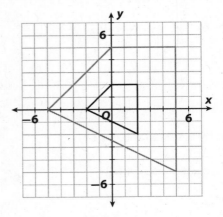

  Ⓐ $(x, y) \rightarrow (1.5x, 1.5y)$

  Ⓑ $(x, y) \rightarrow (2.5x, 2.5y)$

  Ⓒ $(x, y) \rightarrow (3x, 3y)$

  Ⓓ $(x, y) \rightarrow (6x, 6y)$

4. Solve $-a + 7 = 2a - 8$.

  Ⓐ $a = -3$

  Ⓑ $a = -\frac{1}{3}$

  Ⓒ $a = 5$

  Ⓓ $a = 15$

5. An equilateral triangle has a perimeter of 24 centimeters. If the triangle is dilated by a factor of 0.5, what is the length of each side of the new triangle?

  Ⓐ 4 centimeters   Ⓒ 16 centimeters

  Ⓑ 12 centimeters   Ⓓ 48 centimeters

6. Which equation does **not** represent a line with an *x*-intercept of 3?

  Ⓐ $y = -2x + 6$

  Ⓑ $y = -\frac{1}{3}x + 1$

  Ⓒ $y = \frac{2}{3}x - 2$

  Ⓓ $y = 3x - 1$

Gridded Response

7. A car is traveling at a constant speed. After 3 hours, the car has traveled 80 miles. If the car continues to travel at the same constant speed, how many hours will it take to travel 270 miles?

⓪	⓪	⓪	⓪	•	⓪	⓪
①	①	①	①		①	①
②	②	②	②		②	②
③	③	③	③		③	③
④	④	④	④		④	④
⑤	⑤	⑤	⑤		⑤	⑤
⑥	⑥	⑥	⑥		⑥	⑥
⑦	⑦	⑦	⑦		⑦	⑦
⑧	⑧	⑧	⑧		⑧	⑧
⑨	⑨	⑨	⑨		⑨	⑨

MODULE 12 ▸ Transformations and Congruence

Key Vocabulary

center of rotation *(centro de rotación)*

image *(imagen)*

line of reflection *(línea de reflexión)*

preimage *(imagen original)*

reflection *(reflexión)*

rotation *(rotación)*

transformation *(transformación)*

translation *(traslación)*

? ESSENTIAL QUESTION

How can you use transformations and congruence to solve real-world problems?

EXAMPLE

Translate triangle *XYZ* left 4 units and down 2 units. Graph the image and label the vertices.

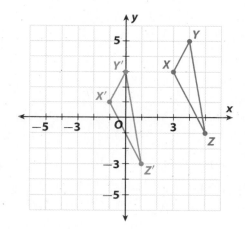

Translate the vertices by subtracting 4 from each *x*-coordinate and 2 from each *y*-coordinate. The new vertices are $X'(-1, 1)$, $Y'(0, 3)$, and $Z'(1, -3)$.

Connect the vertices to draw triangle $X'Y'Z'$.

EXERCISES

Perform the transformation shown. (Lessons 12.1, 12.2, 12.3)

1. Reflection over the *x*-axis

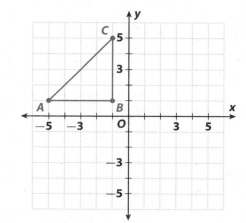

2. Translation 5 units right

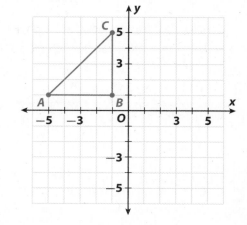

3. Rotation 90° counterclockwise about the origin

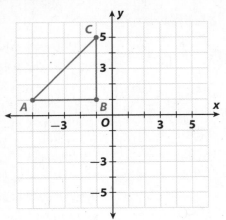

4. Translation 4 units right and 4 units down

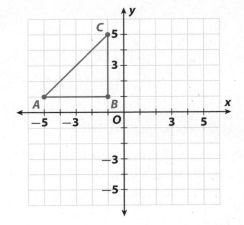

5. Quadrilateral *ABCD* with vertices *A*(4, 4), *B*(5, 1), *C*(5, −1) and *D*(4, −2) is translated left 2 units and down 3 units. Graph the preimage and the image. (Lesson 12.4)

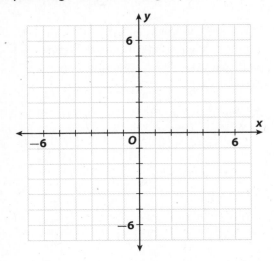

6. Triangle *RST* has vertices at (−8, 2), (−4, 0), and (−12, 8). Find the vertices after the triangle has been reflected over the *y*-axis. (Lesson 12.4)

_____

7. Triangle *XYZ* has vertices at (3, 7), (9, 14), and (12, −1). Find the vertices after the triangle has been rotated 180° about the origin. (Lesson 12.4)

_____

Dilations, Similarity, and Proportionality

Key Vocabulary

center of dilation (*centro de dilatación*)

dilation (*dilatación*)

enlargement (*agrandamiento*)

reduction (*reducción*)

scale factor (*factor de escala*)

? **ESSENTIAL QUESTION**

How can you use dilations, similarity, and proportionality to solve real-world problems?

EXAMPLE

Dilate triangle *ABC* with the origin as the center of dilation and scale factor $\frac{1}{2}$. Graph the dilated image.

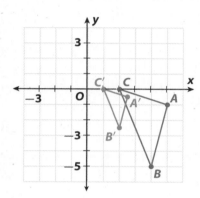

Multiply each coordinate of the vertices of *ABC* by $\frac{1}{2}$ to find the vertices of the dilated image.

$$A(5, -1) \rightarrow A'\left(5 \cdot \frac{1}{2}, -1 \cdot \frac{1}{2}\right) \rightarrow A'\left(2\frac{1}{2}, -\frac{1}{2}\right)$$

$$B(4, -5) \rightarrow B'\left(4 \cdot \frac{1}{2}, -5 \cdot \frac{1}{2}\right) \rightarrow B'\left(2, -2\frac{1}{2}\right)$$

$$C(2, 0) \rightarrow C'\left(2 \cdot \frac{1}{2}, 0 \cdot \frac{1}{2}\right) \rightarrow C'(1, 0)$$

EXERCISES

1. For each pair of corresponding vertices, find the ratio of the *x*-coordinates and the ratio of the *y*-coordinates. (Lesson 13.1)

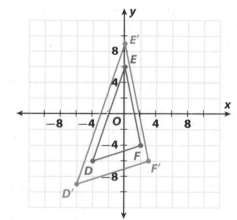

Ratio of *x*-coordinates: _____

Ratio of *y*-coordinates: _____

What is the scale factor of the dilation? _____

2. Andrew's old television had a width of 32 inches and a height of 18 inches. His new television is larger by a scale factor of 2.5. Find the perimeter and area of Andrew's old television and his new television. (Lesson 13.3)

Perimeter of old TV: _____   Perimeter of new TV: _____

Area of old TV: _____   Area of new TV: _____

Dilate each figure with the origin as the center of the dilation. List the vertices of the dilated figure then graph the figure. (Lesson 13.2)

3. $(x, y) \rightarrow \left(\frac{1}{4}x, \frac{1}{4}y\right)$

_____

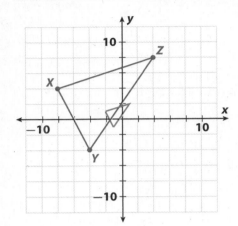

4. $(x, y) \rightarrow (2x, 2y)$

_____

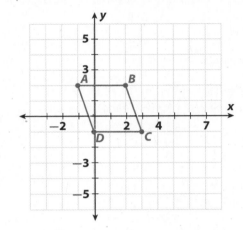

Unit 5 Performance Tasks

1. **CAREERS IN MATH** **Contractor** Fernando is expanding his dog's play yard. The original yard has a fence represented by rectangle *LMNO* on the coordinate plane. Fernando hires a contractor to construct a new fence that should enclose 6 times as much area as the current fence. The shape of the fence must remain the same. The contractor constructs the fence shown by rectangle *L'M'N'O'*.

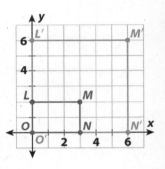

   a. Did the contractor increase the area by the amount Fernando wanted? Explain.

_____

_____

   b. Does the new fence maintain the shape of the old fence? How do you know?

_____

_____

2. A sail for a sailboat is represented by a triangle on the coordinate plane with vertices (0, 0), (5, 0), and (5, 4). The triangle is dilated by a scale factor of 1.5 with the origin as the center of dilation. Find the coordinates of the dilated triangle. Are the triangles similar? Explain.

_____

_____

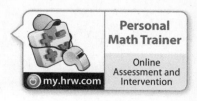
Selected Response

1. What would be the orientation of the figure below after a reflection over the *x*-axis?

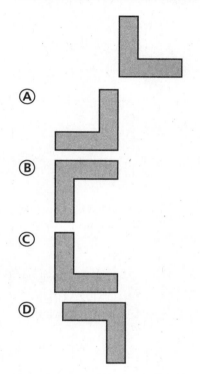

Ⓐ

Ⓑ

Ⓒ

Ⓓ

2. A triangle with coordinates (4, 2), (0, −3), and (−5, 3) is translated 5 units right and rotated 180° about the origin. What are the coordinates of its image?

Ⓐ (9, 2), (−1, −2), (5, −7)

Ⓑ (−10, 3), (−1, 2), (−5, −3)

Ⓒ (2, −1), (−3, −5), (3, −10)

Ⓓ (2, 9), (−3, 5), (3, 0)

3. Quadrilateral *LMNP* has sides measuring 16, 28, 12, and 32. Which could be the side lengths of a dilation of *LMNP*?

Ⓐ 24, 40, 18, 90

Ⓑ 32, 60, 24, 65

Ⓒ 20, 35, 15, 40

Ⓓ 40, 70, 30, 75

4. The table below represents which equation?

x	−1	0	1	2
y	1	−2	−5	−8

Ⓐ $y = x + 2$

Ⓑ $y = -x$

Ⓒ $y = 3x + 6$

Ⓓ $y = -3x - 2$

5. Which of the following is **not** true of a trapezoid that has been translated 8 units down?

Ⓐ The new trapezoid is the same size as the original trapezoid.

Ⓑ The new trapezoid is the same shape as the original trapezoid.

Ⓒ The new trapezoid is in the same orientation as the original trapezoid.

Ⓓ The *y*-coordinates of the new trapezoid are the same as the *y*-coordinates of the original trapezoid.

6. Which represents a reduction?

Ⓐ $(x, y) \rightarrow (0.9x, 0.9y)$

Ⓑ $(x, y) \rightarrow (1.4x, 1.4y)$

Ⓒ $(x, y) \rightarrow (0.7x, 0.3y)$

Ⓓ $(x, y) \rightarrow (2.5x, 2.5y)$

7. Grain is stored in cylindrical structures called silos. Which is the best estimate for the volume of a silo with a diameter of 12.3 feet and a height of 25 feet?

Ⓐ 450 cubic feet

Ⓑ 900 cubic feet

Ⓒ 2970 cubic feet

Ⓓ 10,800 cubic feet

8. A rectangle has vertices (8, 6), (4, 6), (8, −4), and (4, −4). What are the coordinates after dilating from the origin by a scale factor of 1.5?

Ⓐ (9, 6), (3, 6), (9, −3), (3, −3)

Ⓑ (10, 8), (5, 8), (10, −5), (5, −5)

Ⓒ (16, 12), (8, 12), (16, −8), (8, −8)

Ⓓ (12, 9), (6, 9), (12, −6), (6, −6)

9. Two sides of a right triangle have lengths of 56 centimeters and 65 centimeters. The third side is **not** the hypotenuse. How long is the third side?

Ⓐ 9 centimeters

Ⓑ 27 centimeters

Ⓒ 33 centimeters

Ⓓ 86 centimeters

10. Which statement is false?

Ⓐ No integers are irrational numbers.

Ⓑ All whole numbers are integers.

Ⓒ No real numbers are rational numbers.

Ⓓ All integers greater than or equal to 0 are whole numbers.

 Make sure you look at all answer choices before making your decision. Try substituting each answer choice into the problem if you are unsure of the answer.

11. Which inequality represents the solution to $1.5x + 4.5 < 2.75x − 5.5$?

Ⓐ $x > 8$

Ⓑ $x < 8$

Ⓒ $x > 12.5$

Ⓓ $x < 12.5$

Gridded Response

12. In what quadrant would the triangle below be located after a rotation of 90° counterclockwise?

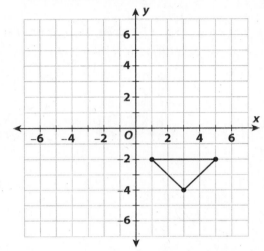

			•		
⓪	⓪	⓪	⓪	⓪	⓪
①	①	①	①	①	①
②	②	②	②	②	②
③	③	③	③	③	③
④	④	④	④	④	④
⑤	⑤	⑤	⑤	⑤	⑤
⑥	⑥	⑥	⑥	⑥	⑥
⑦	⑦	⑦	⑦	⑦	⑦
⑧	⑧	⑧	⑧	⑧	⑧
⑨	⑨	⑨	⑨	⑨	⑨

13. An equilateral triangle has a perimeter of 48 centimeters. If the triangle is dilated by a factor of 0.75, what is the length of each side of the new triangle?

			•		
⓪	⓪	⓪	⓪	⓪	⓪
①	①	①	①	①	①
②	②	②	②	②	②
③	③	③	③	③	③
④	④	④	④	④	④
⑤	⑤	⑤	⑤	⑤	⑤
⑥	⑥	⑥	⑥	⑥	⑥
⑦	⑦	⑦	⑦	⑦	⑦
⑧	⑧	⑧	⑧	⑧	⑧
⑨	⑨	⑨	⑨	⑨	⑨

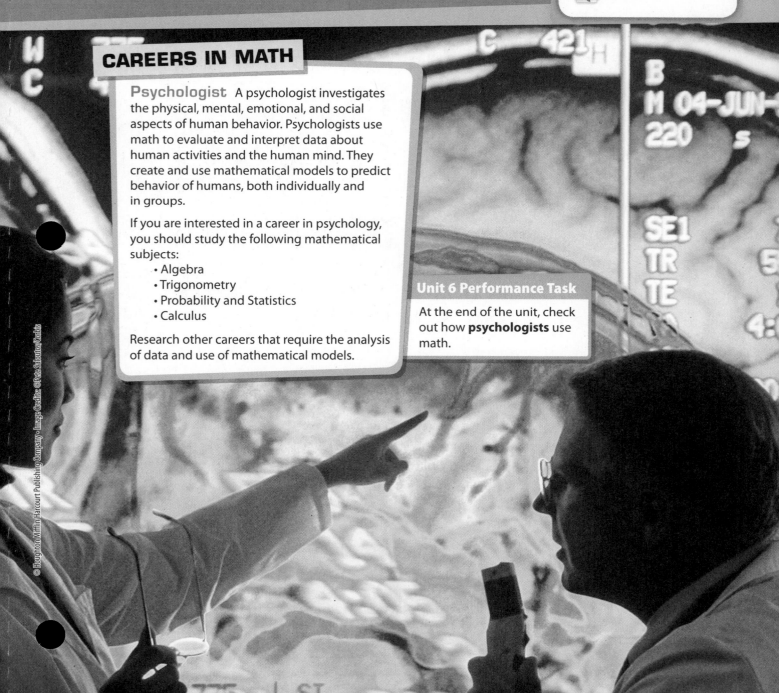

Statistics and Samples

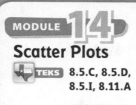

MODULE **14**

Scatter Plots

TEKS 8.5.C, 8.5.D, 8.5.I, 8.11.A

MODULE **15**

Sampling

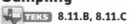

TEKS 8.11.B, 8.11.C

CAREERS IN MATH

Psychologist A psychologist investigates the physical, mental, emotional, and social aspects of human behavior. Psychologists use math to evaluate and interpret data about human activities and the human mind. They create and use mathematical models to predict behavior of humans, both individually and in groups.

If you are interested in a career in psychology, you should study the following mathematical subjects:
- Algebra
- Trigonometry
- Probability and Statistics
- Calculus

Research other careers that require the analysis of data and use of mathematical models.

Unit 6 Performance Task

At the end of the unit, check out how **psychologists** use math.

Vocabulary Preview

Use the puzzle to preview key vocabulary from this unit. Unscramble the circled letters within found words to answer the riddle at the bottom of the page.

```
E  I  F  N  R  B  W  D  F  M  O  (N) J  O  V
N  L  E  L  H  L  D  C  C  W  O  T  R  U  R
O  Y  P  T  R  (E) N  D  L  I  N  E  I  T  W
I  Q  V  M  M  V  I  B  T  U  D  D  B  L  F
T  U  D  K  A  E  B  A  B  R  S  Q  I  I  W
(A) R  Q  O  S  S  L  T  S  M  N  T  B  E  C
I  Y  S  Z  Y  U  (M) P  K  D  G  U  E  R  Q
C  B  T  S  P  B  T  O  B  Q  P  B  H  R  V
O  U  M  O  M  G  V  C  D  W  Q  G  Z  U  E
S  W  P  R  K  V  T  U  E  N  L  M  G  Z  S
S  X  L  E  T  V  U  G  Q  C  A  J  I  G  C
A  D  E  O  A  B  L  W  A  Q  D  R  N  B  U
G  V  J  Q  V  C  X  A  Y  I  V  M  A  Z  W
N  L  F  W  O  M  A  T  L  T  U  Z  B  X  M
R  Y  S  X  G  F  D  E  Y  U  T  U  F  V  G
```

A description of how sets of data are related. (Lesson 14.1)

A set of closely related data. (Lesson 14.1)

A data point that is very different from the rest of the data in the set. (Lesson 14.1)

A straight line that comes closest to the points on a scatter plot (2 words). (Lesson 14.2)

The entire group of objects, individuals, or events in a set of data. (Lesson 15.2)

A sample in which every person, object, or event has an equal chance at being selected (2 words). (Lesson 15.2)

Q: Why doesn't Joe Average have any friends?

A: Because he's so ___ ___ ___ ___!

Scatter Plots

 ESSENTIAL QUESTION

How can you use scatterplots to solve real-world problems?

LESSON 14.1

Scatter Plots and Association

 TEKS 8.5.C, 8.11.A

LESSON 14.2

Trend Lines and Predictions

TEKS 8.5.D, 8.5.I, 8.11.A

Real-World Video

An anthropologist measures dinosaur bones. To estimate a dinosaur's height based on the length of a bone, he can make a scatter plot comparing bone length and height of several dinosaurs.

 my.hrw.com

 GO DIGITAL
my.hrw.com

my.hrw.com

Go digital with your write-in student edition, accessible on any device.

 Math On the Spot

Scan with your smart phone to jump directly to the online edition, video tutor, and more.

X² **Animated Math**

Interactively explore key concepts to see how math works.

 Personal Math Trainer

Get immediate feedback and help as you work through practice sets.

Are YOU Ready?

Complete these exercises to review skills you will need for this module.

Personal Math Trainer

Online Assessment and Intervention

⊙ my.hrw.com

Evaluate Expressions

EXAMPLE   Evaluate $4x + 3$ for $x = 5$.

$4x + 3 = 4(5) + 3$ Substitute the given value for x.

$= 20 + 3$ Multiply.

$= 23$ Add.

Evaluate each expression for the given value of x.

1. $6x - 5$ for $x = 4$

_____

2. $-2x + 7$ for $x = 2$

_____

3. $5x - 6$ for $x = 3$

_____

4. $0.5x + 8.4$ for $x = -1$

_____

5. $\frac{3}{4}x - 9$ for $x = -20$

_____

6. $1.4x + 3.5$ for $x = -4$

_____

Solve Two-Step Equations

EXAMPLE
$$5x + 3 = -7$$
$$\underline{\quad -3 = -3\quad}$$ Subtract 3 from both sides.
$$5x = -10$$
$$\frac{5x}{5} = \frac{-10}{5}$$ Divide both sides by 5.
$$x = -2$$

Solve for x.

7. $3x + 4 = 10$

_____

8. $5x - 11 = 34$

_____

9. $-2x + 5 = -9$

_____

10. $8x + 13 = -11$

_____

11. $4x - 7 = -27$

_____

12. $\frac{1}{2}x + 16 = 39$

_____

13. $\frac{2}{3}x - 16 = 12$

_____

14. $0.5x - 1.5 = -6.5$

_____

© Houghton Mifflin Harcourt Publishing Company

Reading **Start-Up**

Visualize Vocabulary

Use the ✔ words to complete the right column of the chart.

Reviewing Slope	
Mathematical Representation	Review Word
$y = mx + b$	
y	
m	
x	
b	

Understand Vocabulary

Match the term on the left to the correct expression on the right.

1. cluster

2. outlier

3. trend line

A. A data point that is very different from the rest of the data in a set

B. A straight line that comes closest to the points on a scatter plot.

C. A set of closely grouped data.

© Houghton Mifflin Harcourt Publishing Company

Vocabulary

Review Words
- bivariate data *(datos bivariados)*
- data *(datos)*
- ✔ linear equation *(ecuación lineal)*
- ✔ slope *(pendiente)*
- ✔ slope-intercept form of an equation *(forma pendiente-intersección)*
- ✔ x-coordinate *(coordenada x)*
- ✔ y-coordinate *(coordenada y)*
- ✔ y-intercept *(intersección con el eje y)*

Preview Words
- cluster *(agrupación)*
- outlier *(valor extremo)*
- scatter plot *(diagrama de dispersión)*
- trend line *(línea de tendencia)*

Active Reading

Two-Panel Flip Chart Create a two-panel flip chart, to help you understand the concepts in this module. Label each flap with the title of one of the lessons in the module. As you study each lesson, write important ideas under the appropriate flap. Include any sample problems or equations that will help you remember the concepts later when you look back at your notes.

Unpacking the TEKS

Understanding the TEKS and the vocabulary terms in the TEKS will help you know exactly what you are expected to learn in this module.

TEKS 8.5.D

Use a trend line that approximates the linear relationship between bivariate sets of data to make predictions.

What It Means to You

You will use a trend line on a scatterplot to make predictions.

UNPACKING EXAMPLE 8.5.D

Joyce is training for a 10K race. For each of her training runs, she recorded the distance she ran and the time she ran. She made a scatterplot of her data and drew a trend line. Use the trend line to predict how long it would take Joyce to run 4.5 miles.

Distance (mi)	Time (min)
4	38
2	25
1	7
2	16
3	26
5	55
2	20
4	45
3	31

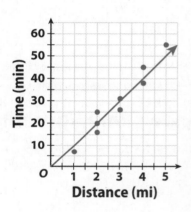

For a distance of 4.5 miles, the trend line shows a distance of 45 minutes. So, it will take Joyce about 45 minutes to run 4.5 miles.

TEKS 8.11.A

Construct a scatterplot and describe the observed data to address questions of association such as linear, non-linear, and no association between bivariate data.

Visit **my.hrw.com** to see all the **TEKS** unpacked.

⊙ my.hrw.com

What It Means to You

You will tell how the data in a scatterplot is related.

UNPACKING EXAMPLE 8.11.A

The scatterplot shows Bob's height at various ages. Describe the type(s) of association between Bob's age and his height. Explain.

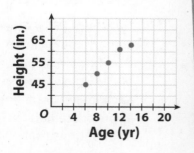

As Bob gets older, his height increases roughly along a straight line on the graph, so the association is positive and basically linear.

LESSON
14.1
Scatter Plots and Association

TEKS
Measurement and data—8.11.A Construct a scatterplot and describe the observed data to address questions of association such as linear, non-linear, and no association between bivariate data. *Also 8.5.C*

ESSENTIAL QUESTION

How can you construct and interpret scatter plots?

EXPLORE ACTIVITY 1 TEKS 8.11.A

Making a Scatter Plot

Recall that a set of bivariate data involves two variables. Bivariate data are used to explore the relationship between two variables. You can graph bivariate data on a *scatter plot*. A **scatter plot** is a graph with points plotted to show the relationship between two sets of data.

The final question on a math test reads, "How many hours did you spend studying for this test?" The teacher records the number of hours each student studied and the grade the student received on the test.

Hours Spent Studying	Test Grade
0	75
0.5	80
1	80
1	85
1.5	85
1.5	95
2	90
3	100
4	90

A Make a prediction about the relationship between the number of hours spent studying and test grades.

_____

_____

_____

B Make a scatter plot. Graph hours spent studying as the independent variable and test grades as the dependent variable.

Reflect

1. What trend do you see in the data?

_____

_____

2. **Justify Reasoning** Do you think that studying for 10 hours would greatly increase a student's grade?

_____

_____

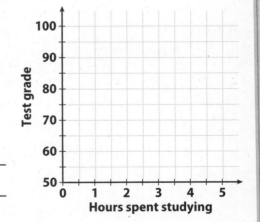

© Houghton Mifflin Harcourt Publishing Company

Interpreting Clusters and Outliers

A **cluster** is a set of closely grouped data. Data may cluster around a point or along a line. An **outlier** is a data point that is very different from the rest of the data in the set.

A scientist gathers information about the eruptions of Old Faithful, a geyser in Yellowstone National Park. She uses the data to create a scatter plot. The data show the length of time between eruptions (interval) and how long the eruption lasts (duration).

A Describe any clusters you see in the scatter plot.

_____

_____

B What do the clusters tell you about eruptions of Old Faithful?

_____

_____

C Describe any outliers you see in the scatter plot.

_____

_____

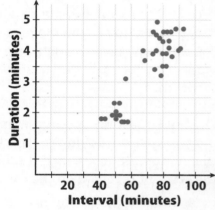

Math Talk

Mathematical Processes

If the point (20, 1) appeared on the scatter plot, would it be an outlier? Explain.

Reflect

3. Suppose the geyser erupts for 2.2 minutes after a 75-minute interval. Would this point lie in one of the clusters? Would it be an outlier? Explain your answer.

_____

_____

_____

4. Suppose the geyser erupts after an 80-minute interval. Give a range of possible duration times for which the point on the scatter plot would not be considered an outlier. Explain your reasoning.

_____

_____

© Houghton Mifflin Harcourt Publishing Company • Image Credits: ©PhotoDisc/ Getty Images

Determining Association

Association describes how sets of data are related. A *positive* association means that both data sets increase together. A *negative* association means that as one data set increases, the other decreases. *No* association means that changes in one data set do not affect the other data set.

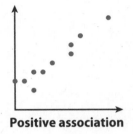

Positive association

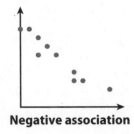

Negative association

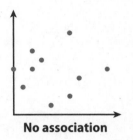

No association

Data that show a positive or negative association and lie basically along a line exhibit a *linear* association. Data that show a positive or negative association but do not lie basically along a line exhibit a *nonlinear* association.

EXAMPLE 1

TEKS 8.5.C, 8.11.A

Susan asked 20 people if they would buy a new product she developed at each of several prices. The scatter plot shows how many of the 20 said "yes" at a given price. Describe the association between price and the number of buyers.

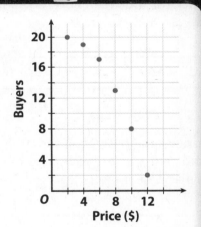

As price increases, the number of buyers decreases. So, there is a negative association. Because the data points do not lie along a line, the association is nonlinear.

Animated Math
⏻ my.hrw.com

Reflect

5. **What If?** Based on the association shown in the scatter plot, what might happen if Susan increased the price to $14?

_____

_____

YOUR TURN

6. The plot shows the reading level and height for 16 students in a district. Describe the association and give a possible reason for it.

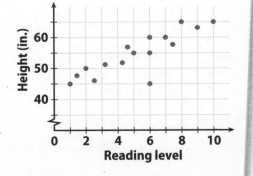

_____

_____

_____

Personal Math Trainer

Online Assessment and Intervention

⏻ my.hrw.com

Bob recorded his height at different ages. The table below shows his data.

Age (years)	6	8	10	12	14
Height (inches)	45	50	55	61	63

1. Make a scatter plot of Bob's data. (Explore Activity 1)

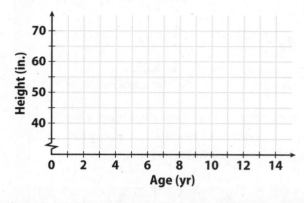

2. Describe the association between Bob's age and his height. Explain the association. (Example 1)

_____

_____

_____

3. The scatter plot shows the basketball shooting results for 14 players. Describe any clusters you see in the scatter plot. Identify any outliers. (Explore Activity 2)

_____

_____

_____

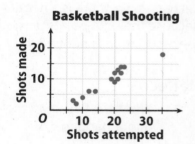

Basketball Shooting

? ESSENTIAL QUESTION CHECK-IN

4. Explain how you can make a scatter plot from a set of bivariate data.

_____

_____

_____

_____

14.1 Independent Practice

 **TEKS** 8.5.C, 8.11.A

Personal Math Trainer

Online Assessment and Intervention

my.hrw.com

Sports Use the scatter plot for 5–8.

Olympic Men's Long Jump Winning Distances

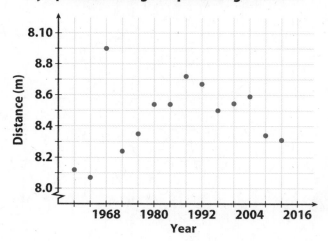

5. Describe the association between the year and the distance jumped for the years 1960 to 1988.

_____

_____

_____

_____

6. Describe the association between the year and the distance jumped for the years after 1988.

_____

_____

_____

_____

7. For the entire scatter plot, is the association between the year and the distance jumped linear or nonlinear? Explain.

_____

_____

_____

_____

_____

8. Identify the outlier and interpret its meaning.

_____

_____

_____

_____

9. Communicate Mathematical Ideas Compare a scatter plot that shows no association to one that shows negative association.

_____

_____

_____

_____

_____

_____

_____

For 10–11, describe a set of real-world bivariate data that the given scatter plot could represent. Define the variable represented on each axis.

10.

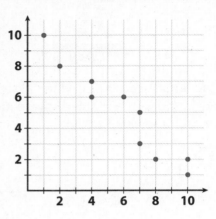

11.

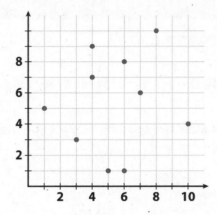

_____

_____

_____

_____

_____

_____

H.O.T. FOCUS ON HIGHER ORDER THINKING

12. Multiple Representations Describe what you might see in a table of bivariate data that would lead you to conclude that the scatter plot of the data would show a cluster.

_____

_____

13. Justify Reasoning Is it possible for a scatter plot to have a positive or negative association that is not linear? Explain.

_____

_____

_____

14. Critical Thinking To try to increase profits, a theater owner increases the price of a ticket by $25 every month. Describe what a scatter plot might look like if x represents the number of months and y represents the profits. Explain your reasoning.

_____

_____

_____

_____

LESSON
14.2
Trend Lines and Predictions

Proportionality—
8.5.D Use a trend line that approximates the linear relationship between bivariate sets of data to make predictions.
Also 8.5.I, 8.11.A

ESSENTIAL QUESTION

How can you use a trend line to make a prediction from a scatter plot?

EXPLORE ACTIVITY 1  **TEKS** 8.5.D, 8.11.A

Drawing a Trend Line

When a scatter plot shows a linear association, you can use a line to model the relationship between the variables. A **trend line** is a straight line that comes closest to the points on a scatter plot.

Joyce is training for a 10K race. For some of her training runs, she records the distance she ran and how many minutes she ran.

A Make a scatter plot of Joyce's running data.

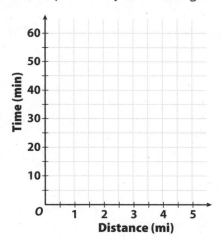

Distance (mi)	Time (min)
4	38
2	25
1	7
2	16
3	26
5	55
2	20
4	45
3	31

B To draw a trend line, use a straight edge to draw a line that has about the same number of points above and below it. Ignore any outliers.

C Use your trend line to predict how long it would take Joyce to run 4.5 miles.

_____

Reflect

1. How well does your trend line fit the data? Explain.

_____

_____

2. Do you think you can use a scatter plot that shows no association to make a prediction? Explain your answer.

_____

_____

Math On the Spot
ⓞ my.hrw.com

Finding the Equation of a Trend Line

You can use two points on a trend line to write an equation in slope-intercept form for the trend line.

EXAMPLE 1

TEKS 8.5.I

The scatter plot and trend line show the relationship between the number of chapters and the total number of pages for several books. Write an equation for the trend line.

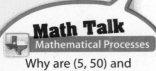

STEP 1 Find the slope of the trend line. The line passes through points (5, 50) and (17, 170).

$m = \dfrac{y_2 - y_1}{x_2 - x_1}$ Use the slope formula.

$m = \dfrac{170 - 50}{17 - 5}$ Substitute (5, 50) for (x_1, y_1) and (17, 170) for (x_2, y_2).

$m = \dfrac{120}{12} = 10$ Simplify.

STEP 2 Find the *y*-intercept of the trend line.

$y = mx + b$ Slope-intercept form

$50 = 10 \cdot 5 + b$ Substitute 50 for y, 10 for m, and 5 for x.

$50 = 50 + b$ Simplify.

$50 - 50 = 50 - 50 + b$ Subtract 50 from both sides.

$0 = b$ Simplify.

STEP 3 Use your slope and *y*-intercept values to write the equation.

$y = mx + b$ Slope-intercept form

$y = 10x + 0$ Substitute 10 for m and 0 for y.

The equation for the trend line is $y = 10x$.

Reflect

3. What type(s) of association does the scatter plot show?

_____

4. What is the meaning of the slope in this situation?

_____

5. What is the meaning of the *y*-intercept in this situation?

_____

YOUR TURN

6. The scatter plot and trend line show the relationship between the number of rainy days in a month and the number of umbrellas sold each month. Write an equation for the trend line.

_____

_____

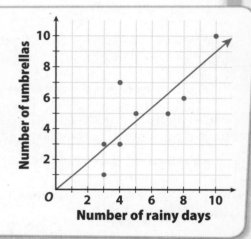

Personal Math Trainer

Online Assessment and Intervention

my.hrw.com

EXPLORE ACTIVITY 2  TEKS 8.5.D

Making Predictions

When you use a trend line or its equation to predict a value between data points that you already know, you *interpolate* the predicted value. When you make a prediction that is outside the data that you know, you *extrapolate* the predicted value.

Use the equation of the trend line in Example 1 to predict how many pages would be in a book with 26 chapters.

Is this prediction an example of interpolation or extrapolation? _____

$y = \boxed{}$ Write the equation for your trend line.

$y = \boxed{}$ Substitute the number of chapters for x.

$y = \boxed{}$ Simplify.

I predict that a book with 26 chapters will have _____ pages.

© Houghton Mifflin Harcourt Publishing Company

Reflect

7. **Make a Prediction** Predict how many pages would be in a book with 14 chapters. Is this prediction an example of interpolation or extrapolation?

_____

8. Do you think that extrapolation or interpolation is more accurate? Explain.

_____

_____

_____

Guided Practice

Angela recorded the price of different weights of several bulk grains. She made a scatter plot of her data. Use the scatter plot for 1–4.

1. Draw a trend line for the scatter plot. (Explore Activity 1)

2. How do you know whether your trend line is a good fit for the data? (Explore Activity 1)

_____

_____

_____

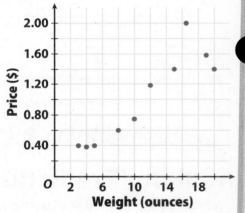

3. Write an equation for your trend line. (Example 1) _____

4. Use the equation for your trend line to interpolate the price of 7 ounces and extrapolate the price of 50 ounces.

(Explore Activity 2) _____

? ESSENTIAL QUESTION CHECK-IN

5. A trend line passes through two points on a scatter plot. How can you use the trend line to make a prediction between or outside the given data points?

_____

_____

_____

14.2 Independent Practice

TEKS 8.5.D, 8.5.I, 8.11.A

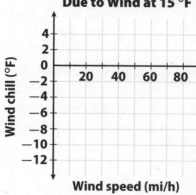

Personal
Math Trainer

Online
Assessment and
Intervention

my.hrw.com

Use the data in the table for Exercises 6–10.

Apparent Temperature Due to Wind at 15 °F						
Wind speed (mi/h)	10	20	30	40	50	60
Wind chill (°F)	2.7	−2.3	−5.5	−7.9	−9.8	−11.4

**Apparent Temperature
Due to Wind at 15 °F**

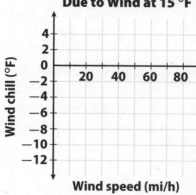

Wind chill (°F)

Wind speed (mi/h)

6. Make a scatter plot of the data and draw a trend line.

7. What type of association does the trend line show?

_____

8. Write an equation for your trend line. _____

9. **Make a Prediction** Use the trend line to predict the wind chill at these wind speeds.

   a. 36 mi/h _____   b. 100 mi/h _____

10. What is the meaning of the slope of the line?

_____

_____

Use the data in the table for Exercises 11–14.

Apparent Temperature Due to Humidity at a Room Temperature of 72 °F						
Humidity (%)	0	20	40	60	80	100
Apparent temperature (°F)	64	67	70	72	74	76

**Apparent Temperature at a
Room Temperature of 72 °F**

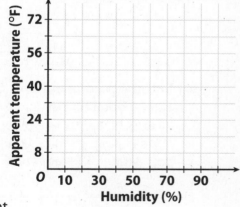

Apparent temperature (°F)

Humidity (%)

11. Make a scatter plot of the data and draw a trend line.

12. Write an equation for your trend line.

_____

13. **Make a Prediction** Use the trend line to predict the apparent temperature at 70% humidity. _____

14. What is the meaning of the *y*-intercept of the line?

_____

© Houghton Mifflin Harcourt Publishing Company

Work Area

15. **Communicate Mathematical Ideas** Is it possible to draw a trend line on a scatter plot that shows no association? Explain.

_____

_____

_____

16. **Critique Reasoning** Sam drew a trend line that had about the same number of data points above it as below it, but did not pass through any data points. He then picked two data points to write the equation for the line. Is this a correct way to write the equation? Explain.

_____

_____

_____

_____

17. Marlene wanted to find a relationship between the areas and populations of counties in Texas. She plotted x (area in square miles) and y (population) for two counties on a scatter plot:

Kent County (903, 808)   Edwards County (2118, 2002)

She concluded that the population of Texas counties is approximately equal to their area in square miles and drew a trend line through her points.

a. **Critique Reasoning** Do you agree with Marlene's method of creating a scatter plot and a trend line? Explain why or why not.

_____

_____

_____

b. **Counterexamples** Harris County has an area of 1778 square miles and a population of about 4.3 million people. Dallas County has an area of 908 square miles and a population of about 2.5 million people. What does this data show about Marlene's conjecture that the population of Texas counties is approximately equal to their area?

_____

_____

_____

_____

Ready to Go On?

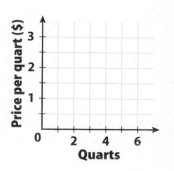

Personal Math Trainer

Online Assessment and Intervention

⏱ my.hrw.com

14.1 Scatter Plots and Association

An auto store is having a sale on motor oil. The chart shows the price per quart as the number of quarts purchased increases. Use the data for 1–2.

Number of quarts	1	2	3	4	5	6
Price per quart ($)	2	1.50	1.25	1.10	1	0.95

1. Use the given data to make a scatter plot.

2. Describe the association you see between the number of quarts purchased and the price per quart. Explain.

_____

_____

_____

14.2 Trend Lines and Predictions

The scatter plot below shows data comparing wind speed and wind chill for an air temperature of 20 °F. Use the scatter plot for 3–5.

3. Draw a trend line for the scatter plot.

4. Write an equation for your trend line.

_____

5. Use your equation to predict the wind chill to the nearest degree for a wind speed of 60 mi/h.

_____

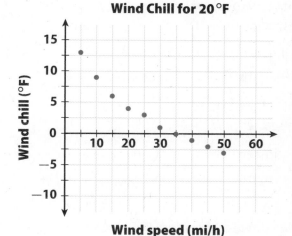

Wind Chill for 20 °F

❓ ESSENTIAL QUESTION

6. How can you use scatter plots to solve real-world problems?

_____

_____

MODULE 14 MIXED REVIEW

Texas Test Prep

Personal
Math Trainer

Online
Assessment and
Intervention

my.hrw.com

Selected Response

1. Which scatter plot could have a trend line whose equation is $y = 3x + 10$?

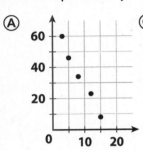

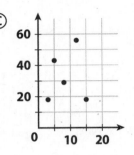

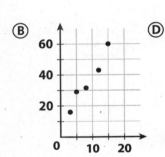

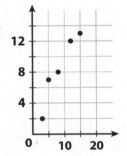

2. What type of association would you expect between a person's age and hair length?

   Ⓐ linear
   Ⓑ negative
   Ⓒ none
   Ⓓ positive

3. Which is **not** shown on the scatter plot?

   Ⓐ cluster
   Ⓑ negative association
   Ⓒ outlier
   Ⓓ positive association

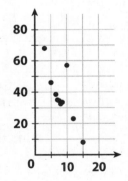

4. A restaurant claims to have served 352,000,000 hamburgers. What is this number in scientific notation?

   Ⓐ 3.52×10^6
   Ⓑ 3.52×10^8
   Ⓒ 35.2×10^7
   Ⓓ 352×10^6

5. Which equation describes the relationship between x and y in the table?

x	−8	−4	0	4	8
y	2	1	0	−1	−2

   Ⓐ $y = -4x$
   Ⓑ $y = -\frac{1}{4}x$
   Ⓒ $y = 4x$
   Ⓓ $y = \frac{1}{4}x$

Gridded Response

6. Predict the number of visitors when the temperature is 102 °F.

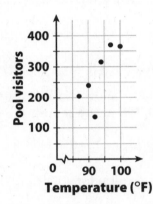

Sampling

? **ESSENTIAL QUESTION**

How can you use sampling to solve real-world problems?

LESSON 15.1

Mean Absolute Deviation

 TEKS 8.11.B

LESSON 15.2

Generating Random Samples

TEKS 8.11.C

my.hrw.com

Real-World Video

Companies collect data to learn how many people are using their products or watching their programs. Data from a sample of consumers helps them decide which products or programs to continue.

GO DIGITAL

my.hrw.com

my.hrw.com

Go digital with your write-in student edition, accessible on any device.

Math On the Spot

Scan with your smart phone to jump directly to the online edition, video tutor, and more.

X^2

Animated Math

Interactively explore key concepts to see how math works.

Personal Math Trainer

Get immediate feedback and help as you work through practice sets.

Are YOU Ready?

Complete these exercises to review skills you will need for this module.

Find the Percent of a Number

EXAMPLE   35% of 40   Write the percent as a decimal. 35% = 0.35

$$\begin{array}{r} 40 \\ \times 0.35 \\ \hline 14 \end{array}$$ Multiply.

Find the percent.

1. 20% of 50 _____

2. 8.5% of 300 _____

3. 175% of 16.8 _____

Solve Proportions

EXAMPLE $\frac{k}{4} = \frac{28}{16}$

$\frac{k}{4} = \frac{28 \div 4}{16 \div 4}$ 16 ÷ 4 = 4, so divide the numerator and denominator by 4.

$\frac{k}{4} = \frac{7}{4}$ 28 ÷ 4 = 7

$k = 7$

Solve for x.

4. $\frac{x}{12} = \frac{24}{36}$ _____

5. $\frac{8}{x} = \frac{16}{7}$ _____

6. $\frac{5}{6} = \frac{x}{18}$ _____

7. $\frac{14}{15} = \frac{x}{75}$ _____

Find Mean

EXAMPLE   21, 17, 25, 19, 21, 23

mean $= \frac{21 + 17 + 25 + 19 + 21 + 23}{6}$ Divide the sum of the data values by the number of values.

$= \frac{126}{6}$

$= 21$

Find the mean of the data.

8. 55, 44, 53, 62, 51: _____

9. 3, 5, 3, 5, 2, 2, 5, 7: _____

Reading Start-Up

Visualize Vocabulary

Use the ✔ words to complete the right column of the chart.

Analyzing Data		
Definition	**Example**	**Review Word**
A group of facts.	The grades of all of the students in a school.	
A tool used to gather information from individuals.	A questionnaire given to all students to find the number of hours each student spends studying in 1 week.	
A value that summarizes a set of unequal values, found through addition and division.	Results of the survey show that students typically spend 5 hours a week studying.	

Understand Vocabulary

Complete the sentences using the preview words.

1. The entire group of objects, individuals, or events is

   the _____.

2. A sample in which every person, object, or event has an equal chance

   at being selected is a _____.

© Houghton Mifflin Harcourt Publishing Company

Active Reading

Layered Book Before beginning the module, create a layered book to help you learn the concepts in this module. Label each flap with lesson titles from this module. As you study each lesson, write important ideas, such as vocabulary and formulas, under the appropriate flap. Refer to your finished layered book as you work on exercises from this module.

Vocabulary

Review Words
- ✔ average *(promedio)*
- ✔ data *(datos)*
- ✔ mode *(moda)*
- range *(rango)*
- statistical question *(pregunta estadística)*

Preview Words
- mean *(media)*
- mean absolute deviation *(desviación absoluta media)*
- measure of center *(medida central)*
- measure of variability *(medida de variación)*
- population *(población)*
- random sample *(muestra aleatoria)*
- range *(rango)*
- relative frequency *(frecuencia relativa)*
- sample *(muestra)*

Unpacking the TEKS

Understanding the TEKS and the vocabulary terms in the TEKS will help you know exactly what you are expected to learn in this module.

 **TEKS 8.11.B**

Determine the mean absolute deviation and use this quantity as a measure of the average distance data are from the mean using a data set of no more than 10 data points.

Key Vocabulary

mean absolute deviation
(desviación absoluta media)
The mean distance between each data value and the mean of the data set.

What It Means to You

You will find the mean absolute deviation (MAD) of a data set and use it to describe the data.

UNPACKING EXAMPLE 8.11.B

The time it took each of ten batteries to burn out when tested in the same flashlight was recorded. Find the mean absolute deviation.

Long Life Batteries (h)									
14.4	12.5	13.9	15.1	12.7	15.7	17.0	16.6	14.3	13.8

The mean is 14.6 hours.

To find the MAD, find the absolute value of the difference between each data value and the mean. Then find the mean of those values.

The MAD is 1.2 hours.

TEKS 8.11.C

Simulate generating random samples of the same size from a population with known characteristics to develop the notion of a random sample being representative of the population from which it was selected.

Key Vocabulary

random sample *(muestra aleatoria)* A sample in which every person, object, or event has an equal chance at being selected.

Visit **my.hrw.com** to see all the **TEKS** unpacked.

ⓗ my.hrw.com

What It Means to You

You will use a random sample to make and compare predictions about a population.

UNPACKING EXAMPLE 8.11.C

The data below shows the number of pairs of shoes owned by the students in Randy's math class. Randy selected 8 values at random, shown by the shaded cells. Use the sample to predict the average number of pairs of shoes owned by someone in his class.

3	2	9	1	7	5	7	9
6	7	9	3	4	2	4	3
1	3	8	6	2	3	3	8

$$\frac{9 + 7 + 6 + 3 + 2 + 3 + 2 + 8}{8} = \frac{40}{8} = 5 \qquad \text{Find the mean.}$$

Randy can predict that the average number of pairs of shoes is 5.

Mean Absolute Deviation

TEKS
Measurement and data—8.11.B Determine the mean absolute deviation and use this quantity as a measure of the average distance data are from the mean using a data set of no more than 10 data points.

? ESSENTIAL QUESTION

How can you determine and use the mean absolute deviation of a set of data points?

EXPLORE ACTIVITY  **TEKS** 8.11.B

Understanding Mean Absolute Deviation

A **measure of center** is a single number used to describe a data set. One measure of center is the **mean**, which is the sum of the data values divided by the number of values in the data set. A **measure of variability** is a single number used to describe the spread of a data set. One measure of variability is the **mean absolute deviation (MAD)**, which is the mean distance between each data value and the mean of the data set.

The data represent the height, in feet, of various buildings. Find the mean absolute deviation for each data set.

A 60, 58, 54, 56, 63, 65, 62, 59, 56, 58

Calculate the mean. Round to the nearest whole number.

| | | |

Complete the table.

Height (ft)	60	58	54	56	63	65	62	59	56	58
Distance from mean										

Calculate the MAD by finding the mean of the values in the second row of the table. Round to the nearest whole number.

| | | |

B 46, 47, 56, 48, 46, 52, 57, 52, 45

Find the mean. Round to the nearest whole number.

| | | |

Complete the table.

Height (ft)	46	47	56	48	46	52	57	52	45
Distance from mean									

Calculate the MAD. Round to the nearest whole number.

Math Talk
Mathematical Processes

What is the difference between a measure of center and a measure of variability?

Reflect

1. **Analyze Relationships** Compare the MADs. How do the MADs describe the distribution of the heights in each group?

_____

_____

Using Mean Absolute Deviation

The mean absolute deviation can be used to answer statistical questions in the real world. Many of these questions may have implications for the operation of various businesses.

Math On the Spot
my.hrw.com

Animated Math
my.hrw.com

EXAMPLE 1   Real World

TEKS 8.11.B

A chicken farmer wants her chickens to all have about the same weight. She is trying two types of feed to see which type produces the best results. All the chickens in Pen A are fed Premium Growth feed, and all the chickens in Pen B are fed Maximum Growth feed. The farmer records the weights of the chickens in each pen in the tables below. Which chicken feed produces less variability in weight?

Pen A: Premium Growth Weights (lb)									
5.8	6.1	5.5	6.6	7.3	5.9	6.3	5.7	6.8	7.1

Pen B: Maximum Growth Weights (lb)									
7.7	7.4	5.4	7.8	6.1	5.2	7.5	7.9	6.3	5.6

STEP 1 Find the mean weight of the chickens in each pen. Round your answers to the nearest tenth.

Pen A: $\dfrac{5.8 + 6.1 + 5.5 + 6.6 + 7.3 + 5.9 + 6.3 + 5.7 + 6.8 + 7.1}{10} \approx 6.3$

Pen B: $\dfrac{7.7 + 7.4 + 5.4 + 7.8 + 6.1 + 5.2 + 7.5 + 7.9 + 6.3 + 5.6}{10} \approx 6.7$

STEP 2 Find the distance from the mean for each of the weights.

The distances from the mean for Pen A are the distance of each weight from 6.3 lb.

Pen A: Premium Growth										
Weight (lb)	5.8	6.1	5.5	6.6	7.3	5.9	6.3	5.7	6.8	7.1
Distance from mean	0.5	0.2	0.8	0.3	1.0	0.4	0	0.6	0.5	0.8

The distances from the mean for Pen B are the distance of each weight from 6.7 lb.

Pen B: Maximum Growth										
Weight (lb)	7.7	7.4	5.4	7.8	6.1	5.2	7.5	7.9	6.3	5.6
Distance from mean	1.0	0.7	1.3	1.1	0.6	1.5	0.8	1.2	0.4	1.1

STEP 3 Calculate the MAD for the chickens in each pen. Round your answers to the nearest tenth.

Pen A: $\dfrac{0.5 + 0.2 + 0.8 + 0.3 + 1.0 + 0.4 + 0 + 0.6 + 0.5 + 0.8}{10} \approx 0.5$ lb

Pen B: $\dfrac{1.0 + 0.7 + 1.3 + 1.1 + 0.6 + 1.5 + 0.8 + 1.2 + 0.4 + 1.1}{10} \approx 1.0$ lb

Since Pen A's MAD is less, Premium Growth feed produces less variability in weight.

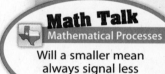

Math Talk
Mathematical Processes

Will a smaller mean always signal less variability?

YOUR TURN

2. Two baristas at a coffee shop each served 10 large coffees. The amount in each large coffee is shown below. Which barista's coffees showed less variability?

Amounts in Barista A's Large Coffees (oz)									
19.1	20.1	20.9	19.6	20.9	19.5	19.2	19.4	20.3	20.9

Amounts in Barista B's Large Coffees (oz)									
20.1	19.6	20.0	20.5	19.8	20.0	20.1	19.7	19.9	20.4

_____

_____

Personal Math Trainer

Online Assessment and Intervention

my.hrw.com

Using a Spreadsheet to Find MAD

Spreadsheets can be used to find the mean absolute deviation of a data set.

EXAMPLE 2  TEKS 8.11.B

A paper mill is testing two paper-cutting machines. Both are set to produce pieces of paper with a width of 8.5 inches. The actual widths of 8 pieces of paper cut by each machine are shown. Use a spreadsheet to determine which machine has less variability and, thus, does a better job.

Widths of Pieces of Paper Cut by Machine A (in.)							
8.502	8.508	8.499	8.501	8.492	8.511	8.505	8.491

Widths of Pieces of Paper Cut by Machine B (in.)							
8.503	8.501	8.498	8.499	8.498	8.504	8.496	8.502

STEP 1 Enter the data values for Machine A into row 1 of a spreadsheet, using cells A to H.

	A	B	C	D	E	F	G	H
1	8.502	8.508	8.499	8.501	8.492	8.511	8.505	8.491
2								
3								

STEP 2 Enter "mean =" into cell A2 and the formula =AVERAGE(A1:H1) into cell B2.

	A	B	C	D	E	F	G	H
1	8.502	8.508	8.499	8.501	8.492	8.511	8.505	8.491
2	mean =	8.501125						
3								

STEP 3 Enter "MAD =" into cell A3 and the formula =AVEDEV(A1:H1) into cell B3.

	A	B	C	D	E	F	G	H
1	8.502	8.508	8.499	8.501	8.492	8.511	8.505	8.491
2	mean =	8.501125						
3	MAD =	0.005375						

The MAD for Machine A is about 0.0054 in.

STEP 4 Repeat Steps 1–3 with the data values for Machine B.

	A	B	C	D	E	F	G	H
1	8.503	8.501	8.498	8.499	8.498	8.504	8.496	8.502
2	mean =	8.500125						
3	MAD =	0.002375						

The MAD for Machine B is about 0.0024 in.

Machine B has less variability, so it does a better job.

YOUR TURN

3. Two aspirin-making devices are set to make tablets containing 0.35 gram of aspirin. The actual amounts in 8 tablets from each device are shown. Use a spreadsheet to determine which device has less variability.

Personal Math Trainer

Online Assessment and Intervention

my.hrw.com

Amounts of Aspirin in Tablets Made by Device A (g)							
0.353	0.351	0.350	0.352	0.349	0.348	0.350	0.346

Amounts of Aspirin in Tablets Made by Device B (g)							
0.349	0.341	0.347	0.358	0.359	0.354	0.339	0.343

_____

Guided Practice

1. A bus route takes about 45 minutes. The company's goal is a MAD of less than 0.5 minute. One driver's times for 9 runs of the route are shown. Did the bus driver meet the goal? (Explore Activity and Example 1)

Times to Complete Bus Route (min)								
44.2	44.9	46.1	45.8	44.7	45.2	45.1	45.3	44.6

a. Calculate the mean of the bus times. _____

b. Calculate the MAD to the nearest tenth. _____

The bus driver **did / did not** meet the company's goal.

2. Below are a different driver's times on the same route. Find the mean and the MAD using a spreadsheet. Enter the data values into row 1 using cells A to I. Enter "mean = " into cell A2 and "MAD =" into cell A3. (Example 2)

Times to Complete Bus Route (min)								
44.4	43.8	45.6	45.9	44.1	45.6	44.0	44.9	45.8

The mean is _____ minutes, and the MAD is _____ minutes.

This time, the bus driver **did / did not** meet the company's goal.

? ESSENTIAL QUESTION CHECK-IN

3. What is the mean absolute deviation and what does it tell you about data sets?

_____

_____

© Houghton Mifflin Harcourt Publishing Company

15.1 Independent Practice

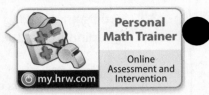

Personal
Math Trainer

Online
Assessment and
Intervention

my.hrw.com

Frank wants to know how many people live in each household in his town. He conducts a random survey of 10 people and asks how many people live in their household. His results are shown in the table.

Number of People per Household									
1	6	2	4	4	3	5	5	2	8

4. Calculate the mean number of people per household. _____

5. Calculate the MAD of the number of people per household. _____

6. What conclusions can you draw about the "typical" number of people in each household? Explain.

_____

_____

_____

_____

Teachers are being trained to standardize the scores they give to students' essays. The same essay was scored by 10 different teachers at the beginning and at the end of their training. The results are shown in the tables.

Scores for Essay at Beginning of Teachers' Training									
76	81	85	79	89	86	84	80	88	79

Scores for Essay at End of Teachers' Training									
79	82	84	81	77	85	82	80	78	83

7. Calculate the MADs for the teachers' scores. Did the teachers make progress in standardizing their scores?

_____

_____

_____

8. **What If?** What would it mean if the teachers had a MAD of 0?

_____

_____

The annual rainfall for Austin, Texas, and San Antonio, Texas, in each of the years from 2002 to 2011 are shown in the tables. Use the data for 9–11.

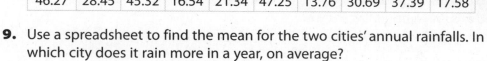

Annual Rainfall for Austin, Texas (in.)									
36.00	21.41	52.27	22.33	34.70	46.95	16.07	31.38	37.76	19.68

Annual Rainfall for San Antonio, Texas (in.)									
46.27	28.45	45.32	16.54	21.34	47.25	13.76	30.69	37.39	17.58

9. Use a spreadsheet to find the mean for the two cities' annual rainfalls. In which city does it rain more in a year, on average?

_____

_____

_____

10. Use your spreadsheet to find the MADs. Use the MADs to compare the distribution of annual rainfall for the two cities.

_____

_____

_____

_____

11. Make a Conjecture Does the information allow you to predict how the future amounts of rainfall for the two cities will compare? Explain.

_____

_____

_____

_____

12. Critical Thinking The life spans of 10 adult mayflies have a mean of 4 hours and a MAD of 2 hours. Fill in the table below with possible values for the life spans. You can use the same value more than once.

Life Spans of Ten Mayflies (h)									

Can any one of the 10 mayflies in the group live for 1 full day? Justify your answer.

_____

_____

Work Area

13. Multistep In a spreadsheet, before entering any data values, first enter "mean =" into cell A2 and the formula =AVERAGE(A1:J1) into cell B2. Next, enter "MAD =" into cell A3 and the formula =AVEDEV(A1:J1) into cell B3. You should see #DIV/0! in cell B2 and #NUM! in cell B3 as shown. Now do the following:

	A	B
1		
2	mean =	#DIV/0!
3	MAD =	#NUM!

a. Enter "1" into cell A1. What do you get for the mean and the MAD of the data set? Explain why this makes sense.

_____

_____

_____

b. Enter "2" into cell B1. What do you get for the mean and the MAD of the data set this time? Explain why this makes sense.

_____

_____

_____

c. Enter the numbers 3 through 10 into cells C1 to J1 and watch the mean and the MAD change. Do they increase, decrease, or stay the same? Explain why this makes sense.

_____

_____

_____

14. Make a Conjecture Each of the values in a data set is increased by 10. Does this affect the MAD of the data set? Why or why not?

_____

_____

_____

15. What If? Suppose a data set contains all negative numbers. Would the MAD for the data set also be negative? Explain.

_____

_____

_____

TEKS
Measurement and data—8.11.C Simulate generating random samples of the same size from a population with known characteristics to develop the notion of a random sample being representative of the population from which it was selected.

 ESSENTIAL QUESTION How can you generate and use random samples to represent a population?

EXPLORE ACTIVITY 1  TEKS 8.11.C

Generating a Random Sample

When information is being gathered about a group, the entire group of objects, individuals, or events is called the **population**. A **sample** is part of the population chosen to represent the entire group.

A sample in which every person, object, or event has an equal chance at being selected is called a **random sample**. A random sample is more likely to be representative of the entire population than other sampling methods.

A store gets a shipment of 1000 light bulbs. Due to a manufacturing problem, 200 of the bulbs are defective, but the store's manager is not aware of this. As she always does, however, the manager will check a sample of the bulbs to look for potential problems. How can she choose a sample of the bulbs to represent the shipment?

A The manager will want to use a random sample to represent the entire shipment. One way to simulate a random sample is to use a graphing calculator to generate random integers.

To simulate picking out random light bulbs between 1 and 1000:

- Press MATH, scroll right and select **PRB**, then select **5: randInt(**.

- Enter the smallest value, comma, largest possible value.

- Hit ENTER to generate random numbers.

randInt (1, 1000)
441
876
198
678

In this specific case, you will enter **randInt** (☐ , ☐)

because there are _____ light bulbs in the shipment.

The numbers that are generated will each represent a bulb in the shipment. Because we know the numbers of defective and working bulbs, we can choose numbers to model the bulbs in the population.

Let numbers 1 to 200 represent bulbs that are _____.

Numbers 201 to 1000 will represent bulbs that are _____.

The manager has a calculator randomly select 4 integers to tell her which bulbs to check. To model this, generate four numbers and record them in the table below. Then tell whether each number represents a defective or a working bulb in the model.

Bulb	Random number generated	Defective or working?
1		
2		
3		
4		

B If the manager's sample matched your results, would it represent the population well? Explain.

_____

Reflect

1. You and your classmates have generated multiple samples. Compare your results to those of your classmates. What do you notice?

_____

2. **Communicate Mathematical Ideas** Why did you and your classmates generate different answers for the number of defective light bulbs?

_____

_____

EXPLORE ACTIVITY 2  **TEKS** 8.11.C

Generating a Larger Random Sample

A The manager wants to use a larger random sample to get better results. This time, collect a sample of 20 light bulbs.

On a separate sheet of paper copy the table from Explore Activity 1 and record your results in the table. You will need rows for 20 light bulbs.

B Does your new sample better represent the shipment than your original sample? Explain.

_____

Math Talk
Mathematical Processes

Which is more likely representative of a population, a small sample or a large sample? Explain.

Reflect

3. You and your classmates have generated multiple samples. Compare your results to those of your classmates. What do you notice?

_____

Generating a Random Sample without Technology

A tree farm has a 100 acre square field arranged in a 10-by-10 array. The farmer wants to know the average number of trees on each acre. Each cell in the table below represents an acre of land. The number in each cell tells how many trees grow on that particular acre.

22	24	27	29	31	24	27	29	30	25
37	22	60	53	62	42	64	53	41	62
61	54	57	34	44	66	39	60	65	40
45	33	64	36	33	51	62	66	42	42
37	34	57	33	47	43	66	33	61	66
66	45	46	67	60	59	51	46	67	48
53	46	35	35	55	56	61	46	38	64
55	51	54	62	55	58	51	45	41	53
61	38	48	48	43	59	64	48	49	47
41	53	53	59	58	48	62	53	45	59

Because counting the trees on all of the acres is too time-consuming, the farmer decides to choose 10 acres at random and find the average number of trees.

A To simulate the random selection, place this page on the floor. Drop 10 small objects onto the chart. Use these numbers for the 10 random acres.

B What is the average number of trees on the 10 acres that were randomly selected?

_____

C Alternately, the farmer decides to choose the 10 acres in the first row. What is the average number of trees on these 10 acres?

_____

> **Math Talk**
> Mathematical Processes
>
> Why does dropping small objects on the grid produce a random sample?

Reflect

4. How do the averages you got with each sampling method compare?

_____

5. How do the averages you got with each sampling method compare to the average for the entire population, which is 48.4?

_____

6. **Communicate Mathematical Ideas** Why do you think the first method gave a closer average than the second method?

_____

_____

Guided Practice

1. A manufacturer gets a shipment of 600 batteries of which 50 are defective. The quality control manager tests a random sample of 30 batteries in each shipment. Simulate the test by generating random numbers between 1 and 600. How well does your sample represent the shipment? Explain. (Explore Activities 1 and 2)

_____

2. The farmer from Explore Activity 3 would like to have a better estimate of the number of trees per acre. This time, the farmer decides to choose 20 acres at random. Use the table to simulate the farmer's random selection and find a new estimated average for the number of trees per acre. (Explore Activity 3)

_____

? ESSENTIAL QUESTION CHECK-IN

3. Why can data from a random sample be used to represent a population? What can happen if a sample is too small or not random?

_____

_____

_____

_____

15.2 Independent Practice

 TEKS 8.11.C

Personal Math Trainer

Online Assessment and Intervention

my.hrw.com

Maurie owns three bagel shops. Each shop sells 500 bagels per day. Maurie asks her store managers to use a random sample to see how many whole-wheat bagels are sold at each store each day. The results are shown in the table. Use the table for 4–6.

	Total bagels in sample	Whole-wheat bagels
Shop A	50	10
Shop B	100	23
Shop C	25	7

4. If you assume the samples are representative, how many whole-wheat bagels are sold at each store?

_____

5. Rank the samples for the shops in terms of how representative they are likely to be. Explain your rankings.

_____

_____

_____

6. Which sample or samples should Maurie use to tell her managers how many whole-wheat bagels to make each day? Explain.

_____

_____

_____

7. In a shipment of 1000 T-shirts, 75 do not meet quality standards. The store manager does not know this but always tests a random sample of each shipment. The table below simulates the manager's random sample of 20 T-shirts to inspect. For the simulation, the integers 1 to 75 represent the below-standard shirts.

124	876	76	79	12	878	86	912	435	91
340	213	45	678	544	271	714	777	812	80

In the sample, how many of the shirts are below quality standards? _____

If the manager assumes his sample is representative and uses it to predict how many of the 1000 shirts are below standard, what will he conclude?

_____

8. Multistep A 64 acre coconut farm is arranged in an 8-by-8 array. Mika wants to know the average number of coconut palms on each acre. Each cell in the table represents an acre of land. The number in each cell tells how many coconut palms grow on that particular acre.

56	54	40	34	44	66	43	65
66	33	42	36	33	51	62	63
33	34	66	33	47	43	66	61
46	35	48	67	60	59	52	67
46	32	64	35	55	47	61	38
45	51	53	62	55	58	51	41
48	38	47	48	43	59	64	54
53	67	59	59	58	48	62	45

a. The numbers in green represent Mika's random sample of 10 acres. What is the average number of coconut palms on the randomly selected acres?

_____

b. Project the number of palms in the entire farm.

_____

FOCUS ON HIGHER ORDER THINKING

Work Area

9. A random sample of 15 of the 78 competitors at a middle school gymnastics competition are asked their height. The data set lists the heights in inches: 55, 57, 57, 58, 59, 59, 59, 59, 59, 61, 62, 62, 63, 64, 66. What is the mean height of the sample? Could you say this is a good estimate of the mean height of all competitors? Why or why not?

_____

_____

_____

10. Critical Thinking The six-by-six grid contains the ages of actors in a youth Shakespeare festival. Describe a method for randomly selecting 8 cells by using number cubes. Then calculate the average of the 8 values you found.

12	15	16	9	21	11
9	10	14	10	13	12
16	21	14	12	8	14
16	20	9	16	19	18
17	14	12	15	10	15
12	20	14	10	12	9

_____

_____

_____

_____

_____

_____

11. Communicating Mathematical Ideas Describe how the size of a random sample affects how well it represents a population as a whole.

_____

_____

Ready to Go On?

15.1 Mean Absolute Deviation

The table shows scores for a gymnastics team. Use the table for 1–3.

Floor Exercise Scores						
Score	8.0	9.0	8.3	8.9	9.1	8.3
Distance from mean						

1. Find the mean of the scores. _____

2. Complete the table to find the distance of each score from the mean.

3. Find the mean absolute deviation. _____

15.2 Generating Random Samples

A manufacturer ships a store 5000 MP3 players, of which 300 are defective. The store manager does not know this but tests a random sample of 10 players to look for problems. A graphing calculator is used to simulate the sample, with 1–300 representing the defective players. The results are shown in the table.

4. Complete the table to tell whether each number generated represents a good or defective player.

5. From this sample, how many defective players

might the manager expect? _____

6. Is the manager's expectation accurate? Explain.

_____

_____

Random number	Good or defective?
13	
2195	
3873	
525	
900	
167	
1094	
1472	
709	
5000	

? ESSENTIAL QUESTION

7. How can you use random samples to solve real-world problems?

_____

_____

Selected Response

1. The radius of a ball is 4 inches. What is the volume of the ball in cubic inches?

Ⓐ 16π in³

Ⓒ $\frac{256\pi}{3}$ in³

Ⓑ $\frac{64\pi}{3}$ in³

Ⓓ $\frac{4096\pi}{3}$ in³

2. A random sample of 30 students were asked to pick their favorite school subject, and 12 of them answered math. There are 480 students in the school. How many students in the school are likely to pick math as their favorite subject?

Ⓐ 120 students

Ⓑ 192 students

Ⓒ 288 students

Ⓓ 360 students

3. For which situation could flipping a coin be used to simulate a random sample?

Ⓐ to predict the number of defective cell phones in a shipment of 2000 phones

Ⓑ to predict the number of days in a month it will rain

Ⓒ to predict the number of blue marbles in a box of 200 marbles

Ⓓ to predict the number of boys or girls born at a hospital in a year

4. Vertex A of triangle ABC is located at the point (2, 5). Which transformation moves vertex A to the point (−2, 5)?

Ⓐ reflection across the x-axis

Ⓑ reflection across the y-axis

Ⓒ $(x, y) \rightarrow (x + 4, y)$

Ⓓ $(x, y) \rightarrow (x - 4, -y)$

5. Which number is closest to $\sqrt{111}$?

Ⓐ −50

Ⓒ 10

Ⓑ −10

Ⓓ 50

6. There are 24 red jellybeans in a bag of 140 jellybeans. Let the integers 1–24 represent the red jellybeans in a calculator simulation of the situation that generates random integers from 1 to 140. A sample of 15 "jellybeans" gives the following:

38	6	69	115	17	53	96	104
21	77	43	29	39	55	71	

Using the sample, which is the best prediction of the number of jellybeans in the bag?

Ⓐ 5

Ⓒ 28

Ⓑ 24

Ⓓ 55

Gridded Response

7. The table below shows the height in meters of several buildings. What is the mean absolute deviation of the data set?

28	32	47	39	38
16	40	35	54	31

⊘	⊘	⊘	⊘	•	⊘	⊘
⓪	⓪	⓪	⓪		⓪	⓪
①	①	①	①		①	①
②	②	②	②		②	②
③	③	③	③		③	③
④	④	④	④		④	④
⑤	⑤	⑤	⑤		⑤	⑤
⑥	⑥	⑥	⑥		⑥	⑥
⑦	⑦	⑦	⑦		⑦	⑦
⑧	⑧	⑧	⑧		⑧	⑧
⑨	⑨	⑨	⑨		⑨	⑨

Study Guide Review

MODULE 14 Scatter Plots

Key Vocabulary
cluster *(agrupación)*
outlier *(valor extremo)*
scatter plot *(diagrama de dispersión)*
trend line *(línea de tendencia)*

? **ESSENTIAL QUESTION**

How can you use scatterplots to solve real-world problems?

EXAMPLE 1

As part of a research project, a researcher made a table of test scores and the number of hours of sleep a person got the night before the test. Make a scatter plot of the data. Does the data show a positive association, negative association, or no association?

Sleep (hours)	Test score
4	30
5	40
6	50
6	70
8	100
9	90
10	100

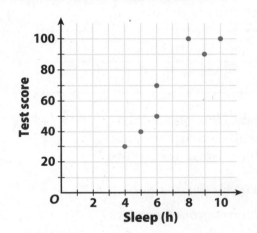

The data show a positive association. Generally, as the number of hours of sleep increases, so do the test scores.

EXAMPLE 2

Write an equation for a trend line of the data shown on the graph.

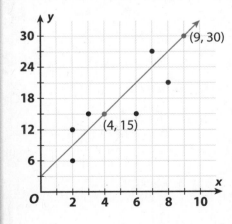

$m = \dfrac{30 - 15}{9 - 4} = 3$ Find the slope.

$15 = 3(4) + b$ Find the y-intercept.

$b = 3$

$y = 3x + 3$ Use the slope and y-intercept to write the equation.

EXERCISES

1. The table shows the income of 8 households, in thousands of dollars, and the number of televisions in each household. (Lesson 14.1)

Income ($1000)	20	20	30	30	40	60	70	90
Number of televisions	4	0	1	2	2	3	3	4

a. Make a scatter plot of the data.

b. Describe the association between income and number of televisions. Are any of the values outliers?

_____

_____

_____

_____

_____

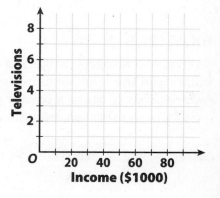

2. The scatter plot shows the relationship between the price of a product and the number of potential buyers. (Lesson 14.2)

a. Draw a trend line for the scatter plot.

b. Write an equation for your trend line.

_____

c. When the price of the product is $3.50, the number of potential buyers will be

about _____.

d. When the price of the product is $5.50, the number of potential buyers will be

about _____.

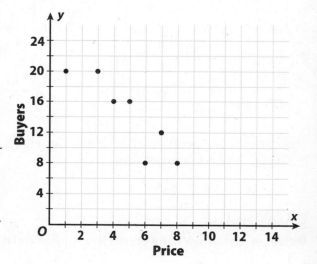

Key Vocabulary
mean absolute deviation
   *(desviación absoluta
   media)*
population *(población)*
random sample *(muestra
   aleatoria)*
sample *(muestra)*

? **ESSENTIAL QUESTION**

How can you use sampling to solve real-world problems?

EXAMPLE

Robert is a waiter. He wants to earn an average of $85 or more in tips each night with no more than $10 variability. His earnings in tips per night for 10 nights are shown in the table. Is Robert meeting his goals?

Robert's Tips per Night									
$92	$70	$105	$89	$90	$90	$110	$72	$71	$98

Mean: $\dfrac{92 + 70 + 105 + 89 + 90 + 90 + 110 + 72 + 71 + 98}{10} = 88.7$

Mean absolute deviation:

$\dfrac{3.3 + 18.7 + 16.3 + 0.3 + 1.3 + 1.3 + 21.3 + 16.7 + 17.7 + 9.3}{10} = 10.62$

On average, Robert is making $88.70 in tips per night, which is more than $85. His earnings have a mean absolute deviation of $10.62, which is higher than $10. He is not meeting his goals.

EXERCISES

1. Find the mean and mean absolute deviation of the set of data. Round to the nearest hundredth. (Lesson 15.1)

Distance per day (mi) driven by Juan						
12	9	7	7	11	10	7

Mean: _____   Mean absolute deviation: _____

2. A pottery store gets a shipment of 1500 dishes and wants to estimate how many dishes are broken. The manager will use a random sample to represent the entire shipment. In actuality, 18% of the dishes are broken. (Lesson 15.2)

You will simulate the manager's test by generating random numbers between 1 and 1500. Explain what the generated numbers will mean.

_____

_____

Use the graphing calculator function randInt(1,1500) to generate 30 numbers.

According to the sample, how many broken dishes should the manager expect to find in the shipment? _____

1. 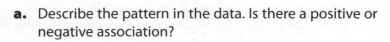 **CAREERS IN MATH** **Psychologist** A psychologist gave a test to 15 women of different ages to measure their short-term memory. The test score scale goes from 0 to 24, and a higher score means that the participant has a better short-term memory. The scatter plot shows the results of this study.

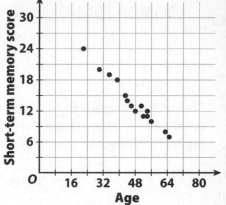

a. Describe the pattern in the data. Is there a positive or negative association?

_____

_____

b. Draw a line of best fit on the scatter plot and estimate its slope. Interpret the slope in the context of the problem.

_____

_____

c. In another test, a 70 year-old woman scored 8. Does your line of best fit predict a higher or lower score? What may have happened?

_____

_____

2. Tara and Makina are friends and study partners who decide to compare their math test scores for the semester.

Tara's grades: 80, 95, 85, 70, 90   Makina's grades: 75, 90, 95, 75, 100

a. Find the mean of each girl's test scores. Show your work.

_____

_____

b. Find the mean absolute deviation (MAD) for each girl. Show your work.

c. Who the better test scores? Who is more consistent? Explain.

_____

_____

UNIT 6 MIXED REVIEW

Texas Test Prep

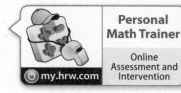

Personal
Math Trainer

Online
Assessment and
Intervention

my.hrw.com

Selected Response

Use the data set below for 1–2.

26	30	45	43	26
14	28	33	56	29

1. What is the mean of the data set?

Ⓐ 14 Ⓒ 33

Ⓑ 26 Ⓓ 42

2. What is the mean absolute deviation?

Ⓐ 2

Ⓑ 4

Ⓒ 6

Ⓓ 9

3. What type of association is there between the speed of a car and the distance the car travels in a given time at that speed?

Ⓐ cluster

Ⓑ negative association

Ⓒ no association

Ⓓ positive association

4. Using 3.14 for π, what is the volume of the sphere to the nearest tenth?

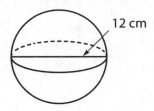

12 cm

Ⓐ 508.7 cubic centimeters

Ⓑ 678.2 cubic centimeters

Ⓒ 904.3 cubic centimeters

Ⓓ 2713 cubic centimeters

Read graphs and diagrams carefully. Look at the labels for important information.

5. Which scatter plot could have a trend line given by the equation $y = -7x + 90$?

Ⓐ
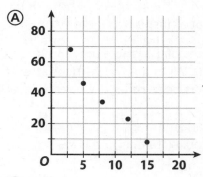

Ⓑ
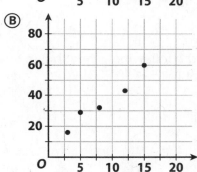

Ⓒ
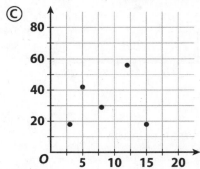

Ⓓ
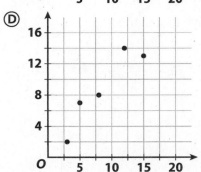

6. For which situation could flipping a coin **not** be used as a simulation to generate a random sample?

(A) to predict the number of wins a team will have in a season

(B) to predict whether the number of times the number rolled on a standard number cube will be even or odd

(C) to predict the number of people who will attend an event

(D) to predict the number of boys or girls born at a hospital in a month

7. The vertices of a triangle are (11, 9), (7, 4), and (1, 11). What are the vertices after the triangle has been reflected over the *y*-axis?

(A) (9, 11), (4, 7), (11, 1)

(B) (11, −9), (7, −4), (1, −11)

(C) (9, 11), (4, 7), (11, 1)

(D) (−11, 9), (−7, 4), (−1, 11)

8. Which of the following is **not** shown on the scatter plot below?

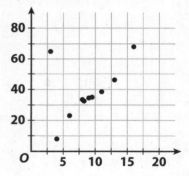

(A) cluster

(B) negative association

(C) outlier

(D) positive association

Gridded Response

9. A random sample of 45 students was asked to pick their favorite type of shoe, and 18 of them answered sandals. There are 390 students in the school. How many are likely to pick sandals as their favorite type of shoe?

Estimate your answer before solving the question. Use your estimate to check the reasonableness of your answer.

10. Bert took a handful of buttons from a bag. Out of the 27 buttons in his hand, 12 were brown. How many brown buttons should Bert expect to find in the bag if there are a total of 180 buttons?

Personal Financial Literacy

 MODULE 16

Managing Your Money and Planning for Your Future

TEKS 8.12.A, 8.12.B, 8.12.C, 8.12.D, 8.12.E, 8.12.F, 8.12.G

CAREERS IN MATH

Organic Farmer An organic farmer uses ecological principles to grow and maintain crops and never uses synthetic pesticides or fertilizers. Organic farmers use math to calculate crop yields, business costs, and profits, and to compute how much of a crop to grow on a given piece of land. They also use math to estimate water needs, labor, time to harvest, and amount to plant.

If you are interested in a career as an organic farmer, you should study the following mathematical subjects:
- Basic Math
- Geometry
- Business Math

Research other careers that require calculating business costs and profits.

Unit 7 Performance Task

At the end of the unit, check out how **organic farmers** use math.

Vocabulary Preview

Use the puzzle to preview key vocabulary from this unit. Unscramble the circled letters within found words to answer the riddle at the bottom of the page.

Across

2. College funding awards for students based on achievement. (Lesson 16.4)

4. Payment card you can use to make purchases, and the money is deducted immediately from a bank account. (Lesson 16.4)

5. College funding awards from the government or other organizations, usually for students who need money the most. (Lesson 16.4)

Down

1. The original amount of money deposited or saved. (Lesson 16.2)

3. Payment card you can use to make purchases, then pay a bill at the end of a billing cycle. (Lesson 16.4)

Q: Why did the man put his money in the freezer?

A: Because he wanted ___ ___ ___ ___,

___ ___ ___ ___ ___ ___ ___ ___!

Managing Your Money and Planning for Your Future

MODULE 16

ESSENTIAL QUESTION

How can you manage your money and plan for a successful financial future?

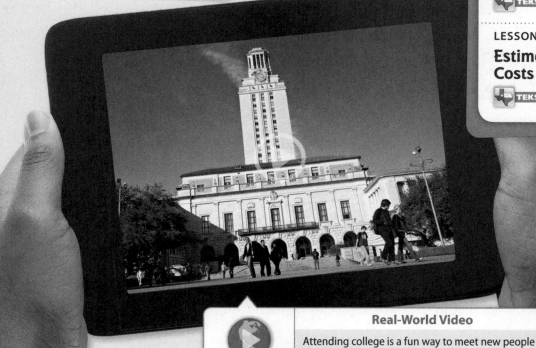

LESSON 16.1
Repaying Loans
TEKS 8.12.A, 8.12.B, 8.12.E

LESSON 16.2
Saving and Investing
TEKS 8.12.C, 8.12.D

LESSON 16.3
Analyzing Financial Situations
TEKS 8.12.E, 8.12.F

LESSON 16.4
Estimating College Costs and Payments
TEKS 8.12.G

Real-World Video

Attending college is a fun way to meet new people and learn new ideas. To pay your tuition, you might use grants, scholarships, savings, loans, or participate in a work-study program

my.hrw.com

GO DIGITAL
my.hrw.com

my.hrw.com

Go digital with your write-in student edition, accessible on any device.

Math On the Spot

Scan with your smart phone to jump directly to the online edition, video tutor, and more.

Animated Math

Interactively explore key concepts to see how math works.

Personal Math Trainer

Get immediate feedback and help as you work through practice sets.

Are YOU Ready?

Complete these exercises to review skills you will need for this module.

Multiply with Fractions and Decimals

EXAMPLE

$$\begin{array}{r} 2.53 \\ \times\ 1.6 \\ \hline 1518 \\ +\ 253 \\ \hline 4.048 \end{array}$$

Multiply as you would with whole numbers.

Count the total number of decimal places in the two factors.

Write the same total number of decimal places in the product.

Multiply.

1. $\begin{array}{r} 4.04 \\ \times\ 23 \\ \hline \end{array}$

2. $\begin{array}{r} 6.3 \\ \times\ 4.3 \\ \hline \end{array}$

3. $\begin{array}{r} 29.4 \\ \times\ 5.4 \\ \hline \end{array}$

4. $\begin{array}{r} 0.45 \\ \times\ 0.86 \\ \hline \end{array}$

Find the Percent of a Number

EXAMPLE 6.5% of 24

Write the percent as a decimal. 6.5% = 0.065

$$\begin{array}{r} 24 \\ \times\ 0.065 \\ \hline 1.56 \end{array}$$

Multiply.

Find the percent.

5. 4% of 40 _____

6. 7% of 300 _____

7. 4.3% of 1,200 _____

Use of Parentheses

EXAMPLE $40(1 + 0.08)^2 = 40(1.08)^2$

Perform operations inside parentheses first.

$= 40(1.1664)$ Simplify exponents.

$= 46.656$ Multiply.

Evaluate. Round to the nearest hundredth.

8. $120(1 + 0.02)^2$ _____

9. $450(1 + 0.05)^2$ _____

10. $900(1 + 0.03)^2$ _____

11. $75(1 + 0.01)^2$ _____

Reading Start-Up

Visualize Vocabulary

Use the ✔ words to complete the graphic organizer. You will put one word in each box.

Ways to Pay for College

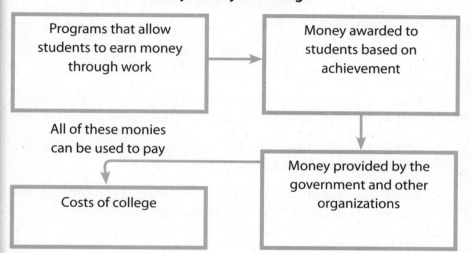

| Programs that allow students to earn money through work | → | Money awarded to students based on achievement |

All of these monies can be used to pay

| Costs of college | | Money provided by the government and other organizations |

Understand Vocabulary

Complete the sentences using the preview words.

1. The amount of money paid by banks and others to use money in an account is _____.

2. _____ is earned on an annual basis using the formula $I = Prt$.

© Houghton Mifflin Harcourt Publishing Company

Vocabulary

Review Words

checking account *(cuenta corriente)*

credit card *(tarjeta de crédito)*

debit card *(tarjeta de débito)*

deposit *(depósito)*

✔ grants *(beca)*

principal *(capital)*

✔ scholarships *(becas)*

✔ tuition *(matrícula)*

✔ work-study programs *(programas de trabajo y estudio)*

Preview Words

compound interest *(interés compuesto)*

interest *(interés)*

simple interest *(interés simple)*

Active Reading

Tri-Fold Before beginning the module, create a tri-fold to help you learn the concepts and vocabulary in this module. Fold the paper into three sections. Label the columns "What I Know," "What I Need to Know," and "What I Learned." Complete the first two columns before you read. After studying the module, complete the third column.

Unpacking the TEKS

Understanding the TEKS and the vocabulary terms in the TEKS will help you know exactly what you are expected to learn in this module.

 TEKS 8.12

Develop an economic way of thinking and problem solving useful in one's life as a knowledgeable consumer and investor.

Key Vocabulary

debit card *(tarjeta de débito)*
A plastic card used to purchase goods or services. The money is deducted immediately from your bank account.

credit card *(tarjeta de crédito)*
A plastic card used to purchase goods or services. You receive a monthly bill, and you will pay interest on the balance.

simple interest *(interés simple)*
Interest paid only on the principal.

compound interest *(interés compuesto)* Interest on the principal and interest an account has earned.

What It Means to You

You will learn how each of the following standards related to 8.12 are designed to help you to understand how to manage your money and plan for your future.

8.12.A Solve real-world problems comparing how interest rate and loan length affect the cost of credit.

8.12.C Explain how small amounts of money invested regularly, including money saved for college and retirement, grow over time.

8.12.E Identify and explain the advantages and disadvantages of different payment methods.

8.12.F Analyze situations to determine if they represent financially responsible decisions and identify the benefits of financial responsibility and the costs of financial irresponsibility.

Visit **my.hrw.com** to see all the **TEKS** unpacked.

my.hrw.com

16.1 Repaying Loans

TEKS
Personal financial literacy—8.12.A Solve real-world problems comparing how interest rate and loan length affect the cost of credit. *Also 8.12.B, 8.12.E*

Math On the Spot
my.hrw.com

? **ESSENTIAL QUESTION**

How do you calculate the cost of repaying a loan?

Comparing Interest Rates

How much does it cost to borrow money? When you use a credit card or get a loan from a bank, the cost of borrowing the money depends on two factors. The first is the interest rate that you pay. The second is the time that you take to pay off the total amount.

Interest is the money that you pay to borrow money or use credit. The interest rate determines in part the cost of a loan or of purchases on a credit card.

EXAMPLE 1   TEKS 8.12.A, 8.12.B

Credit Card

A In September, Alex charged his textbooks, clothes, and some downloads on his credit card. He received a bill from his credit card company for $1000. The interest rate on his card is 21%. He is going to pay in 3 monthly payments. He wants to know how much this loan will cost him in interest.

Use an online calculator. Enter these numbers:

> Loan amount: $1000
> Loan term: 3 months   *The calculator converts to 0.25 year.*
> Interest rate: 21% per year

Click CALCULATE.

> Monthly payment: $345.07

What is Alex's total repayment?

> $345.07 monthly payment × 3 months = $1035.21

The credit card company loaned Alex $1000, and he paid $1035.21 back to the credit card company. What was the cost of this loan?

> Interest paid = $1035.21 − $1000 = $35.21   *The cost of the loan*

Math Talk
Mathematical Processes

In addition to the interest you pay to borrow money, what other costs may there be when you take out a loan?

B Barry takes out a loan from his bank for $1000 to buy a bicycle. The interest rate on his loan is 9%. He is going to pay the total amount in 3 monthly payments. Use an online calculator to find the cost of his loan.

What is Barry's total repayment and the cost of his loan?

> $338.35 monthly payment × 3 months = $1015.05

> Interest paid = $1015.05 − $1000 = $15.05   *The cost of the loan*

Reflect

1. **What If?** If Alex had saved $333.34 a month for 3 months, how much money would he have? If he had used his savings instead of his credit card, how much less would his purchases have cost him?

   _____

2. How much less did Barry's loan, at an interest rate of 9%, cost than Alex's loan at 21%?

   _____

3. Barry looks into the cost of repaying an easy access loan for $1000. The up-front cost of the loan is $3 for every $20, plus Barry will owe $1000 at the end of the loan. How much will this loan cost Barry?

   _____

YOUR TURN

Use an online calculator to fill in the blanks for the easy access loans.

4. Loan amount: $5000   Monthly payment: _____

   Loan term: 2 years   Total repayment: _____

   Interest rate: 7%   Interest paid: _____

5. Loan amount: $5000   Monthly payment: _____

   Loan term: 2 years   Total repayment: _____

   Interest rate: 21%   Interest paid: _____

Comparing Loan Lengths

You saw in Example 1 how the interest rate affects the cost of borrowing money. The time taken to repay the loan also affects the cost.

EXAMPLE 2   ⭐ TEKS 8.12.A, 8.12.B

A Susan has a balance of $1000 on her credit card. She stops using her card and pays the minimum monthly amount until the loan is paid off.

Use an online calculator. Enter these numbers:

   Loan amount: $1000
   Loan term: 93 months
   Interest rate: 18% per year

Click CALCULATE.   Monthly payment: $20.01

What is Susan's total repayment?

$20.01 monthly payment × 93 months = $1860.93

What was the cost of this loan?

Interest paid = $1860.93 − $1000 = $860.93   *The cost of the loan*

B Laura also has a balance of $1000 at 18% interest on her credit card. She stops using her card to pay off the balance. She wants to pay as much as she can each month to pay off the loan as quickly as she can.

Use an online calculator. Enter these numbers:

Loan amount: $1000
Loan term: 3 years
Interest rate: 18% per year

Click CALCULATE.   Monthly payment: $36.15

What is Laura's total repayment?

$36.15 monthly payment × 36 months = $1301.40

What was the cost of this loan?

Interest paid = $1301.40 − $1000 = $301.40   *The cost of the loan*

Reflect

6. **What If?** If Susan had put $20 in her savings account each month, how long would it take her to save a total of $1000? Compare this to the time she took to pay off her credit card loan of $1000.

_____

_____

7. Laura paid off her debt in 36 months while Susan took 93 months to pay off her debt of the same amount. How much less did Laura pay in interest than Susan did?

_____

YOUR TURN

Use an online calculator to fill in the blanks.

8. Loan amount: $5000   Monthly payment: _____

Loan term: 2 years   Total repayment: _____

Interest rate: 15%   Interest paid: _____

9. Loan amount: $5000   Monthly payment: _____

Loan term: 4 years   Total repayment: _____

Interest rate: 15%   Interest paid: _____

Personal Math Trainer

Online Assessment and Intervention

my.hrw.com

1. Kyle is going to take out a loan for $1500 for 2 years. He wants to know how much more it will cost him in interest if he uses his credit card, at 20% interest, instead of borrowing from the bank at 11% interest. Find the difference in the cost of these two choices. (Example 1)

Enter the numbers in an online calculator and fill in the blanks.

Credit Card

Loan amount: $_____

Loan term: _____ months

Interest rate: _____% per year

Monthly payment: $_____

$_____ × 24 months =

Total repayment: $_____

Interest paid: $_____

Bank Loan

Loan amount: $_____

Loan term: _____ months

Interest rate: _____% per year

Monthly payment: $_____

$_____ × 24 months =

Total repayment: $_____

Interest paid: $_____

Kyle would pay $_____ less in interest if he borrows from the bank than if he borrows using his credit card.

2. How much less will Kyle pay in interest if he borrows $1500 at 11% for 1 year instead of for 2 years? (Example 2)

Monthly payment: $_____

$_____ × _____ months = Total repayment: $_____

Interest paid: $_____

Kyle will pay $_____ less for a loan that lasts 1 year instead of 2.

? ESSENTIAL QUESTION CHECK-IN

3. How do you calculate the cost of repaying a loan using an online calculator?

_____

_____

_____

_____

_____

16.1 Independent Practice

 TEKS 8.12.A, 8.12.B, 8.12.E

Personal
Math Trainer

Online
Assessment and
Intervention

my.hrw.com

Claudia is going to buy a used car for $10,000. She can finance it at the car dealer for 14% interest, or she can get a loan from the bank at 8% interest for 3 years. If she chooses to finance with the car dealer, she can choose either a 3-year loan or a 5-year loan. Use an online calculator.

4. Find the amount of Claudia's monthly payment for these choices.

   a. 14% for 3 years: _____   **c.** 8% for 3 years: _____

   b. 14% for 5 years: _____

5. Find the amount of Claudia's total repayment for these choices.

   a. 14% for 3 years: _____   **c.** 8% for 3 years: _____

   b. 14% for 5 years: _____

6. Find the amount that Claudia would pay in interest for these choices.

   a. 14% for 3 years: _____   **c.** 8% for 3 years: _____

   b. 14% for 5 years: _____

7. What is the difference in interest cost between the car dealer loan at 14% for 3 years and the bank loan at 8% for 3 years?   _____

8. What is the difference in interest cost between the car dealer loan for 3 years and the car dealer loan for 5 years?   _____

9. If Claudia wants the lowest possible monthly payment, which option should she choose?   _____

10. If Claudia wants the lowest possible cost for the loan, which option should she choose?   _____

11. Communicate Mathematical Ideas With Claudia's loan, does loan length or interest rate have the greater effect on the cost of the interest for the loan? Explain.

_____

_____

_____

12. Jess takes out an easy access loan for $200. The up-front cost of the loan is $4 for every $20, plus Jess will owe $200 at the end of the loan. How much will this loan cost Jess?   _____

Use an online calculator for 13–16.

13. **Persevere in Problem Solving** Christopher is thinking about charging a $2000 computer on his credit card at an interest rate of 21%. He realizes that if he takes *m* months to pay off this debt, he will have paid just over twice the original price. What is the value of *m*?

_____

14. **Make a Conjecture** Lara wants to buy a sewing machine so she can sell quilts that she makes. The machine costs $1500. She has $200 each month that she can use for the sewing machine. What choice would you advise Lara to make about how to pay for the machine? Explain.

_____

_____

_____

_____

_____

15. **Multistep** Pat can get a student loan of $10,000 for 10 years at an interest rate of 7% or borrow the same amount for 5 years at an interest rate of 4%. Which do you think Pat should do and why?

_____

_____

_____

_____

16. **Analyze Relationships** What do you need to know in order to decide which choice is better when you are borrowing money? What do you need to consider when you make your choice?

_____

_____

_____

_____

16.2 Saving and Investing

TEKS
Personal financial literacy— 8.12.D Calculate and compare simple interest and compound earnings. *Also* 8.12.C.

ESSENTIAL QUESTION

How can you save money by investing small amounts of money regularly?

EXPLORE ACTIVITY 1 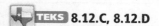 TEKS 8.12.C, 8.12.D

Calculating Simple Interest

Interest is money paid by banks and others for the use of depositors' money. **Simple interest** is earned using the formula $I = Prt$, where I is the amount of interest, P is the principal, or the original amount deposited, r is the interest rate expressed as a decimal, and t is the time in years. Simple interest is paid at the end of the term based only on the principal at the beginning.

Adan makes regular deposits to a savings account to save money for college. He deposits $1000 at the start of each year into an account that pays 4% simple interest at the end of each year. He does not deposit the interest.

A How much interest does Adan's account earn the first year?

$I = Prt$ Use the formula for simple interest.

$I = 1000 \times \boxed{} \times 1 = \boxed{}$ Substitute and simplify.

Adan's account earns _____ the first year.

B Complete the table to show how the interest earned grows over time.

Deposit phase	Beginning balance for new phase	Amount deposited	New balance	Amount of interest earned (at 4%)
1	$0	$1000	$1000	$40
2	$1000	$1000	$2000	$80
3	$2000	$1000	$3000	$120
4	$3000	$1000		
5		$1000		
6		$1000		
7		$1000		
8		$1000		
9		$1000		
10		$1000		

Reflect

1. How much interest did Adan's account earn from the initial deposit to the end of year 5? from the start of year 6 to the end of year 10? How do these values compare? Explain.

_____

_____

_____

2. What was the total amount saved from the initial deposit to the end of year 5? from the start of year 6 to the end of year 10? Include the amount contributed and the interest.

_____

_____

EXPLORE ACTIVITY 2 Real World | TEKS 8.12.C, 8.12.D

Calculating Compound Interest

Compound interest is interest paid not only on the principal but also on any interest that has already been earned. Every time interest is calculated, the interest is added to the principal for future interest calculations. The calculation can be made more than once a year, but in this lesson only interest compounded annually will be found.

The formula for compound interest is $A = P(1 + r)^t$, where P is the principal, r is the interest rate expressed as a decimal, t is the time in years, and A is the amount in the account after t years if no withdrawals were made.

Lilly makes regular deposits to a savings account to save money for retirement. She deposits $1000 each year, and her account earns interest compounded annually at a rate of 4%.

A How much interest does Lilly earn the first year?

$A = P(1 + r)^t$ Use the formula for compound interest.

 $A = 1000 \times \left(1 + \boxed{}\right)^1$ Substitute.

$A = \boxed{}$ Simplify.

So, Lilly's account earns _____ − $1000 = _____ the first year.

B Complete the table to show how the amount in the account accumulates over time. Round all values to the nearest cent.

Deposit phase	Beginning balance for new phase	Amount deposited	New balance	Amount of interest earned (at 4%)	Ending balance
1	$0	$1,000	$1,000	$40	$1,040
2	$1,040	$1,000	$2,040	$81.60	$2,121.60
3	$2,121.60	$1,000	$3,121.60		
4		$1,000			
5		$1,000			
6		$1,000			
7		$1,000			
8		$1,000			
9		$1,000			
10		$1,000			

Reflect

3. How much interest did Lilly's account earn from the initial deposit to the end of year 5? from the start of year 6 to the end of year 10?

_____

4. Compare the interest earned during the two five-year periods. Explain the difference.

_____

_____

_____

_____

5. Compare the final balance in this Explore Activity to the total amount deposited and earned in interest in Explore Activity 1 (see Reflect question 2). What can you conclude?

_____

_____

_____

Comparing Simple and Compound Interest

In this example, you will compare simple and compound interest in a situation where no additional deposits are made.

EXAMPLE 1 **TEKS** 8.12.D

Suppose you have two savings accounts, both with a principal of $100 and an interest rate of 5%, but one earns simple interest and one earns interest compounded annually. Which account will earn more interest after 10 years?

STEP 1 Find the amount of simple interest earned in 10 years.

$I = Prt$	Use the formula for simple interest.
$I = 100 \times 0.05 \times 10$	Substitute 100 for P, 0.05 for r, and 10 for t.
$I = 50$	Simplify.

The account earning simple interest will earn $50.

STEP 2 Find the amount of interest compounded annually earned in 10 years.

$A = P(1 + r)^t$	Use the formula for compound interest.
$A = 100(1 + 0.05)^{10}$	Substitute 100 for P, 0.05 for r, and 10 for t.
$A = 162.89$	Simplify. Round to the nearest cent.

Subtract the principal of $100 to find the interest earned, $62.89.

The account earning interest compounded annually will earn $62.89.

STEP 3 Compare the interest earned in each account.

The account that earns interest compounded annually earns $62.89, which is $12.89 more than the $50 of simple interest earned.

Personal Math Trainer

Online Assessment and Intervention

⊙ my.hrw.com

YOUR TURN

6. Marlena saved $50 in an account earning 3.5% simple interest. How much more interest would her account earn in 10 years if her account earned interest compounded annually instead of simple interest?

_____

16.2 Independent Practice

TEKS 8.12.C, 8.12.D

Personal Math Trainer

Online Assessment and Intervention

my.hrw.com

1. Gina deposits $150 at the start of each year into a college savings account that pays 4% simple interest at the end of each year. She does not deposit the interest she earns each year. How much total interest will Gina earn on her deposits through the end of the fifth year? (Explore Activity 1)

_____

2. Fredo deposits $75 each year in an account earning 3% interest compounded annually. If he deposits an additional $75 per year and does not make any withdrawals, how much interest will the account earn in the fourth year? (Explore Activity 2)

_____

3. Huan deposited $850 into a college savings account earning 4.8% interest compounded annually. He also deposited $850 into a second account earning 4.8% simple interest. He made no additional deposits. (Example 1)

   a. How much interest does the first account earn in 10 years?

   _____

   b. How much interest does the second account earn in 10 years?

   _____

   c. After 10 years, which account earned more interest? How much more?

   _____

   _____

   _____

4. Andreas invested $1000 in a savings account. After 4 years, the account had earned a total of $112 simple interest without any additional deposits. What was his interest rate?

_____

5. Hei has $1500 in a retirement account earning 5% interest compounded annually. Each year after the first, she makes additional deposits of $1500. After 5 years, what was her account balance if she did not make any withdrawals?

_____

6. Lester deposited $400 into a savings account earning 4.5% simple interest, and $450 into an investment account earning 3.2% interest compounded annually. What was the total interest he earned in 3 years? Justify your reasoning.

_____

_____

7. Randee invested $1000 for college in an account earning 5% simple interest. When she withdrew the investment, she had earned a total of $550 in interest. How long was the money invested? Justify your reasoning.

_____

_____

_____

_____

8. Critical Thinking Is it possible for an amount of money invested in an account earning simple interest to earn more interest than the same amount of money invested at the same rate in an account earning interest compounded annually? Explain.

_____

_____

_____

_____

_____

H.O.T. FOCUS ON HIGHER ORDER THINKING

Work Area

9. Multiple Representations The graph shows how the values of two accounts increase over time. The line represents $50 invested in an account paying 5% simple interest, and the curve represents $50 invested in an account paying 5% interest compounded annually. Write an equation for the line and for the curve. Assume no additional deposits were made to either account.

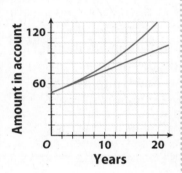

_____

10. Critique Reasoning Marco says he will earn more interest on his $100 savings if he gets 4% interest compounded annually than if he gets 5% simple interest. How many years does he have to keep the money in the bank without withdrawing any to be right? Justify your reasoning.

_____

_____

_____

_____

11. Critique Reasoning Parker invested $6,500, part at 6% interest compounded annually and part at 5% simple interest. He earned three times as much interest in the account paying compound interest as the account paying simple interest. Can Parker model this situation using the equation $x(1 + 0.06)^2 = 3(6500 - x)(0.05)(2)$ where x is the initial amount in the 6% account and $6500 - x$ is the amount in the 5% account? Explain.

_____

_____

_____

TEKS
Personal financial literacy—
8.12.F Analyze situations to determine if they represent financially responsible decisions and identify the benefits of financial responsibility and the cost of financial irresponsibility.
Also 8.12.E

ESSENTIAL QUESTION

How do you analyze financial situations to determine if they represent financially responsible decisions?

EXPLORE ACTIVITY **TEKS** 8.12.E

Exploring Different Payment Methods

There are several ways to pay for goods and services. These payment methods include cash, stored-value cards, debit cards, credit cards, money orders, and checks.

Research the similarities and differences between stored-value cards, also known as prepaid cards, debit cards, and credit cards.

A Use an Internet search engine to find images of the three types of cards. How are they similar and different in appearance?

_____

_____

_____

_____

B What information is on each card?

Stored-value card: _____

Debit card: _____

Credit card: _____

C When you use a stored-value card, debit card, or credit card, the money you spend is coming from different places. From where is the money deducted when you use each card?

_____

_____

_____

_____

_____

Math Talk
Mathematical Processes

What are some common uses of stored-value cards?

D Do you need to have an account at a bank to have each type of card?

_____

_____

E Research the fees associated with each type of card, such as activation fees, ATM fees, annual fees, and late payment fees. Describe the possible fees associated with each type of payment method.

Stored-value card _____

_____

Debit card _____

_____

Credit card _____

Reflect

1. What are the advantages and disadvantages of using a credit card?

_____

_____

_____

_____

2. What are the advantages and disadvantages of using a debit card?

_____

_____

_____

_____

Identify the payment method used in each transaction as a stored-value card, a debit card, or a credit card.

3. Stan buys a television and pays for it over the next 3 months.

_____

4. Ingra buys a cup of coffee, and the money is immediately withdrawn

from her bank account. _____

5. Yun used a $20 bus pass to ride the bus.

_____

Analyzing Situations for Financial Responsibility

Before making a monetary decision, it is important to consider whether your decision is financially responsible or financially irresponsible.

There are benefits to making financially responsible decisions, such as having more money in savings and having no debt or low debt. Financially irresponsible decisions can negatively affect your chance to buy a car, rent an apartment, own a house, and pay for college.

Math On the Spot
my.hrw.com

EXAMPLE 1 Real World

TEKS 8.12.F

Determine if the decision described was financially responsible or financially irresponsible. Explain your answer.

A Katarina had $100 in cash to spend on a $55 ink cartridge. When Katarina got to the office supply store, she noticed a sale on ink cartridges, 1 for $55 or 2 for $70. She purchased two for $70.

Katarina made a financially responsible decision.

Reason 1: Katarina saved $40 on the second ink cartridge.

Reason 2: She spent cash, so she will not owe money on her purchase.

B Melissa is renting an apartment for $850 a month. In August she had $2100 in her checking account. She used her credit card to pay rent and spent $1800 from her savings on a second flat-screen television.

Melissa made a financially irresponsible decision.

Reason 1: Melissa had enough money in her checking account to pay rent. Instead, she used her credit card to pay rent and may now have to pay interest on her card.

Reason 2: A second flat-screen television is not a necessity.

Math Talk
Mathematical Processes

What are some monetary and nonmonetary benefits of making financially responsible decisions?

Reflect

6. Don has been saving to buy a used truck for his lawn care business. He has $5,200 in his business savings account. The truck he wants costs $6000, and there is a possibility of financing at an interest rate of 7.5%. What financial advice would you give Don?

_____

_____

_____

_____

YOUR TURN

Tom has $524 in savings. His car needs new tires. Tom bought new racing tires for his car for $1400 with his credit card.

7. Was Tom's decision financially responsible or financially irresponsible? Explain your answer.

_____

_____

8. What could Tom have done differently?

_____

Guided Practice

Identify the payment method used in each transaction as cash, a credit card, a debit card, or a stored-value card. (Explore Activity)

1. Trina received a gift card to an electronics store and used it to buy a video game. _____

2. Sue gives $5 to a street vendor for a necklace. _____

3. Steve sets up an online payment for his cable bill that withdraws $50 from his checking account. _____

Determine if the decisions described are financially responsible or financially irresponsible. Explain your answers. (Example 1)

4. John was just laid off from his job. He has $750 in savings. To make himself feel better, he buys a new bike for $650 with his credit card.

_____

_____

5. Maria and Pat are recently married and work for the same company. They each pay $45 per month for health insurance. Pat combined their insurance for a new rate of $74 per month.

_____

_____

? ESSENTIAL QUESTION CHECK-IN

6. What are the characteristics of financially responsible decisions?

_____

16.3 Independent Practice

Personal Math Trainer

Online Assessment and Intervention

🔵 my.hrw.com

TEKS 8.12.E, 8.12.F

Research the similarities and differences of checks and money orders. Then answer 7–10.

7. What is a check? What is a money order?

_____

_____

_____

_____

_____

8. When someone writes a check, where is the money coming from?

_____

_____

9. When someone pays with a money order, where is the money coming from?

_____

_____

10. Do you think it is more secure to have someone pay you with a check or a money order? Explain.

_____

_____

_____

_____

_____

11. Matt is saving for a new computer. Matt's uncle offers to pay him $15 an hour to clean out his garage. Matt decides to go play soccer with his friends instead. Do you think Matt made the right decision? Why or why not?

_____

_____

_____

12. Amy owns her own business as a landscaper of homes and office buildings. On average, maintaining a homeowner's yard takes 2 hours per month, and Amy is paid $300 per month. The office buildings require 35 hours of landscaping per month and pay $2800 monthly. Which type of client do you think Amy prefers? Explain your answer.

_____

_____

_____

13. **Analyze Relationships** Fred and Wilma are buying a house. They have enough money in savings to pay for it directly. However, they have an opportunity to get a loan for the total price of the house at a 3% annual interest rate. (This means they will have to pay an extra 3% of annual interest over time.) If they put the cash they have in savings into other investments, they expect to earn 5% annual interest. How should Fred and Wilma pay for their house? Explain.

_____

_____

_____

14. **Critical Thinking** Nikola has received two job offers. The first is for an online company that pays $20 per hour. The work is interesting and lets him work from home, allowing him to spend more time with his kids. The second offer is at a factory an hour away. It is hard and repetitive work that pays $25 per hour. Which job should Nikola take? What factors should he consider besides the hourly pay in making his decision?

_____

_____

_____

15. **Critique Reasoning** Elena has learned to analyze whether decisions are financially responsible or not. For all of her future decisions, she plans to choose the option that is most financially responsible. Do you think this is a good idea? Explain.

_____

_____

_____

_____

Estimating College Costs and Payments

TEKS
Personal financial literacy—8.12.G Estimate the cost of a two-year and four-year college education, including family contribution, and devise a periodic savings plan for accumulating the money needed to contribute to the total cost of attendance for at least the first year of college.

? ESSENTIAL QUESTION

How do you estimate the cost of a college education?

Estimating the Cost of a College Education

The cost of a college education is affected by many factors, such as if you attend school in state or out of state and if you plan to live on campus, off campus, or at home. The total cost of a college education includes the cost of tuition, room and board, and textbooks.

Math On the Spot
my.hrw.com

EXAMPLE 1 Real World

TEKS 8.12.G

June wants to attend Texas A&M University-Kingsville, near Corpus Christi, Texas. She is 18, single, does not have any dependents, and lives in Dallas. She was raised by her single father, a contractor who makes $81,000 per year and pays roughly 12% income tax. For the past 4 years, June has worked part time at the local bookstore, earning a taxable annual income of $15,000, which is taxed at roughly 8%. June has 2 brothers, both of whom are in middle school.

How much should June expect to spend if she plans on completing a four-year degree program at A&M University-Kingsville while living in on-campus housing?

STEP 1 Find the cost of attending Texas A&M University-Kingsville for 1 year using the values in the table.

Other costs can include parking, transportation, and entertainment.

Tuition & Fees	$6,940
Room & Board	$7,086
Books	$1,300
Other	$5,170
Total	**$20,496**

STEP 2 Compute the cost of attending the university for 4 years.

$20,496 × 4 = $81,428

The estimated cost of June attending for 4 years is $81,984.

Reflect

1. How can June help to pay for her education?

_____

_____

_____

_____

YOUR TURN

2. June is also considering attending Del Mar College in Corpus Christi to get a 2-year associate's degree. Estimate the cost of June attending Del Mar College. Use the college's website or other online tool to find the figures for an out-of-district student.

Tuition & Fees	
Room & Board	
Books	
Other	
Total	

_____

_____

_____

3. Suppose June earns an associate's degree from Del Mar and then transfers to Texas A&M University-Kingsville for two more years to complete a bachelor's degree. Estimate the total amount that the 4 years of school will cost.

_____

_____

_____

4. Approximately how much less would it cost June to attend Del Mar for two years and A&M Kingsville for two years than to attend A&M Kingsville for four years?

_____

_____

Devising a Savings Plan for College

You can reduce the cost of your college education by applying for grants and scholarships. Another way to lower the cost of a college education is to start a college savings account.

EXPLORE ACTIVITY  TEKS 8.12.G

As we saw in Example 1, it will cost June an estimated $81,984 to attend Texas A&M University-Kingsville for 4 years. Let's apply the savings from June's scholarship, the money her father can contribute to her education, and the funds from her college savings account, to find a more accurate estimated total remaining cost.

A June received a scholarship, and has been awarded $2,000 each year for 4 years. Find the new estimated total cost of June's college education.

After subtracting the funds from the scholarship from the total cost of her college education, what estimated amount will June pay?

_____

B June's father has put aside $11,000 for June's college expenses. Find the new estimated total remaining cost of June's education.

After applying her father's contribution to her education expenses, what estimated remaining amount will June pay?

_____

C At the beginning of each of the 4 years of high school, June put $4500 of her bookstore income into a savings account. The account earns interest at a rate of 2.5%, compounded annually. Complete the table to find how much June has in her college savings account at the beginning of her freshman year of college.

Year	Beginning balance	Amount deposited	New balance	Amount of interested earned (at 2.5%)	Ending balance
1	$0	$4,500	$4,500	$4,500 × 0.025 = $112.50	$4,612.50
2					$9,340.31
3					$14,186.32
4					$19,153.48

After applying June's savings to her education expenses, what estimated remaining amount will June pay?

_____

© Houghton Mifflin Harcourt Publishing Company

Reflect

5. Does June have enough in her savings account to cover her first year at Texas A&M University-Kingsville without help from her father or a scholarship? What about with the scholarship?

_____

_____

_____

_____

6. If June had been able to deposit $5,000 a year instead of $4,500, earning the same annual interest rate of 2.5%, would she have enough saved to pay for her first year?

_____

Guided Practice

Ronan, a 19-year-old male from Texas, has been accepted at the University of Texas at Austin. If he attends the University of Texas, he plans to live at home with his mother, a single parent. His mother is a nurse who makes roughly $60,000 a year and pays roughly 13% in taxes annually. Ronan has never had a job. (Example 1, Explore Activity)

1. Use the table and an online tool to estimate the cost of Ronan attending the University of Texas for 1 year.

2. Estimate the cost of Ronan getting a 4-year degree from the University of Texas. _____

3. Ronan has been granted a scholarship for $1,500 per year. His mother has saved $21,000 for Ronan's college education. Recalculate the estimated remaining cost of Ronan's degree.

_____

Tuition & Fees	
Room & Board	
Books	
Other	
Total	

❓ ESSENTIAL QUESTION CHECK-IN

4. What are some things to consider when estimating the cost of college?

_____

_____

_____

© Houghton Mifflin Harcourt Publishing Company

16.4 Independent Practice

TEKS 8.12.G

Personal
Math Trainer

Online
Assessment and
Intervention

my.hrw.com

5. At the beginning of each of the last two years, Laura put $4800 from her earnings as a part-time cashier during high school into a college savings account earning 1.2% interest compounded annually. Now she is applying for school and needs to know how much she has in her account. Complete the table to determine how much money Laura has saved.

Year	Beginning balance	Amount deposited	New balance	Amount of interest earned (at 1.2%)	Ending balance
1					
2					

_____

6. At the beginning of each of the last three years, Lucas put $7000 from his earnings as a waiter into a college savings account that earned 1.5% interest compounded annually. Now he will spend an estimated $18,000 to attend his local community college for 2 years and not take out a student loan. Complete the table to determine whether Lucas has saved enough money to attend a community college.

Year	Beginning balance	Amount deposited	New balance	Amount of interest earned (at 1.5%)	Ending balance
1					
2					
3					

_____

_____

7. Find a college grant online.

a. Grant Name: _____

b. Describe the application process.

_____

_____

c. How much money does the grant award?

_____

_____

8. Find a college scholarship.

a. Name of Scholarship: _____

_____

b. Describe the application process.

_____

_____

c. How much money does the scholarship award?

_____

_____

_____

H.O.T. FOCUS ON HIGHER ORDER THINKING

9. Critical Thinking Having a savings plan is important even if you are not currently planning on attending college. Describe your savings plan including stating a goal, how much you plan to save, and how you plan to save your money.

_____

_____

_____

_____

10. Make a Conjecture A CD, or certificate of deposit, is similar to a savings account, but it requires the depositor to leave the money in the bank for a fixed period of time. There is a penalty for withdrawing money from the CD before the time period is over. The interest rates on CDs are generally higher than those for savings accounts. When would it be a good idea to put money in a CD to save for college? Would you put all of your savings into a CD? Explain your answer.

_____

_____

_____

_____

_____

Work Area

Ready to Go On?

16.1 Repaying Loans

Dustin is taking out a loan for $2000 and wants to know how much money he will save by taking a 2-year loan at 14% interest instead of 20% interest. (Use an online calculator.)

1. What is the total repayment for the 20% loan? _____

2. What is the total repayment for the 14% loan? _____

3. How much can Dustin save? _____

16.2 Saving and Investing

4. Cecilia has $800 in an account earning 4.5% simple interest. How much more interest would her account earn in 7 years with annually compounded interest? _____

16.3 Analyzing Financial Situations

5. Byron has $250 in his savings account. He starts a new job next week and spends $300 on tickets to a sporting event to celebrate. Is his decision financially responsible or financially irresponsible? Explain.

_____

_____

_____

16.4 Estimating College Costs and Payments

6. At the beginning of each of the last two years, Alfonso put $4200 from his earnings as a part-time pizza delivery driver into a college savings account earning 2.4% interest compounded annually. Complete the table to determine how much money Alfonso has saved.

Year	Beginning balance	Amount deposited	New balance	Amount of interest earned (at 2.4%)	Ending balance
1					
2					

Personal
Math Trainer

Online
Assessment and
Intervention

my.hrw.com

Selected Response

1. Which interest rate and time period result in the lowest total loan repayment for a $4000 loan?

Ⓐ 3 years at 11%

Ⓑ 3 years at 13%

Ⓒ 4 years at 8%

Ⓓ 4 years at 11%

2. Which equation represents a nonproportional relationship?

Ⓐ $y = -5x$ Ⓒ $y = \frac{1}{5}x$

Ⓑ $y = 5x + 0$ Ⓓ $y = 5x - 5$

3. Jemarcus starts with $1200 in a college savings account. His account earns interest at a rate of 1.8% compounded annually. How much money is in the account after 6 years?

Ⓐ $1221.60

Ⓑ $1265.97

Ⓒ $1329.60

Ⓓ $1335.57

4. Which equation relates x and y for the set of ordered pairs (4, 1), (8, 2), (12, 3)?

Ⓐ $y = \frac{1}{4}x$ Ⓒ $y = x - 3$

Ⓑ $y = 4x$ Ⓓ $y = x - 9$

5. Danielle received a gift card to a clothing store and uses it to buy a pair of jeans. Which payment method did she use?

Ⓐ cash

Ⓑ credit card

Ⓒ debit card

Ⓓ stored-value card

6. Ashley is considering attending the state university to obtain a 4-year bachelor's degree. For one year, the tuition and fees are $9890, room and board are $8250, and books are $680. What will be the total of these costs over the 4 years of obtaining the degree?

Ⓐ $18,140   Ⓒ $37,640

Ⓑ $18,820   Ⓓ $75,280

7. Triangle ABC, with vertices A(2, 3), B(4, −5), and C(6, 8), is reflected across the x-axis to form triangle A'B'C'. What are the coordinates of triangle A'B'C' ?

Ⓐ A'(2, −3), B'(4, 5), C'(6, −8)

Ⓑ A'(−2, 3), B'(−4, −5), C'(−6, 8)

Ⓒ A'(−2, −3), B'(−4, 5), C'(−6, −8)

Ⓓ A'(2, −3), B'(4, −11), C'(6, 2)

Gridded Response

8. A cone-shaped cup has a height of 3 inches and a volume of 9 cubic inches. What is the length in inches of the diameter of the cone? Round your answer to the nearest hundredth.

				•		
⓪	⓪	⓪	⓪		⓪	⓪
①	①	①	①		①	①
②	②	②	②		②	②
③	③	③	③		③	③
④	④	④	④		④	④
⑤	⑤	⑤	⑤		⑤	⑤
⑥	⑥	⑥	⑥		⑥	⑥
⑦	⑦	⑦	⑦		⑦	⑦
⑧	⑧	⑧	⑧		⑧	⑧
⑨	⑨	⑨	⑨		⑨	⑨

© Houghton Mifflin Harcourt Publishing Company

MODULE 16 Managing Your Money and Planning for Your Future

Key Vocabulary
compound interest *(interés compuesto)*
interest *(interés)*
simple interest *(interés simple)*

? ESSENTIAL QUESTION

How can you manage your money and plan for a successful financial future?

EXAMPLE 1

Clayton has $5,000 in an account earning simple interest at a rate of 2.5% per year. His wife Candice has $5,000 in an account earning interest at a rate of 2.3% compounded annually. How much interest did each account earn over 15 years? Which account is worth more after 15 years?

Clayton — Simple Interest

$I = Prt$

$I = \$5,000 \times 0.025 \times 15$

$I = \$1,875$

Candice — Compound Interest

$A = P(1 + r)^t$

$A = \$5,000(1.023)^{15}$

$A = \$7,032.42$

Clayton earned $1,875 in interest over 15 years for a total of $6,875 in his savings account. Candice earned $7,032.42 − $5,000 = $2,032.42 in interest for a total of $7,032.42 in her account. Candice earned more interest and has more money in her savings account.

EXAMPLE 2

Lee earns an annual salary of $42,000. He has $2,300 in savings and $1,500 in credit card debt. Lee finances a new truck with monthly payments of $525 and a down payment of $1,300 that he takes out of savings. Was Lee's decision financially responsible or financially irresponsible?

Lee made a financially irresponsible decision.

Reason 1: If Lee loses his job, he does not have enough savings to cover his car payments for more than 4 months.

Reason 2: Lee could have continued driving his current truck and used the money in savings to pay off his credit card debt.

EXERCISES

1. Sheri is going to take out a loan for $4,000 that she plans to pay back in 2 years. She wants to know how much more it will cost her in interest if she uses her credit card at 18% interest instead of borrowing from the bank at 10% interest. Use an online calculator to find the total repayment for each loan and the difference in the cost of these two choices. (Lesson 16.1)

_____

_____

2. You are trying to decide which account to put $3,500 into for the next 6 years. One account has an interest rate of 2.9% and is compounded annually. The other account has a simple interest rate of 3.1%. Which account will earn more interest over 6 years, and how much more interest will it earn? (Lesson 16.2)

_____

3. Maria has $120 to spend on food for the week. She goes out to a restaurant to eat dinner with her friends and spends $62 on the meal. Did Maria make a financially responsible decision or a financially irresponsible decision? Explain your answer. (Lesson 16.3)

_____

_____

4. Use an online tool to estimate the cost for one year at a 4-year university and one year at a 2-year college in Texas. (Lesson 16.4)

	4-year university	**2-year college**
Tuition & Fees		
Room & Board		
Books		
Other		
Total		

a. Find the cost of attending the university for four years.

_____

_____

b. Find the cost of attending the two-year college and transferring to the university for your final two years of school.

_____

_____

1. **CAREERS IN MATH** Organic Farmer Carlos is an organic farmer, and his business is doing so well that he his thinking of expanding in the next few years. He decides to start saving for this expansion and is going to put $8,200 into a savings account. At his credit union, he has two choices for savings accounts: Simple Savers that earns 2% simple interest per year, and Super Savers which earns 1.95% interest, compounded annually.

   a. How much will Carlos have after 2 years if he chooses the Simple Savers account? Show your work.

   _____

   b. How much will Carlos have after 2 years if he chooses the Super Savers account? Show your work.

   _____

   c. Which account would you recommend Carlos use and why?

   _____

   _____

   d. If Carlos decides to keep the money in the savings account for 5 years, would you change your recommendation? Why or why not?

   _____

   _____

   _____

2. Kay wants a new television. She sees an advertisement in the newspaper for a rent-to-own store, where for $80 a month she can rent a new television. And, if she rents for 18 months, she will own the television outright. Kay is considering this option, because she doesn't have enough money to purchase a television but she can pay $80 a month.

   a. If Kay rents the television for 18 months, how much will she pay in total for the television?

   _____

   b. The same television sells for $429 at an electronics store. How much more will Kay end up paying if she rents the television for 18 months than if she buys it outright?

   _____

c. What financially responsible recommendation would you give to Kay about purchasing the television?

_____

_____

_____

_____

3. Anastasia is a high school senior who wants to be an architect. She was accepted at a four-year university and was offered a scholarship of $17,800 per year. The costs per year at this university are shown in the table.

Tuition & Fees	$17,400
Room & Board	$10,350
Books and Materials	$850

She can also attend a community college for the first two years. The tuition for the community college is $1,150 per year. She would need to rent an apartment and buy her food, which she estimates will cost $400 a month for the apartment and $210 a month for food. She would still need to buy books and materials at $850 a year.

a. How much will it cost Anastasia to attend the university for all four years of college, assuming she has her scholarship all four years? Show how you got your answer.

_____

_____

b. How much will it cost Anastasia to attend the community college for the first two years, and to attend the university for the last two years? Show your work.

_____

_____

_____

c. Give one reason in favor of going to the university for her entire college career, and one reason in favor of going two years to the community college and two years to the university.

_____

_____

_____

Selected Response

1. Which interest rate and time period result in the lowest total loan repayment for a $5,000 loan?

Ⓐ 3 years at 10%

Ⓑ 3 years at 13%

Ⓒ 4 years at 8%

Ⓓ 4 years at 11%

2. Which of the relationships below is a function?

Ⓐ
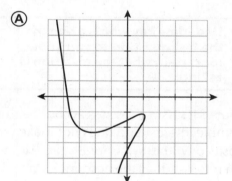

Ⓑ
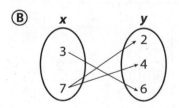

Ⓒ (6, 3), (5, 0), (1, 2), (0, 7), (−1, 6)

Ⓓ

x	5	6	5	8
y	5	7	9	11

3. Amanda used her PIN to complete a transaction at a department store. Which payment method does this describe?

Ⓐ gift card

Ⓑ credit card

Ⓒ debit card

Ⓓ stored-value card

4. What is the surface area of the rectangular prism?

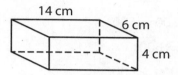

Ⓐ 160 cm²

Ⓑ 164 cm²

Ⓒ 328 cm²

Ⓓ 392 cm²

5. Rianna opens a savings account with $900. Her account earns interest at a rate of 1.3% compounded annually. How much money is in the account after 4 years?

Ⓐ $46.80

Ⓑ $47.72

Ⓒ $946.80

Ⓓ $947.72

Hot Tip! Some answer choices, called **distracters, may seem correct because they are based on common errors made in calculations.**

6. Richard took a handful of pencils from a large box. Out of the 15 pencils in his hand, 4 were glittery. How many glittery pencils should Richard expect to find in the box if there are a total of 240 pencils?

Ⓐ 16 glittery pencils

Ⓑ 32 glittery pencils

Ⓒ 64 glittery pencils

Ⓓ 96 glittery pencils

© Houghton Mifflin Harcourt Publishing Company

7. Yvonne started running 8 minutes after Cassie started. Cassie was running at a rate of 500 feet per minute. Yvonne was running at a rate of 600 feet per minute. Which equation could you solve to find how long it will take Yvonne to catch up to Cassie?

Ⓐ $600t + 3 = 500t$

Ⓑ $600t + 4,800 = 500t$

Ⓒ $500t + 3 = 600t$

Ⓓ $500t + 4,000 = 600t$

8. Leah is planning on attending a public university to earn a four year bachelor's degree. For one year, the tuition and fees are $10,220, room and board is $6250, and books are $540. At these rates, how much should Leah expect four years of school to cost?

Ⓐ $16,470

Ⓑ $17,010

Ⓒ $34,020

Ⓓ $68,040

9. The square below is dilated under the dilation $(x, y) \rightarrow (0.25x, 0.25y)$.

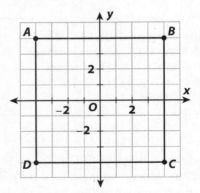

What are the coordinates of A'?

Ⓐ $(-4, -4)$

Ⓑ $(-1, -1)$

Ⓒ $(-2, -2)$

Ⓓ $(4, -4)$

Gridded Response

10. Fletcher took out a $4,500 loan at 14% interest for 3 years. Use an online calculator to find his monthly payment.

> **Hot Tip!**
>
> **Underline key words given in the test question so you know for certain what the question is asking.**

11. Pat puts $1,310 in a savings account earning 2% simple interest and does not make any deposits or withdrawals for 8 years. How much interest does the account earn?

Selected Answers

MODULE 1

LESSON 1.1

Your Turn

6. 8, −8 **7.** 10, −10
8. $\frac{1}{3}$, $-\frac{1}{3}$ **9.** 12 ft

Guided Practice

1. irrational numbers **2.** 0.875
3. 0.85 **4.** 0.72 **5.** 2.375 **6.** 5.$\overline{6}$
7. 2.8 **8.** 7, −7 **9.** 12, −12
10. 20, −20 **11.** $\frac{1}{4}$, $-\frac{1}{4}$
12. $\frac{2}{3}$, $-\frac{2}{3}$ **13.** $\frac{3}{2}$, $-\frac{3}{2}$ **14.** 5.85
15. 9.05 **16.** 6.75 **17.** 10.15
18. −8.45 **19.** −4.35 **20.** 3.2; 3.1;
3.2; 3.2; The ratio is about 3.15.

Independent Practice

23. 0.1$\overline{6}$ **25.** 98.$\overline{6}$ **26.** 2.65 cm
29. 17 ft **31.** terminating
33. 120 in. **35.** 6.45

37. High: 5 is much closer to 4
than to 9. A better estimate would
be 2.2 or 2.3. **39.** 225; the square
roots are 15 and −15, so −15
− (−15) = 30.

LESSON 1.2

Your Turn

1. rational, real **2.** irrational,
real **3.** False. Every integer is
a rational number, but every
rational number is not an integer.
Rational numbers such as $\frac{3}{5}$ and
$-\frac{5}{2}$ are not integers. **4.** False. Real
numbers are either rational or
irrational numbers. Integers are
rational numbers, so no integers
are irrational numbers. **5.** Real
numbers; the amount can be any
number greater than 0. **6.** Real
numbers; the number of seconds
left can be any number less than 0.

Guided Practice

1. rational, real **2.** whole, integer,
rational, real **3.** irrational, real
4. rational, real **5.** whole, integer,
rational, real **6.** integer, rational,
real **7.** rational, real **8.** integer,
rational, real **9.** True. Whole
numbers are a subset of the set
of rational numbers and can
be written as a quotient with
a denominator of 1. **10.** True.
Whole numbers are rational
numbers. **11.** Integers; the
change can be a whole dollar
amount and can be positive or
negative. **12.** Rational numbers;
the ruler is marked every
$\frac{1}{16}$th inch.

Independent Practice

15. whole, integer, rational,
real **17.** rational, real **19.** whole,
integer, rational, real **21.** Integers;
the scores are counting numbers,
their opposites, and zero.
23. Whole; the diameter is $\frac{\pi}{\pi}$ =
1 mile. **25.** rational number
27. Sample answer: If the
calculator shows a terminating
decimal, the number is rational.
Otherwise, you cannot tell
because you see only a few digits.

LESSON 1.3

Your Turn

3. > **4.** < **5.** $\sqrt{3}$, $\sqrt{5}$, 2.5

6. $\sqrt{75}$, π^2, 10

7. $3\frac{1}{2}$ mi, 3.$\overline{45}$ mi, $\frac{10}{3}$ mi, $\sqrt{10}$ mi

Guided Practice

1. < **2.** > **3.** < **4.** < **5.** >
6. < **7.** > **8.** > **9.** 1.7; 1.8; 1.75;
6.28; 1.5; $\sqrt{3}$; 2π **10.** $1 + \frac{\pi}{2}$ km,
2.5 km, $\frac{12}{5}$ km, $\sqrt{17}$ −2 km

Independent Practice

13. π, $\sqrt{10}$, 3.5 **15.** −3.75, $\frac{9}{4}$, $\sqrt{8}$, 3
17a. $\sqrt{60} \approx$ 7.7.5, $\frac{58}{8} =$ 7.25,
7.$\overline{3} \approx$ 7.33, $7\frac{3}{5} =$ 7.60, so the
average is 7.4825 km. **b.** They
are nearly identical. $\sqrt{56}$ is
approximately 7.4833…
19. Sample answer: $\sqrt{31}$
21a. between $\sqrt{7} \approx$ 2.65 and
$\sqrt{8} \approx$ 2.82 **b.** between $\sqrt{9} \approx$ 3
and $\sqrt{10} \approx$ 3.16 **23.** 2; rational
numbers can have the same
location, and irrational numbers
can have the same location, but
they cannot share a location.

MODULE 2

LESSON 2.1

Your Turn

3. 6.4×10^3 **4.** 5.7×10^{11}
5. 9.461×10^{12} km **8.** 7,034,000,000
9. 236,000 **10.** 5,000,000 g

Guided Practice

1. 5.8927×10^4 **2.** 1.304×10^9
3. 6.73×10^6 **4.** 1.33×10^4
5. 9.77×10^{22} **6.** 3.84×10^5
7. 400,000 **8.** 1,849,900,00
9. 6,410 **10.** 84,560,00
11. 800,000 **12.** 90,000,000,000
13. 54,00 s **14.** 7,600,000 cans

Independent Practice

17. 2.2×10^5 lb **19.** 4×10^4 lb
21. 5×10^4 lb **23.** $108\frac{1}{3}$ hours or
108 hours and 20 minutes
25. 4.6×10^3 **27a.** None of the
girls has the correct answer.
b. Polly and Samantha have the

decimal in the wrong place; Esther miscounted the number of places the decimal moved. **29.** The speed of a car because it is likely to be less than 100. **31.** Is the first factor greater than 1 and less than 10? Is the second factor a power of 10?

LESSON 2.2

Your Turn

4. 8.29×10^{-5} **5.** 3.02×10^{-7}
6. 7×10^{-6} m **9.** 0.000001045
10. 0.000099 **11.** 0.01 m

Guided Practice

1. 4.87×10^{-4} **2.** 2.8×10^{-5}
3. 5.9×10^{-5} **4.** 4.17×10^{-2}
5. 2×10^{-5} **6.** 1.5×10^{-5}
7. 0.00002 **8.** 0.000003582
9. 0.00083 **10.** 0.0297
11. 0.0000906 **12.** 0.00004
13. 1×10^{-4}
14. 0.00000000000000000000000017

Independent Practice

17. 1.3×10^{-3} cm **19.** 4.5×10^{-3} cm **21.** 8×10^{-4} cm
23. 7 cm = 0.07 m, 7 cm = 7×10^{0} cm; 0.07 m = 7×10^{-2} m

The first factors are the same; the exponents differ by 2. **25.** If the exponent on 10 is positive, the number is greater than 1. **27.** Negative, because a ladybug would weigh less than 1 ounce. **29.** 0.000000000125 **31.** 71,490,000 **33.** 3,397,000 **35.** 5.85×10^{-3} m, 1.5×10^{-2} m, 2.3×10^{-2} m, 9.6×10^{-1} m, 1.2×10^{2} m **37.** The number will be very large because you are dividing a large number by a decimal value less than 1.

 # UNIT 2 Selected Answers

MODULE 3

LESSON 3.1

Your Turn

3. $y = 15x$ **4.** 6 miles hiked in 5 hours **5.** $y = \frac{6}{5}x$

Guided Practice

1. is **2.** constant of proportionality **3a.** The pairs (weeks, days) are (2, 14), (4, 28), (8, 56), (10, 70). **b.** the time in weeks; the time in days; $y = 7x$ **4.** The pairs (oxygen atoms, hydrogen atoms) are (5, 10), (17, 34), (120, 240); $y = 2x$ **5.** $y = 30x$

Independent Practice

7. No; the ratios of the numbers in each column are not equal.
9a. Sample answer: The account had a balance of $100 to begin with. **b.** Sample answer: Have Ralph open the account with no money to begin with and then put $20 in every month. **11.** $y = 105$
13a. The pairs (distance, time) are (10, 1), (20, 2), (30, 3), (40, 4), (50, 5). **b.** $y = \frac{1}{10}x$, where y is the time in minutes and x is the distance in inches. **c.** 8.5 minutes **15.** For $S = 1$, $P = 4$ and $A = 1$; For $S = 2$, $P = 8$ and $A = 4$; For $S = 3$, $P = 12$ and $A = 9$; For $S = 4$, $P = 16$ and $A = 16$; For $S = 5$, $P = 20$ and $A = 25$. **a.** Yes. The ratio of the perimeter of a square to its side length is always 4. **b.** No. The ratio of the area of a square to its side length is not constant.

LESSON 3.2

Your Turn

1. 36, 13, −10; variable **4.** +3; +4; $\frac{3}{4}$

Guided Practice

1. constant **2.** variable
3. variable **4.** constant **5.** 200; 1;

200; 1; 200 **6.** 200 ft per min
7. −2 **8.** $\frac{3}{2}$

Independent Practice

11. 15 miles per hour
13a. 1 gallon every 5 minutes, or 0.2 gal/min **b.** 25 minutes
15.

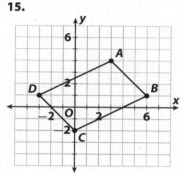

a. slope $\overline{AB} = -1$; slope $\overline{BC} = \frac{1}{2}$; slope $\overline{CD} = -1$; slope $\overline{DA} = \frac{1}{2}$
b. The slopes of the opposite sides are the same. **c.** Yes; opposite sides still have the same slope. **17.** Sample answer: One line has a positive slope and one has a negative slope. The lines are equally steep, but one slants upward left to right and the other slants downward left to right.

LESSON 3.3

Your Turn

2. His unit rate and the slope of a graph of the ride both equal $\frac{1}{5}$ mi/min.

Tomas's Ride

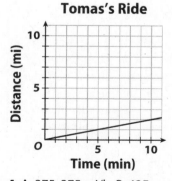

4. A: 375, 375 mi/h; B: 425, 425 mi/h; B is flying faster.

Guided Practice

1. slope = unit rate = $\frac{5}{6}$ mi/h
2. slope = unit rate = $\frac{4}{5}$ mi/h
3. Clark is faster. From the equation, Henry's rate is equal to 0.5, or $\frac{1}{2}$ mile per hour. Clark's rate is the slope of the line, which is $\frac{3}{2}$, or 1.5 miles per hour.
4. $y = 15x$ **5.** $y = \frac{3}{8}x$

Independent Practice

7a. The pairs (time, distance) are (4, 3), (8, 6), (12, 9), (16, 12), (20, 15).
b.

Migration Flight

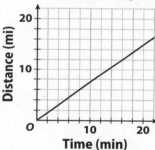

c. $\frac{3}{4}$; The unit rate of migration of the goose and the slope of the graph both equal $\frac{3}{4}$ mi/min.
9a. Machine 1: slope = unit rate = $\frac{0.6}{1}$ = 0.6 gal/s; Machine 2: slope = unit rate = $\frac{3}{4}$ = 0.75 gal/s
b. Machine 2 is working at a faster rate since 0.75 > 0.6. **11.** slope = unit rate = 4.75. If the graph of a proportional relationship passes through the point (1, r), then r equals the slope and the unit rate, which is $4.75/min. **13.** 243 gallons; The unit rate is $\frac{36}{2}$ = 18 gal/min. So, $1\frac{1}{2}$ min. after 12 min., an additional $18 \times 1\frac{1}{2}$ = 27 gal. will be pumped in. The total is 216 + 27 = 243 gal.

LESSON 3.4

Your Turn

1. yes; $y = 1.9x$ **3.** $y = 4x$, where x is gallons of gasoline and y is ounces of oil; 26 ounces

Guided Practice

1. not a direct variation **2.** yes; $y = 20x$ **3.** yes; $y = 3.1x$ **4.** yes; $y = 0.0725x$ **5.** $y = \frac{1}{16}x$; 3.5 cups **6.** $y = 4x$; 100 calories

Independent Practice

9. C **11.** For $S = 1$, $P = 4$ and $A = 1$; For $S = 2$, $P = 8$ and $A = 4$; For $S = 3$, $P = 12$ and $A = 9$; For $S = 5$, $P = 20$ and $A = 25$; For $S = 9$, $P = 36$ and $A = 81$. **a.** Yes; the perimeter is always the side length multiplied by 4, so $y = 4x$. **b.** No; the ratio of the area to the side length is not constant. **c.** 8 border pieces cover the 12 feet around, so $8 \times 99 = 15.92$; 3 bags of soil cover 9 sq. feet, so $3 \times 4.99 = 14.97$. She spends $15.92 + 14.97 = \$30.89$. **13.** No. There is not enough information to conclude that it is a direct variation. The graph may not be a line and may not include the origin. **15.** The first equation; the slope of the second direct variation is less than the slope of the first one.

MODULE 4

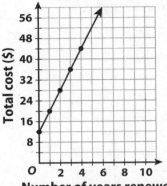

LESSON 4.1

Your Turn

1. Sample answer: (2, 20), (3, 32), (4, 44), (5, 36) **3.** (−1, 3), (0, 1), (1, −1), (2, −3)

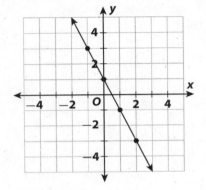

Guided Practice

1. (−2, 1), (−1, 3), (0, 5), (1, 7), (2, 9) **2.** (−8, −8), (0, −5), (8, −2), (16, 1), (24, 4) **3.** Undefined, 3.5, 2.75, 2.5, 2.375; The ratio $\frac{y}{x}$ is not constant. **4.** The graph is a line, but it does not pass through the origin. **5.** (−2, −3), (−1, −2), (0, −1), (1, 0), (2, 1)

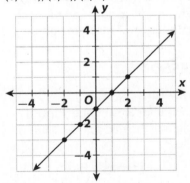

Independent Practice

7. Set of unconnected points; you cannot buy a fractional part of a lunch. **9a.** Sample answer: For (x, y) where x is number of years renewed and y is total cost in dollars: (0, 12), (1, 20), (2, 28), (3, 36), (4, 44)

b.

Magazine Subscription Costs

c. The graph does not include the origin. Also, the ratio of the total cost and number of years is not constant. **d.** No; the number of years must be a whole number, so total cost goes up in $8 increments. **11.** Sample answer: In a table, the ratios $\frac{y}{x}$ will not be equal; a graph will not pass through the origin; an equation will be in the form $y = mx + b$ where $b \neq 0$. **13.** At most one: A line representing a proportional relationship must pass through the origin. A line parallel to it cannot also pass through the origin.

LESSON 4.2

Your Turn

1. $m = 5$; $b = 12$ **2.** $m = 7$; $b = 1$

Guided Practice

1. −2; 1 **2.** 5; −15 **3.** $\frac{3}{2}$; −2 **4.** −3; 9 **5.** 3; 1 **6.** −4; 140

Independent Practice

9a. $5 to park; $12 per hour **b.** $23.50; (3.5 hours × $12 per hour + $5) ÷ 2 = $23.50 **11.** Rate of change is constant from 1 to 2 to 3, but not from 3 to 4. **13.** Express the slope m between a random point (x, y) on the line and the point $(0, b)$ where the line crosses the y-axis. Then solve the equation for y.

15. After parking 61 cars; John earns a fixed weekly salary of $300 plus $5 for each car he parks. He earns the same in fees as his fixed salary for parking 300 ÷ 5 = 60 cars.

LESSON 4.3

Your Turn

2.

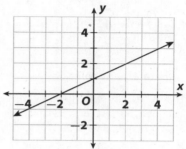

3.

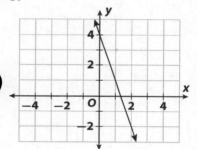

4.

5. The new graph has the same y-intercept but a slope of −200 instead of −300.

6. The calories left to burn will decrease more slowly with each hour of exercise, so it will take longer for Ken to meet his goal.

7. The y-intercept would not change, but the slope would become −600, which is much steeper. The line would intersect the x-axis when x = 4 hours.

1. $\frac{1}{2}$; −3

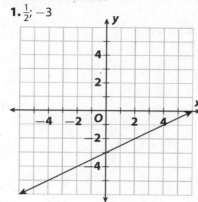

2. −2; 2

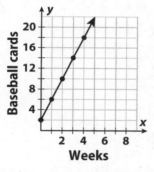

3a. Slope = 4; y-intercept = 2; you start with 2 cards and add 4 cards each week.

b. The points with coordinates that are not whole numbers; you will not buy part of a baseball card and you are buying only once a week.

5a.

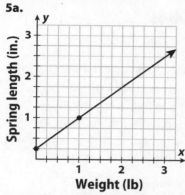

b. The slope, 0.75, means that the spring stretches by 0.75 inch with each additional pound of weight. The y-intercept, 0.25, is the unstretched length of the spring in inches. **c.** 1.75 inches; no; the length with a 4-pound weight is 3.25 in., not 3.5 in.

7. (0, 8), (1, 7), (2, 6), (3, 5) **9.** (0, −3), (1, −1.5), (2, 0), (3, 1.5) **11.** (0, −5), (3, −3), (6, −1), (9, 1) **13a.** Yes; a slope of 3 or $\frac{3}{1}$ means a positive vertical change of 3 and a positive horizontal change of 1. **b.** m = 3 so $3 is the charge per visit; b = 50 so the membership fee is $50.

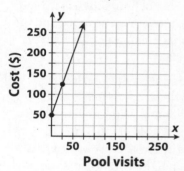

c. 50 visits **15.** Yes; plot the point and use the slope to find a second point. Then draw a line through the two points.

LESSON 4.4

Your Turn

1. nonproportional
2. proportional
5. proportional
6. nonproportional
7. nonproportional
8. proportional

9. nonproportional
10. proportional
11. Test-Prep Center A's charges are proportional, but B's are not. Center B offers a coupon for an initial credit, but its hourly rate, $25, is higher than Center A's hourly rate of $20. So, Center B will cost more in the long run.

Guided Practice
1. Proportional; the line includes the origin. **2.** Nonproportional; the line does not include the origin. **3.** Nonproportional; when the equation is written in the form $y = mx + b$, the value of b is not 0.
4. Proportional; when the equation is written in the form $y = mx + b$, the value of b is 0.
5. Proportional; the quotient of y and x is constant, 4, for every number pair. **6.** No, because when the equation $y = mx + b$ is written for the values, the value of b is not 0. **7.** Sample answer: The rating is proportional to the number of households watching: the quotient of the rating and the number of households is always 0.0000008.

Independent Practice
9a. Nonproportional; the graph does not pass through the origin, so $b \neq 0$. **b.** $m = 0.5$, $b = 10$; each cup of sports drink weighs a half pound. The empty cooler weighs 10 pounds. **11.** Proportional; this equation has the form $y = mx + b$ where $b = 0$.
15a. No; from Equation B, the y-intercept is 273.15, not 0, so the graph does not include the origin. From Table C, the quotient of K and C is not constant.
b. No; Equation A is in the form $y = mx + b$, with F instead of y and C instead of x. The value of b is 32, not 0, so the relationship is not proportional.

LESSON 4.5

Your Turn
3. $(-1, 3)$

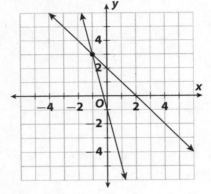

4. $(1, 3)$

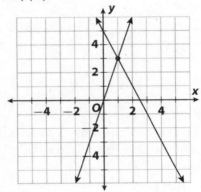

6a. $x + y = 6$ and $2x + 4y = 20$; $y = -x + 8$ and $y = -0.5x + 5$
b.

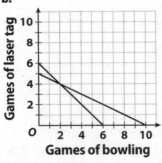

c. Marquis will bowl 2 games and play 4 games of laser tag.

Guided Practice
1. $(3, 5)$

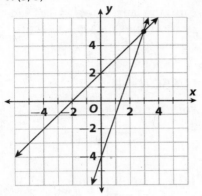

2. infinitely many solutions

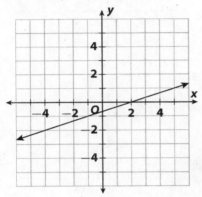

3a. $y = -x + 15$ **b.** $y = -0.5x + 10$
c.

d. 10 spelling questions and 5 vocabulary questions

Independent Practice
5. system of equations
7a. $y = 2.50x + 2$; $y = 2x + 4$
b. The solution is $(4, 12)$. The cost at both alleys will be the same for 4 games bowled, $12.

Cost of Bowling

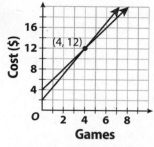

11. Infinitely many; Rearranging the left side of the 2nd equation and subtracting $3a$ from both sides gives $-ax + ay = -3a$. Dividing both sides by $-a$ gives $x - y = 3$. The equations describe the same line.

MODULE 5

LESSON 5.1

Your Turn

3. $y = -2.5x + 25$ **5.** $y = 0.5x + 10$

Guided Practice

1a. the length of the necklace in inches **b.** the total number of beads in the necklace
c. $y = 5x + 27$ **2.** $\frac{0 - 300}{5 - 0} = \frac{-300}{5} = -60$; 300; $y = -60x + 300$
3. temperature; chirps per minute; $\frac{100 - 76}{65 - 59} = \frac{24}{6} = 4$; -160; $y = 4x - 160$

Independent Practice

5. $y = 30x$ **7.** $m = 0.125$; the diver ascends at a rate of 0.125 m/s
9. $y = 0.125x - 10$ **11.** $y = 20x + 12$ **13.** $m = 500$; $b = 1000$
15. The amount of money in the savings account increases by $500 each month. **17.** The rate of change would not be constant. Using different pairs of points in the slope formula would give different results.

LESSON 5.2

Your Turn
1. $m = 15,000$; $b = 0$; $y = 15,000x$

Water Released from Hoover Dam

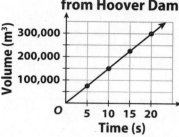

4. $p = 75n + 250$ **5.** $c = 0.50d + 40$

Guided Practice
1. $m = -1.25$; $b = 20$; $y = -1.25x + 20$

Bus Pass Balance

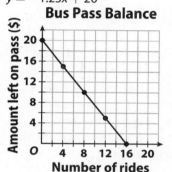

2. $m = \frac{51 - 59}{2000 - 0} = \frac{-8}{2000} = -0.004$
3. $b = 59$ **4.** $y = -0.004x + 59$
5. $y = -0.004(5000) + 59 = 39°F$

Independent Practice
7. $m = 2$; $b = 8$; $C = 2t + 8$
9a. $y = -1.5x + 30$ **b.** The number of dollars left decreases as the number of car washes increases. **c.** 20; after 20 washes there is no money left on the card.
11. $y = -2x + 6$ **13a.** No, the change between weeks is constant, but the change in the amount of rain is not constant. **b.** No; there is no apparent pattern in the table. **15.** 0; Jaíme's graph contained (0, 0). Since Jayla's data were the same, but with x and y switched, her graph also contained (0, 0).

LESSON 5.3

Your Turn
1. $y = 4x + 20$ **2.** $y = 240x$
6. $30 **7.** $48.75 **8.** $600

Guided Practice
1. $y = 30x$ **2.** $y = 2.5x + 2$ **3.** $y = 20x + 30$; $140 **4.** Yes, because

the graph has a constant rate of change. **5.** No, because the graph does not have a constant rate of change.

Independent Practice
7. Yes, because the rate of change is constant. **9.** Linear; the rate of change is the cost of a DVD, which is constant. **11.** Not linear; the rate of change in the area of a square increases as the side length increases. **13.** The relationship is linear; the equation of the linear relationship is $y = 0.125x$, so the Mars Rover would travel 7.5 feet in 60 seconds. **15.** Because $x = 6$ lies halfway between $x = 4$ and $x = 8$, so the y-value should lie halfway between the corresponding y-values. **17.** Find the equation of the linear relationship using the slope and given point, and then insert any x-value to find a y-value on the graph of the line.

MODULE 6

LESSON 6.1

Your Turn
4. Function; each input value is paired with only one output value. **5.** Not a function; the input value is paired with more than one output value. **7.** Function; each input value is paired with only one output value. **8.** Not a function; the input value 8 is paired with more than one output value.
10. Not a function; input values are paired with more than one output values; (70,165) and (70, 178)

Guided Practice
1. $20x$; 200 **2.** $\frac{x}{2}$; 15 **3.** $2.25x$; 27.00 **4.** Function; each input value is paired with only one output value **5.** Not a function; the input value 4 is paired with more than one output value.
6. Yes; each input value is paired with only one output value.

© Houghton Mifflin Harcourt Publishing Company

Independent Practice

9. Not a function; the input value 5 is paired with more than one output value. **11a.** There is only one number of bacteria for each number of hours, so each input is paired with only one output. **b.** Yes. Each input value would still be paired with only one output value. **13.** Yes. Each input value (the weight) is paired with only one output value (the price). **15.** It does not represent a function. For the input values to be paired with all four output values, at least one of the input values would be paired with more than one output value.

LESSON 6.2

Your Turn

2. proportional

3. $(x, y) = (0, 0), (3, 2), (6, 4), (9, 6)$; linear; proportional

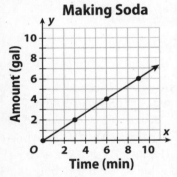
Making Soda

Guided Practice

1. $(-1, 7), (1, 3), (3, -1), (5, -5)$; linear

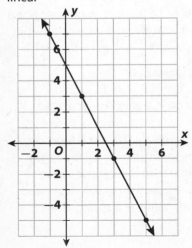

2. $(-2, -2), (-1, 1), (0, 2), (1, 1), (2, -2)$; nonlinear

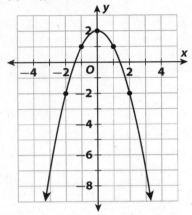

3. No; the equation cannot be written in the form $y = mx + b$, and the graph of the solutions is not a line. **4.** Yes; the equation can be written in the form $y = mx + b$, and the graph of the solutions is a line.

Independent Practice

7. No. The relationship is not linear because x is squared, so it will not be proportional. **9a.** Yes. The graph of the solutions lie in a line.

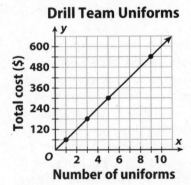
Drill Team Uniforms

b. $720
11. Disagree; the equation can be written in the form $y = mx + b$ where m is 0, and the graph of the solutions is a horizontal line.
13. The relationship is linear if the points all lie on the same line, and proportional if it is linear and a line through the points passes through the origin. **15.** Applying the Distr. Prop gives $y + 3 = 6x + 3$, or $y = 6x$. This is in the form $y = mx + b$ with $b = 0$, so it is linear and proportional.

LESSON 6.3

Your Turn

1. Buying at the bookstore is more expensive.

Guided Practice

1. The second method (159 bpm vs. 150 bpm) gives the greater heart rate. **2.** Heart rate and age are nonproportional for each method. **3.** Students pay a $40 fee and $5 per hour.

4.

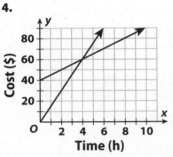

5. With both plans, it costs $60 for 4 hours of tutoring. **6.** Plan 2 ($90 vs. $150) is cheaper for 10 hours of tutoring. **7.** Cost and time are proportional for Plan 1 and nonproportional for Plan 2.

Independent Practice

9. Scooter B (15 gallons vs. 18 gallons) uses fewer gallons of gas. **11.** the first plan **13.** The camera at the second store; the cost at the first store is $290 and the cost at the second store is $260. **15.** Since the rate per visit is the same, the monthly cost of Gym A is always more than Gym B. **17.** $y = -24x + 8$ is changing more quickly because even though -24 is less than -21, the absolute value of -24 is greater than the absolute value of -21.

UNIT 3 Selected Answers

MODULE 7

LESSON 7.1

Your Turn
5. 72° **6.** 108° **7.** 108°

Guided Practice
1. ∠VWZ **2.** alternate interior
3. 80° **4.** 100° **5.** same-side interior

Independent Practice
7. ∠1 and ∠5, ∠2 and ∠6, ∠3
and ∠7, ∠4 and ∠8 **9.** alternate
interior angles **11.** 30°
13. 110° **15.** 78° **17.** 132°; the
48° angle is supplementary to
the larger angle because the two
angles are same-side interior
angles. **19.** ∠6 and ∠2 are corr.,
so m∠2 = 125°. ∠6 and ∠3 are alt.
int., so m∠3 = 125°. ∠3 and ∠7
are corr., so m∠7 = 125°. ∠6 and
∠4 are same-side int., so m∠4 =
180° − 125°, or 55°. ∠4 and ∠8 are
corr., so m∠8 = 55°. ∠4 and ∠5
are alt. int., so m∠5 = 55°. ∠1 and
∠5 are corr., so m∠1 = 55°.
21. 3 angles; 4 angles; no

LESSON 7.2

Your Turn
4. 53° **5.** 90° **8.** 78°; 68°

Guided Practice
1. 71° **2.** 30° **3.** 88°; 29°; 63°
4. 90°; 45°; 45° **5.** 40°; 76°; 64°
6. 129°; 32°; 19°

Independent Practice
9. 60°; 30° **11.** 98°; 55°; 27° **13.**
60°; 90°; 30; 150 **15.** No; the
measure of an obtuse angle is
greater than 90°. If a triangle had
two obtuse angles, the sum of
their measures would be greater
than 180°, the sum of the angle
measures of a triangle. **17a.**
360° **b.** The sum of the angle
measures of a quadrilateral is 360°.

Any quadrilateral can be divided
into two triangles, so the sum of its
angle measures is $2 \times 180° = 360°$.

LESSON 7.3

Your Turn
3. The triangles are not similar
because only one angle is
congruent. The angle measures of
the triangles are 70°, 58°, and 52°
and 70°, 61°, and 49°. **5.** 8 inches
6. 21 ft

Guided Practice
1. 41°, 109°, and 30°; 41°, 109°,
and 30°; two angles; two angles;
similar **2.** 7.5; 23.5; 17.2
3. congruent; alternate interior
angles; congruent; alternate
interior angles; AA Similarity;
similar

Independent Practice
5. m∠B = 42°, m∠F = 69°, m∠H =
64°, m∠K = 53° **7.** ∠J ≅ ∠A,
∠L ≅ ∠B, and ∠K ≅ ∠C **9.** 25 feet
11. In the first line, Ryan should
have added 19.5 and 6.5 to get
a denominator of 26 for the
expression on the right side to get
the correct value of 13.6 cm for *h*.

MODULE 8

LESSON 8.1

Your Turn
4. 50 ft **5.** 9 in. **6.** $r = \sqrt{228}$, so
the greatest length is 15 in.

Guided Practice
1. 10^2, 676, 26 **2a.** 1700
2b. 41.2 in.; yes

Independent Practice
5. 11.5 in. **7.** 14.1 in. **9.** 12 feet
11. 52.8 ft; $12^2 + 39^2 = c^2$, so 144
+ 1521 = c^2, 1665 = c^2, and 40.8 ≈
c. Adding this to the height of the

bottom of the tree: 40.8 + 12 =
52.8 ft. **13.** $\sqrt{x^2 + x^2}$ (or $\sqrt{2x^2}$ or
$x\sqrt{2}$); if $a = x$ and $b = x$, then
$x^2 + x^2 = c^2$. Thus, $c = \sqrt{x^2 + x^2}$.

LESSON 8.2

Your Turn
2. not a right triangle **3.** a right
triangle **4.** right triangle **5.** not
a right triangle **6.** Yes; 140^2 +
$480^2 = 250,000$; $500^2 = 250,000$;
250,000 = 250,000 **7.** No; 18^2 +
$19^2 = 685$, $25^2 = 625$, 685 ≠
625 **8.** No; there are no pairs of
whole numbers whose squares
add to $12^2 = 144$.

Guided Practice
1a. 6; 8, 10 **b.** 6, 8, 10; 26, 64, 100;
100, 100; is **2.** 9, 12, 16; 9, 12, 16;
81, 144, 256; 225, 256; is not
3. Yes; $2.5^2 + 6^2 = 42.25$, $6.5^2 =$
42.25, 42.25 = 42.25

Independent Practice
5. right triangle **7.** not a right
triangle **9.** not a right triangle
11. right triangle **13.** not a right
triangle **15.** No; $13^2 + 14^2 = 365$,
$15^2 = 225$, and 365 ≠ 225.
17. No; $6^2 + 10^2 = 136$, $12^2 = 144$,
and 136 ≠ 144. **19.** Yes; since
$0.75^2 + 1^2 = 1.25^2$, the triangles
are right triangles. Adjoining them
at their hypotenuses will form a
rectangle with sides 1 m and
0.75 m. **21.** Yes **23.** The diagonals
should measure $\sqrt{90^2 + 48^2} = 102$
yards if the sides of the field meet
at right angles.

LESSON 8.3

Your Turn
1. 6.5 units **4.** approximately
214.7 meters

Guided Practice
1. 5.8 units **2.** 13 units
3. 103.6 miles

Independent Practice

7a. $ET = \sqrt{113}$ units **b.** Let $(x_1, y_1) = (-3, 4)$ and $(x_2, y_2) = (4, -4)$. Substitute the coordinates into the Distance Formula and then simplify. **9.** (5, 0), (4, 3), (3, 4), (0, 5), (−3, 4), (−4, 3), (−5, 0), (−4, −3), (−3, −4), (0, −5), (3, −4), (4, −3); The points would form a circle.

11.

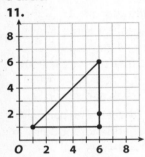

Let $(x_1, y_1) = (6, 6)$, and $(x_2, y_2) = (1, 1)$. Use the Distance Formula to show that hypotenuse $= \sqrt{50} \approx 7.1$.

LESSON 9.1

Your Turn

4. 471 in³ **5.** 602.9 ft³ **6.** 452.2 in³

Guided Practice

1. two congruent circles that lie in parallel planes **2.** Sample answer: 427 in³; there are 61 cubes on the bottom of the cylinder. The height is 7 cubes. $V = 61 \times 7 = 427$ in³ **3.** 6; 15; 36; 15; 1695.6; 1695.6 **4.** 1.35; 15.5

Independent Practice

7. 1205.8 in **9.** 942 in² **11.** 803.8 m² **13.** 6838.9 in² **15.** 339,120 m² **17.** 57.7 in² **19.** Divide the diameter by 2 to find the radius. Substitute the volume and radius in $V = \pi r^2 h$ and solve for h.

LESSON 9.2

Your Turn

4. 942 cm² **5.** 12.6 ft² **6.** about 19,300,000 m²

Guided Practice

1. 45; 10; 450; 450; 150; 150 **2.** 54 m²; the volume of a cylinder is 3 times the volume of a cone with a congruent base and height. **3.** 65.9 ft² **4.** 113,982 in² **5.** 141.3 in² **6.** 13,083.3 m²

Independent Practice

9. 25.1 in² **11.** 94.2 m² **13.** 167.5 in² **15.** 628 in² **17.** 6 cm **19a.** either the diameter or the radius of the base **b.** No; the cone is tapered from top to bottom. An equal volume of sand has a smaller radius and a greater height as the sand rises. **21.** Since the radius and height of the cones and cylinder are the same, it will take 3 cones to equal the volume of the cylinder.

LESSON 9.3

Your Turn

2. 4186.7 cm² **3.** 20.6 m² **6.** 904.3 in²

Guided Practice

1. the same distance **2.** radius **3.** 4.2 in² **4.** 4,186.7 cm² **5.** 14.1 ft² **6.** 4.2 yd² **7.** 12.8 in² **8.** 407.5 in² **9a.** $\frac{1}{3}$; the ball takes up $\frac{2}{3}$ of the space so $\frac{1}{3}$ is empty. **b.** $(2r)^3 = 8r^3$ **c.** Almost $\frac{1}{2}$; the empty space is $8r^3 - \frac{4}{3}\pi r^3$, or about $3.81r^2$, and $\frac{3.81}{8} \approx 0.48$. **10.** Find the radius. Then substitute r into the formula $V = \frac{4}{3}\pi r^3$ and simplify.

Independent Practice

11. 124.7 m² **13.** 904.3 in² **15.** 5572.5 in² **17.** 5389 cm² **19.** 1766.3 cm² **21.** Divide $V = \frac{4}{3}\pi r^3$ by 2 to find the volume of the hemisphere: $V = \frac{2}{3}\pi r^3$. Add the volume of the cylinder, $V = h = \pi r^3$: $V = \frac{2}{3}\pi r^3 + \pi r^3 = \frac{5}{3}\pi r^3$. **23.** 12.3 in² **25.** The cylindrical glass; the cylinder has a volume of πr^3, the hemisphere's volume is $\frac{2}{3}\pi r^3$, and the cone's volume is $\frac{1}{3}\pi r^3$. **27.** About 16 feet; 136 is 8 times 17, so the volume must be

8 times as big. Because $2^3 = 8$, this means the radius, and thus the diameter, must be twice as big.

LESSON 10.1

Your Turn

1. 1,728 square inches **2.** 240 cm², 288 cm² **3.** 126 in², 156 in²

Guided Practice

1. 162 in², 202 in² **2.** 100 ft², 148 ft² **3.** 254 in² **4.** 54.6 cm²

Independent Practice

7. 576 in²; 672 in² **9.** 72 ft²; 84 ft² **11.** 504 in²; 672 in² **13.** 5 in. **15.** 235 ft² **17.** about 2100 mm² **19.** 1680 cm²

LESSON 10.2

Your Turn

2. 489.8 cm²; 415.9 cm² **3.** 109.9 ft²; 186.8 ft² **4.** 62.8 in², 87.9 in²

Guided Practice

1. 5; 31.4; 8; 251.2; 25; 157; 157; 251.2; 408.2

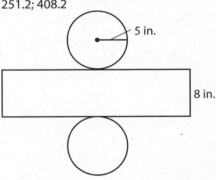

2. 9; 24

Independent Practice

5. 80.1 in², 94.2 in² **7.** 201 in², 301.4 in² **9.** 241.8 in², 549.5 in² **11.** 56 cm² **13.** Total surface area includes all surfaces. Lateral does not include bases. **15.** 66 ft² **17.** 192π in²

MODULE 11

LESSON 11.1

Your Turn

2. 64 weeks

Guided Practice

1. $x = -4$ **2.** $x = 5$ **3.** 4 personal training sessions

Independent Practice

7a. $12 + 5x = 18 + 3x; x = 3$; 3 hours **b.** Darlene's Dog Sitting; the cost would be $33, as opposed to $37 at Derrick's Dog Sitting. **9.** $3x - 2 = x + 10; x = 6$ **11.** $8x - 20 = x + 15; x = 5$ **13.** $9x + 3 = 7x + 19; x = 8$; 75 chairs **15.** $3x + 6 = 5x + 2; x = 2$; 6 laps

LESSON 11.2

Your Turn

3. $k = -35$ **4.** $4 = -\frac{9}{16}$ **5.** $1.9x = 1.3x + 37.44$; 62.4 lb

Guided Practice

1a. $60 + 50.45x = 57.95x$ **b.** $x = 8$; 8 months **2.** $n = 28$ **3.** $b = 60$ **4.** $m = 33$ **5.** $t = -0.8$ **6.** $w = 12$ **7.** $p = -2$

Independent Practice

11. 60 tiles **13a.** 100 mi **b.** $80 **17.** $C = 1.8C + 32$; $-40°F = -40°C$ **19.** When you attempt to solve the equation, you eliminate the variable from both sides of the equation, leaving a false statement such as $-30 = 24$. Since the statement is false, the equation must not have a solution. **21.** No; his equation gives 3, 4, and 5 as the integers. The correct equation is $k + (k + 2) + (k + 4) = 4k$, which gives $k = 6$ and the integers 6, 8, 10.

LESSON 11.3

Your Turn

2. $68 + 4h > 74 + 2h, h > 3$; after 3 hours

Guided Practice

1a. $525 + 75w < 150w$ **b.** after 7 weeks **2.** $150 - 7x = 120 - 5x$; after 15 days

Independent Practice

5a. $100 + 4p < 7p$ **b.** $p > 33.33$; at least 34 pizzas **9.** $x + 20 > 4x - 1; x > 7$ **11.** Cameron's forgot to reverse the inequality symbol when dividing both sides by -4.

LESSON 11.4

Your Turn

1. $\frac{3}{4}x > x - 5; x < 20$ **3.** after 7 days

Guided Practice

1. $\frac{3}{4}x < 6 + x; x > -24$ **2.** $11 + \frac{1}{5}x > \frac{3}{4}x; x < 20$ **3.** $9.95m < 4.95m + 49.95$; $m < 9.99$; between 0 and 9 months

Independent Practice

7. 4 hours or less **11.** more than $25,000 **13a.** No; the point (6, 11) lies above the line. **b.** $x > -\frac{15}{4}$; every point on the line $y = 2\frac{1}{2}$ for which the x-value is greater than $-\frac{15}{4}$ is a solution of the inequality. **15.** When x is between -1.5 and 1.5; $|x|$ for $a > 0$ whenever x is between $-a$ and a.

UNIT 5 Selected Answers

MODULE 12

LESSON 12.1

Your Turn
4.

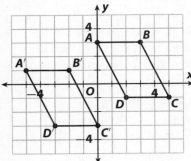

Guided Practice
1. transformation **2.** preimage; image **3.** The orientation will be the same. **4.** They are congruent.
5.

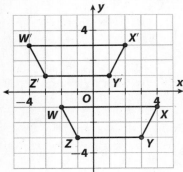

Independent Practice
7a.

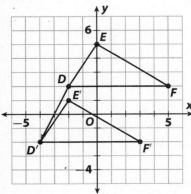

b. The translation moved the triangle 2 units to the left and 4 units down. **c.** They are congruent.
9.

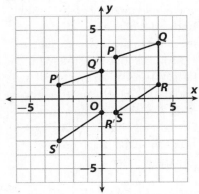

11. The hot air balloon was translated 4 units to the right and 5 units up.
13a.–c.

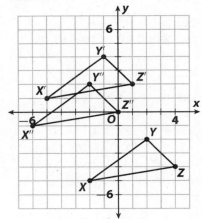

d. The original triangle was translated 4 units up and 4 units to the left.

LESSON 12.2

Your Turn
4.

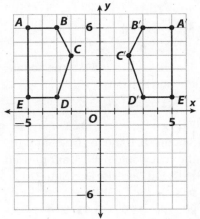

Guided Practice
1. line of reflection
2a.

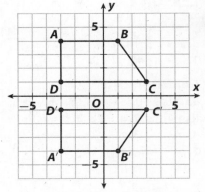

b. They are congruent. **c.** The orientation would be reversed horizontally: the figure from left to right in the preimage would match the figure from right to left in the image.

Independent Practice
5. C and D **7.** Since each triangle is either a reflection or translation of triangle C, they are all congruent. **9.** Yes; if the point lies on the line of reflection, then the image and the preimage will be the same point.

11a.–c.

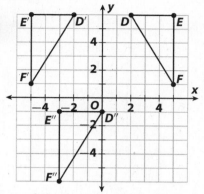

d. Sample answer: Translate triangle *DEF* 7 units down and 2 units to the left. Then reflect the image across the *y*-axis.

LESSON 12.3

Your Turn

6.–7.

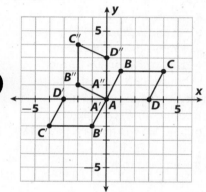

8. 2, −4

Guided Practice

1. point **2.** The triangle is turned 90° to the left about vertex *E*.
3. Yes, the figures are congruent.
4.

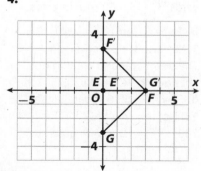

5.

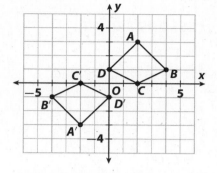

Independent Practice

7a. *ABC* was rotated 90° counterclockwise. **b.** *A'* (3, 1); *B'* (2, 3); *C'* (−1, 4) **9.** 180° rotation
11. 90° clockwise **13.** 90° counterclockwise
15.

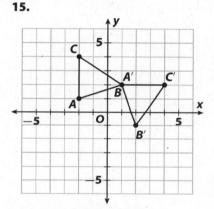

17. 2 times; 1 time; 4 times
19. If *A* is at the origin, then so is *A'* for any rotation about the origin. Otherwise, *A'* is on the *x*-axis for 90° and 270° rotations and on the *y*-axis for a 180° rotation.

LESSON 12.4

Your Turn

1. (−6, −5), (−6, 0), (−3, −5), and (−3, 0); the rectangle is translated 6 units to the left and 3 units down. **2.** *A'*(−2, −6), *B'*(0, −5), and *C'*(3, 1) **4.** *J'*(4, −2), *K'*(−5, 1), and *L'*(−2, 2)

Guided Practice

1. *X'*(3, −2), *Y'*(5, 0), and *Z'*(7, −6)

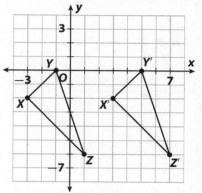

2. The *x*-coordinate remains the same, while the *y*-coordinate changes sign. **3.** The triangle is rotated 90° clockwise.

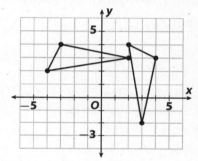

Independent Practice

5. $(x, y) \rightarrow (x + 5, y − 2)$; translation of 2 units to the left and 5 units down **7.** $(x, y) \rightarrow (x − 3.2, y + 1)$; *Y'*(4.3, 6), *Z'*(5.8, 5)
9. The rectangle is translated 2 units to the left and 4 units down.

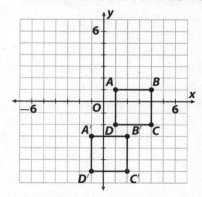

11. $(x, y) \rightarrow (x + 0.5, y − 0.25)$
13a. (−5, −5); *x* and *y* are equal, so switching *x* and *y* has no effect on the coordinates. **b.** $y = x$ **c.** The triangle is reflected across the line $y = x$.

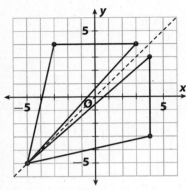

15a. $A''(1, 0)$, $B''(0, 3)$, and $C''(4, 3)$
b. $(x, y) \rightarrow (x + 3, y + 2)$

MODULE 13

LESSON 13.1

Your Turn
5. The scale factor is 0.5.

Guided Practice
1. 2; 2 **2.** equal; equal **3.** 2
4. congruent **5.** 2

Independent Practice
7. No; the ratios of the lengths of the corresponding sides are not equal. **9.** Yes; a dilation produces an image similar to the original figure. **11.** Yes; each coordinate of triangle $U'V'W'$ is $\frac{3}{4}$ times the corresponding coordinate of triangle UVW. **13.** changed; same; same **15.** same; changed; same
17. 3 **19.** Locate the corresponding vertices of the triangles, and draw lines connecting each pair. The lines will intersect at the center of dilation.

LESSON 13.2

Your Turn
5. $(x, y) \rightarrow \left(\frac{1}{3}x, \frac{1}{3}y\right)$

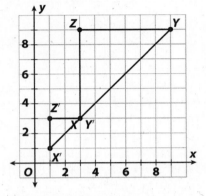

Guided Practice
1.

PreImage	Image
(2, 0)	(3, 0)
(0, 2)	(0, 3)
(−2, 0)	(−3, 0)
(0, −2)	(0, −3)

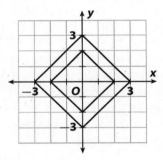

2.

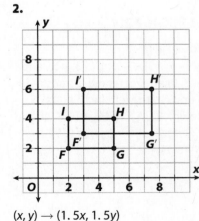

$(x, y) \rightarrow (1.5x, 1.5y)$

3.

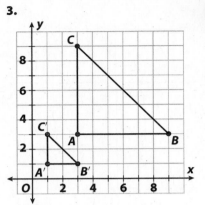

$(x, y) \rightarrow \left(\frac{1}{3}x, \frac{1}{3}y\right)$

Independent Practice
5. Green square: $(x, y) \rightarrow (2x, 2y)$; Purple square $(x, y) \rightarrow \left(\frac{1}{2}x, \frac{1}{2}y\right)$
7. $(x, y) \rightarrow \left(\frac{2}{3}x, \frac{2}{3}y\right)$ **9a.** The scale factor is 48. **b.** 48 inches or 4 feet **c.** $(x, y) \rightarrow (48x, 48y)$
d. $Q'(2.5, 2.5)$, $R'(8.75, 2.5)$, $S'(8.75, 6.25)$, and $T'(2.5, 6.25)$
e. Dimensions on blueprint: 6.25 in. by 3.75 in. Dimensions in house: 25 ft by 15 ft **11.** The crew member's calculation is incorrect. The scale factor is $\frac{1}{20}$, not $\frac{1}{12}$. **13.** The figure is dilated by a factor of 2, but the orientation of the figure is rotated 180°.

LESSON 13.3

Your Turn
2. 1152 square inches

Guided Practice
1. 60; 225 **2.** 36; 72 **3.** 320 yards **4.** $\frac{2}{5}$ **5.** 960 square yards

Independent Practice
7. Yes. The scale factor is 1. The perimeter and area do not change. **9.** 9 cm **11a.** 0.75 inch
b. 6 inches **c.** 36 square inches
13. No; the area of $W'X'Y'Z'$ is $108 \cdot \left(\frac{1}{3}\right)^2 = 12$ square units.

UNIT 6 Selected Answers

MODULE 14

LESSON 14.1

Your Turn

6. Positive and basically linear: older students would be taller and read at a higher level.

Guided Practice

1.

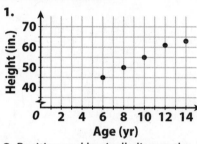

2. Positive and basically linear; the plot shows Bob's height increasing as he gets older. **3.** There is a cluster for 20–23 shots attempted and a lesser one for 7–14 shots attempted; (35, 18) is an outlier.

Independent Practice

5. A generally positive linear association: as the year increases, so does the winning distance.
7. Nonlinear; the points generally rise up to 1988 and then fall from 1988 to 2012, so there is no overall linear pattern. **13.** Yes; for example, the points may appear to lie along a rising or falling curve, or may generally rise or fall, but not in a way that suggests a linear association.

LESSON 14.2

Your Turn

6. Sample answer: $y = \frac{9}{10}x$

Guided Practice

Answers for 1–4 may vary slightly.

1.

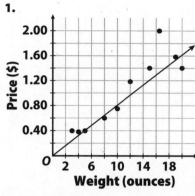

2. Most data points are close to the trend line, with about the same number of points above and below the line. **3.** $y = 8.2x$
4. $0.57; $4.10

Independent Practice

Answers for 6–14 may vary slightly.

7. negative; basically linear
9a. about −6°F **b.** about −22°F
11.

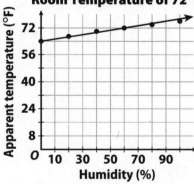

Apparent Temperature at a Room Temperature of 72 °F

13. about 73°F **17a.** No; two data points are not enough to create a scatter plot or trendline. A random sample of many counties should be used. **b.** Marlene's conjecture is incorrect. Harris and Dallas counties are counterexamples to Marlene's original conclusion.

MODULE 15

LESSON 15.1

Your Turn

2. The MAD for Barista A is 0.6 oz, and for Barista B is 0.2 oz, so Barista B's coffees showed less variability.
3. A: MAD ≈ 0.0017; B: MAD ≈ 0.0063; A has less variability.

Guided Practice

1. did
a. 45.1 min
b. 0.4 min
2. 44.9; 0.733333; did not

Independent Practice

5. 1.6 people
7. The MAD at the beginning was about 3.7, and at the end it was about 2.1, so they made progress.
9. The mean for Austin is 31.855 in., and for San Antonio is 30.459 in.; Austin.
13a. mean = 1, MAD = 0; Because 1 is the only data value, it is the mean of the data set and does not deviate from the mean.
b. mean = 1.5, MAD = 0.5; $1 + 2 = 3$, and $3 \div 2 = 1.5$. Also, both 1 and 2 are 0.5 away from 1.5.
c. Increase; the values are getting larger, so the mean increases, and they are getting more spread out, so the MAD increases.
15. No; the absolute differences from the mean are nonnegative, so their mean, or the MAD, is nonnegative.

Selected Answers

LESSON 15. 2

Independent Practice

5. Shop B's sample is most representative because it is the largest sample. Shop C's sample is least representative because it is the smallest. **7.** 2; that about 100 of the 1000 shirts are below standard **9.** 60 inches; yes; the sample is random and fairly large compared to the number of competitors. **11.** The larger the random sample, the more likely it is to represent the population well.

UNIT 7 Selected Answers

MODULE 16

LESSON 16.1

Your Turn

4. $223.86; $5372.64; $372.64
5. $256.93; $6166.32; $1166.32
8. $242.43; $5818.32; $818.32
9. $139.15; $6679.20; $1679.20

Guided Practice

1. Credit Card: 1500; 24; 20; 76.34; 76.34; 1832.16; 332.16 Bank Loan: 1500; 24; 11; 69.91; 69.91; 1677.84; 177.84 Kyle pays $154.32 less in interest if he borrows from the bank. **2.** 132.57; 132.57; 12; 1590.84; 90.84; 87

Independent Practice

5a. $12,304.08 **b.** $13,960.80
c. $11,280.96 **7.** $1023.12
9. 14% for 5 years
11. loan length **13.** 91 months

LESSON 16.2

Your Turn

6. $3.03

Independent Practice

1. $90 **3a.** $508.41 **b.** $408
c. The account with compounded interest earned $100.41 more interest. **5.** $8702.87 **7.** 11 years; substituting in $I = Prt$ gives $550 = 1000(0.05)t$, or $550 = 50t$. Dividing both sides by 50 gives a time of $t = 11$ years. **9.** Line: $y = 50 + 50(0.05)(x)$; Curve: $y = 50(1 + 0.05)^x$ **11.** No; the left side of the equation represents the total amount in the compound interest account, not just the interest. It should be $x(1 + 0.06)^2 - x$.

LESSON 16.3

Guided Practice

1. stored-value card **2.** cash
3. debit card **5.** Responsible; the new rate will save them $16 per month; $(45 \times 2) - 74 = 16$.

Independent Practice

9. The money has already been paid to a bank or lending institution by the purchaser of the money order.

LESSON 16.4

Independent Practice

5. Year 1: $0; $4800; $4800; $57.60; $4857.60; Year 1: $4857.60; $4800; $9657.60; $115.89; $9773.49; Laura has saved $9,773.49 for college.

Glossary/Glosario

A

ENGLISH	SPANISH	EXAMPLES
absolute value The distance of a number from zero on a number line; shown by | |.	**valor absoluto** Distancia a la que está un número de 0 en una recta numérica. El símbolo del valor absoluto es | |.	$|-5| = 5$
accuracy The closeness of a given measurement or value to the actual measurement or value.	**exactitud** Cercanía de una medida o un valor a la medida o el valor real.	
acute angle An angle that measures greater than 0° and less than 90°.	**ángulo agudo** Ángulo que mide mas de 0° y menos de 90°.	
acute triangle A triangle with all angles measuring less than 90°.	**triángulo acutángulo** Triángulo en el que todos los ángulos miden menos de 90°.	
Addition Property of Equality The property that states that if you add the same number to both sides of an equation, the new equation will have the same solution.	**Propiedad de igualdad de la suma** Propiedad que establece que puedes sumar el mismo número a ambos lados de una ecuación y la nueva ecuación tendrá la misma solución.	$14 - 6 = 8$ $\underline{+6 \quad +6}$ $14 = 14$
Addition Property of Opposites The property that states that the sum of a number and its opposite equals zero.	**Propiedad de la suma de los opuestos** Propiedad que establece que la suma de un número y su opuesto es cero.	$12 + (-12) = 0$
additive inverse The opposite of a number.	**inverso aditivo** El opuesto de un número.	The additive inverse of 5 is −5.
adjacent angles Angles in the same plane that have a common vertex and a common side.	**ángulos adyacentes** Ángulos en el mismo plano que comparten un vértice y un lado.	
algebraic expression An expression that contains at least one variable.	**expresión algebraica** Expresión que contiene al menos una variable.	$x + 8$ $4(m - b)$
algebraic inequality An inequality that contains at least one variable.	**desigualdad algebraica** Desigualdad que contiene al menos una variable.	$x + 3 > 10$ $5a > b + 3$

ENGLISH	SPANISH	EXAMPLES

alternate exterior angles For two lines intersected by a transversal, a pair of angles that lie on opposite sides of the transversal and outside the other two lines.

ángulos alternos externos Dadas dos rectas cortadas por una transversal, par de ángulos no adyacentes ubicados en los lados opuestos de la transversal y fuera de las otras dos rectas.

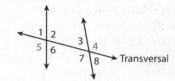

∠4 and ∠5 are alternate exterior angles.

alternate interior angles For two lines intersected by a transversal, a pair of nonadjacent angles that lie on opposite sides of the transversal and between the other two lines.

ángulos alternos internos Dadas dos rectas cortadas por una transversal, par de ángulos no adyacentes ubicados en los lados opuestos de la transversal y entre de las otras dos rectas.

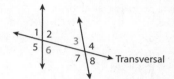

∠3 and ∠6 are alternate interior angles.

angle A figure formed by two rays with a common endpoint called the vertex.

ángulo Figura formada por dos rayos con un extremo común llamado vértice.

angle bisector A line, segment, or ray that divides an angle into two congruent angles.

bisectriz de un ángulo Línea, segmento o rayo que divide un ángulo en dos ángulos congruentes.

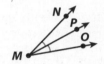

arc An unbroken part of a circle.

arco Parte continua de un círculo.

area The number of square units needed to cover a given surface.

área El número de unidades cuadradas que se necesitan para cubrir una superficie dada.

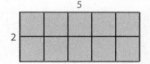

arithmetic sequence An ordered list of numbers in which the difference between consecutive terms is always the same.

sucesión aritmética Lista ordenada de números en la que la diferencia entre términos consecutivos es siempre la misma.

The sequence 2, 5, 8, 11, 14 ... is an arithmetic sequence.

association A description of how data sets are related.

asociación Descripción de cómo se relaciona un conjunto de datos.

Associative Property (of Addition) The property that states that for all real numbers a, b, and c, the sum is always the same, regardless of their grouping.

Propiedad asociativa (de la suma) Propiedad que establece que para todos los números reales a, b y c, la suma siempre es la misma sin importar cómo se agrupen.

$$a + b + c = (a + b) + c = a + (b + c)$$

Glossary/Glosario

Associative Property (of Multiplication) The property that states that for all real numbers *a, b,* and *c,* their product is always the same, regardless of their grouping.

Propiedad asociativa (de la multiplicación) Propiedad que establece que para todos los números reales *a, b* y *c,* el producto siempre es el mismo, sin importar cómo se agrupen.

$a \cdot b \cdot c = (a \cdot b) \cdot c = a \cdot (b \cdot c)$

---

average The sum of a set of data divided by the number of items in the data set; also called *mean.*

promedio La suma de los elementos de un conjunto de datos dividida entre el número de elementos del conjunto. También se llama media.

Data set: 4, 6, 7, 8, 10

Average: $\frac{4+6+7+8+10}{5}$

$= \frac{35}{5} = 7$

B

back-to-back stem-and-leaf plot A stem-and-leaf plot that compares two sets of data by displaying one set of data to the left of the stem and the other to the right.

diagrama doble de tallo y hojas Diagrama de tallo y hojas que compara dos conjuntos de datos presentando uno de ellos a la izquierda del tallo y el otro a la derecha.

Data set A: 9, 12, 14, 16, 23, 27
Data set B: 6, 8, 10, 13, 15, 16, 21

Set A		Set B
9	0	6 8
6 4 2	1	0 3 5 6
7 3	2	1

Key: |2| 1 means 21
7 |2| means 27

---

bar graph A graph that uses vertical or horizontal bars to display data.

gráfica de barras Gráfica en la que se usan barras verticales u horizontales para presentar datos.

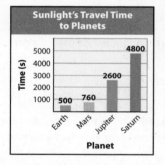

---

base When a number is raised to a power, the number that is used as a factor is the base.

base Cuando un número es elevado a una potencia, el número que se usa como factor es la base.

$3^5 = 3 \cdot 3 \cdot 3 \cdot 3 \cdot 3$; 3 is the base.

---

base (of a polygon or three-dimensional figure) A side of a polygon; a face of a three-dimensional figure by which the figure is measured or classified.

base (de un polígono o figura tridimensional) Lado de un polígono; cara de una figura tridimensional según la cual se mide o se clasifica la figura.

Bases of a cylinder

Bases of a prism

Base of a cone

Base of a pyramid

Glossary/Glosario

biased question A question that leads people to give a certain answer.

pregunta tendenciosa pregunta que lleva a las personas a dar una respuesta determinada

---

biased sample A sample that does not fairly represent the population.

muestra no representativa Muestra que no representa adecuadamente la población.

---

binomial A polynomial with two terms.

binomio Polinomio con dos términos.

$x + y$
$2a^2 - 3$
$4m^3n^2 + 6mn^4$

---

bisect To divide into two congruent parts.

trazar una bisectriz Dividir en dos partes congruentes.

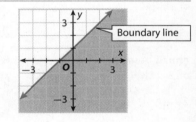

$\overrightarrow{JK}$ bisects $\angle LJM$.

---

bivariate data A set of data that is made of two paired variables.

datos bivariados Conjunto de datos compuesto de dos variables apareadas.

---

boundary line The set of points where the two sides of a two-variable linear inequality are equal.

línea de límite Conjunto de puntos donde los dos lados de una desigualdad lineal con dos variables son iguales.

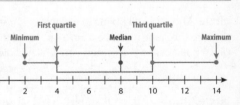

---

box-and-whisker plot A graph that shows how data are distributed by using the median, quartiles, least value, and greatest value; also called a *box plot*.

gráfica de mediana y rango Gráfica para demostrar la distribución de datos utilizando la mediana, los cuartiles y los valores menos y más grande; también llamado gráfica de caja.

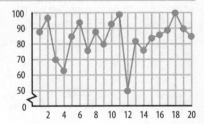

---

break (graph) A zigzag on a horizontal or vertical scale of a graph that indicates that some of the numbers on the scale have been omitted.

discontinuidad (gráfica) Zig-zag en la escala horizontal o vertical de una gráfica que indica la omisión de algunos de los números de la escala.

C

capacity The amount a container can hold when filled.

capacidad Cantidad que cabe en un recipiente cuando se llena.

A large milk container has a capacity of 1 gallon.

Celsius A metric scale for measuring temperature in which 0 °C is the freezing point of water and 100 °C is the boiling point of water; also called *centigrade*.

Celsius Escala métrica para medir la temperatura, en la que 0 °C es el punto de congelación del agua y 100 °C es el punto de ebullición. También se llama *centígrado*.

Glossary/Glosario

center (of a circle) The point inside a circle that is the same distance from all the points on the circle.

centro (de un círculo) Punto interior de un círculo que se encuentra a la misma distancia de todos los puntos de la circunferencia.

center of dilation The point of intersection of lines through each pair of corresponding vertices in a dilation.

centro de una dilatación Punto de intersección de las líneas que pasan a través de cada par de vértices correspondientes en una dilatación.

center of rotation The point about which a figure is rotated.

centro de una rotación Punto alrededor del cual se hace girar una figura.

central angle An angle formed by two radii with its vertex at the center of a circle.

ángulo central de un círculo Ángulo formado por dos radios cuyo vértice se encuentra en el centro de un círculo.

chord A segment with its endpoints on a circle.

cuerda Segmento de recta cuyos extremos forman parte de un círculo.

circle The set of all points in a plane that are the same distance from a given point called the center.

círculo Conjunto de todos los puntos en un plano que se encuentran a la misma distancia de un punto dado llamado centro.

circle graph A graph that uses sectors of a circle to compare parts to the whole and parts to other parts.

gráfica circular Gráfica que usa secciones de un círculo para comparar partes con el todo y con otras partes.

circuit A path in a graph that begins and ends at the same vertex.

circuito Una trayectoria en una gráfica que empieza y termina en el mismo vértice.

circumference The distance around a circle.

circumferencia Distancia alrededor de un círculo.

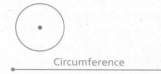

Glossary/Glosario

ENGLISH	SPANISH	EXAMPLES

clockwise A circular movement to the right in the direction shown.

en el sentido de las manecillas del reloj Movimiento circular en la dirección que se indica.

---

cluster A set of closely grouped data.

agrupación Conjunto de datos bien agrupados.

---

clustering A condition that occurs when data points in a scatter plot are grouped more in one part of the graph than another.

arracimando Una condición que ocurre cuando los datos están apiñando en una parte de una diagrama de dispersión mas que en otras partes.

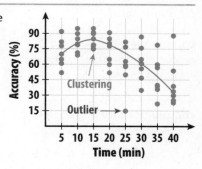

---

coefficient The number that is multiplied by the variable in an algebraic expression.

coeficiente Número que se multiplica por la variable en una expresión algebraica.

5 is the coefficient in 5*b*.

---

combination An arrangement of items or events in which order does not matter.

combinación Agrupación de objetos o sucesos en la que el orden no es importante.

For objects *A*, *B*, *C*, and *D*, there are 6 different combinations of 2 objects: *AB, AC, AD, BC, BD, CD*.

---

commission A fee paid to a person for making a sale.

comisión Pago que recibe una persona por realizar una venta.

---

commission rate The fee paid to a person who makes a sale expressed as a percent of the selling price.

tasa de comisión Pago que recibe una persona por hacer una venta, expresado como un porcentaje del precio de venta.

A commission rate of 5% on a sale of $10,000 results in a commission of $500.

---

common denominator A denominator that is the same in two or more fractions.

común denominador Denominador que es común a dos o más fracciones.

The common denominator of $\frac{5}{8}$ and $\frac{2}{8}$ is 8.

---

common factor A number that is a factor of two or more numbers.

factor común Número que es factor de dos o más números.

8 is a common factor of 16 and 40.

---

common multiple A number that is a multiple of each of two or more numbers.

común múltiplo Número que es múltiplo de dos o más números.

15 is a common multiple of 3 and 5.

---

common ratio The ratio each term is multiplied by to produce the next term in a geometric sequence.

razón común Razón por la que se multiplica cada término para obtener el siguiente término de una sucesión geométrica.

In the geometric sequence 32, 16, 8, 4, 2, …, the common ratio is $\frac{1}{2}$.

Commutative Property (of Addition) The property that states that two or more numbers can be added in any order without changing the sum.

Propiedad conmutativa (de la suma) Propiedad que establece que sumar dos o más números en cualquier orden no altera la suma.

$8 + 20 = 20 + 8; a + b = b + a$

Commutative Property (of Multiplication) The property that states that two or more numbers can be multiplied in any order without changing the product.

Propiedad conmutativa (de la multiplicación) Propiedad que establece que multiplicar dos o más números en cualquier orden no altera el producto.

$6 \cdot 12 = 12 \cdot 6; a \cdot b = b \cdot a$

compatible numbers Numbers that are close to the given numbers that make estimation or mental calculation easier.

números compatibles Números que están cerca de los números dados y hacen más fácil la estimación o el cálculo mental.

To estimate $7,957 + 5,009$, use the compatible numbers 8,000 and 5,000:
$8,000 + 5,000 = 13,000$

complement The set of all outcomes in the sample space that are not the event.

complemento La serie de resultados que no están en el suceso.

Experiment: rolling a number cube
Sample space: {1, 2, 3, 4, 5, 6}
Event: rolling a 1, 3, 4, or 6
Complement: rolling a 2 or 5

complementary angles Two angles whose measures add to 90°.

ángulos complementarios Dos ángulos cuyas medidas suman 90°.

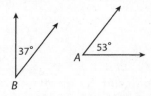

The complement of a 53° angle is a 37° angle.

composite figure A figure made up of simple geometric shapes.

figura compuesta Figura formada por figuras geométricas simples.

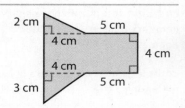

composite number A number greater than 1 that has more than two whole-number factors.

número compuesto Número mayor que 1 que tiene más de dos factores que son números cabales.

4, 6, 8, and 9 are composite numbers.

compound interest Interest earned or paid on principal and previously earned or paid interest.

interés compuesto Interés que se gana o se paga sobre el capital y los intereses previamente ganados o pagados.

If $100 is put into an account with an interest rate of 5% compounded monthly, then after 2 years, the account will have $100\left(1 + \frac{0.05}{12}\right)^{12 \cdot 2} = \$110.49$

cone A three-dimensional figure with one vertex and one circular base.

cono Figura tridimensional con un vértice y una base circular.

congruence transformation A transformation that results in an image that is the same shape and the same size as the original figure.

transformación de congruencia Una transformación que resulta en una imagen que tiene la misma forma y el mismo tamaño como la figura original.

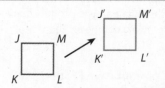

congruent Having the same size and shape; the symbol for congruent is ≅.

congruentes Que tienen la misma forma y el mismo tamaño expresado por ≅.

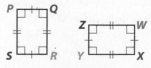

$PQRS \cong WXYZ$

congruent angles Angles that have the same measure.

ángulos congruentes Ángulos que tienen la misma medida.

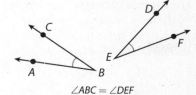

$\angle ABC = \angle DEF$

---

congruent figures See *congruent*.

figures congruentes Vea *congruente*.

---

congruent segments Segments that have the same length.

segmentos congruentes Segmentos que tienen la misma longitud.

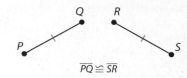

$\overline{PQ} \cong \overline{SR}$

---

conjecture A statement believed to be true.

conjetura Enunciado que se supone verdadero.

---

constant A value that does not change.

constante Valor que no cambia.

$3, 0, \pi$

---

constant of variation The constant k in direct and inverse variation equations.

constante de variación La constante k en ecuaciones de variación directa e inversa.

$y = 5x$
↑
constant of variation

---

continuous graph A graph made up of connected lines or curves.

gráfica continua Gráfica compuesta por líneas rectas *o* curvas conectadas.

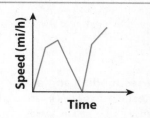

---

convenience sample A sample based on members of the population that are readily available.

muestra de conveniencia Una muestra basada en miembros de la población que están fácilmente disponibles.

---

conversion factor A fraction whose numerator and denominator represent the same quantity but use different units; the fraction is equal to 1 because the numerator and denominator are equal.

factor de conversión Fracción cuyo numerador y denominador representan la misma cantidad pero con unidades distintas; la fracción es igual a 1 porque el numerador y el denominador son iguales.

$\frac{24 \text{ hours}}{1 \text{ day}}$ and $\frac{1 \text{ day}}{24 \text{ hours}}$

---

coordinate One of the numbers of an ordered pair that locate a point on a coordinate graph.

coordenada Uno de los números de un par ordenado que ubica un punto en una gráfica de coordenadas.

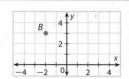

The coordinates of *B* are (−2, 3).

Glossary/Glosario

ENGLISH	SPANISH	EXAMPLES
coordinate plane A plane formed by the intersection of a horizontal number line called the *x*-axis and a vertical number line called the *y*-axis.	**plano cartesiano** Plano formado por la intersección de una recta numérica horizontal llamada eje *x* y otra vertical llamada eje *y*.	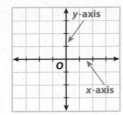
correlation The description of the relationship between two data sets.	**correlación** Descripción de la relación entre dos conjuntos de datos.	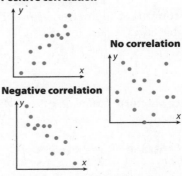
correspondence The relationship between two or more objects that are matched.	**correspondencia** La relación entre dos o más objetos que coinciden.	∠*A* and ∠*D* are corresponding angles. $\overline{AB}$ and $\overline{DE}$ are corresponding sides.
corresponding angles (for lines) For two lines intersected by a transversal, a pair of angles that lie on the same side of the transversal and on the same sides of the other two lines.	**ángulos correspondientes (en líneas)** Dadas dos rectas cortadas por una transversal, el par de ángulos ubicados en el mismo lado de la transversal y en los mismos lados de las otras dos rectas.	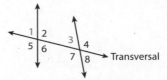 ∠1 and ∠3 are corresponding angles.
corresponding angles (of polygons) Angles in the same relative position in polygons with an equal number of sides.	**ángulos correspondientes (en polígonos)** Ángulos en la misma posición formaron cuando una tercera línea interseca dos líneas.	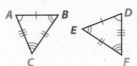 ∠*A* and ∠*D* are corresponding angles.
corresponding sides Matching sides of two or more polygons.	**lados correspondientes** Lados que se ubican en la misma posición relativa en dos o más polígonos.	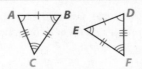 $\overline{AB}$ and $\overline{DE}$ are corresponding sides.
counterclockwise A circular movement to the left in the direction shown.	**en sentido contrario a las manecillas del reloj** Movimiento circular en la dirección que se indica.	

Glossary/Glosario

ENGLISH	SPANISH	EXAMPLES
counterexample An example that proves that a conjecture or statement is false.	**contraejemplo** Ejemplo que demuestra que una conjetura o enunciado es falso.	
cube (geometric figure) A rectangular prism with six congruent square faces.	**cubo (figura geométrica)** Prisma rectangular con seis caras cuadradas congruentes.	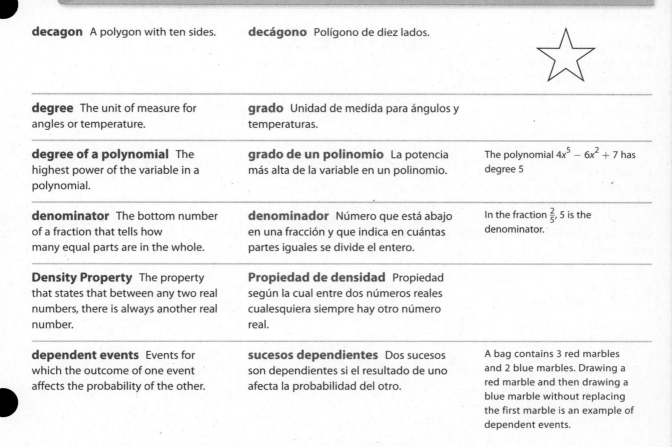
cube (in numeration) A number raised to the third power.	**cubo (en numeración)** Número elevado a la tercera potencia.	$2^3 = 2 \cdot 2 \cdot 2 = 8$ 8 is the cube of 2.
cumulative frequency The sum of successive data items.	**frecuencia acumulativa** La suma de datos sucesivos.	
customary system of measurement The measurement system often used in the United States.	**sistema usual de medidas** El sistema de medidas que se usa comúnmente en Estados Unidos.	inches, feet, miles, ounces, pounds, tons, cups, quarts, gallons
cylinder A three-dimensional figure with two parallel, congruent circular bases connected by a curved lateral surface.	**cilindro** Figura tridimensional con dos bases circulares paralelas y congruentes, unidas por una superficie lateral curva.	

D

decagon A polygon with ten sides.	**decágono** Polígono de diez lados.	
degree The unit of measure for angles or temperature.	**grado** Unidad de medida para ángulos y temperaturas.	
degree of a polynomial The highest power of the variable in a polynomial.	**grado de un polinomio** La potencia más alta de la variable en un polinomio.	The polynomial $4x^5 - 6x^2 + 7$ has degree 5
denominator The bottom number of a fraction that tells how many equal parts are in the whole.	**denominador** Número que está abajo en una fracción y que indica en cuántas partes iguales se divide el entero.	In the fraction $\frac{2}{5}$, 5 is the denominator.
Density Property The property that states that between any two real numbers, there is always another real number.	**Propiedad de densidad** Propiedad según la cual entre dos números reales cualesquiera siempre hay otro número real.	
dependent events Events for which the outcome of one event affects the probability of the other.	**sucesos dependientes** Dos sucesos son dependientes si el resultado de uno afecta la probabilidad del otro.	A bag contains 3 red marbles and 2 blue marbles. Drawing a red marble and then drawing a blue marble without replacing the first marble is an example of dependent events.

ENGLISH	SPANISH	EXAMPLES
dependent variable The output of a function; a variable whose value depends on the value of the input, or independent variable.	**variable dependiente** Salida de una función; variable cuyo valor depende del valor de la entrada, o variable independiente.	For $y = 2x + 1$, y is the dependent variable. input: x output: y
diagonal A line segment that connect two nonadjacent vertices of a polygon.	**diagonal** Segmento de recta que une dos vértices no adyacentes de un polígono.	
diameter A line segment that passes through the center of a circle and has endpoints on the circle, or the length of that segment.	**diámetro** Segmento de recta que pasa por el centro de un círculo y tiene sus extremos en la circunferencia, o bien la longitud de ese segmento.	
dilation A transformation that enlarges or reduces a figure.	**dilatación** Transformación que agranda o reduce una figura.	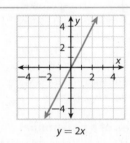
dimensions (geometry) The length, width, or height of a figure.	**dimensiones (geometría)** Longitud, ancho o altura de una figura.	
dimensions (of a matrix) The number of horizontal rows and vertical columns in a matrix.	**dimensiones (de una matriz)** Número de filas y columnas que hay en una matriz.	
direct variation A linear relationship between two variables, x and y, that can be written in the form $y = kx$, where k is a nonzero constant.	**variación directa** Relación lineal entre dos variables, x e y, que puede expresarse en la forma $y = kx$, donde k es una constante distinta de cero.	 $y = 2x$
discount The amount by which the original price is reduced.	**descuento** Cantidad que se resta del precio original de un artículo.	
discrete graph A graph made up of unconnected points.	**gráfica discreta** Gráfica compuesta de puntos no conectados.	**Cost of Photo Printing**

© Houghton Mifflin Harcourt Publishing Company

Glossary/Glosario

disjoint events See *mutually exclusive*.

sucesos disjuntos Vea *mutuamente excluyentes*.

Distributive Property For all real numbers a, b, and c, $a(b + c) = ab + ac$, and $a(b - c) = ab - ac$.

Propiedad distributiva Dados los números reales a, b, y c, $a(b + c) = ab + ac$, y $a(b - c) = ab - ac$.

$5 \cdot 21 = 5(20 + 1) = (5 \cdot 20) + (5 \cdot 1)$

---

dividend The number to be divided in a division problem.

dividendo Número que se divide en un problema de división.

In $8 \div 4 = 2$, 8 is the dividend.

---

divisible Can be divided by a number without leaving a remainder.

divisible Que se puede dividir entre un número sin dejar residuo.

18 is divisible by 3.

Division Property of Equality The property that states that if you divide both sides of an equation by the same nonzero number, the new equation will have the same solution.

Propiedad de igualdad de la división Propiedad que establece que puedes dividir ambos lados de una ecuación entre el mismo número distinto de cero, y la nueva ecuación tendrá la misma solución.

---

divisor The number you are dividing by in a division problem.

divisor El número entre el que se divide en un problema de división.

In $8 \div 4 = 2$, 4 is the divisor.

---

dodecahedron A polyhedron with 12 faces.

dodecaedro Poliedro de 12 caras.

---

domain The set of all possible input values of a function.

dominio Conjunto de todos los posibles valores de entrada de una función.

The domain of the function $y = x^2 + 1$ is all real numbers.

---

double-bar graph A bar graph that compares two related sets of data.

gráfica de doble barra Gráfica de barras que compara dos conjuntos de datos relacionados.

© Houghton Mifflin Harcourt Publishing Company

Glossary/Glosario

double-line graph A line graph that shows how two related sets of data change over time.

gráfica de doble línea Gráfica lineal que muestra cómo cambian con el tiempo dos conjuntos de datos relacionados.

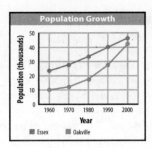

edge The line segment along which two faces of a polyhedron intersect.

arista Segmento de recta donde se intersecan dos caras de un poliedro.

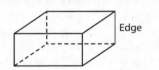

endpoint A point at the end of a line segment or ray.

extremo Un punto ubicado al final de un segmento de recta o rayo.

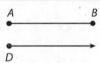

enlargement An increase in size of all dimensions in the same proportions.

agrandamiento Aumento de tamaño de todas las dimensiones en las mismas proporciones.

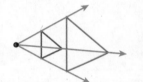

entries (of a matrix) Individual entries in a matrix.

elementos (de una matriz) Entradas individuales de una matriz.

equally likely Outcomes that have the same probability.

resultados igualmente probables Resultados que tienen la misma probabilidad de ocurrir.

When tossing a coin, the outcomes "heads" and "tails" are equally likely.

equation A mathematical sentence that shows that two expressions are equivalent.

ecuación Enunciado matemático que indica que dos expresiones son equivalentes.

$x + 4 = 7$
$6 + 1 = 10 - 3$

equilateral triangle A triangle with three congruent sides.

triángulo equilátero Triángulo con tres lados congruentes.

equivalent Having the same value.

equivalentes Que tienen el mismo valor.

equivalent expression Equivalent expressions have the same value for all values of the variables.

expresión equivalente Las expresiones equivalentes tienen el mismo valor para todos los valores de las variables.

$4x + 5x$ and $9x$ are equivalent expressions.

equivalent fractions Fractions that name the same amount or part.

fracciones equivalentes Fracciones que representan la misma cantidad o parte.

$\frac{1}{2}$ and $\frac{2}{4}$ are equivalent fractions.

Glossary/Glosario

equivalent ratios Ratios that name the same comparison. — **razones equivalentes** Razones que representan la misma comparación. — $\frac{1}{2}$ and $\frac{2}{4}$ are equivalent ratios.

estimate (n) An answer that is close to the exact answer and is found by rounding or other methods. **(v)** To find such an answer. — **estimación (s)** Una solución aproximada a la respuesta exacta que se halla mediante el redondeo u otros métodos. **estimar (v)** Hallar una solución aproximada a la respuesta exacta. — 500 is an estimate for the sum $98 + 287 + 104$.

evaluate To find the value of a numerical or algebraic expression. — **evaluar** Hallar el valor de una expresión numérica o algebraica. — Evaluate $2x + 7$ for $x = 3$.
$2x + 7$
$2(3)+ 7$
$6 + 7$
13

event An outcome or set of outcomes of an experiment or situation. — **suceso** Un resultado o una serie de resultados de un experimento o una situación. — When rolling a number cube, the event "an odd number" consists of the outcomes 1, 3, and 5.

expanded form A number written as the sum of the values of its digits. — **forma desarrollada** Número escrito como suma de los valores de sus dígitos. — 236,536 written in expanded form is $200,000 + 30,000 + 6,000 + 500 + 30 + 6$.

experiment (probability) In probability, any activity based on chance (such as tossing a coin). — **experimento (probabilidad)** En probabilidad, cualquier actividad basada en la posibilidad, como lanzar una moneda. — Tossing a coin 10 times and noting the number of "heads"

experimental probability The ratio of the number of times an event occurs to the total number of trials, or times that the activity is performed. — **probabilidad experimental** Razón del número de veces que ocurre un suceso al número total de pruebas o al número de que se realiza el experimento. — Kendra attempted 27 free throws and made 16 of them. Her experimental probability of making a free throw is $\frac{\text{number made}}{\text{number attempted}} = \frac{16}{27} \approx 0.59$.

exponent The number that indicates how many times the base is used as a factor. — **exponente** Número que indica cuántas veces se usa la base como factor. — $2^3 = 2 \times 2 \times 2 = 8$; 3 is the exponent.

exponential decay An exponential function of the form $f(x) = a \cdot r^x$ in which $0 < r < 1$. — **decremento exponencial** Función exponencial del tipo $f(x) = a \cdot r^x$ en la cual $0 < r < 1$.

exponential form A number is in exponential form when it is written with a base and an exponent. — **forma exponencial** Se dice que un número está en forma exponencial cuando se escribe con una base y un exponente. — 4^2 is the exponential form for $4 \cdot 4$.

exponential function A nonlinear function in which the variable is in the exponent. — **función exponencial** Función no lineal en la que la variable está en el exponente. — $f(x) = 4^x$

exponential growth An exponential function of the form $f(x) = a \cdot r^x$ in which $r > 1$. — **crecimiento exponencial** Función exponencial del tipo $f(x) = a \cdot r^x$ en la cual $r > 1$.

Glossary/Glosario

expression A mathematical phrase that contains operations, numbers, and/or variables.

expresión Enunciado matemático que contiene operaciones, números y/o variables.

$6x + 1$

exterior angle (of a polygon) An angle formed by one side of a polygon and the extension of an adjacent side.

ángulo extreno de un polígono Ángulo formado por un lado de un polígono y la prolongación del lado adyacente.

F

face A flat surface of a polyhedron.

cara Superficie plana de un poliedro.

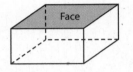
Face

factor A number that is multiplied by another number to get a product.

factor Número que se multiplica por otro para hallar un producto.

7 is a factor of 21 since $7 \cdot 3 = 21$.

factorial The product of all whole numbers except zero that are less than or equal to a number.

factorial El producto de todos los números cabales, excepto cero, que son menores que o iguales a un número.

$4 \text{ factorial} = 4! = 4 \cdot 3 \cdot 2 \cdot 1$

Fahrenheit A temperature scale in which 32 °F is the freezing point of water and 212 °F is the boiling point of water.

Fahrenheit Escala de temperatura en la que 32° F es el punto de congelación del agua y 212° F es el punto de ebullición.

fair When all outcomes of an experiment are equally likely, the experiment is said to be fair.

justo Se dice de un experimento donde todos los resultados posibles son igualmente probables.

When tossing a coin, heads and tails are equally likely, so it is a fair experiment.

Fibonacci sequence The infinite sequence of numbers (1, 1, 2, 3, 5, 8, 13,...); starting with the third term, each number is the sum of the two previous numbers; it is named after the thirteenth-century mathematician Leonardo Fibonacci.

sucesión de Fibonacci La sucesión infinita de números (1, 1, 2, 3, 5, 8, 13…); a partir del tercer término, cada número es la suma de los dos anteriores. Esta sucesión lleva el nombre de Leonardo Fibonacci, un matemático del siglo XIII.

1, 1, 2, 3, 5, 8, 13, . . .

first differences A sequence formed by subtracting each term of a sequence from the next term.

primeras diferencias Sucesión que se forma al restar cada término de una sucesión del término siguiente.

For the sequence 4, 7, 10, 13, 16, . . ., the first differences are all 3.

first quartile The median of the lower half of a set of data; also called *lower quartile*.

primer cuartil La mediana de la mitad inferior de un conjunto de datos. También se llama *cuartil inferior*.

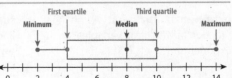

ENGLISH	SPANISH	EXAMPLES

FOIL An acronym for the terms used when multiplying two binomials: the First, Outer, Inner, and Last terms.

FOIL Sigla en inglés de los términos que se usan al multiplicar dos binomios: los primeros, los externos, los internos, y los últimos (First, Outer, Inner, Last).

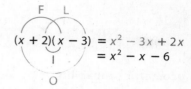

$$(x + 2)(x - 3) = x^2 - 3x + 2x$$
$$= x^2 - x - 6$$

---

formula A rule showing relationships among quantities.

fórmula Regla que muestra relaciones entre cantidades.

$A = \ell w$ is the formula for the area of a rectangle.

---

fractal A structure with repeating patterns containing shapes that are like the whole but are of different sizes throughout.

fractal Estructura con patrones repetidos que contiene figuras similares al patrón general pero de diferente tamaño.

---

fraction A number in the form $\frac{a}{b}$, where $b \neq 0$.

fracción Número escrito en la forma $\frac{a}{b}$, donde $b \neq 0$.

$\frac{2}{3}$

---

frequency The number of times the value appears in the data set.

frecuencia Cantidad de veces que aparece el valor en un conjunto de datos.

Data set: 5, 6, 6, 7, 8, 9
The data value 6 has a frequency of 2.

---

frequency table A table that lists items together according to the number of times, or frequency, that the items occur.

tabla de frecuencia Una tabla en la que se organizan los datos de acuerdo con el número de veces que aparece cada valor (o la frecuencia).

Data set: 1, 1, 2, 2, 3, 5, 5, 5
Frequency table:

Data	Frequency
1	2
2	2
3	1

---

function An input-output relationship that has exactly one output for each input.

función Regla que relaciona dos candidates de forma que a cada valor de entrada corresponde exactamente un valor de salida.

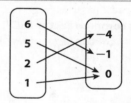

---

function notation The notation used to describe a function.

notación de función Notación que se usa para describir una función.

Equation: $y = 2x$
Function notation: $f(x) = 2x$

---

function table A table of ordered pairs that represent solutions of a function.

tabla de función Tabla de pares ordenados que representan soluciones de una función.

x	3	4	5	6
y	7	9	11	13

Fundamental Counting Principle If one event has m possible outcomes and a second event has n possible outcomes after the first event has occurred, then there are $m \cdot n$ total possible outcomes for the two events.

Principio fundamental de conteo Si un suceso tiene m resultados posibles y otro suceso tiene n resultados posibles después de ocurrido el primer suceso, entonces hay $m \cdot n$ resultados posibles en total para los dos sucesos.

There are 4 colors of shirts and 3 colors of pants. There are $4 \cdot 3 = 12$ possible outfits.

Glossary/Glosario

G

Glossary/Glosario

geometric probability A form of theoretical probability determined by a ratio of geometric measures such as lengths, areas, or volumes.

probabilidad geométrica Método para calcular probabilidades basado en una medida geométrica como la longitud o el área.

The probability of the pointer landing on red is $\frac{80}{360}$, or $\frac{2}{9}$.

geometric sequence An ordered list of numbers that has a common ratio between consecutive terms.

sucesión geométrica Lista ordenada de números que tiene una razón común entre términos consecutivos.

The sequence 2, 4, 8, 16 . . . is a geometric sequence.

graph of an equation A graph of the set of ordered pairs that are solutions of the equation.

gráfica de una ecuación Gráfica del conjunto de pares ordenados que son soluciones de la ecuación.

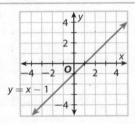

$y = x - 1$

great circle A circle on a sphere such that the plane containing the circle passes through the center of the sphere.

círculo máximo Círculo de una esfera tal que el plano que contiene el círculo pasa por el centro de la esfera.

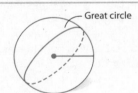

Great circle

greatest common factor (GCF) The largest common factor of two or more given numbers.

máximo común divisor (MCD) El mayor de los factores comunes compartidos por dos o más números dados.

The GCF of 27 and 45 is 9.

H

height In a pyramid or cone, the perpendicular distance from the base to the opposite vertex.

altura En una pirámide o cono, la distancia perpendicular desde la base al vértice opuesto.

h

In a triangle or quadrilateral, the perpendicular distance from the base to the opposite vertex or side.

En un triángulo o cuadrilátero, la distancia perpendicular desde la base de la figura al vértice o lado opuesto.

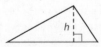

h

In a prism or cylinder, the perpendicular distance between the bases.

En un prisma o cilindro, la distancia perpendicular entre las bases.

h

ENGLISH	SPANISH	EXAMPLES

hemisphere A half of a sphere.

hemisferio La mitad de una esfera.

---

heptagon A seven-sided polygon.

heptágono Polígono de siete lados.

---

hexagon A six-sided polygon.

hexágono Polígono de seis lados.

---

histogram A bar graph that shows the frequency of data within equal intervals.

histograma Gráfica de barras que muestra la frecuencia de los datos en intervalos iguales.

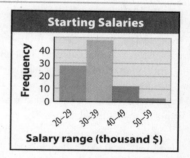

---

hypotenuse In a right triangle, the side opposite the right angle.

hipotenusa En un triángulo rectángulo, el lado opuesto al ángulo recto.

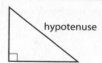

hypotenuse

Identity Property (of One) The property that states that the product of 1 and any number is that number.

Propiedad de identidad (del uno) Propiedad que establece que el producto de 1 y cualquier número es ese número.

$4 \cdot 1 = 4$
$-3 \cdot 1 = -3$

Identity Property (of Zero) The property that states the sum of zero and any number is that number.

Propiedad de identidad (del cero) Propiedad que establece que la suma de cero y cualquier número es ese número.

$4 + 0 = 4$
$-3 + 0 = -3$

---

image A figure resulting from a transformation.

imagen Figura que resulta de una transformación.

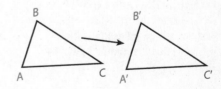

---

improper fraction A fraction in which the numerator is greater than or equal to the denominator.

fracción impropia Fracción cuyo numerador es mayor que o igual al denominador.

$\frac{17}{5}, \frac{3}{3}$

Glossary/Glosario

ENGLISH	SPANISH	EXAMPLES
independent events Events for which the outcome of one event does not affect the probability of the other.	**sucesos independientes** Dos sucesos son independientes si el resultado de uno no afecta la probabilidad del otro.	A bag contains 3 red marbles and 2 blue marbles. Drawing a red marble, replacing it, and then drawing a blue marble is an example of independent events.
independent variable The input of a function; a variable whose value determines the value of the output, or dependent variable.	**variable independiente** Entrada de una función; variable cuyo valor determina el valor de la salida, o variable dependiente.	For $y = 2x + 1$, x is the dependent variable. input: x output: y
indirect measurement The technique of using similar figures and proportions to find a measure.	**medición indirecta** La técnica de usar figuras semejantes y proporciones para hallar una medida.	
inductive reasoning Using a pattern to make a conclusion.	**razonamiento inductivo** Uso de un patrón para sacar una conclusión.	
inequality A mathematical sentence that shows the relationship between quantities that are not equivalent.	**desigualdad** Enunciado matemático que muestra una relación entre cantidades que no son equivalentes.	$5 < 8$ $5x + 2 \geq 12$
input The value substituted into an expression or function.	**valor de entrada** Valor que se usa para sustituir una variable en una expresión o función.	For the function $y = 6x$, the input 4 produces an output of 24.
inscribed angle An angle formed by two chords with its vertex on a circle.	**ángulo inscrito** Ángulo formado por dos cuerdas cuyo vértice está en un círculo.	
integers The set of whole numbers and their opposites.	**enteros** Conjunto de todos los números cabales y sus opuestos.	$\ldots -3, -2, -1, 0, 1, 2, 3, \ldots$
interest The amount of money charged for borrowing or using money.	**interés** Cantidad de dinero que se cobra por el préstamo o uso del dinero.	
interior angles Angles on the inner sides of two lines cut by a transversal.	**ángulos internos** Ángulos en los lados internos de dos líneas intersecadas por una transversal.	 $\angle 1$ is an interior angle.
interquartile range (IQR) The difference of the third (upper) and first (lower) quartiles in a data set, representing the middle half of the data.	**rango intercuartil (RIC)** Diferencia entre el tercer cuartil (superior) y el primer cuartil (inferior) de un conjunto de datos, que representa la mitad central de los datos.	 Interquartile range: $36 - 23 = 13$
intersecting lines Lines that cross at exactly one point.	**líneas secantes** Líneas que se cruzan en un solo punto.	

Glossary/Glosario

ENGLISH	SPANISH	EXAMPLES
interval The space between marked values on a number line or the scale of a graph.	**intervalo** El espacio entre los valores marcados en una recta numérica o en la escala de una gráfica.	
inverse operations Operations that undo each other: addition and subtraction, or multiplication and division.	**operaciones inversas** Operaciones que se cancelan mutuamente: suma y resta, o multiplicación y división.	Addition and subtraction are inverse operations: $5 + 3 = 8; 8 - 3 = 5$ Multiplication and division are inverse operations: $2 \cdot 3 = 6; 6 \div 3 = 2$
inverse variation A relationship in which one variable quantity increases as another variable quantity decreases; the product of the variables is a constant.	**variación inversa** Relación en la que una cantidad variable aumenta a medida que otra cantidad variable disminuye; el producto de las variables es una constante.	$xy = 7, y = \frac{7}{x}$
irrational number A number that cannot be expressed as a ratio of two integers or as a repeating or terminating decimal.	**número irracional** Número que no se puede expresar como una razón de dos enteros ni como un decimal periódico o finito.	$\sqrt{2}, \pi$
isolate the variable To get a variable alone on one side of an equation or inequality in order to solve the equation or inequality.	**despejar la variable** Dejar sola la variable en un lado de una ecuación o desigualdad para resolverla.	$x + 7 = 22$ $\frac{-7 \quad -7}{x \quad = 15}$ $\frac{12}{3} = \frac{3x}{3}$ $4 = x$
isometric drawing A representation of a three-dimensional figure that is drawn on a grid of equilateral triangles.	**dibujo isométrico** Representación de una figura tridimensional que se dibuja sobre una cuadrícula de triángulos equiláteros.	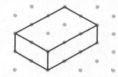
isosceles triangle A triangle with at least two congruent sides.	**triángulo isósceles** Triángulo que tiene al menos dos lados congruentes.	

lateral area The sum of the areas of the lateral faces of a prism or pyramid, or the area of the lateral surface of a cylinder or cone.	**rango intercuartil (RIC)** área lateral Suma de las áreas de las caras laterales de un prisma o pirámide, o área de la superficie lateral de un cilindro o cono.	 Lateral area = area of the 5 rectangular faces

Glossary/Glosario

ENGLISH	SPANISH	EXAMPLES
lateral face In a prism or a pyramid, a face that is not a base.	**cara lateral** En un prisma o pirámide, una cara que no es la base.	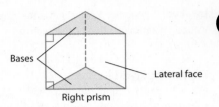
lateral surface In a cylinder, the curved surface connecting the circular bases; in a cone, the curved surface that is not a base.	**superficie lateral** En un cilindro, superficie curva que une las bases circulares; en un cono, la superficie curva que no es la base.	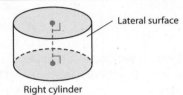
least common denominator (LCD) The least common multiple of two or more denominators.	**mínimo común denominador (mcd)** El mínimo común múltiplo más pequeño de dos o más denominadores.	The LCD of $\frac{3}{4}$ and $\frac{5}{6}$ is 12.
least common multiple (LCM) The smallest whole number, other than zero, that is a multiple of two or more given numbers.	**mínimo común múltiplo (mcm)** El menor de los números cabales, distinto de cero, que es múltiplo de dos o más números dados.	The LCM of 6 and 10 is 30.
legs In a right triangle, the sides that include the right angle; in an isosceles triangle, the pair of congruent sides.	**catetos** En un triángulo rectángulo, los lados adyacentes al ángulo recto. En un triángulo isósceles, el par de lados congruentes.	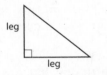
like fractions Fractions that have the same denominator.	**fracciones semejantes** Fracciones que tienen el mismo denominador.	$\frac{5}{12}$ and $\frac{7}{12}$ are like fractions.
like terms Terms with that have the same variable raised to the same exponents.	**términos semejantes** Términos que contienen las mismas variables elevada a las mismas exponentes.	In the expression $3a^2 + 5b + 12a^2$, $3a^2$ and $12a^2$ are like terms.
line A straight path that has no thickness and extends forever.	**línea** Un trazo recto que no tiene grosor y se extiende infinitamente.	
line graph A graph that uses line segments to show how data changes.	**gráfica lineal** Gráfica que muestra cómo cambian los datos mediante segmentos de recta.	
line of best fit A straight line that comes closest to the points on a scatter plot.	**línea de mejor ajuste** La línea recta que más se aproxima a los puntos de un diagrama de dispersión.	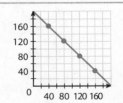

Glossary/Glosario

line of reflection A line that a figure is flipped across to create a mirror image of the original figure.

línea de reflexión Línea sobre la cual se invierte una figura para crear una imagen reflejada de la figura original.

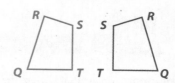

line of symmetry A line that divides a figure into two congruent reflected halves.

eje de simetría Línea que divide una figura en dos mitades reflejas.

line plot A number line with marks or dots that show frequency.

diagrama de acumulación Recta numérica con marcas o puntos que indican la frecuencia.

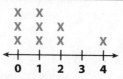

Number of pets

line segment A part of a line consisting of two endpoints and all points between them.

segmento de recta Parte de una línea que consiste en dos extremos y todos los puntos entre éstos.

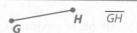

line symmetry A figure has line symmetry if one half is a mirror image of the other half.

simetría axial Una figura tiene simetría axial si una de sus mitades es la imagen reflejada de la otra.

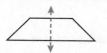

linear equation An equation whose solutions form a straight line on a coordinate plane.

ecuación lineal Ecuación cuyas soluciones forman una línea recta en un plano cartesiano.

$y = 2x + 1$

linear function A function whose graph is a straight line.

función lineal Función cuya gráfica es una línea recta.

$y = x - 1$

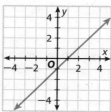

linear inequality A mathematical sentence using $<$, $>$, $\leq$, or $\geq$ whose graph is a region with a straight-line boundary.

desigualdad lineal Enunciado matemático en que se usan los símbolos $<$, $>$, $\leq$, o $\geq$ y cuya gráfica es una región con una línea de límite recta.

literal equation An equation that contains two or more variables.

ecuación literal Ecuación que contiene dos o más variables.

$d = rt$
$A = bh$

Glossary/Glosario

major arc An arc that is more than half of a circle.

arco mayor Arco que es más de la mitad de un círculo.

$\widehat{ADC}$ is a major arc of the circle.

---

matrix A rectangular arrangement of data enclosed in brackets.

matriz Arreglo rectangular de datos encerrado entre corchetes.

$$\begin{bmatrix} 1 & 0 & 3 \\ -2 & 2 & -5 \\ 7 & -6 & 3 \end{bmatrix}$$

---

mean The sum of a set of data divided by the number of items in the data set; also called *average*.

media La suma de todos los elementos de un conjunto de datos dividida entre el número de elementos del conjunto. También se llama promedio.

Data set: 4, 6, 7, 8, 10
Mean:
$$\frac{4+6+7+8+10}{5} = \frac{35}{5} = 7$$

---

mean absolute deviation (MAD) The mean distance between each data value and the mean of the data set.

desviación absoluta media (DAM) Distancia media entre cada dato y la media del conjunto de datos.

---

measure of center A measure used to describe the middle of a data set; the mean, median, and mode are measures of center. Also called measure of central tendency.

medida de tendencia dominante Medida que describe la parte media de un conjunto de datos; la media, la mediana y la moda son medidas de tendencia dominante.

---

median The middle number, or the mean (average) of the two middle numbers, in an ordered set of data.

mediana El número intermedio o la media (el promedio) de los dos números intermedios en un conjunto ordenado de datos.

Data set: 4, 6, 7, 8, 10
Median: 7

---

metric system of measurement A decimal system of weights and measures that is used universally in science and commonly throughout the world.

sistema métrico de medición Sistema decimal de pesos y medidas empleado universalmente en las ciencias y de uso común en todo el mundo.

centimeters, meters, kilometers, gram, kilograms, milliliters, liters

---

midpoint The point that divides a line segment into two congruent line segments.

punto medio El punto que divide un segmento de recta en dos segmentos de recta congruentes.

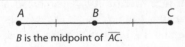

B is the midpoint of $\overline{AC}$.

---

minor arc An arc that is less than half of a circle.

arco menor Arco que es menor que la mitad de un círculo.

$\widehat{AC}$ is the minor arc of the circle.

mixed number A number made up of a whole number that is not zero and a fraction.	**número mixto** Número compuesto por un número cabal distinto de cero y una fracción.	$4\frac{1}{8}$
mode The number or numbers that occur most frequently in a set of data; when all numbers occur with the same frequency, we say there is no mode.	**moda** Número o números más frecuentes en un conjunto de datos; si todos los números aparecen con la misma frecuencia, no hay moda.	Data set: 3, 5, 8, 8, 10 Mode: 8
monomial A number or a product of numbers and variables with exponents that are whole numbers.	**monomio** Un número o un producto de números y variables con exponentes que son números cabales.	$3x^2y^4$
Multiplication Property of Equality The property that states that if you multiply both sides of an equation by the same number, the new equation will have the same solution.	**Propiedad de igualdad de la multiplicación** Propiedad que establece que puedes multiplicar ambos lados de una ecuación por el mismo número y la nueva ecuación tendrá la misma solución.	$3 \cdot 4 = 12$ $3 \cdot 4 \cdot 2 = 12 \cdot 2$ $24 = 24$
Multiplication Property of Zero The property that states that for all real numbers a, $a \cdot 0 = 0$ and $0 \cdot a = 0$.	**Propiedad de multiplicación del cero** Propiedad que establece que para todos los números reales a, $a \cdot 0 = 0$ y $0 \cdot a = 0$.	
multiplicative inverse A number times its multiplicative inverse is equal to 1; also called *reciprocal*.	**inverso multiplicativo** Un número multiplicado por su inverso multiplicativo es igual a 1. También se llama *recíproco*.	The multiplicative inverse of $\frac{4}{5}$ is $\frac{5}{4}$.
multiple The product of any number and a nonzero whole number is a multiple of that number.	**múltiplo** El producto de cualquier número y un número cabal distinto de cero es un múltiplo de ese número.	
mutually exclusive Two events are mutually exclusive if they cannot occur in the same trial of an experiment.	**mutuamente excluyentes** Dos sucesos son mutuamente excluyentes cuando no pueden ocurrir en la misma prueba de un experimento.	When rolling a number cube, rolling a 3 and rolling an even number are mutually exclusive events.

N

| **negative correlation** Two data sets have a negative correlation if one set of data values increases while the other decreases. | **correlación negativa** Dos conjuntos de datos tienen correlación negativa si los valores de un conjunto aumentan a medida que los valores del otro conjunto disminuyen. | 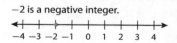 |
| **negative integer** An integer less than zero. | **entero negativo** Entero menor que cero. | -2 is a negative integer.
$\overset{\longleftarrow}{\underset{-4\ -3\ -2\ -1\ \ 0\ \ 1\ \ 2\ \ 3\ \ 4}{\vert\ \ \vert\ \ \vert\ \ \vert\ \ \vert\ \ \vert\ \ \vert\ \ \vert\ \ \vert}}$ |

Glossary/Glosario

net An arrangement of two-dimensional figures that can be folded to form a polyhedron.

plantilla Arreglo de figuras bidimensionales que se doblan para formar un poliedro.

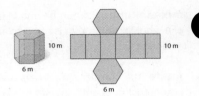

network A set of points and the line segments or arcs that connect the points.

red Conjunto de puntos y los segmentos de recta o arcos que los conectan.

no correlation Two data sets have no correlation when there is no relationship between their data values.

sin correlación Caso en que los valores de dos conjuntos no muestran ninguna relación.

nonlinear function A function whose graph is not a straight line.

función no lineal Función cuya gráfica no es una línea recta.

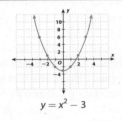

$y = x^2 - 3$

nonlinear relationship A relationship between two variables in which the data do not increase or decrease together at the same rate.

relación no lineal Relación entre dos variables en la cual los datos no aumentan o disminuyen al mismo tiempo a una tasa constante.

nonterminating decimal A decimal that never ends.

decimal infinito Decimal que nunca termina.

$0.\overline{3}$

numerator The top number of a fraction that tells how many parts of a whole are being considered.

numerador El número de arriba de una fracción; indica cuántas partes de un entero se consideran.

$\frac{4}{5}$ ← numerator

numerical expression An expression that contains only numbers and operations.

expresión numérica Expresión que incluye sólo números y operaciones.

$(2 \cdot 3) + 1$

obtuse angle An angle whose measure is greater than 90° but less than 180°.

ángulo obtuso Ángulo que mide más de 90° y menos de 180°.

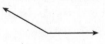

obtuse triangle A triangle containing one obtuse angle.

triángulo obtusángulo Triángulo que tiene un ángulo obtuso.

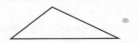

octagon An eight-sided polygon.

octágono Polígono de ocho lados.

odds A comparison of the number of ways an event can occur and the number of ways an event can *not* occur.

probabilidades Comparación del numero de las maneras que puede ocurrir un suceso y el numero de maneras que no puede ocurrir el suceso.

---

odds against The ratio of the number of unfavorable outcomes to the number of favorable outcomes.

probabilidades en contra Razón del número de resultados no favorables al número de resultados favorables.

The odds against rolling a 3 on a number cube are 5:1.

---

odds in favor The ratio of the number of favorable outcomes to the number of unfavorable outcomes.

probabilidades a favor Razón del número de resultados favorables al número de resultados no favorables.

The odds in favor of rolling a 3 on a number cube are 1:5.

---

opposites Two numbers that are an equal distance from zero on a number line; also called *additive inverse*.

opuestos Dos números que están a la misma distancia de cero en una recta numérica. También se llaman *inversos aditivos*.

5 and −5 are opposites.

5 units · 5 units

−6 −5 −4 −3 −2 −1 0 1 2 3 4 5 6

---

order of operations A rule for evaluating expressions: First perform the operations in parentheses, then compute powers and roots, then perform all multiplication and division from left to right, and then perform all addition and subtraction from left to right.

orden de las operaciones Regla para evaluar expresiones: primero se hacen las operaciones entre paréntesis, luego se hallan las potencias y raíces, después todas las multiplicaciones y divisiones de izquierda a derecha, y por último, todas las sumas y restas de izquierda a derecha.

$4^2 + 8 \div 2$	Evaluate the power.
$16 + 8 \div 2$	Divide.
$16 + 4$	Add.
20	

---

ordered pair A pair of numbers that can be used to locate a point on a coordinate plane.

par ordenado Par de números que sirven para ubicar un punto en un plano cartesiano.

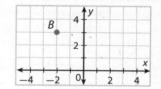

The coordinates of *B* are (−2, 3).

---

origin The point where the *x*-axis and *y*-axis intersect on the coordinate plane; (0, 0).

origen Punto de intersección entre el eje *x* y el eje *y* en un plano cartesiano: (0, 0).

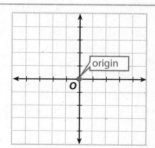

---

orthogonal views A drawing that shows the top, bottom, front, back, and side views of a three-dimensional object.

vista ortogonal Un dibujo que muestra la vista superior, inferior, frontal, posterior y lateral de un objeto de tres dimensiones.

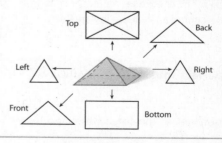

---

outcome (probability) A possible result of a probability experiment.

resultado (en probabilidad) Posible resultado de un experimento de probabilidad.

When rolling a number cube, the possible outcomes are 1, 2, 3, 4, 5, and 6.

Glossary/Glosario

outlier A value much greater or much less than the others in a data set.	**valor extremo** Un valor mucho mayor o menor que los demás valores de un conjunto de datos.	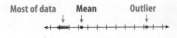
output The value that results from the substitution of a given input into an expression or function.	**valor de salida** Valor que resulta después de sustituir una variable por un valor de entrada determinado en una expresión o función.	For the function $y = 6x$, the input 4 produces an output of 24.

parabola The graph of a quadratic function.	**parábola** Gráfica de una función cuadrática.	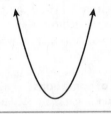
parallel lines Lines in a plane that do not intersect.	**líneas paralelas** Líneas que se encuentran en el mismo plano pero que nunca se intersecan.	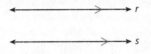
parallelogram A quadrilateral with two pairs of parallel sides.	**paralelogramo** Cuadrilátero con dos pares de lados paralelos.	
pentagon A five-sided polygon.	**pentágono** Polígono de cinco lados.	
percent A ratio comparing a number to 100.	**porcentaje** Razón que compara un número con el número 100.	$45\% = \frac{45}{100}$
percent change The amount stated as a percent that a number increases or decreases.	**porcentaje de cambio** Cantidad en que un número aumenta o disminuye, expresada como un porcentaje.	
percent decrease A percent change describing a decrease in a quantity.	**porcentaje de disminución** Porcentaje de cambio en que una cantidad disminuye.	An item that costs $8 is marked down to $6. The amount of the decrease is $2 and the percent of decrease is $\frac{2}{8} = 0.25 = 25\%$.
percent increase A percent change describing an increase in a quantity.	**porcentaje de incremento** Porcentaje de cambio en que una cantidad aumenta.	The price of an item increases from $8 to $12. The amount of the increase is $4 and the percent of increase is $\frac{4}{8} = 0.5 = 50\%$.
perfect square A square of a whole number.	**cuadrado perfecto** El cuadrado de un número cabal.	$5^2 = 25$, so 25 is a perfect square.
perimeter The distance around a polygon.	**perímetro** Distancia alrededor de un polígono.	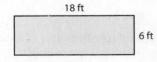

perimeter $= 18 + 6 + 18 + 6 = 48$ ft

Glossary/Glosario

ENGLISH	SPANISH	EXAMPLES

permutation An arrangement of items or events in which order is important.

permutación Arreglo de objetos o sucesos en el que el orden es importante.

For objects A, B, and C, there are 6 different permutations: ABC, ACB, BAC, BCA, CAB, CBA.

---

perpendicular bisector A line that intersects a segment at its midpoint and is perpendicular to the segment.

mediatriz Línea que cruza un segmento en su punto medio y es perpendicular al segmento.

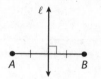

---

perpendicular lines Lines that intersect to form right angles.

líneas perpendiculares Líneas que al intersecarse forman ángulos rectos.

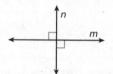

---

pi (π) The ratio of the circumference of a circle to the length of its diameter; $\pi \approx 3.14$ or $\frac{22}{7}$.

pi (π) Razón de la circunferencia de un círculo a la longitud de su diámetro; $\pi \approx 3.14$ ó $\frac{22}{7}$.

---

plane A flat surface that has no thickness and extends forever.

plano Superficie plana que no tiene ningún grueso y que se extiende por siempre.

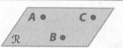

---

point An exact location that has no size.

punto Ubicación exacta que no tiene ningún tamaño.

$P \bullet$

---

point-slope form The equation of a line in the form of $y - y_1 = m(x - x_1)$, where m is the slope and (x_1, y_1) is a specific point on the line.

forma de punto y pendiente Ecuación lineal del tipo $y - y_1 = m(x - x_1)$, donde m es la pendiente y (x_1, y_1) es un punto específico de la línea.

$y - 3 = 2(x - 3)$

---

polygon A closed plane figure formed by three or more line segments that intersect only at their endpoints (vertices).

polígono Figura plana cerrada, formada por tres o más segmentos de recta que se intersecan sólo en sus extremos (vértices).

---

polyhedron A three-dimensional figure in which all the surfaces or faces are polygons.

poliedro Figura tridimensional cuyas superficies o caras tiene forma de polígonos.

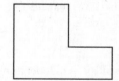

---

polynomial One monomial or the sum or difference of monomials.

polinomio Un monomio o la suma o la diferencia de monomios.

$2x^2 + 3xy - 7y^2$

---

population The entire group of objects or individuals considered for a survey.

población Grupo completo de objetos o individuos que se desea estudiar.

In a survey about study habits of middle school students, the population is all middle school students.

Glossary/Glosario

ENGLISH	SPANISH	EXAMPLES
positive correlation Two data sets have a positive correlation when their data values increase or decrease together.	**correlación positiva** Dos conjuntos de datos tienen una correlación positiva cuando los valores de ambos conjuntos aumentan o disminuyen al mismo tiempo.	
positive integer An integer greater than zero.	**entero positivo** Entero mayor que cero.	 2 is a positive integer.
power A number produced by raising a base to an exponent.	**potencia** Número que resulta al elevar una base a un exponente.	$2^3 = 8$, so 2 to the 3rd power is 8.
preimage The original figure in a transformation.	**imagen original** Figura original en una transformación.	
prime factorization A number written as the product of its prime factors.	**factorización prima** Un número escrito como el producto de sus factores primos.	$10 = 2 \cdot 5$, $24 = 2^3 \cdot 3$
prime number A whole number greater than 1 that has exactly two factors, itself and 1.	**número primo** Número cabal mayor que 1 que sólo es divisible entre 1 y él mismo.	5 is prime because its only factors are 5 and 1.
principal The initial amount of money borrowed or saved.	**capital** Cantidad inicial de dinero depositada o recibida en préstamo.	
principal square root The nonnegative square root of a number.	**raíz cuadrada principal** Raíz cuadrada no negativa de un número.	$\sqrt{25} = 5$; the principal square root of 25 is 5.
prism A polyhedron that has two congruent, polygon-shaped bases and other faces that are all parallelograms.	**prisma** Poliedro con dos bases congruentes con forma de polígono y caras con forma de paralelogramo.	
probability A number from 0 to 1 (or 0% to 100%) that describes how likely an event is to occur.	**probabilidad** Un número entre 0 y 1 (ó 0% y 100%) que describe qué tan probable es un suceso.	A bag contains 3 red marbles and 4 blue marbles. The probability of randomly choosing a red marble is $\frac{3}{7}$.
proper fraction A fraction in which the numerator is less than the denominator.	**fracción propia** Fracción en la que el numerador es menor que el denominador.	$\frac{3}{4}, \frac{1}{12}, \frac{7}{8}$
proportion An equation that states that two ratios are equivalent.	**proporción** Ecuación que establece que dos razones son equivalentes.	$\frac{2}{3} = \frac{4}{6}$
proportional relationship A relationship between two quantities in which of the ratio of one quantity to the other quantity is constant.	**relación proporcional** Relación entre dos cantidades en que la razón de una cantidad a la otra es constante.	

© Houghton Mifflin Harcourt Publishing Company

ENGLISH	SPANISH	EXAMPLES
protractor A tool for measuring angles.	**transportador** Instrumento para medir ángulos.	
pyramid A polyhedron with a polygon base and triangular sides that all meet at a common vertex.	**pirámide** Poliedro cuya base es un polígono; tiene caras triangulares que se juntan en un vértice común.	
Pythagorean Theorem In a right triangle, the square of the length of the hypotenuse is equal to the sum of the squares of the lengths of the legs.	**Teorema de Pitágoras** En un triángulo rectángulo, la suma de los cuadrados de los catetos es igual al cuadrado de la hipotenusa.	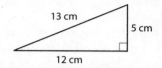 $5^2 + 12^2 = 13^2$ $25 + 144 = 169$
Pythagorean triple A set of three positive integers a, b, and c such that $a^2 + b^2 = c^2$.	**Tripleta de Pitágoras** Conjunto de tres números enteros positivos de cero a, b y c tal que $a^2 + b^2 = c^2$.	3, 4, 5 because $3^2 + 4^2 = 5^2$

ENGLISH	SPANISH	EXAMPLES
quadrant The x- and y-axes divide the coordinate plane into four regions. Each region is called a quadrant.	**cuadrante** El eje x y el eje y dividen el plano cartesiano en cuatro regiones. Cada región recibe el nombre de cuadrante.	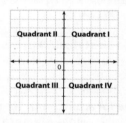
quadratic function A function of the form $y = ax^2 + bx + c$, where $a \neq 0$.	**función cuadrática** Función del tipo $y = ax^2 + bx + c$, donde $a \neq 0$.	$y = x^2 - 6x + 8$
quadrilateral A four-sided polygon.	**cuadrilátero** Polígono de cuatro lados.	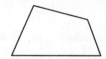
quarterly Four times a year.	**trimestral** Cuatro veces al año.	
quartile Three values, one of which is the median, that divide a data set into fourths.	**cuartil** Cada uno de tres valores, uno de los cuales es la mediana, que dividen en cuartos un conjunto de datos.	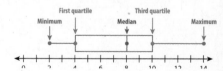
quotient The result when one number is divided by another.	**cociente** Resultado de dividir un número entre otro.	In $8 \div 4 = 2$, 2 is the quotient.

Glossary/Glosario

radical symbol The symbol $\sqrt{\ }$ used to represent the nonnegative square root of a number.

símbolo de radical El símbolo $\sqrt{\ }$ con que se representa la raíz cuadrada no negativa de un número.

---

radius A line segment with one endpoint at the center of the circle and the other endpoint on the circle, or the length of that segment.

radio Segmento de recta con un extremo en el centro de un círculo y el otro en la circunferencia, o bien se llama radio a la longitud de ese segmento.

Radius

---

random numbers In a set of random numbers, each number has an equal chance of appearing.

muestra aleatoria Muestra en la que cada individuo u objeto de la población tiene la misma posibilidad de ser elegido.

---

random sample A sample in which each individual or object in the entire population has an equal chance of being selected.

números aleatorios En un conjunto de números aleatorios, todos los números tienen la misma probabilidad de ser seleccionados.

---

range (in statistics) The difference between the greatest and least values in a data set.

rango (en estadística) Diferencia entre los valores máximo y mínimo de un conjunto de datos.

Data set: 3, 5, 7, 7, 12
Range: $12 - 3 = 9$

---

range (of a function) The set of all possible output values of a function.

rango (en una función) El conjunto de todos los valores posibles de una función.

The range of $y = |x|$ is $y \geq 0$.

---

rate A ratio that compares two quantities measured in different units.

tasa Una razón que compara dos cantidades medidas en diferentes unidades.

The speed limit is 55 miles per hour or 55 mi/h.

---

rate of change A ratio that compares the amount of change in a dependent variable to the amount of change in an independent variable.

tasa de cambio Razón que compara la cantidad de cambio de la variable dependiente con la cantidad de cambio de la variable independiente.

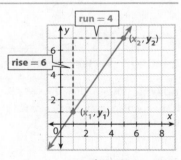

Rate of change $= \dfrac{\text{change in } y}{\text{change in } x} = \dfrac{6}{4} = \dfrac{3}{2}$

---

rate of interest The percent charged or earned on an amount of money; see *simple interest*.

tasa de interés Porcentaje que se cobra por una cantidad de dinero prestada o que se gana por una cantidad de dinero ahorrada; ver *interés simple*.

ratio A comparison of two quantities by division.	**razón** Comparación de dos cantidades mediante una división.	12 to 25, $12{:}25$, $\frac{12}{25}$
rational number Any number that can be expressed as a ratio of two integers.	**número racional** Número que se puede escribir como una razón de dos enteros.	6 can be expressed as $\frac{6}{1}$. 0.5 can be expressed as $\frac{1}{2}$.
ray A part of a line that starts at one endpoint and extends forever in one direction.	**rayo** Parte de una línea que comienza en un extremo y se extiende de manera infinitamente en una dirección.	
real number A rational or irrational number.	**número real** Número racional o irracional.	
reciprocal One of two numbers whose product is 1; also called *multiplicative inverse*.	**recíproco** Uno de dos números cuyo producto es igual a 1. También se llama *inverso multiplicativo*.	The reciprocal of $\frac{2}{3}$ is $\frac{3}{2}$.
rectangle A parallelogram with four right angles.	**rectángulo** Paralelogramo con cuatro ángulos rectos.	
rectangular prism A polyhedron whose bases are rectangles and whose other faces are parallelograms.	**prisma rectangular** Poliedro cuyas bases son rectángulos y cuyas caras tienen forma de paralelogramo.	
reduction A decrease in the size of all dimensions.	**reducción** Disminución de tamaño en todas las dimensiones de una figura.	
reflection A transformation of a figure that flips the figure across a line.	**reflexión** Transformación que ocurre cuando se invierte una figura sobre una línea.	
regular polygon A polygon with congruent sides and angles.	**polígono regular** Polígono con lados y ángulos congruentes.	
regular pyramid A pyramid whose base is a regular polygon and whose lateral faces are all congruent.	**pirámide regular** Pirámide que tiene un polígono regular como base y caras laterales congruentes.	
relation A set of ordered pairs.	**relación** Conjunto de pares ordenados.	$(0, 5)$, $(0, 4)$, $(2, 3)$, $(4, 0)$
relative frequency The frequency of a specific data value divided by the total number of data values in the set.	**frecuencia relativa** La frecuencia de un valor dividido por el número total de los valores en el conjunto.	

Glossary/Glosario

ENGLISH	SPANISH	EXAMPLES
relatively prime Two numbers are relatively prime if their greatest common factor (GCF) is 1.	**primo relativo** Dos números son primos relativos si su máximo común divisor (MCD) es 1.	8 and 15 are relatively prime.
repeating decimal A decimal in which one or more digits repeat infinitely.	**decimal periódico** Decimal en el que uno o más dígitos se repiten infinitamente.	$0.757575\ldots = 0.\overline{75}$
remote interior angle An interior angle of a polygon that is not adjacent to the exterior angle.	**ángulo interno remoto** Ángulo interno de un polígono que no es adyacente al ángulo externo.	
rhombus A parallelogram with all sides congruent.	**rombo** Paralelogramo en el que todos los lados son congruentes.	
right angle An angle that measures 90°.	**ángulo recto** Ángulo que mide exactamente 90°.	
right cone A cone in which a perpendicular line drawn from the base to the tip (vertex) passes through the center of the base.	**cono regular** Cono en el que una línea perpendicular trazada de la base a la punta (vértice) pasa por el centro de la base.	Axis Right cone
right triangle A triangle containing a right angle.	**triángulo rectángulo** Triángulo que tiene un ángulo recto.	
rise The vertical change when the slope of a line is expressed as the ratio $\frac{rise}{run}$, or "rise over run."	**distancia vertical** El cambio vertical cuando la pendiente de una línea se expresa como la razón $\frac{distancia\ vertical}{distancia\ horizontal}$, o "distancia vertical sobre distancia horizontal".	For the points (3, −1) and (6, 5), the rise is $5 - (-1) = 6$.
rotation A transformation in which a figure is turned around a point.	**rotación** Transformación que ocurre cuando una figura gira alrededor de un punto.	
rotational symmetry A figure has rotational symmetry if it can be rotated less than 360° around a central point and coincide with the original figure.	**simetría de rotación** Ocurre cuando una figura gira menos de 360° alrededor de un punto central sin dejar de ser congruente con la figura original.	90° 90° 90° 90°

Glossary/Glosario

ENGLISH	SPANISH	EXAMPLES

run The horizontal change when the slope of a line is expressed as the ratio $\frac{rise}{run}$, or "rise over run."

distancia horizontal El cambio horizontal cuando la pendiente de una línea se expresa como la razón $\frac{distancia\ vertical}{distancia\ horizontal}$, o "distancia vertical sobre distancia horizontal".

For the points $(3, -1)$ and $(6, 5)$, the run is $6 - 3 = 3$.

sales tax A percent of the cost of an item that is charged by governments to raise money.

impuesto sobre la venta Porcentaje del costo de un artículo que los gobiernos cobran para recaudar fondos.

same-side interior angles A pair of angles on the same side of a transversal and between two lines intersected by the transversal.

ángulo internos del mismo lado Dadas dos rectas cortadas por una transversal, par de ángulos ubicados en el mismo lado de la transversal y entre las dos rectas.

sample A part of the population.

muestra Una parte de la población.

sample space All possible outcomes of an experiment.

espacio muestral Conjunto de todos los resultados posibles de un experimento.

When rolling a number cube, the sample space is 1, 2, 3, 4, 5, 6.

scale The ratio between two sets of measurements.

escala La razón entre dos conjuntos de medidas.

1 cm: 5 mi

scale drawing A drawing that uses a scale to make an object smaller than (a reduction) or larger than (an enlargement) the real object.

dibujo a escala Dibujo en el que se usa una escala para que un objeto se vea menor (reducción) o mayor (agrandamiento) que el objeto real al que representa.

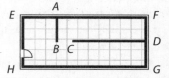

A blueprint is an example of a scale drawing.

scale factor The ratio used to enlarge or reduce similar figures.

factor de escala Razón empleada para agrandar o reducir figuras semejantes.

scale model A proportional model of a three-dimensional object.

modelo a escala Modelo proporcional de un objeto tridimensional.

scalene triangle A triangle with no congruent sides.

triángulo escaleno Triángulo que no tiene lados congruentes.

scatter plot A graph with points plotted to show a possible relationship between two sets of data.

diagrama de dispersión Gráfica de puntos que muestra una posible relación entre dos conjuntos de datos.

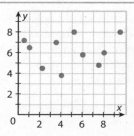

Glossary/Glosario

ENGLISH	SPANISH	EXAMPLES
scientific notation A method of writing very large or very small numbers by using powers of 10.	**notación científica** Método que se usa para escribir números muy grandes o muy pequeños mediante potencias de 10.	$12{,}560{,}000{,}000{,}000 = 1.256 \times 10^{13}$
second quartile The median of a set of data.	**segundo cuartil** Mediana de un conjunto de datos.	Data set: 4, 6, 7, 8, 10 Second quartile: 7
segment A part of a line between two endpoints.	**segmento** Parte de una línea entre dos extremos.	$\overline{GH}$
sequence An ordered list of numbers.	**sucesión** Lista ordenada de números.	2, 4, 6, 8, 10, …
self-selected sample A sample in which members choose to be in the sample.	**muestra auto-seleccionada** Una muestra en la que los miembros eligen participar.	A store provides survey cards for customers who choose to fill them out.
side A line bounding a geometric figure; one of the faces forming the outside of an object.	**lado** Línea que delimita las figuras geométricas; una de las caras que forman la parte exterior de un objeto.	
similar Figures with the same shape but not necessarily the same size are similar.	**semejantes** Figuras que tienen la misma forma, pero no necesariamente el mismo tamaño.	
similarity transformation A transformation that results in an image that is the same shape, but not necessarily the same size, as the original figure.	**transformación de semejanza** Una transformación que resulta en una imagen que tiene la misma forma, pero no necesariamente el mismo tamaño como la figura original.	
simple interest A fixed percent of the principal. It is found using the formula $I = Prt$, where P represents the principal, r the rate of interest, and t the time.	**interés simple** Un porcentaje fijo del capital. Se calcula con la fórmula $I = Cit$, donde C representa el capital, i, la tasa de interés y t, el tiempo.	$100 is put into an account with a simple interest rate of 5%. After 2 years, the account will have earned $I = 100 \cdot 0.05 \cdot 2 = \$10$.
simplest form A fraction is in simplest form when the numerator and denominator have no common factors other than 1.	**mínima expresión** Una fracción está en su mínima expresión cuando el numerador y el denominador no tienen más factor común que 1.	Fraction: $\frac{8}{12}$ Simplest form: $\frac{2}{3}$
simplify To write a fraction or expression in simplest form.	**simplificar** Escribir una fracción o expresión numérica en su mínima expresión.	
simulation A model of an experiment, often one that would be too difficult or too time-consuming to actually perform.	**simulación** Representación de un experimento, por lo general, de uno cuya realización sería demasiado difícil o llevaría mucho tiempo.	

ENGLISH	SPANISH	EXAMPLES

slant height (of a right cone) The distance from the vertex of a right cone to a point on the edge of the base.

altura inclinada (de un cono recto) Distancia desde el vértice de un cono recto hasta un punto en el borde de la base.

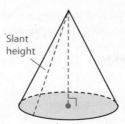

Slant height

---

slant height (of a regular pyramid) The distance from the vertex of a regular pyramid to the midpoint of an edge of the base.

altura inclinada (de una pirámide) Distancia desde el vértice de una pirámide hasta el punto medio de una arista de la base.

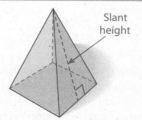

Slant height

Regular pyramid

---

slope A measure of the steepness of a line on a graph; the rise divided by the run.

pendiente Medida de la inclinación de una línea en una gráfica. Razón de la distancia vertical a la distancia horizontal.

$\text{Slope} = \frac{\text{rise}}{\text{run}} = \frac{3}{4}$

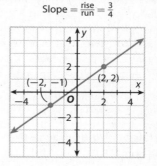

$(-2, -1)$ $(2, 2)$

---

slope-intercept form A linear equation written in the form $y = mx + b$, where m represents slope and b represents the y-intercept.

forma de pendiente-intersección Ecuación lineal escrita en la forma $y = mx + b$, donde m es la pendiente y b es la intersección con el eje y.

$y = 6x - 3$

---

solution of an equation A value or values that make an equation true.

solución de una ecuación Valor o valores que hacen verdadera una ecuación.

Equation: $x + 2 = 6$
Solution: $x = 4$

---

solution of an inequality A value or values that make an inequality true.

solución de una desigualdad Valor o valores que hacen verdadera una desigualdad.

Inequality: $x + 3 \geq 10$
Solution: $x \geq 7$

---

solution of a system of equations A set of values that make all equations in a system true.

solución de un sistema de ecuaciones Conjunto de valores que hacen verdaderas todas las ecuaciones de un sistema.

System: $\begin{cases} x + y = -1 \\ -x + y = -3 \end{cases}$
Solution: $(1, -2)$

---

solution set The set of values that make a statement true.

conjunto solución Conjunto de valores que hacen verdadero un enunciado.

Inequality: $x + 3 \geq 5$
Solution set: $x \geq 2$

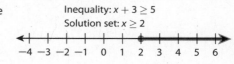

---

solve To find an answer or a solution.

resolver Hallar una respuesta o solución.

Glossary/Glosario

sphere A three-dimensional figure with all points the same distance from the center.

esfera Figura tridimensional en la que todos los puntos están a la misma distancia del centro.

square A rectangle with four congruent sides.

cuadrado Rectángulo con cuatro lados congruentes.

square (numeration) A number raised to the second power.

cuadrado (en numeración) Número elevado a la segunda potencia.

In 5^2, the number 5 is squared.

square root A number that is multiplied by itself to form a product is called a square root of that product.

raíz quadrada El número que se multiplica por sí mismo para formar un producto se denomina la raíz cuadrada de ese producto.

A square root of 16 is 4, because $4^2 = 4 \cdot 4 = 16$.
Another square root of 16 is -4 because $(-4)^2 = (-4)(-4) = 16$.

stem-and-leaf plot A graph used to organize and display data so that the frequencies can be compared.

diagrama de tallo y hojas Gráfica que muestra y ordena los datos, y que sirve para comparar las frecuencias.

Stem	Leaves
3	2 3 4 4 7 9
4	0 1 5 7 7 7 8
5	1 2 2 3

Key: 3|2 means 3.2

straight angle An angle that measures 180°.

ángulo llano Ángulo que mide exactamente 180°.

substitute To replace a variable with a number or another expression in an algebraic expression.

sustituir Reemplazar una variable por un número u otra expresión en una expresión algebraica.

Substituting 3 for m in the expression $5m - 2$ gives $5(3) - 2 = 15 + 2 = 13$.

Subtraction Property of Equality The property that states that if you subtract the same number from both sides of an equation, the new equation will have the same solution.

Propiedad de igualdad de la resta Propiedad que establece que puedes restar el mismo número de ambos lados de una ecuación y la nueva ecuación tendrá la misma solución.

$$
\begin{array}{r}
14 - 6 = 8 \\
\underline{-6 = -6} \\
14 - 12 = 2
\end{array}
$$

supplementary angles Two angles whose measures have a sum of 180°.

ángulos suplementarios Dos ángulos cuyas medidas suman 180°.

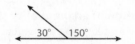

surface area The sum of the areas of the faces, or surfaces, of a three-dimensional figure.

área total Suma de las áreas de las caras, o superficies, de una figura tridimensional.

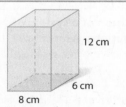

Surface area $= 2(8)(12) + 2(8)(6) + 2(12)(6) = 432 \text{ cm}^2$

Glossary/Glosario

system of equations A set of two or more equations that contain two or more variables.

sistema de ecuaciones Conjunto de dos o más ecuaciones que contienen dos o más variables.

$$\begin{cases} x + y = -1 \\ -x + y = -3 \end{cases}$$

---

systematic sample A sample of a population that has been selected using a pattern.

muestra sistemática Muestra de una población, que ha sido elegida mediante un patrón.

To conduct a phone survey, every tenth name is chosen from the phone book.

term (in an expression) The parts of an expression that are added or subtracted.

término (en una expresión) Las partes de una expresión que se suman o se restan.

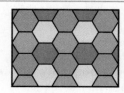

---

term (in a sequence) An element or number in a sequence.

término (en una sucesión) Elemento o número de una sucesión.

5 is the third term in the sequence 1, 3, 5, 7, 9, …

---

terminating decimal A decimal number that ends, or terminates.

decimal finito Decimal con un número determinado de posiciones decimales.

6.75

---

tessellation A repeating pattern of plane figures that completely cover a plane with no gaps or overlaps.

teselado Patrón repetido de figuras planas que cubren totalmente un plano sin superponerse ni dejar huecos.

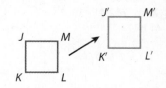

---

theoretical probability The ratio of the number of ways an event can occur to the number of equally likely outcomes.

probabilidad teórica Razón del número de las maneras que puede ocurrir un suceso al numero total de resultados igualmente probables.

When rolling a number cube, the theoretical probability of rolling a 4 is $\frac{1}{6}$.

---

third quartile The median of the upper half of a set of data; also called *upper quartile*.

tercer cuartil La mediana de la mitad superior de un conjunto de datos. También se llama *cuartil superior*.

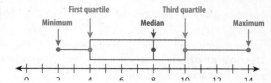

---

transformation A change in the size or position of a figure.

transformación Cambio en el tamaño o la posición de una figura.

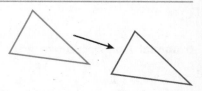

---

translation A movement (slide) of a figure along a straight line.

traslación Desplazamiento de una figura a lo largo de una línea recta.

Glossary/Glosario

transversal A line that intersects two or more lines.

transversal Línea que cruza dos o más líneas.

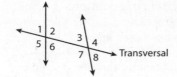

Transversal

---

trapezoid A quadrilateral with exactly one pair of parallel sides.

trapecio Cuadrilátero con un par de lados paralelos.

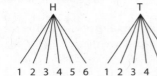

---

tree diagram A branching diagram that shows all possible combinations or outcomes of an event.

diagrama de árbol Diagrama ramificado que muestra todas las posibles combinaciones o resultados de un suceso.

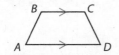

---

trend line A line on a scatter plot that helps show the correlation between data sets more clearly.

línea de tendencia Línea en un diagrama de dispersión que sirve para mostrar la correlación entre conjuntos de datos más claramente. *ver también* línea de mejor ajuste.

---

trial Each repetition or observation of an experiment.

prueba Una sola repetición u observación de un experimento.

When rolling a number cube, each roll is one trial.

Triangle Inequality Theorem The theorem that states that the sum of the lengths of any two sides of a triangle is greater than the length of the third side.

Teorema de Desigualdad de Triángulos El teorema dice que la suma de cualquier dos lados de un triangulo es mayor que la longitud del lado tercero.

Can form a triangle   Cannot form a triangle

Triangle Sum Theorem The theorem that states that the measures of the angles in a triangle add up to 180°.

Teorema de la suma del triángulo Teorema que establece que las medidas de los ángulos de un triángulo suman 180°.

---

triangular prism A polyhedron whose bases are triangles and whose other faces are parallelograms.

prisma triangular Poliedro cuyas bases son triángulos y cuyas demás caras tienen forma de paralelogramo.

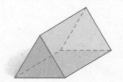

---

trinomial A polynomial with three terms.

trinomio Polinomio con tres términos.

$4x^2 + 3xy - 5y^2$

---

two-way table A table that displays two-variable data by organizing it into rows and columns.

tabla de doble entrada Una tabla que muestran los datos de dos variables por organizándolos en columnas y filas.

		Preference		
		Inside	Outside	Total
Pet	Cats	35	15	50
	Dogs	20	30	50
	Total	55	45	100

unit conversion The process of changing one unit of measure to another.

conversión de unidades Proceso que consiste en cambiar una unidad de medida por otra.

---

unit conversion factor A fraction used in unit conversion in which the numerator and denominator represent the same amount but are in different units.

factor de conversión de unidades Fracción que se usa para la conversión de unidades, donde el numerador y el denominador representan la misma cantidad pero están en unidades distintas.

$\frac{60 \text{ min}}{1 \text{ h}}$ or $\frac{1 \text{ h}}{60 \text{ min}}$

---

unit price A unit rate used to compare prices.

precio unitario Tasa unitaria que sirve para comparar precios.

Cereal costs $0.23 per ounce.

---

unit rate A rate in which the second quantity in the comparison is one unit.

tasa unitaria Una tasa en la que la segunda cantidad de la comparación es la unidad.

10 cm per minute

variability The spread of values in a set of data.

variabilidad Amplitud de los valores de un conjunto de datos.

The data set {1, 5, 7, 10, 25} has greater variability than the data set {8, 8, 9, 9, 9}.

---

variable A symbol used to represent a quantity that can change.

variable Símbolo que representa una cantidad que puede cambiar.

In the expression $2x + 3$, x is the variable.

Venn diagram A diagram that is used to show relationships between sets.

diagrama de Venn Diagrama que muestra las relaciones entre conjuntos.

Transformations
Rotations

---

vertex On an angle or polygon, the point where two sides intersect; on a polyhedron, the intersection of three or more faces; on a cone or pyramid, the top point.

vértice En un ángulo o polígono, el punto de intersección de dos lados; en un poliedro, el punto de intersección de tres o más caras; en un cono o pirámide, la punta.

A is the vertex of $\angle CAB$.

---

vertical angles A pair of opposite congruent angles formed by intersecting lines.

ángulos opuestos por el vértice Par de ángulos opuestos congruentes formados por líneas secantes.

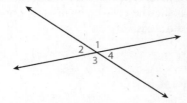

$\angle 1$ and $\angle 3$ are vertical angles.

Glossary/Glosario

ENGLISH	SPANISH	EXAMPLES

vertical line test A test used to determine whether a relation is a function. If any vertical line crosses the graph of a relation more than once, the relation is not a function.

prueba de la línea vertical Prueba utilizada para determinar si una relación es una función. Si una línea vertical corta la gráfica de una relación más de una vez, la relación no es una función.

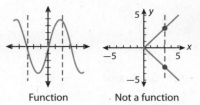

Function   Not a function

---

volume The number of cubic units needed to fill a given space.

volumen Número de unidades cúbicas que se necesitan para llenar un espacio.

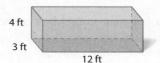

Volume = $3 \cdot 4 \cdot 12 = 144 \text{ ft}^3$

---

weighted average A mean that is calculated by multiplying each data value by a weight, and dividing the sum of these products by the sum of the weights.

promedio ponderado Promedio que se calcula por multiplicando cada valor de datos por un peso, y dividiendo la suma de estos productos por la suma de los pesos.

If the data values 0, 5, and 10 are assigned the weights 0.1, 0.2, and 0.7, respectively, the weighted average is:
$$\frac{0(0.1) + 5(0.2) + 10(0.7)}{0.1 + 0.2 + 0.7} = \frac{8}{1}$$

---

x-axis The horizontal axis on a coordinate plane.

eje x El eje horizontal del plano cartesiano.

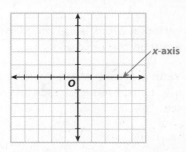

x-axis

---

x-coordinate The first number in an ordered pair; it tells the distance to move right or left from the origin (0, 0).

coordenada x El primer número de un par ordenado; indica la distancia que debes moverte hacia la izquierda o la derecha desde el origen, (0, 0).

5 is the x-coordinate in (5, 3).

---

x-intercept The x-coordinate of the point where the graph of a line crosses the x-axis.

intersección con el eje x Coordenada x del punto donde la gráfica de una línea cruza el eje x.

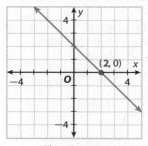

(2, 0)

The x-intercept is 2.

Glossary/Glosario

Y

_y_-axis The vertical axis on a coordinate plane.

eje _y_ El eje vertical del plano cartesiano.

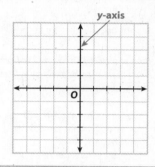

_y_-coordinate The second number in an ordered pair; it tells the distance to move up or down from the origin (0, 0).

coordenada _y_ El segundo número de un par ordenado; indica la distancia que debes avanzar hacia arriba o hacia abajo desde el origen, (0, 0).

3 is the _y_-coordinate in (5, 3).

_y_-intercept The _y_-coordinate of the point where the graph of a line crosses the _y_-axis.

intersección con el eje _y_ Coordenada _y_ del punto donde la gráfica de una línea cruza el eje _y_.

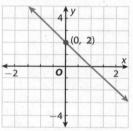

The _y_-intercept is 2.

Z

zero pair A number and its opposite, which add to 0.

par nulo Un número y su opuesto, cuya suma es 0.

18 and −18

Glossary/Glosario

Index

Index

graphing, 101–106
  slope-intercept form of an equation, 95–100
for proportional vs. nonproportional
  relationships, 108
systems of, solved by graphing, 115–122
writing
  from a description, 131
  from situations and graphs, 129–134
  in slope-intercept form, 129
  from a table, 135–140

linear functions
  determining, 165
  graphing, 164

linear relationships, 141–148
  and bivariate data, 144–145
  equations of. *See* linear equations
  making predictions with, 142–143
  nonproportional, 89–94
    on graphs, 91, 92, 101–106
    on tables, 89, 90

line of reflection, 339

loans, repaying, 441–446

Longhorn Band, 247

Look for a Pattern, 63, 105, 308

Los Angeles, California, 184

M

Make a Conjecture, 14, 43, 44, 64, 66, 82, 94,
  106, 119, 148, 174, 198, 206, 207, 232, 238,
  245, 320, 335, 341, 344, 347, 350, 356, 368,
  376, 419, 420, 446, 464

Make a Prediction, 14, 99, 168, 404, 405

Mali, 46

manipulatives
  algebra tiles, 297, 298, 300
  centimeter cubes, 245
  centimeter ruler, 375
  8-by-8 array, 426
  grid paper, 227, 230
  inch cubes, 248
  nets, 269, 275, 278
  rulers, 13, 334, 346
  square tiles, 165
  tape measure, 10
  10-by-10 array, 423
  three-dimensional figures, 251
  tracing paper, 195

mapping diagrams, 156–157

Mars, 44

Mars Rover, 147

mathematical processes
  *Mathematical processes are a central focus of this
  course and are found throughout this book.*
  Analyze Relationships, 8, 26, 38, 44, 63, 64, 70,
    76, 82, 90, 93, 113, 140, 162, 174, 199, 200,
    206, 213, 222, 226, 250, 252, 256, 257, 280,
    302, 307, 338, 340, 344, 356, 414, 446, 458
  Classifying Numbers, 37
  Communicate Mathematical Ideas, 20, 26, 38,
    43, 64, 70, 94, 100, 108, 134, 148, 162, 168,
    173, 198, 206, 214, 250, 274, 276, 280, 299,
    320, 338, 345, 350, 354, 374, 399, 406, 424,
    426, 445

Counterexamples, 406
Critical Thinking, 20, 40, 76, 97, 106, 122, 197,
  206, 214, 252, 338, 344, 356, 368, 373, 400,
  419, 426, 452, 458, 464
Critique Reasoning, 20, 26, 44, 70, 82, 94, 100,
  148, 198, 214, 232, 252, 256, 308, 314, 374,
  380, 406, 452, 458
Draw Conclusions, 19, 20, 38, 43, 76, 102, 161,
  168, 198, 206, 228, 232, 302, 308, 320, 380
Error Analysis, 168
Explain the Error, 20, 38, 106, 148, 302, 308
Explain Why, 11
Justify Reasoning, 20, 38, 41, 43, 100, 162,
  168, 174, 199, 213, 214, 225, 232, 238, 301,
  395, 400
Look for a Pattern, 63, 105, 308
Make a Conjecture, 14, 43, 44, 64, 66, 82, 94,
  106, 119, 148, 174, 198, 206, 207, 232, 238,
  245, 320, 335, 341, 344, 347, 350, 356, 368,
  376, 419, 420, 446, 464
Make a Prediction, 14, 99, 168, 404, 405
Mathematical Reasoning, 114
Math Talk. *Math Talk appears in most lessons.
  See, for example,* 8, 16, 22, 34, 41, 60
Multiple Representations, 43, 69, 114, 161, 273,
  280, 400, 452
Multistep, 13, 14, 37, 69, 99, 121, 122, 147, 205,
  213, 226, 237, 252, 255, 261, 274, 279, 307,
  319, 320, 338, 380, 420, 426, 446
Persevere in Problem Solving, 226, 238, 261,
  280, 302, 446
Problem Solving, 14, 350, 379
Reason Abstractly, 70
Reflect. *Reflect appears in most lessons. See, for
  example,* 8, 10, 11, 16, 22, 33
Represent Real-World Problems, 14, 63, 114,
  134, 167, 213, 225, 232, 238, 313, 314, 373,
  379
What If?, 22, 72, 108, 137, 156, 161, 209, 211,
  279, 304, 314, 342, 397, 418, 420, 442, 443
What's the Error?, 250

Mathematical Reasoning, 114

Math History, 26

Math On the Spot. *Math On the Spot is available
online for every example.*

Math Talk. *Math Talk appears in most lessons. See,
for example,* 8, 16, 22, 34, 41, 60, 72, 96

mean, 413–415

mean absolute deviation (MAD), 412–420

measurement
  and dilations, 375–380
  to estimate pi, 12
  mean absolute deviation, 413–420
  ratios of distance measures, 60
  rounding and errors in, 247
  rulers, 13

measure of center, 413

measure of variability, 413–420

miles, 59–60

Mixed Review. *See* Texas Test Prep

modeling
  algebra tiles, 297, 298, 300
  centimeter cubes, 245

grid paper, 227, 230
inch cubes, 248
nets, 269, 275, 278
square tiles, 165
with three-dimensional figures, 251

money orders, 457

Moon, 44, 45, 61

Multiple Representations, 43, 69, 114, 161,
  273, 280, 400, 452

Multistep, 13, 14, 37, 69, 99, 121, 122, 147, 205,
  213, 226, 237, 252, 255, 261, 274, 279, 307,
  319, 320, 338, 380, 420, 426, 446

N

negative numbers, and square roots, 8

**New England Aquarium, Boston,
Massachusetts,** 249

nonlinear relationships, 144, 165–166

nonproportional relationships
  linear, representing, 89–94
    with graphs, 91, 101–106
    with tables, 89
  proportional relationships vs., 107–114
  comparing, 110–111
  using equations, 108
  using graphs, 107
  using tables, 109
  slope and *y*-intercept
    determining, 95–100
    graphing with, 101–106
  systems of linear equations solved by graphing,
    115–122

number lines, 14
  pi on, 11
  plotting real numbers on, 22, 23

numbers
  integers, 8, 15
  irrational, 6, 9
    approximating, 10–11
    approximating pi, 10–11, 22
    comparing, 21
    estimating, 9–10, 12
    as real numbers, 15
  names applied to, 15–16, 19
  rational, 2, 6, 7, 296
    equations with, 303–308
    in equations with variables on both sides,
      303–308
    expressed as decimals, 7–8
    in inequalities, 315–320
    in inequalities with variables on both sides,
      315–320
    as real numbers, 15
  real, 2, 6
    classifying, 15–16
    ordering, 21–26
    sets of, 15–20
  whole, 15
  writing
    in scientific notation, 34, 36, 40, 42
    in standard notation, 35, 36, 41, 42

© Houghton Mifflin Harcourt Publishing Company

Index

Index

© Houghton Mifflin Harcourt Publishing Company

Index

Index

TABLE OF MEASURES

METRIC

Length

1,000 millimeters (mm) = 1 meter (m)

100 centimeters (cm) = 1 meter

10 millimeters = 1 centimeter

10 decimeters (dm) = 1 meter

1 kilometer (km) = 1000 meters

Capacity

1,000 milliliters (mL) = 1 liter (L)

100 centiliters (cL) = 1 liter

10 deciliters (dL) = 1 liter

1 kiloliter (kL) = 1,000 liters

Mass

1,000 milligrams (mg) = 1 gram (g)

100 centigrams (cg) = 1 gram

10 decigrams (dg) = 1 gram

1 kilogram (kg) = 1,000 grams

CUSTOMARY

Length

1 foot (ft) = 12 inches (in.)

1 yard (yd) = 3 feet

1 yard = 36 inches

1 mile (mi) = 5,280 feet

1 mile = 1,760 yards

Capacity

1 cup (c) = 8 fluid ounces (fl oz)

1 pint (pt) = 2 cups

1 quart (qt) = 2 pints

1 quart = 4 cups

1 gallon (gal) = 4 quarts

Weight

1 pound (lb) = 16 ounces (oz)

1 ton (T) = 2,000 pounds

TIME

1 minute (min) = 60 seconds (s)

1 hour (hr) = 60 minutes

1 day = 24 hours

1 week (wk) = 7 days

1 year (yr) = 12 months (mo)

1 year = 52 weeks

1 year = 365 days

1 leap year = 366 days

FORMULAS

Perimeter

Rectangle $P = 2\ell + 2w$ or
$P = 2(\ell + w)$

Square $P = 4s$

Circumference

Circle $C = 2\pi r$ or $C = \pi d$

Area

Circle $A = \pi r^2$

Parallelogram $A = bh$

Rectangular $A = \ell w$ or $A = bh$

Square $A = s^2$

Rhombus $A = \frac{1}{2} d_1 d_2$ or

$A = \frac{d_1 d_2}{2}$

Trapezoid $A = \frac{1}{2}(b_1 + b_2)h$ or

$A = \frac{(b_1 + b_2)h}{2}$

Triangle $A = \frac{1}{2} bh$ or $A = \frac{bh}{2}$

Volume

Cylinder $V = Bh$ or $V = \pi r^2 h$

Cube $V = s^3$

Rectangle prism $V = Bh$ or $V = \ell wh$

Triangular prism $V = Bh$

Cone $V = \frac{1}{3} Bh$ or $V = \frac{1}{3} \pi r^2 h$

Pyramid $V = \frac{1}{3} Bh$

Sphere $V = \frac{4}{3} \pi r^3$

Surface Area

Cylinder:

  Lateral $L = Ch$ or $L = 2\pi rh$

  Total $S = 2B + L$ or $S = 2\pi r^2 + 2\pi rh$

Prism:

  Lateral $L = Ph$

  Total $S = 2B + L$ or $S = 2B + Ph$

Other

Distance traveled $d = 2r$

Interest (simple) $I = Prt$

Pythagorean Theorem $a^2 + b^2 = c^2$

SYMBOLS

$\neq$	is not equal to	π	pi: (about 3.14)
$\approx$	is approximately equal to	$\perp$	is perpendicular to
10^2	ten squared; ten to the second power	$\parallel$	is parallel to
		$\overleftrightarrow{AB}$	line AB
$2.\overline{6}$	repeating decimal 2.66666...	$\overrightarrow{AB}$	ray AB
$\lvert -4 \rvert$	the absolute value of negative 4	$\overline{AB}$	line segment AB
$\sqrt{}$	square root	$m\angle A$	measure of $\angle A$